DOG
BOATS
AT WAR

The author on the bridge of MGB 658.

DOG BOATS
AT WAR

**A HISTORY OF THE OPERATIONS OF
THE ROYAL NAVY D CLASS FAIRMILE
MOTOR TORPEDO BOATS AND MOTOR GUNBOATS
1939–1945**

L.C. REYNOLDS, OBE, DSC

Foreword by ADMIRAL OF THE FLEET LORD LEWIN

SUTTON PUBLISHING

in association with
THE IMPERIAL WAR MUSEUM

IMPERIAL WAR
MUSEUM

First published in the United Kingdom in 1998 by
Sutton Publishing Limited · Phoenix Mill
Thrupp · Stroud · Gloucestershire · GL5 2BU
in association with the Imperial War Museum

British Library Cataloguing in Publication Data
A catalogue record for this book is available from the British Library

ISBN 0 7509 1817 9

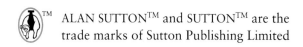

Typeset in 10/13 pt Sabon.
Typesetting and origination by
Sutton Publishing Limited.
Printed in Great Britain by
Butler & Tanner, Frome, Somerset.

CONTENTS

Foreword   vi

Author's Note   vii

Introduction   ix

MTB/MGB Class Data   x

Chapter 1   The Urgency of War   1
Chapter 2   Operations Begin   14
Chapter 3   The 30th (Norwegian) MTB Flotilla, June 1942 to October 1943   29
Chapter 4   Mediterranean Operations, March to October 1943   44
Chapter 5   Home Waters, May 1943 to May 1944   72
Chapter 6   Norwegian Operations, September 1943 to May 1945   104
Chapter 7   Mediterranean Operations, October 1943 to July 1944   120
Chapter 8   Home Waters, June 1944 to May 1945   158
Chapter 9   MTB 718, Clandestine Operations to the Shores of Brittany and Norway   192
Chapter 10   Mediterranean Operations, August 1944 to May 1945   209
Chapter 11   C Class MGBs, SGBs and Camper and Nicholsons MGBs   241

Epilogue   254

Glossary   259

Appendix 1   Notes   260

Appendix 2   Tables: 1. Awards of Decorations   266
                       2. War Losses   273
                       3. The Dog Boat Flotillas   274

Appendix 3   Bibliography   279

Index   283

FOREWORD

BY ADMIRAL OF THE FLEET LORD LEWIN

To the majority of those who served in the Navy in the last war, the exploits of our Coastal Forces were almost a closed book. Operating away from the main naval bases, from small harbours like Felixstowe, Yarmouth, Newhaven and Dartmouth, we rarely met them; manned almost entirely by peacetime volunteer reserves and wartime sailors, they were virtually a private navy. Once in 'the boats' they stayed in, and would never, if they could help it, transfer to what they regarded as the Pusser Navy. Early responsibility, small close-knit crews, the chance to get to grips with the enemy, attracted the best men from the home country and an almost disproportionate number from the countries of the Old Commonwealth. What little those of us serving in destroyers and bigger ships heard of their dramatic deeds filled us, young as we were, with envy.

Maritime warfare in narrow seas does not change. Throughout our history small craft have played a major and vital part, defending our coastal shipping and attacking that of the enemy. The employment of our Coastal Forces in the Second World War on frustrating convoy escort, the interception of enemy shipping and the brisk and bloody action at close quarters this usually entailed, hazardous clandestine landings on hostile shores, all these operations would have been recognized by the men who manned the brigs and cutters of the Napoleonic wars. Like their forebears the crews of the gunboats were, in the words of Conrad, men of courage, initiative and hardihood. It is interesting but not surprising to note that of those who survived many also served with distinction in their chosen careers after the war.

Some have written of their experiences, fine leaders like Robert Hichens, Peter Scott and Peter Dickens among them, and gripping accounts they are. But until now no one has gathered together a complete record of even one class of gunboat. This Len Reynolds has now achieved, for the Dog Boats in which he served. A truly mammoth task of research that has taken him eight years, this book is not just a fascinating account of the Dog Boats' war but a historic archive for which future maritime historians will have every reason to be grateful.

Author's Note

This history of the D class Fairmile MTBs and MGBs in the Second World War is the result of eight years of research.

Quite apart from seeking out the somewhat fragmented and incomplete official record, I have been able to contact several hundred veterans who served in the boats. They completed questionnaires and sent me letters, notes, lists and anecdotes, and in so doing not only filled many of the gaps but also breathed life and warmth into the record. I acknowledge and thank all who helped in this way, particularly Douglas Hunt of the MTB/MGB Officers' Association, and Harold Pickles and Pieter Jansen, newsletter editors of the Coastal Forces Veterans' Association, who made this approach possible.

Throughout my research and during the writing my main support has been from Geoffrey Hudson, the Official Historian of the Coastal Forces Veterans' Association, who has been compiling his own records of boats and flotillas for many years. He has an unparalleled knowledge of the construction details of every type of MTB, all of which he has generously been willing to share with me.

The long period of research was greatly assisted by a grant from the Caird Fund of the National Maritime Museum, whose chairman at the time, Admiral of the Fleet The Lord Lewin, gave me considerable support and encouragement, and whose staff were always very helpful. Similarly, Dr Christopher Dowling of the Imperial War Museum was largely responsible for my embarking upon the project and has since become my principal 'patron', seeing the book through to publication. Mrs Janet Mihell of the museum has been invaluable in editing the text with great skill.

The staff of the Naval Historical Branch, the Public Record Office at Kew, and the Royal Naval Museum at Portsmouth have all given me generous help and advice. The Royal Norwegian Navy's Museum at Horten provided information and photographs. John Lambert generously allowed me to use some of his excellent drawings of Dog Boats.

I record with great appreciation my debt to the following whose direct help will be obvious from a perusal of the text and the notes, and apologize to those who sent me material which helped but is not quoted: Colonel Medoc Antunac; Captain S.M. Barnes DSC USN (Retd); T. Barrett DSM; L.H. Blaxell OBE DSC; the late D.G. Bradford DSO DSC; Captain W. Chatterton Dickson RN (Retd); Lady Bligh; Sir Walter Blount DSC; R.W.V. Board; P. Boissier; C. Burke DSC RCNVR; M.W. Coan; the late Fred Coombes DSM; H.F. Cooper; P. Coney; G.G. Connell; L.D. Conquest; Commander C.W.S. Dreyer DSO DSC; A. Falconer; J. Fearon; J.Y. Ferguson; Lord Fisher; Daniel Frka; H. Garmsen; Rear Admiral Bj Grimstvedt (RNorN); Vice Admiral H.B. Gundersen (RNorN); J. Hargreaves; R. Harrison; J.W. Harrop; M. Hayes; F. Hewitt; Sir Derrick Holden-Brown; the late K. Horlock DSC; I. Kinross; T.E. Ladner DSC QC; G. Lesslie; A.H. Lewis; E. Lonsdale DSC; F. Loy; the late A.D. McIlwraith CdeG GkWC; C. McIntyre; G. Manning; C. Milner

DSM; R. Morgan; Rear Admiral Sir Morgan Giles DSO OBE GM; P. O'Hare DSM; J.P. Perkins DSC; the late Dudley Pope; D.G.E. Probert DSC; Wallis Randall; A.T. Robinson; T.M. Robinson; K. Rogers; R. Seddon DSC; Lord Strathcona & Mount Royal; the late G.V. Surtees; Randall Tomlinson; Robert Tough; the late Sir Fred Warner GCVO KCMG; R. Westwood.

Most of all, I thank my wife who has supported me tirelessly, through eight years of endeavour as 'secretary-receptionist', and in this fiftieth year of our marriage has mastered the art of word processing and produced a very high quality manuscript. In this she was helped considerably by the technical assistance of two friends, Mr Roger Battye and Mr Colin Daniel, and by Mr Desmond Wilton's careful checking of the text.

Few researchers and authors have, I suspect, gained as much advantage from personal experience in their subject as I have enjoyed. I had the privilege of serving in one of the Dog Boats for nearly three years, joining her only a few weeks after the class first made an impact on the operational scene. I had, I am told, the unique experience not only of remaining in the one boat from commissioning to paying off, but also of being her Navigating Officer (as a Midshipman), then her First Lieutenant and Gunnery Officer, and ultimately her Commanding Officer at the age of twenty-one. I believe this has helped me to tackle a daunting task, especially, as a 'Mediterranean' Officer, when writing of the Dog Boats in home waters and Norway. I ask for the forbearance of those who detect inaccuracies, especially in areas where the official record is particularly scanty.

I should perhaps justify my use of several somewhat unusual ways of referring to boats and individual officers in an account that seeks to satisfy historians more accustomed to greater formality. First, although RN, RNR, SANF(V) and officers from the Canadian, Australian and New Zealand Naval Volunteer Reserve have the appropriate letters after their names (unless they are referred to frequently), because the great majority of officers were RNVR this has been omitted after their names. Then, as Coastal Forces had a particular camaraderie among its officers, and indeed first names were often used as R/T call signs, those names are often given after a first formal reference, to attempt to capture the appropriate atmosphere.

Similarly, in order to avoid constant repetition, the designation MTB or MGB is only used before a boat's number where this is of operational importance. All the boats were numbered in the 600 and 700 sequence until the last 28 of the class, numbered from 5001.

Notes from the text appear in two categories. In order to assist other researchers and readers wishing to see original texts, sources of information are usually marked in the text as footnotes. Longer and more complex notes are marked with a different symbol – e.g. Note 1/Appendix 1 that signifies Note 1, which will be found in Appendix 1. Abbreviations commonly used are shown at the beginning of that section.

L.C. Reynolds

INTRODUCTION

It is rare that a new concept in ship construction, even in war, can be developed and brought into being so quickly that it makes a significant contribution operationally. But that is the truth behind the story of the Fairmile 'D' class motor torpedo boats and motor gunboats, often known as 'Dog Boats'.

They were initially conceived in 1941 with the specific purpose of combating the highly regarded German schnellboote, which had steel hulls and high-speed diesel engines giving a top speed of over 40 knots.

Strangely, although the schnellboote were known in the German Navy as S-boats, they were always called E-boats in Allied circles – the 'E' standing rather quaintly for 'enemy'.

The Dog Boats began to emerge from the boat yards of Britain in the spring of 1942, by the end of the war, they were regarded as the most heavily armed motor boats in the navies of the world: powerful, capable of long-range operations and of sustained independence. There were 228 of them built and they operated in home waters, off Norway and in the Mediterranean with equal success.

Their crews displayed – and still reveal – a strong bond of loyalty for their boats and shipmates. Perhaps this bond was due in large part to the closeness with which the three officers and thirty men lived, crammed into a 115-ft plywood hull alongside four massive supercharged engines and thousands of gallons of 100 octane petrol. There was no segregation here; the officers and crew lived within feet of each other and shared the same food. They were also all young, the CO and the coxswain often the only men on board aged more than twenty-five.

The Dog Boats fought in over 300 actions, and sank and damaged innumerable enemy ships. Thirty-seven of them were lost, mostly in battle or destroyed by mines as they ventured through the minefields to launch close attacks on the enemy's coasts.

These, then, were the vessels and the men in this story of human endeavour during war. It tells of countless acts of selfless devotion to the high standards of the naval service, by men and boys who served the Royal Navy and their country when called to war from their offices and factories, and even from their schools.

It is dedicated to the 273 officers and men who gave their lives in the Dog Boats.

The Fairmile D Class MTB/MGB: Class Data

Dimensions
Length overall	115 ft	0 in
Length waterline	110 ft	0 in
Beam	20 ft	10 in
Draught	4ft	9 in

Displacement
Designed	85 tons
Actual	105 tons

Main engines

4 Packard, 12 cylinder, 1,250 b.h.p. supercharged 4M 2,500 petrol engines.

Speed
Actual maximum (105 tons)	
with reduction gear	32 knots
with direct drive	30 knots
Actual continuous	
with reduction gear	27 knots
with direct drive	25 knots

Fuel capacity	5,200 gallons
Range at max. continuous speed	506 nautical miles
Silencers	Dumbflow

Specimen engine revolutions
1,000 r.p.m.	12 knots
1,500 r.p.m.	17 knots
1,800 r.p.m.	21 knots
2,000 r.p.m.	25 knots
2,400 r.p.m.	30 knots

Complement	3 officers
	30–32 crew

A dirty night in prospect. (Courtesy, Harold Garland)

CHAPTER 1

THE URGENCY OF WAR

The 'Dog Boats' – the D class Fairmile MTBs and MGBs – formed one of the classes of wooden boat produced by the Fairmile Marine Company. The history of that company is a tribute to one man's vision and drive and to the positive and speedy decision-making that resulted from the existence of an urgent requirement: exactly the conditions which existed in 1939. It is remarkable that such decisions had to be taken with so little long-term planning to make rapid expansion possible, and that the man, Noel Macklin, should be there ready to take risks and invest money, even before the slow response and reactionary thinking of the Admiralty had taken only faltering steps.

This story of the operations of the Dog Boats would not be complete without a brief reference to the organization and system which led to the astonishing achievement of their production.

Noel Macklin had a background of naval service in the First World War, and of car racing and flying between the wars. It was his

A Dog Boat at speed.

success with car construction in the 1930s, when models such as the Invicta and the Railton car were produced by his Fairmile Engineering Company in sheds behind his house at Fairmile, Cobham, that put him in a position to respond when he read that imminent war would require an immediate and urgent need for small anti-submarine vessels.

He quickly discovered that lessons were to be learned from the experience of fulfilling precisely the same requirements in the First World War. In 1915, orders had been placed with Elco in New Jersey for 550 motor launches (MLs) of 75–80 ft in length, capable of 19 knots and an average radius of action of 750 miles. These had been delivered, by a remarkable feat of production, by November 1916. In retrospect, however, the Royal Navy considered that a vessel of 100–200 ft length,

designed more significantly for the weather conditions in home waters, would have been preferable. With this in mind, Macklin began to apply his extraordinary energy and breadth of vision to the concept of building mass-produced wooden boats in a multitude of small boat yards. He formed the Fairmile Marine Company, assembled a team of experts, and had soon decided on a prototype of a 110-ft hard chine motor launch designed for a maximum speed of 25 knots. Despite a very negative early Admiralty response to this initiative, Macklin had sufficient confidence in his concept to set about building a prototype. Fairmile's records show that the Admiralty finally placed an order for ML 100 on 27 July 1939 and she was 'laid off' at Woodnutt's yard on the Isle of Wight, 'laid down' on 29 September and completed on 21 March 1940.

A look underneath – rudders and propellers.

A very significant figure in the design of the Fairmile boats was William John Holt, at that time the head of the boat section in the Department of Naval Construction (DNCD). He recognized the huge potential of the Fairmile production organization, and threw himself into the task of designing developments of that first motor launch, designated the Fairmile 'A', of which twelve were built and were used mainly as minelayers.

It was his design for a round bilge motor launch that was accepted and went into production immediately as the Fairmile 'B'. This became the versatile and ubiquitous 'ML', which served all over the world in large numbers and with great distinction.

The additional capital required for even the first few dozen boats led to a quite remarkable agreement with the Admiralty. The Fairmile Marine Company retained its name and considerable freedom in commercial activity but became a Government Agency with guaranteed firm contracts.

The stage was set, with amazing speed and unorthodox supply sources, for the rapid expansion of orders and consideration of new designs, and Holt set about the task of using these early ideas and the Fairmile system to provide a significant new element in another field. The Navy's fleet of motor torpedo boats (MTBs) and motor gunboats (MGBs) had until this time been thought of as primarily consisting of 'short' boats, usually of 60–80 ft in length. These MTBs and MGBs were faster and more powerfully armed than the MLs, and their role was to attack enemy shipping and to counteract the threat of the German Navy's E-boats, which had the advantage of high speed provided by powerful lightweight diesel engines.

Just as Macklin had taken a commercial risk to produce a prototype, so the Vosper Company, the British Power Boat Company and the Thornycroft Organisation had been producing early MTBs, MASBs (motor anti-submarine boats) and MGBs for the navies of the world. The onset of war found the Admiralty commandeering boats under construction for other nations, to add to the handful of boats very tentatively ordered from 1935 onwards and initially deployed in Malta and Hong Kong.

It was rapidly concluded that there was a need to reinforce the 'short boats' with a new design of 'long' boats (over 100 ft) to provide a more stable gun platform, an ability to withstand heavier seas, and room for a greatly increased armament.

The first Fairmile 'long' boats with greater power were ordered in August 1940 as motor launches, and were a development from the early A class. They were designated C class and began coming off the construction line in June 1941. Almost at once, they were reclassed as motor gunboats, and the twenty-four boats of the class were numbered from 312 to 335. They were to do valiant service not only as escorts for East Coast convoys, but for clandestine operations: indeed MGB 314 entered naval history as the headquarters ship for the St Nazaire raid.

Throughout the construction period of the C class boats, and with growing confidence in the Fairmile system of mass production, the Admiralty, using the expertise of William John Holt, were designing and testing a new hull design for a boat of greater power.[1]

Holt's concept for the next development of the Fairmile MTB/MGB was to marry a destroyer bow to a fast motor boat stern capable of accepting the greater power of four engines. He was working on this before the end of 1939. The aim was to obtain less pounding when driven at high speed into a head sea, and

[1] J. Lambert and A. Ross, 'The Fairmile "D" MTB', *Allied Coastal Forces in World War Two*, vol. 1, Fairmile Designs.

MGB 601, the prototype, under construction. Planking up the bow.
(Courtesy, Tough's Boatyard)

also to produce a dry boat forward by ploughing over the bow wave. This form had been tested experimentally to compare it with the round bilge form already developed.

The result was a semi-hard chine design with a sharp bow and very distinctive flare, with a wide flat transom which lent itself well to the arrangement of four shafts and propellers.

Holt later acknowledged that it was found that problems arose when it was necessary to maintain higher speeds into short steep sea conditions; then the plywood frames forward tended to break. This was tackled successfully by doubling the number of frames forward, and reinforcing parts of the hull with steel angle bars. The hull proved capable of providing the required greater speed, longer range, and heavier armament with a steady gun platform, and was acknowledged as a success.[2]

This, then, was the D class Fairmile, soon to be known as the 'Dog Boat'. The boats of the class were allocated the numbers 601 onwards.

[2] Paper by W.J. Holt to Institute of Naval Architects, 1947.

Sadly, this design did not lead to beauty. Compared with the sleek yacht-like hull of the Fairmile 'B' motor launch, the Dog Boat was at first sight ugly – much beamier and very squat. Indeed, one CO joining his boat and remembering it was prefabricated, was heard to mutter, 'Is that the boat or the box it was delivered in?'

By March 1941, the design was ready, and orders given for twelve motor gunboats, with the prototype MGB 601 laid down at Tough Brothers' yard at Teddington on 1 June 1941. Within a few weeks, the order was increased to forty boats, to be built at fifteen boat yards. The first thirty-two boats were planned to be gunboats and had no torpedo scallops cut into the hull forward of the bridge, but almost at once it was recognized that some might be completed as MTBs. The boats from 633 onwards had scallops incorporated, and could receive 21-in torpedo tubes, even though some were completed as MGBs. By November 1941, the order had been increased to 100 boats, and four more yards were building Dog Boats.

A feature of the construction of the class was the ease with which modifications could be introduced, proving the value of the prefabrication techniques and the flexibility of both planning and execution by the Fairmile method. This was quickly demonstrated when the decision was made to complete four of the first eight flotillas (each of eight boats) as MTBs rather than MGBs. Armament varied as new weapons and mountings became available, and it was not long before the Dog Boat was recognized as the most powerfully armed fast motor boat in the navies of the world.

The early flotillas soon settled to a 'normal' configuration. The common elements were the 2-pdr pom-pom on the focs'le and the twin 0.5-in mountings on each

A visit to Tough's yard by the First Lord of the Admiralty, Mr A.V. Alexander, illustrates the importance accorded to the Dog Boat programme. (Courtesy, Tough's Boatyard)

side of the bridge, with twin Vickers .303 machine-guns in the bridge wings. The MTBs had their two 21-in torpedoes, and a twin Oerlikon aft, while the MGBs mounted their twin Oerlikon on the coach roof and had a hand-operated Hotchkiss 6-pdr aft. This gun of ancient vintage, laid and trained by something akin to bicycle chains, proved in action to be accurate and effective when manned by a well-trained crew, and was greatly respected.

Later, some of the MGBs in the Mediterranean replaced the twin 0.5-in turrets with single Oerlikons; a power-operated semi-automatic 6-pdr replaced the pom-pom and the manual 6-pdr, and there were many local adaptations and experiments.

To complete the picture of this new concept of a brutal striking force, the early Dog Boats were powered by four Packard 4M-2500 marine petrol engines giving 1,250 b.h.p. at 2,400 r.p.m. They were the first MTBs to have four engines. Certainly, to be in the engine room when all four engines were running at high revs was to the uninitiated a frightening experience: somehow the dedicated motor mechanics and stokers found it exhilarating! The engines ran on 100 octane fuel, and the crews had quickly to get used to living within feet of 5,000 gallons of this highly volatile liquid whose vapour mixed with air could explode easily, given a spark from a faulty electrical system. The wardroom after bulkhead, for instance, was within

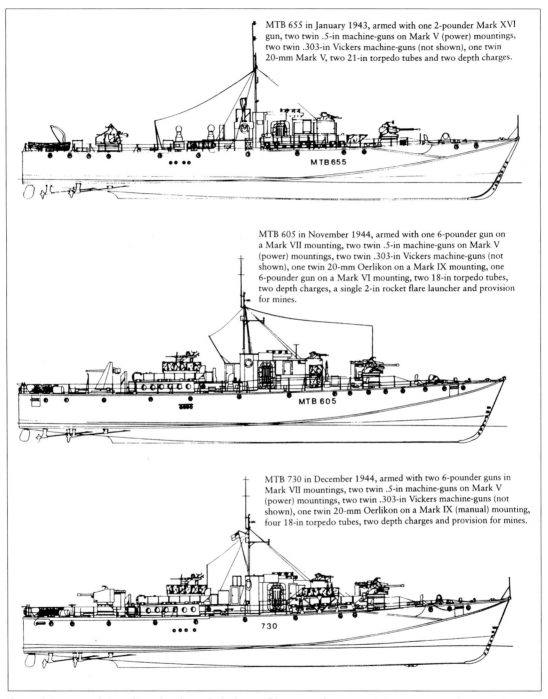

MTB 655 in January 1943, armed with one 2-pounder Mark XVI gun, two twin .5-in machine-guns on Mark V (power) mountings, two twin .303-in Vickers machine-guns (not shown), one twin 20-mm Mark V, two 21-in torpedo tubes and two depth charges.

MTB 605 in November 1944, armed with one 6-pounder gun on a Mark VII mounting, two twin .5-in machine-guns on Mark V (power) mountings, two twin .303-in Vickers machine-guns (not shown), one twin 20-mm Oerlikon on a Mark IX mounting, one 6-pounder gun on a Mark VI mounting, two 18-in torpedo tubes, two depth charges, a single 2-in rocket flare launcher and provision for mines.

MTB 730 in December 1944, armed with two 6-pounder guns in Mark VII mountings, two twin .5-in machine-guns on Mark V (power) mountings, two twin .303-in Vickers machine-guns (not shown), one twin 20-mm Oerlikon on a Mark IX (manual) mounting, four 18-in torpedo tubes, two depth charges and provision for mines.

The Fairmile D Motor Torpedo Boats: three outlines showing the development of the armament from January 1943 (MTB 655), November 1944 (605) to December 1944 (730) by which time they mounted four 18-inch torpedo tubes in addition to a very heavy gun armament. (Courtesy, John Lambert)

MGB 601 in March 1942, armed with one 2-pounder Mark XV gun, two twin .5-in machine-guns on Mark V (power) mountings, two twin .303-in Vickers machine-guns (not shown), one twin 20-mm Oerlikon Mark V, a Holman projector and two depth charges.

MGB 660 in October 1943, as modified for operations in the eastern Mediterranean, armed with one 2-pounder Mark XVI gun, two single 20-mm Oerlikons on Mark IIA mountings, two twin .303-in Vickers machine-guns (not shown), one twin 20-mm Oerlikon Mark V, one 6-pounder gun on a Mark VI (manual) mounting and four depth charges.

MGB 658 in February 1945, armed with two 6-pounder guns on Mark VII mountings, two single 20-mm Oerlikons on Mark IIA mountings, two twin .303-in Vickers machine-guns (not shown), one twin 20-mm Oerlikon on a Mark V (power) mounting and two depth charges.

The Fairmile D Motor Gun Boat: three outlines showing the development of the armament from March 1942 (601), October 1943 (658) to February 1945 (660). Except in the Mediterranean, where the gun boats remained as such, all other MGBs became 'general purpose' boats, mostly mounting torpedo tubes. (Courtesy, John Lambert)

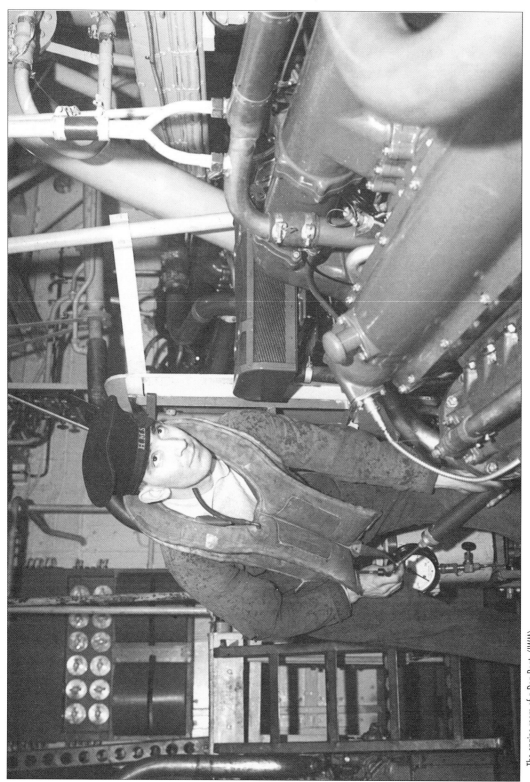

The engine room of a Dog Boat. (IWM)

inches of six copper tanks, each surrounded by a self-sealing compound, and each holding nearly 400 gallons. The petty officers' and stokers' messes down aft were similarly close to the after tank space, with another five tanks.

Descriptions thus far have been of hull and armament and engines: a power pack within the confines of thin plywood. But it was the men manning the boats who created their spirit and effectiveness, and gave them their vibrant purpose.

Indeed, these were the first MTBs and MGBs that were designed to have a crew which lived aboard and could be self-sufficient for long periods. That decision had its critics, including the legendary Commander-in-Chief Mediterranean, Admiral A.B.C. Cunningham who, paying his first and unannounced visit to a Dog Boat newly arrived in Algiers, muttered sharp imprecations about MTBs which were so full of clutter by virtue of living accommodation, that they were too slow to be effective.

But those words were quickly refuted as the benefits became rapidly evident. The ability to undertake much longer patrols and, for example, to remain off a beachhead for days supported only by transfers of water and fuel were exemplified during the Invasion of Sicily, and 'ABC' was soon sending congratulatory messages![3]

For those responsible for organizing the manning of this new generation of much larger boats, with their complement of three officers and thirty men, the rapid expansion of manpower requirements posed very real problems. The increasing demand caused by the regular arrival from the boat yards of short MTBs and MGBs, and MLs and HDMLs, was now compounded by this proportionately greater need of the larger boats.

The Naval Psychological Service had already been involved in devising methods of identifying suitable candidates from the mass of officers and men coming out of initial training, given the specific qualities needed in a branch of the service where youth, physical resilience, quick reactions and mental toughness were all deemed essential requirements.

The middle of 1942 in Coastal Forces was indeed the start of a remarkable expansion in required manpower. It also happened to be a time when those yachtsmen and seafaring amateurs who had flocked in 1938 and 1939 to the RNVR had proved themselves in many types of small boat. The early MTBs had nearly all been commanded by young RN officers but very quickly the RNVR men began to get commands, and the Canadians, Australians and New Zealanders came through strongly, too. (Note 1, Appendix 1)

So, command of the new Dog Boats went generally to RNVR officers who had spent two years in either short boats or in MLs and who had proved their worth in seamanship and aggression. They tended to be in their mid-twenties, although some were older, but even at twenty-five they were frequently the oldest men aboard.

First Lieutenants came broadly from a different background. They were mostly in an age group that had come into the Navy as ratings, had been commissioned in 1941 and then gained perhaps a year or less of experience in short boats. The Third Officers (usually known as 'Pilot' because normally they had the responsibility of navigating the boat) were however invariably straight from training, and were commonly nineteen or twenty years old – either fresh-faced midshipmen with their maroon patches, or sub-lieutenants with brightly gleaming new gold braid on their sleeves. It was a fact that every week, the Officers' Training Ship at

[3] See chapter four.

A bow view of Fairmile D class Motor Gun Boat: MGB 673 in May 1943. (Courtesy, John Lambert)

The crew of 721 on their messdeck. (Courtesy, Alan Benson)

Hove, HMS *King Alfred*, was turning out over a hundred young officers. Of these, it was normal that fifteen of the top twenty in the pass out list should be allocated to Coastal Forces, presumably because it was inevitable that they would almost immediately be navigating boats on operations which would be physically and mentally demanding – quite definitely a job for the young and bright.

This group was given one special 'perk' before being thrown in at the deep end. They alone were sent to Royal Naval College, Greenwich, for two weeks on what was irreverently known as the 'knife and fork' course. Few remembered afterwards any special benefits of that fortnight other than the proximity of London and the opportunity of dining in unaccustomed splendour in the Painted Hall, served by delightful Wren stewards. But at least it eased the transition

from lower deck to wardroom and was greatly appreciated. They spent the next three weeks at Whale Island on gunnery instruction, and at Roedean College near Brighton on a torpedo course, before making the long train journey north to Fort William. There, at HMS *St Christopher*, the Coastal Forces training base, they were instructed in specifically relevant aspects of what they were about to do. They all remembered the aircraft recognition sessions with the renowned yachtsman and author Alan Villiers, and benefited from instruction by young officers, often recovering from wounds, who only weeks before had been in command of an MTB.

The problems of manning at this stage of the war (in mid-1942) were probably seen most dramatically in the composition of crews. The keystone of any crew was the coxswain, and in the Dog Boats he was invariably a Petty Officer and almost always

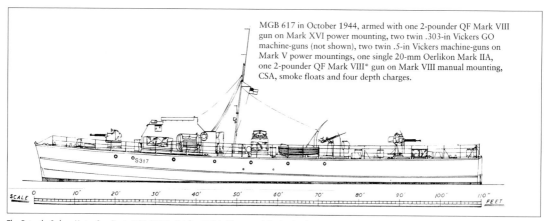

MGB 617 in October 1944, armed with one 2-pounder QF Mark VIII gun on Mark XVI power mounting, two twin .303-in Vickers GO machine-guns (not shown), two twin .5-in Vickers machine-guns on Mark V power mountings, one single 20-mm Oerlikon Mark IIA, one 2-pounder QF Mark VIII* gun on Mark VIII manual mounting, CSA, smoke floats and four depth charges.

The Fairmile C class Motor Gun Boat: MGB 317 in October 1944. (Courtesy, John Lambert)

Packard engine being lowered into position through the hatch.
(Courtesy, W. Last)

he had a General Service (i.e., career Navy) background. He brought the seamanship and man-management skills which were so necessary, especially when his crew were largely raw recruits.

He was supported by a 'second coxswain' – normally a Leading Seaman – with perhaps two years of Coastal Forces experience behind him. After that, he was lucky if he had two or three Able Seamen with salt in their veins: the rest of the upper deck crew were Ordinary Seamen straight from training. Their job was to man the guns and to maintain the boat in a shipshape and seamanlike condition. The boats had no signalman – the Pilot and First Lieutenant were expected to cope with light or flag signals – but carried a Telegraphist ('Sparks') and a Radar Operator. Rather strangely, there was no cook: morale on board often reflected the coxswain's success in persuading one of the seamen to take on that very important role with a modicum of competence.

Below decks in the engine room crew there was a Petty Officer (or Chief) Motor Mechanic, and a Leading MM, with four stokers, only one of whom might have some experience. So, in a crew of thirty-two, the CO

A contrast of scale: a Dog Boat and the battleship *King George V*. (Courtesy, I. Kinross)

might be lucky when he commissioned his boat to have six or seven hands with any experience. The other twenty-five were raw material for him to train and mould into an efficient unit as quickly as possible. His coxswain was therefore vital to his success, their relationship literally a matter of life or death, with the possibility of action only days away.

It was these untried boats and men that formed the first Dog Boat flotillas, and were thrust rapidly into the realities of war.

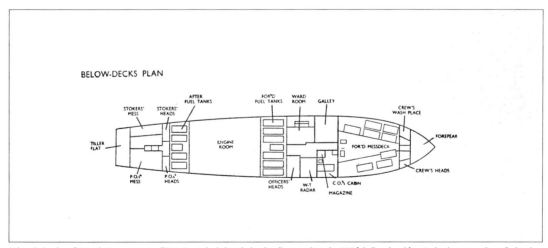

Below decks plan of Fairmile D: common to all Dog Boats the below decks plan illustrates how the 115-ft hull enclosed four Packard engines, eleven fuel tanks and accommodation for three or four officers and thirty to thirty-four other crew members. (Courtesy, John Lambert)

CHAPTER 2

OPERATIONS BEGIN

When the Dog Boats began to come off the slipways of their boat yards in the spring of 1942, they joined a rapidly growing force of short MTBs and MGBs which, until a few months earlier, had been desperately short of resources.

The war had begun with only a handful of MTBs in commission, and most of these were in the 1st Flotilla in Malta and the 2nd Flotilla in Hong Kong. The 1st Flotilla was brought home at the end of 1939 through the French canals, and was joined after the fall of France, Holland and Norway by a number of boats being built for other navies, which were rapidly requisitioned by the Admiralty. What they lacked in technical quality and armament was compensated by the dash and seamanship of their RN Commanding Officers, and they formed flotillas based in Felixstowe and Dover. They distinguished themselves at Dunkirk but had few opportunities to prove their worth until 1941, when with increasing numbers, re-armament, greater experience and the arrival of the first British Power Boat MGBs, things began to change.

Coastal Forces had begun to discern more specific objectives. Much effort was needed to protect British coastal convoys from the attacks of E-boats but the boats were also taking the offensive, and attacking enemy convoys as they crept along the coasts of the Channel and North Sea.

Because of the numerous escorts protecting those convoys, tactics had developed which involved combined attacks by units of MTBs and MGBs working together. The MGBs would try to engage the attention of the escorts to enable the MTBs to make their torpedo attacks on the larger targets. The 'short' gunboats had often lacked the fire-power to inflict crippling damage on many of the escorts but were led with such skill and aggression by Senior Officers like Robert Hichens, Dickie Richards, Stewart Gould and Bremer Horne that they scored many notable victories over the E-boats and R-boats they came across.

This enabled the MTBs to get to grips with the larger targets, and gradually, and especially in the Dover Strait, the MTBs began to score torpedo hits.

The Fairmile 'C' MGBs – the first 'long' boats and the forerunners of the Dog Boats – had begun to operate from Yarmouth and Dover by the autumn of 1941 and had added a new dimension of fire-power to the convoy protection role. By the end of 1941, there were seven MTB flotillas and seven MGB flotillas of short boats in home waters so that 1942 at last saw the build up of Coastal Forces that had been so long awaited.

It was augmented by another group of boats of new design, the steam gunboats (SGBs) which were completed early in 1942 and had

Two C class MGBs set out on patrol. (IWM)

MGBs 334 and 323 pick up two Danish boys attempting to sail to Britain across the North Sea to escape the occupation. (Courtesy, J. Carr)

MGB 605 at speed after refit. (Courtesy, Tough's Boatyard)

their first actions in June. They were mini-destroyers in aspect and, gallantly led, they had their successes and were much involved in the Dieppe Raid in August. But they proved, until given additional armour to protect their steam plant, to be very vulnerable, and for several reasons the decision was taken not to order more of this design.

Another significant step forward was the establishment of HMS *Bee* at Weymouth. Flotillas and individual boats could 'work up' there as they were commissioned, and crews were indeed worked hard at all hours of the day and night to prepare them for the operations to come.

This was the background against which the first Dog Boats made their appearance in Coastal Forces. The prototype, MGB 601, was completed on 9 March 1942, well in advance of the others being built, and she was entrusted to Allan Gotelee RNVR, an experienced officer and a solicitor in private life. Before flotillas were formed, 601 found herself attached to a group of C class MGBs operating from Dover and on 20 July a unit of three MGBs led by Lt H.P. (Pat) Cobb RNVR in 328, with 322 (Lt A. (Tony) Price RNVR) and 601 set out from Dover to search for enemy patrols south of Boulogne.[1]

Shortly after midnight, the group was vectored to intercept an enemy convoy off Cap Gris Nez which had been picked up by the Dover radar. It proved to be a merchant ship escorted by armed trawlers ahead and astern with an outer screen of E-boats and

[1] MO10221; ADM 199/782 at PRO.

16

A German R-boat. (Courtesy, the late J. Mannooch)

R-boats (the German equivalent of the Royal Navy's MLs). The SO asked Dover Command if MTBs were available, as this was clearly a torpedo target, but the sea conditions were not favourable for short boats, so Cobb decided to make a direct attack, possibly having the intention of dropping a depth charge under the bow of the merchant ship.

Sub-Lt Lionel Blaxell RNVR, who was the First Lieutenant of MGB 322, wrote an eye-witness account of this action:

> We had, in fact, run through an outer screen of E-boats before turning parallel to the main target. Cobb's boat began to close, and 322 and 601 followed in. We all opened fire, and hits from all three boats could be seen on the bridge of the target. Suddenly, all hell let loose: having penetrated the screen, all the escorts were now firing at us from – it seemed – every direction. As we passed very close to the main target, there was an enormous flash and flames from the position of Cobb's boat (328) and we did not see her again.

We later discovered she had been sunk, and Cobb was killed.[2]

Blaxell was wounded, and 322 hit many times by 40-mm and 20-mm shells, and contact with 601 was lost. In fact, 601 had also been severely damaged, and Gotelee badly wounded. Gallantly, she continued to harry the convoy for nearly an hour, inflicting damage to the main target and escorts alike, before limping back to Dover. Blaxell adds a postscript:

> I found myself in the same hospital ward as Allan Gotelee. He had had a close shave: a 20-mm armour-piercing shell had come through the rear of the bridge, narrowly missing Gotelee and his Coxswain. It had splintered against the forward bridge bulkhead, and he collected some of it in his leg. He had also found that the shell had been deflected off a silver hip-flask in the pocket of his bridge coat:

[2] From, *Through the Hawse Pipe, 1939–1946*, L.H. Blaxell, OBE DSC.

MGB 601 sinks alongside at Dover after action damage. (Courtesy, Tough's Boatyard)

he showed me the groove in it and was sure it had saved his right hip joint.

The official report on damage to 601 records twenty-six hits by 20-mm shells. The machinery was undamaged, and she returned to Dover under her own power. The report is particularly interesting in that it records precisely the damage effected by each shell: most left a 4–6-in hole in the hull. It also reveals that all power-operated turrets were put out of action as hydraulic leads were cut. Casualties were one man killed and all three officers wounded.[3]

There was an unexpected sequel to this action. Three days later, alongside in Dover, 601 was destroyed by an explosion and fire. The enquiry report established that the probable cause was a result of one of the fuel tanks being hit in the action, and the petrol

(and subsequently vapour) being trapped between the tank and the self-sealing compound. This emphasized the need for extreme caution, and led to a number of valuable lessons being learned. One change that was received most gratefully by later Dog Boat crews was to ensure that open flame (paraffin) cooking apparatus should be replaced by electrical units.

It must be said that this was a sad start to the operations of Dog Boats but 601 had proved a doughty opponent for a heavily escorted convoy, operational experience had been gained, and the need for modifications in equipment learned. These proved of great value to the boats coming from the boat yards.

But only three weeks later there was to be another blow. The second Dog Boat to be completed was 609, early in June 1942. She was allocated to the 17th MGB Flotilla at Yarmouth, where the Senior Officer, Lt Cdr Duff-Still RNVR was standing by to

[3] BR2054: Reports of Damage.

receive his boats as they completed trials and working up. 609's CO, Alan McIlwraith, describes how 609 set off from HMS *Bee*, the working-up base, but was ordered to put in to Dover and to operate with the C class MGBs there for a short time:

We did a couple of night patrols off the French coast but made no contact with the enemy. On 16 August, 609 set off on another patrol, following MGB 330, whose CO – and leader of the unit – was Derek Sidebottom. MGB 331 (Lt N.R. Weekes) was third in line.

In fact, this was no normal patrol: it turned out to be one of the most gallant and bruising MGB actions of the war. Twenty to thirty R-boats had set out from Calais to lay mines mid-Channel, and Sidebottom's unit and another of short MGBs, led by Lt 'Dickie' Richards, left Dover hell-bent to intercept them. The long boats were the first to sight the enemy, and Sidebottom led his unit in to attack at close range, astonished that the six R-boats they saw at first made no effort to respond. The engagement when it began was so fierce, the range so close and the visibility so clear, that all British boats suffered damage and casualties, while pouring devastating broadsides at the two R-boats at the rear of the line. Sidebottom, with all his guns out of action, rammed the R-boat last in line, and 609 and 331 went on firing at the other enemy boats until they too had so many guns disabled and crew wounded that they had to disengage: 609 had three engines out of action, two men killed and two mortally wounded, and all three officers and eight of the crew wounded. Casualties were also high in the two Cs, with both COs wounded, but the last two R-boats in line were unquestionably near to sinking.

A camouflaged R-boat. (Courtesy, S.C. Minette)

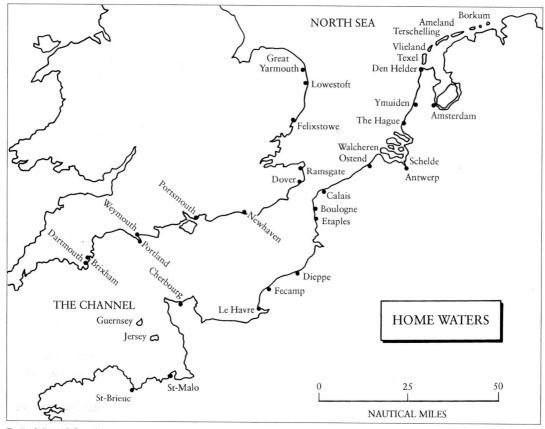

The North Sea and Channel.

Richards and his short gunboats then began their attack, and set the leading boat on fire, boarded it, and took fifteen prisoners. The following day, an MTB patrol picked up nine more Germans in a raft, from the R-boat that had been rammed. All the boats returned to harbour but 609 had no controls, no compass, no charts, and only one engine. McIlwraith remembers that they found Dover with the help of the North Star![4]

Without doubt the heavy fire-power of this second Dog Boat to be commissioned had added a new dimension to the attack but all

[4] Letter in 1988 from A.D. McIlwraith, CO of MGB 609.

the boats concerned had shown great gallantry. 609 was paid off for extensive repairs, but was recommissioned in 1943.

Following these two aggressive but expensive introductions to action by the Dog Boats, the autumn of 1942 saw the build up of the first four Dog Boat Flotillas.

The 17th MGB Flotilla has already been mentioned. It was commanded by Lt Cdr Henry Duff-Still RNVR and based at Yarmouth.

The COs were:

601 Lt A.A. Gotelee RNVR
603 Lt F.R. Lightoller RNVR
604 Lt J.O. King RNVR
605 Lt Cdr.H. Duff-Still RNVR

606 Lt E.D. Truman RNVR
607 Lt R.M. Marshall RNVR
609 Lt A.D. McIlwraith RNVR
610 Lt D.G.E. Probert RNVR
612 Lt P.A. Williams RNVR

The 18th MGB Flotilla, commanded by Lt H.P. Byrne RN, was based first at Portsmouth and then at Newhaven.

The COs were:

602 Lt J.D. Robinson RNVR
608 Lt J.H. Hodder RNVR
611 Lt A.C.N. Chapman RNVR
611 Lt I.D. Lyle RNVR
613 Lt H.W. Paton RNVR
614 Lt P.E. Mason RNVR
615 Lt T.W. Boyd DSO RNVR
616 Lt H.P. Byrne RN

The 30th MTB Flotilla was manned by Royal Norwegian Navy officers and men, with RN telegraphists. The flotilla was based at Lerwick in the Shetland Islands, and its operations will be described in a chapter devoted entirely to the extraordinary exploits of its boats.

Finally, the 31st MTB Flotilla, which was commanded by Lt I.R.P. (Giles) Goodden RN and based at Yarmouth, formed up in the New Year of 1943.

The COs were:

617 Lt C.J. Fleming RNVR
621 Lt I.R.P. Goodden RN
622 Lt P.F.S. Gould DSC RN
624 Lt K. Gemmell RNVR
628 Lt A.A. Gotelee DSC RNVR
628 Lt R.E. Cunningham RNVR
629 Lt C.A. Law RCNVR
630 Lt G.A. Guthrie RNVR
632 Lt P.A. Berthon DSC RNVR

The selection of the COs named above for these demanding new commands proved by subsequent results to have been entirely justified. Almost without exception they went on to make significant contributions to the record of Coastal Forces, and between them they were, by the end of the war, to receive three DSOs, twenty-two DSCs, and a hatful of 'mentions'.

The three 'home' flotillas were effectively operational by the end of 1942 or the start of 1943, and spent weeks on valuable but often frustrating and boring convoy protection patrols. The lifeblood of Britain depended to a great extent on the movement of supplies by frequent convoys along the Channel and up the east coast of England. These were vulnerable to attack by E-boats, and the new Dog Boats proved to be valuable additions to the stretched resources of escorts. They would be stationed on the seaward side of the convoy routes with the dual task of intercepting E-boats before they had the chance of attacking convoys, or catching them on their way home.

The task was made more frustrating by the fact that the E-boats were ordered to conserve their destructive potential by avoiding action with Coastal Forces escorts, using their speed and low silhouette to achieve this. Of course there were many occasions when they were surprised and thus trapped into action, but they were difficult to catch if given any sort of start. The short MGBs had the speed to catch them but at this stage of the war lacked sufficient fire-power to press home their attacks unless they could – as the legendary Robert Hichens (Appendix 1, Note 2) frequently accomplished – lie in wait for their return into their home ports. The Dog Boats, however, with their 30 knots maximum speed, lacked the pace to catch them but had the fire-power to destroy them given the chance.

Mixed in with the defensive patrols were offensive forays to the far shore, which for the Yarmouth-based boats meant a long flog, often in appalling weather and bad sea conditions.

In February 1943, this monotony was interrupted for three of the boats of the 17th Flotilla. The Senior Officer, Henry Duff-Still in 605, with Peter Williams in 612, and Douglas Probert in 610, had been sent north to Scotland for a special operation. Williams had, before his appointment as CO of 612, been in command of MGB 325, attached temporarily to an Admiralty department headed by Captain Frank Slocum RN. Slocum's designation was DDOD(I) – Deputy Director Operations Division (Irregular) – and his responsibility was to operate naval units carrying out clandestine tasks. Coastal Forces craft were used occasionally, and later a flotilla was formed to specialize in this work.

The three boats sailed to Aberdeen, where they found that they were to be involved in Operation Cabaret. The background to this was the tremendous need to bring Swedish steel products from neutral Sweden through the German blockade of the Skagerrak. Two Norwegian ships, the *Lionel* and the *Dicto*, were already loaded, having been forced back to Gothenburg in the ill-fated Operation Performance the previous year. They had sailed to Hakefjord, a small fjord near Vinga, and were awaiting an escort and the delivery of Oerlikon and Lewis guns, and Merchant Navy gunners, to make their breakout possible. The delivery of weapons and men was codenamed Operation Cabaret, and the three MGBs had been selected to carry it out. (Appendix 1, Note 3)

The three Dogs sailed on 4 February to attempt the hazardous passage through the Skagerrak to Sweden. They reached the entrance to the Skagerrak with weather conditions deteriorating markedly, when a signal was received abandoning the operation. It had little to do with the sea

conditions. The Admiralty had received information that heavy German Naval units had sailed south from Norway. The boats were recalled but faced mountainous seas, and all three suffered damage to their forward frames and spent some weeks undergoing repairs.

Although this was a disappointing end to a potentially very significant operation, the contribution of Coastal Forces boats did not end there, even if Dog Boats were not used. A new breed of 'long' MGBs originally ordered from Camper and Nicholsons by the Turkish Navy was under construction at Gosport. They were powered by three Paxman diesel engines, and were thought to be suitable for use as blockade-runners. Five of them were registered under the red ensign and commanded by Merchant Navy officers, and this fleet undertook the hazardous and politically delicate task of slipping through the well-defended waters of the Skagerrak. Between November 1943 and March 1944, vital cargoes totalling 347 tons of machine tools, high-speed steels and major loads of roller- and ball-bearings were delivered. They were acknowledged by the Minister of Supply as being of enormous importance to the war effort and to the build up to the invasion of Europe.[5]

Throughout the winter, the 30th MTB Flotilla manned by Norwegians had already experienced the rigours of the northern waters, and had been battling with the two enemies, the German Navy and the sea, with considerable success.

But in home waters, spring was on its way, and in March 1943 an increase in the proportion of offensive operations rather than convoy protection patrols led to a spate of actions which finally established the Dog Boats as very

[5] *The Blockade Busters*, Ralph Barker.

In line ahead leaving for patrol. (Courtesy, A.T. Robinson)

powerful and effective newcomers to the Coastal Forces scene.

The 31st MTB Flotilla, the first of the D class MTB flotillas in home waters, was based at HMS *Midge*, Great Yarmouth. The boats were working up and then gathering at their base during January and February 1943, and very soon after beginning patrols off the Dutch coast had two successes within a few days, early in March.

The normal pattern of operations for any flotilla was to make up units of different boats each night. Obviously the Senior Officer could not be at sea night after night, and his half-leader (the senior CO) frequently led a unit. So it was that on the 9/10 March, Lt Ken Gemmell in MTB 624 was leading a unit, followed by 617 (Lt C.J. Fleming) and 622 (Lt Frank Carr).

Gemmell was a noted yachtsman who, in 1938, had won the Royal Ocean Racing Club's race from Dover to Christiansund in Norway, against opposition from nine of

Germany's crack yachting team. Frank Carr, in a similar mould, had been a racing motorist: he had taken over 622 in December when Stewart Gould had been given command of the 32nd MTB Flotilla, destined for the Mediterranean.

The boats left Yarmouth with orders to carry out an offensive sweep off Terschelling. Earlier in the day, a reconnaissance aircraft had reported a westbound enemy convoy of eleven ships north of Wangeroog. The unit arrived in the area at about 2300, and almost at once made contact with a group of armed trawlers. Assuming these vessels to be the screen for the convoy, Gemmell altered course to avoid them but his unit was sighted and the enemy opened heavy fire. A lively action ensued in which the Dog Boats set one of the escorts (now known to be Vps 1247 and 1248) on fire.

While disengaging, 617 became separated from the other two MTBs, but 624 and 622 found the convoy that in fact was composed

Lt K. Gemmell (right) with others of the 31st MTB Flotilla.

of eight merchant ships and was very heavily escorted by four M class minesweepers of the 1st Flotilla and four Vps.[6]

Gemmell's two boats attacked from the port side of the convoy, and four torpedoes were fired at a tanker of about 6,500 tons and two hits were claimed.

By this time they were under very heavy fire, and 622 was hit and disabled. 624 made smoke and attempted to close and give assistance, only to be met by what appeared to be a destroyer, and was beaten off. It was later learned that 622 was abandoned and on fire and sank, the survivors being rescued by Vp 1300, becoming prisoners of war. 624 and 617 returned to Yarmouth with only superficial damage.[7]

[6] German auxiliary patrol vessels, literally 'Vorpostenboote'.
[7] ROP at PRO, ADM 199/537; MO3486; search file at NHB for loss of MTB 622.

Three nights later on 12/13 March, Lt Gemmell, once again leading a unit of the 31st Flotilla, had another great success, achieving the most unusual feat of carrying out an unobserved approach, a successful torpedo attack, and a withdrawal all without any fire from the enemy. Quite naturally it is often assumed that MTBs always attacked at high speed. In fact the majority of attacks began at low speed as quietly as possible to avoid detection: once sighted, of course, speed became essential.

On this occasion, Gemmell's unit had been alerted that an enemy convoy was moving down the Dutch coast, again off Terschelling. By midnight, in good visibility, they had sighted the convoy at long range and identified three merchant ships and a considerable escorting force. The three boats – this time, Gemmell in 624 had 628 (Ronald Cunningham) and 617 (with Bill

Beynon in temporary command) – stopped to plot the enemy course and to give Gemmell the chance to issue orders. They moved in slowly, getting closer and closer and astonished that they were not seen. At 3,000 yards the executive signal was given, and the three boats turned in at right angles, now in line abreast, and each boat moved towards its target, each CO's eyes glued to his torpedo sight. Each one fired when 'on', and five torpedoes shot towards their targets (for some reason 628 only got one off).

The reward was three resounding 'thumps' and smoke billowing from two of the targets but memories returned to the events of three nights earlier. The withdrawal had still to be achieved, and surely the escorts would see them and the hail of shells would whistle round their ears. But no! They turned to port together and crept away unseen, and the only reaction was a star-shell fired in the wrong direction.

It had been a beautifully executed attack and it was later established that two ships were indeed sunk. Intelligence reports after the war confirmed that the two were SS *Liege* (4,398 tons) and SS *Hermod* (1,495 tons). (Appendix 1, Note 4)

There was another unusual consequence of these two actions. For the first, Gemmell and Carr won DSCs, and DSMs were awarded to A/B William Wilson of 624, and A/B Harry Leader of 622, the latter for his bravery in fighting the fire which ultimately led to 622's sinking. For the second, no awards were made and indeed no publicity allowed, as if the Admiralty wanted to keep the enemy guessing. But the men of Coastal Forces, and especially the 31st MTB Flotilla, were well aware of a splendid success.

March saw one more action by boats of the 31st Flotilla. This time the unit was led

in 629 by Lt C.A. (Tony) Law, a Canadian who was later to be Senior Officer of an all-Canadian short boat flotilla which achieved great distinction in 1944. He was followed by 628, commanded by Lt Ronald Cunningham. This patrol, on 22/23 March, was once again off Terschelling and the engagement began when a unit of short MTBs attempting to attack a convoy was driven off. Tony Law, leading the northern group, made two attacks. In the first he met heavy fire and could only get close enough to inflict damage on one escort. The second led to a long-range torpedo attack from which no results were claimed, and both 629 and 628 were slightly damaged. But later post-war intelligence confirmed that an enemy trawler was damaged in the first clash.

The Dog Boats of all three 'home' flotillas stepped up their level of patrol activity considerably in the months of April and May 1943, and benefited from the growing experience of their crews and the increase in confidence in their boats felt by the COs. Much of the work from Yarmouth still involved the frequently fruitless manning of the line eight miles east of the convoy route, to intercept attacks by E-boats, but most nights there were also offensive patrols off the Dutch coast, where the enemy convoys were well protected by heavily armed and numerous escorts. But Lt Cdr Duff-Still, leading his 17th MGB Flotilla boats, achieved several notable successes with gun actions. 606, 607 and 603 damaged an escort trawler and possibly sank it on 27 March; two weeks later, 606, 603, 610 and 612 had another close brush with escorts but were unable to penetrate the screen.

Now that Yarmouth housed both an MGB and an MTB flotilla of Dog Boats, mixed units could be sent out. This put into practice the tactics that the short boat flotillas had been developing, particularly under Robert Hichens at Felixstowe and in the radar directed flotillas at Dover. The additional flexibility this gave, allowing units to make the type of attack most likely to succeed against the targets which were encountered, led in the autumn of 1943 to a major decision to convert the majority of MGBs – both short and long – into MTBs. Although this policy was under discussion in the spring, the experience being gained in April and May off the Dutch coast was proving valuable.

On both 19 and 30 April, Duff-Still led units made up from his 17th MGB Flotilla and the 31st MTB Flotilla. On both occasions the gunboats occupied the attention of the escorts, allowing the torpedo boats to get their torpedoes away but sadly no hits were obtained. The fire-power of a unit of Dog Boats attacking together was proving to be a new dimension in close gun attacks: four boats in close formation could bring such an intense battery to bear that targets were being set on fire and faltering in their ability to respond. The action on 30 April was very unusual indeed in that it took place in daylight.

The telegraphist aboard MTB 630 (Tom Barrett DSM) recalls:

On 30 April eight boats of the 17th and 31st Flotillas left Yarmouth to patrol the northern area of the Dutch coast. 621 had

Steering a good course.

26

to turn back with an engine defect, but we split into two sections. MTB 624 and MGBs 606 and 612 set off to patrol the outer convoy route off Vlieland and Terschelling, while MTBs 632 and 630, with MGBs 605 and 610 covered the inner convoy route. Both units, having found no targets, turned for home at about 0500, but soon after, as dawn broke and the Dutch coast was still well in sight, our inshore group sighted four enemy vessels. They looked like flak ships – large and menacing escorts which in daylight would heavily outgun the Dog Boats.

Duff-Still's report[8] reveals that he decided to attempt an attack by bluff: there was no other way to get close in, and without an element of surprise the battle would be too one-sided. He turned his boats directly towards the enemy hoping to pass the unit off as E-boats. Who else would be reckless enough to close in daylight? Tom Barrett continues:

630 was the last boat in line, and incredibly the enemy did not open fire until our four boats had had the chance to strike first and strike hard. The first target did not even fire a shot at us – all her guns must have been disabled very quickly. The next two were severely mauled but they and the fourth gun-coaster soon began to reply with their larger calibre guns and that was when a shell hit the bridge and caused heavy casualties. The captain (Lt Guthrie), the starboard Vickers' gunner and the starboard 0.5-in gunner were all killed instantly. The First Lieutenant, Sub-Lt Goddard, was so badly injured that he

died next day in hospital, and eight others (including the Navigating Officer, Sub-Lt Dalziel, and the Coxswain) were wounded, many of them seriously.

A/B George Lesslie throws some light on his captain's intentions.

Lt Guthrie, as 630 was last in line and the first attack had been so successful that return fire had dwindled, decided to attempt a depth charge attack on the fourth escort, and closed at speed. He shouted to me 'Lesslie – tell them to release manually' and as I turned back after doing that, the shell hit the bridge.[9]

It was Sub-Lt W.G. Dalziel, the Navigating Officer, who, although wounded himself, got to the bridge and with the help of the unwounded crew members, extricated the boat and linked up with the rest of the unit. The action had gone on for over half an hour, and Duff-Still was able to pause and watch as one of the enemy craft sank and two others burned furiously. It was 1645 before the unit got back to Yarmouth, with Dalziel, despite his wounds, still on the bridge of 630. Small wonder that he was awarded the DSC for his courage and devotion to duty. Also listed in the *London Gazette* of 6 July 1943 were DSMs for five of the crew (including Telegraphist Tom Barrett) and a posthumous Mention in Despatches for Graham Guthrie, the CO. In a separate entry, in the same gazette, Lt Cdr Henry Duff-Still was rewarded for 'leading coastal forces actions in April and May 1943' by the award of the Distinguished Service Order, joining the growing number of comparatively junior Coastal Forces officers to be so honoured.

---

[8] ROP at PRO in ADM 199/537; MO5493.

[9] Quoted from a letter to the author.

Each of the flotillas had further brushes with the enemy in May, both off the Dutch coast and in the Channel, but in the interests of chronology it is necessary to go back to the winter of 1942/3 and record the activities of the 30th MTB Flotilla, manned by officers and men of the Royal Norwegian Navy.

CHAPTER 3

THE 30TH (NORWEGIAN) MTB FLOTILLA

(Appendix 1, Note 5)

JUNE 1942 TO OCTOBER 1943

Very early in the war the officers and men of the Royal Norwegian Navy made it clear that they wished to be involved in the activities of the MTBs of Coastal Forces. Indeed, some boats were on order from British boat yards before the Germans invaded Norway in April 1940.

Two early Norwegian 60-ft Vosper MTBs (Norwegian numbers 5 and 6) joined the 11th MTB Flotilla at Dover, but both were lost by mid-1941. They were replaced by MTB 56, a 75-ft Thornycroft boat commanded by Lt Per Danielsen, and although 56 did not have any successful actions while operating from Dover, strangely enough her CO and ship's company did. A Norwegian report tells the story:

On 9 September 1941, as MTB 56 was non-operational, Per Danielsen and his men were ordered to take over the available MTB 54 and to join other British boats then in action against a convoy off the French coast. The British boats were attacking from seaward while MTB 54 attacked independently from inshore of the convoy. Her torpedoes hit and sank a 5,000-ton merchant vessel. It was probably a unique event in the history of the Royal Navy that an enemy ship was sunk by a unit flying the white ensign with a non-British CO and ship's company.[1]

The Norwegian Navy and its young MTB officers at the time were quite certain that the Norwegian coast, with its narrow passages between islands into the channels called the Inner Leads, must be an ideal hunting ground for their boats. Per Danielsen and his boat MTB 56 were chosen to demonstrate the accuracy of that belief. An operation was planned involving the towing of MTB 56 from Scapa Flow by the old Norwegian destroyer *Draug* to a point just outside the islands. This was

[1] ROP at PRO in ADM 199/675; MO14924.

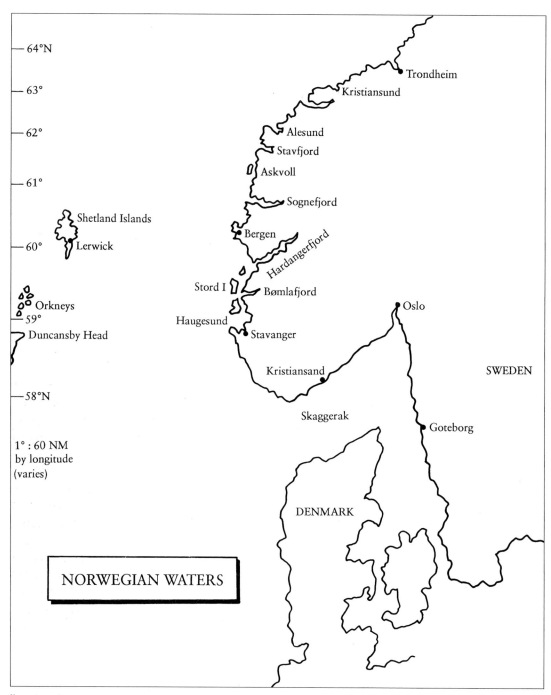

64°N

63°

62°

61°

Shetland Islands

60° Lerwick

Orkneys

59°

Duncansby Head

58°N

1° : 60 NM
by longitude
(varies)

Trondheim

Kristiansund

Alesund

Stavfjord

Askvoll

Sognefjord

Bergen

Hardangerfjord

Stord I

Bømlafjord

Haugesund

Stavanger

Oslo

Kristiansand

SWEDEN

Skaggerak

Goteborg

DENMARK

NORWEGIAN WATERS

Norwegian waters.

Boats of the Norwegian manned MTB flotilla in Lerwick Harbour, Shetland. (R. Nor. Navy Museum)

safely accomplished on 1 October 1941, and under cover of darkness 56 entered the Inner Leads only a few miles south of the city of Bergen. She moored up alongside an island and was covered by camouflage nets and bushes. The next evening, she took up a patrol position and soon a tanker was observed *en route* for Bergen, escorted by two minesweepers. Two torpedoes were fired, both hit the target, and the tanker caught fire and blew up. It was later discovered that she was the MV *Borgny* and that she was carrying 3,500 tons of aviation spirit for the German air force. MTB 56 managed to avoid an attack by the escorts, and returned safely to Lerwick in company with the *Draug*.[2]

It had been a brilliantly successful execution of a new and bold concept of attack, and it set the pattern for future operations. It also had the effect of forcing

the Germans to deploy extensive counter measures. However, it was recognized that there would be a greater advantage in using boats with longer range and better ability to withstand the appalling weather of the northern sea in winter.

It was this realization that led to the allocation of the very first Dog Boat MTB Flotilla, the 30th, to the Royal Norwegian Navy, to operate from Lerwick in the Shetland Islands through the winter of 1942/3. After MTB 56 (and indeed MTB 54) had led the way, several other short boats were commissioned by the Norwegians during 1942, and were based at Portland and Portsmouth where they were employed for training purposes. They provided the nucleus of the crews that manned the Dog Boats as they came from the boat yards between June and September, worked up at Weymouth at HMS *Bee*, and gathered in Lerwick under their Senior Officer, Lt R. Tamber RNorN.

---

[2] Report by Royal Norwegian Navy.

For the period from November 1942 to August 1943, the following boats made up the flotilla, and their COs (all RNorN or RNorNR) were to prove worthy upholders of the great seagoing traditions of the Norwegian Navy and people.

618   Lt A.H. Andresen
623   Lt A. Haavik
      Lt P.E. Danielsen
625   Lt K. Hjellestad
626   Lt K. Bogeberg
620   Lt A. Prebensen
631   Lt E. Matland
627   Lt H. Henriksen
619   S-Lt H.L. Henriksen
653   Lt E. Matland
      Lt R. Tamber
(653 replaced 631 later)
      Lt Ch. Herlofsen
      Lt B. Christiansen

Lt Tamber initially had the dual responsibility of being both SO of the 30th Flotilla and Senior Norwegian Naval Officer (SNNO) Lerwick. Later, as the base staff increased dramatically to keep the boats operational, he was able to concentrate solely on leading the flotilla, and Commander T. Horve RNorN, already decorated for services as CO of a destroyer, took over as SNNO.

The command structure in Shetland was similar to that in other commands: SNNO was operationally responsible to the Naval Officer in Charge (NOIC) Lerwick, who, until July 1944, was Captain Bell Salter RN. He in turn worked under direction from Admiral Commanding Orkney and Shetland (ACOS) at Lyness.

The operations planned for the boats were largely dictated by intelligence coordinated by Norwegian officers in Lerwick. One feature of the planning greatly appreciated by the

Leaving Lerwick for the Norwegian fjords. (R. Nor. Navy Museum)

A close up of the camouflage netting used when boats hid in the fjords. (R. Nor. Navy)

Dog Boat COs was their involvement at all stages, which led to confidence that the operational plans were realistic, with a good chance of success.

In fact, the intelligence received came from a number of sources and it reflected the determination of the Norwegian people to help in every way possible in the fight against the German occupying forces. The Resistance Movement continually passed information, and refugees from Norway crossed the North Sea in many small boats to the Shetland Islands and brought valuable details of troop concentrations and coastal defensive installations such as radar and lookout stations and coastal batteries.

The agents ashore reported by radio on the composition of convoys and their move-ments, and were also often able to verify the results of successful operations.

All this led to the establishment of a set of ground rules for the operations, dictated by distance and the nature of the Norwegian coast, in particular of the Inner Leads sheltered by hundreds of islands.

First the boats had to cross the North Sea undetected by enemy aircraft. Clearly, this passage had normally to be made in daylight hours to enable the next phase to be made in darkness. The boats, usually in pairs or threes, would take up an open formation one or two miles apart to make a less visible wake from the air. They would adjust their speed so as to be 20 to 30 nautical miles off the coast at nightfall. Then with the help of still visible mountainous features, a reasonably accurate initial position could be established, enabling

On lookout duty ashore. (R. Nor. Navy Museum)

a stealthy and unobserved entry to the Inner Leads. Unless this was achieved, the Germans could easily re-route convoys and hunt for the boats with a good chance of success. The main entrances to the Inner Leads, through the major fjords, were in most cases out of the question, due to the numerous and highly efficient German posts. It was therefore necessary for the boats to use narrow and undefended inlets among the islands to penetrate unobserved to the Leads.

This task, which would otherwise have been extraordinarily difficult for the navigators, was made possible by the availability of men eminently qualified to help. Many of those serving in the flotilla were fishermen, or seamen with excellent knowledge of the local coastal areas where they had previously earned their living. On most operations, therefore, the COs

had navigational advisors aboard intimately familiar with the particular area targeted.

Once in the Leads, the boats needed to find a good lurking position close to the shore, so as to be in the shadow of land. The precipitous nature of many of the shorelines, with deep water close inshore and often some vegetation at the water's edge, made this possible. The boats avoided locations close to populated areas and local seaborne traffic. Once alongside, masts could be hinged down and nets stretched over the superstructure, covered wherever possible by bushes and small trees. All this had to be achieved before daybreak, and often lookouts were put ashore to watch the sea and land approaches.

It was of course impossible to use the guns from under the camouflage nets; to do so anyway would have revealed a boat's position. This feeling of helplessness was quite a strain, especially when enemy aircraft flew over. But there was, on the other hand, a compensating psychological effect of the awareness of being in one's own country. This was particularly strong in the extremely patriotic Norwegians who deeply resented the occupation of their homeland.

In fact, through all the operations of the Norwegian Dog Boat flotillas, there is no record of camouflaged boats being detected by the enemy. But there was one great hazard which was hard to stomach, the need to avoid contact with the civilians ashore. Occasionally, boats were faced with the dilemma of local fishermen coming alongside! The policy was to be as nice as possible to them, invite them on board, serve them coffee and food and impress upon them that what they had seen and heard should not be mentioned to anybody. Quite often the visitors provided useful information on the German coastal activities. In some cases there were even touching meetings between MTB crew members and men from their own families.

With secrecy so essential, these encounters with local civilians were considered undesirable, and they left an uneasy feeling. It was not that the visitors were considered unreliable or possible informers, but they lived in such isolated localities and were so cut off from the realities of the war that they could be naïve. There was one extraordinary example which shows how potentially dangerous such contacts could be.

In February 1943, MTBs 619 and 631 had been lying hidden for several days due to very bad weather. They had received visitors on board and it soon became obvious that news of their presence was spreading quite widely. Eventually one of the visitors told the crew that they wanted to repay the hospitality they had received on board, and were planning a party! They had cleaned out a nearby barn and intended to hire an accordion player from a village a few miles away. They had even arranged to bring in a number of pretty girls as dancing partners for the crews. Needless to say, regardless of the weather, the boats were on their way back to Lerwick the same evening, having been in Norway for eight days.

There was a general saying among the boats' crews that the real enemy was not the Germans but the sea. Soon after operations began in 1942, it became all too evident that the early Dog Boats had not been built to withstand the awesome seas and weather conditions involved in these northern patrols in winter. Frames tended to break when the bows had to punch into typical westerly gales especially perhaps on return passages. The lessons were learned, and later boats were specially strengthened but most of the 30th Flotilla had in turn to undertake time-consuming repairs and refits in Scotland.

It was, of course, a real problem that the time span involved in an outward passage and several days lurking meant that weather forecasts which had been reliable when the boats set out for Norway, had little relevance to the conditions they met on the return to Lerwick. A rule of thumb developed that units should not leave Lerwick when seas above Force 4 were running. If the weather worsened on the outward passage, they were expected to turn back. But once they set out on the return voyage after a period of operations, with fuel getting low, they knew there was no turning back. They had to carry on, irrespective of the danger of breaking down and being at the mercy of the sea. There were a number of examples of fearsome voyages with recorded wind velocities of up to 130 m.p.h.

Fuelling from cans. (R. Nor. Navy Museum)

Fuel was always a significant matter on every operation. The shortest round trip on Norwegian patrols was 400 miles, and anything more than that required additional petrol to be carried on deck in 5-gallon cans. As there was an operational need to stretch German defensive measures over more and more of the coastline – which in turn slowed down the German convoys – some very long patrols reaching much further north were carried out that involved round trips of up to 800 miles.

The maximum extra petrol load was 4,000 gallons. This was regarded by crews with dislike and apprehension as it not only restricted the use of guns, but it was a great hazard when under the threat of air attack. It also led to an additional chore in dangerous conditions as it was vital to refill the outer tanks (the most vulnerable) from the deck tins, before entering the Inner Leads. The other method of reducing petrol consumption was for available patrol vessels to tow boats when extreme ranges were contemplated but as bad weather might necessitate the discontinuation of the tow, it was regarded as an unreliable method and was rarely used.

As in every sphere of naval operations, there were many patrols, often long and arduous, where no contact with the enemy was made. But the 30th MTB Flotilla under its Norwegian SO, Lt Ragnvald Tamber, distinguished itself in the winter of 1942/3 before the home flotillas had begun to register their first successes. In many ways, there was a special urgency among the Norwegians as exiles to take the war to the occupying force, and this together with the need to take advantage of the long winter nights, led to early successes.

After several fruitless patrols, the flotilla was rewarded on 28 November 1942. MTB 620 (Lt Aksel Prebensen) and 623 (Lt A. Haavik) approached the German convoy assembly port of Askvoll, north of Sognefjord, expecting it to be well protected. But they found the inshore navigation lights burning brightly and had no trouble in entering the harbour undetected. They were able to sink two merchant vessels that were later identified as SS *Harvest Hude* and SS *Herva*. They left the harbour pursued only by a few desultory rounds aimed in their general direction. This first success for the flotilla, so early in its history, was a great boost to morale.[3]

In January 1943, after a period of very bad weather, Tamber led his flotilla in a complex series of linked raids with the overall code name of Operation Cartoon. The purpose was the destruction of a mining facility producing copper for the German war industries. This mine was situated on the island of Stord, not far from the city of Haugesund.

The operation had an unusual first phase. Two officers from the flotilla, dressed as fishermen, crossed the North Sea in a fishing boat to carry out a reconnaissance. They went ashore and thoroughly inspected the objective and its approaches, taking photographs and making sketches. One delightful (if scary) aspect of their daring visit was the way the German sentries took their lines and were generally helpful as they came to the jetty!

Two weeks later, seven boats of the flotilla converged on the general area of the raid. MTBs 618 (Lt Alf Andresen) and 623 (Lt Haavik) were despatched to carry out a

Lt Ragnald Tamber R. Nor. Navy, SO 30th (Norwegian) MTB flotilla and CO MTB 619. (R. Nor. Navy)

diversionary attack on a German lookout station 25 miles north of Stord, which was successfully accomplished.

In a similar covering feint, 620 (Lt Aksel Prebensen), 625 (Lt Karl Hjellestad) and 631 (Lt E. Matland) proceeded eastward deep into a fjord. They set fire to a herring oil factory by gunfire, took on several shore batteries and laid some mines in the convoy channel. In the middle of all these activities, the German merchant vessel SS *Ilse L.M. Russ* had the misfortune to choose this moment to come along. She was engaged by gunfire, set on fire, grounded and burnt out.

The main assault on Stord was carried out by fifty specially trained raiders who embarked in all seven boats but eventually

3 From Summary of Actions at NHB.

Relaxing ashore close to the camouflaged boat hidden deep in a fjord. (R. Nor. Navy Museum)

transferred to 626 (Lt Knut Bogeberg) and 627 (Lt H. Henriksen). Twenty-five Norwegian commandos were put aboard 626, and twenty-five British commandos aboard 627. In command of the raiding party was Major Fynn RN.

The reconnaissance party had established that machine-gun posts were manned, and that there were two 4-in guns on the jetty where the MTBs intended to land their troops. 626 fired her two torpedoes at the jetty, partly destroying both it and the 4-in guns, and then attacked with blistering gunfire before putting her commandos ashore. 627 followed in with her troops, who methodically prepared all the German machinery, housing and equipment for demolition. The raid was not without

opposition, and some casualties were sustained, but the aim was totally achieved. It was later estimated that it would take twelve months to get the mine back into working condition.

All the boats returned safely to Lerwick and even this phase had its success: 625 and 631 shot down a Ju88 aircraft that attacked them.[4]

It appears that the raid had its repercussions at a high level in the enemy command. At the direction of Hitler's War HQ, the area commander was court-martialled for 'lack of readiness'. The German Admiral in Bergen made the following accurate observation in his war

[4] CF Periodic Review 1,2/1943; Summary of Actions.

diary: 'The operation must have been planned and carried out by an enemy with superior intelligence of the area.'

Another example of a classic lurking operation took place on 13 March. MTBs 619 (with the SO, Lt Ragnvald Tamber in command) and 631 (Lt E. Matland) were lying camouflaged alongside an island from where it was possible to overlook the activities inside the convoy assembly port of Floro, which was known to be only lightly defended. During the first day no enemy movements were observed. The next day, a convoy of three merchant vessels with escorts were seen at anchor.

As darkness fell, the boats prepared to attack through very intricate waters. Once inside the harbour, 619 fired her torpedoes and sank the German merchant vessel SS *Optima*. Following close behind, 631 had to proceed through the wreck in order to get at another vessel. It is not known whether she fired her torpedoes or whether, if she did, they hit or missed but on her way out of the harbour, she grounded. With the assistance of 619, frantic efforts were made to get her off, but all to no avail. As a German escort vessel was approaching and opened heavy fire, 619 took off 631's ship's company and tried to destroy her with gunfire. Sadly, at this time no demolition charges were fitted. Eventually 631 had to be left behind and 619 got back to Lerwick after a very miserable crossing in bad weather.[5]

631 was naturally an important capture for the Germans, as it provided them with valuable intelligence. She was towed to Bergen and was taken into service and renumbered 'S 631' – 'S' being the normal prefix for S-boats (E-boats). There is no evidence that she was engaged in any actions against Coastal Forces.

It will be remembered that the guidelines which dictated the planning of operations included the need for undetected entry to the Leads, and indeed no aerial detection in the approach across the North Sea. Even so, such was the enthusiasm and aggression of the flotilla officers and the operating team that the patrols continued into the summer of 1943, when there was virtually no dark period.

An example of this that turned out successfully took place on 4 June 1943 when MTBs 626 (Lt Knut Bogeberg) and 620 (Lt Aksel Prebensen) attacked a convoy just south of Bergen and torpedoed and sank the merchant vessel SS *Altenfels*, which was carrying 8,000 tons of iron ore. The two boats had been lying camouflaged for two days within a heavily defended area on the doorstep of the city of Bergen, with an enemy airbase in the vicinity and considerable local seaborne traffic. After the sinking of the *Altenfels*, the boats engaged the escort (an M class minesweeper) and severely damaged her. As they withdrew, they were fired on by no less that five coastal batteries and sustained both fatalities and casualties, including the SO, Lt Tamber. They were perhaps lucky to get away and back to Lerwick without further damage.[6]

In retrospect, the Norwegian authorities, acknowledging the success and the daring which led to it, considered that the planners had underrated the probable counter-measures. They also felt that this attitude of overconfident aggression may have been a contributing factor to the tragedy of MTB 345 soon after.

Although 345 was not a Dog Boat – indeed she was an experimental Thornycroft 55-ft boat, displacing only 16 tons – she was added to the 30th MTB Flotilla for specific

[5] Summary of Actions; MO53055; War History Case (WHC) 7942.

[6] Summary of Actions; MO53614; WHC 7942.

The only known photograph of MTB 345, discovered and captured in July when all the crew were executed by the Gestapo. (R. Nor. Navy Museum)

operational purposes, and for that reason, her short, sad and ill-fated commission deserves a mention here. She was very similar to the 1919 CMBs that had achieved fame when they penetrated Kronstadt Harbour in the Gulf of Finland in August 1919, and sank first the cruiser *Oleg* and then later two Russian battleships and a destroyer, severely damaging a cruiser. (Appendix 1, Note 6)

MTB 345 had a very limited range: she could only make one single crossing of the North Sea and needed either to be towed or supported by a craft which could refuel her. However it was believed that because of her very small size she could easily be camouflaged and, when attacking, would be very difficult to detect. So, once again in defiance of the guidelines that discounted summer operations, she made her first patrol in June 1943, supported by fuel and provisions brought over by MTB 653. She

patrolled for an incredible twelve days, mostly in daylight, camouflaging as necessary for rest and maintenance. Unfortunately, and to the intense disappointment of her crew and especially her enthusiastic CO Lt Alf H. Andresen, she made no contact with any enemy shipping.

She tried again in July and on the 24th she left Lerwick with MTB 620 in support. This time they were spotted by enemy aircraft, and it is almost certain that they were observed by a coastal lookout station on entering the Inner Leads. At midnight, 620 started transferring fuel, and there was an exchange of fire with a Blohm und Voss flying boat that certainly compromised 345's position. 620 returned to base and 345 remained under camouflage for four days. By this time, German patrol vessels had closed access to the sea and aircraft were circling. Eventually, a landing party attacked

A Christmas tree brought over to Lerwick from Norway. (R. Nor. Navy)

from the shore and after a short but fierce fight during which three of 345's crew were wounded, the boat was captured. The prisoners were taken to Bergen and interrogated. Next day they were handed over to the Gestapo and on the morning of 30 July the eight men were executed. Their bodies were attached to depth charges and thrown overboard in the fjord south of Bergen. (Appendix 1, Note 7)

When these tragic events became known to the flotilla, they made a deep impression. They were not deterred from future operations, indeed the resolve of these patriotic and aggressive crews was hardened, but certainly operations were conducted with greater prudence, and (for example) the use of camouflage for an extended period became far less frequent. Quite properly, the absence of darkness through the rest of the summer of 1943 led to the suspension of patrols until September.

But concern that other ways must be found to hinder German sea traffic at this time led to experiments using the Dog Boats as carriers for the one-man midget submarines (Welman craft) and for the two-man human torpedoes (Chariots) which were seen as better ways of attacking shipping in harbour.

A number of boats were modified to provide davits for lifting the craft inboard and outboard. MGB 675, which on commissioning in July 1943 was not allocated to an MTB flotilla but attached as a tender to the 12th Submarine Flotilla, was the first boat to be fitted with the davits. This involved the removal of the 6-pdr gun aft. In September she sailed to Lerwick with two Chariots aboard. Simultaneously, other boats in the 30th (about to become the 54th) Norwegian MTB Flotilla were being prepared and trained to carry Chariots and Welman craft at Lerwick.

675, escorted by Norwegian Dog Boats, was the first to undertake a Chariot operation in mid-October. The intention was to attack shipping in Askvoll. The weather was terrible and 675 – by now on her own – was forced to lie up in a fjord under camouflage. When she ventured out, she was tracked and finally attacked by aircraft and severely damaged, with dead and wounded among the crew. She bravely struggled back to Dunbar on the east coast of Scotland, a voyage of 400 miles, on one engine and with no compass.

There were other attacks attempted by the Dog Boats carrying Chariots and Welman craft but none was successful, and the operations were effectively brought to a close by the loss of 686 (of the 34th/58th Flotilla) and 626 (of the 30th/54th Flotilla) by fire and explosion on 22 November. This tragedy occurred alongside at Lerwick just as they were leaving for the Norwegian coast to recover Welman drivers who were hiding ashore after abandoning their craft. They were eventually rescued by MTB 653 but not until February 1944, despite several attempts. (Appendix 1, Note 8)

It was at this time, October 1943, that the policy decisions to re-constitute the Dog Boat flotillas, giving them new numbers and converting the MGBs in home waters to MTBs, were being implemented.

This affected the Norwegian Flotilla as all others, and the 30th MTBs became the 54th Flotilla, with Lt Ragnvald Tamber RNorN continuing as Senior Officer right through to April 1944.

On the east coast, the 17th MGB Flotilla became the 50th MTB Flotilla, and Lt Cdr G.L. Cotton took over as Senior Officer, while the 31st MTB

Flotilla was renumbered as the 55th MTB Flotilla. From 1 September 1943 to late in 1944 the Senior Officer was Lt Cdr Donald Gould Bradford RNR. (Appendix 1, Note 9)

To complete the picture, the 18th MGB Flotilla operating in the Channel became the 51st MTB Flotilla, with Lt Cdr Ian D. Lyle RNVR (who had taken over from Lt H.P. Byrne RN early in 1943) continuing a long and distinguished period as Senior Officer.

But before the narrative takes up the activities of these boats, together with other newly formed flotillas, it is proper to go back to the early spring of 1943 when the Dog Boats that had been earmarked for service in the Mediterranean were about to begin their colourful, and very different, commissions.

CHAPTER 4

MEDITERRANEAN OPERATIONS

MARCH TO OCTOBER 1943

From 1941 to March 1943, the Coastal Forces' presence in the Mediterranean had been confined to the short boats of the 10th and 15th MTB Flotillas, augmented by the 7th MTB Flotilla in late 1942. Much of their effort had been concentrated in the Eastern Mediterranean, where HMS *Mosquito* had been developed as the Coastal Forces base in Alexandria. From there, the first small Thornycroft boats had almost all been lost at Crete in December 1941, after which they were re-equipped with US-built Elco boats. They had then ranged along the desert coast in support of the Eighth Army. They had chafed with frustration at the problems of shortage of spares and maintenance of their boats but most of all at the lack of targets and often inadequate range available to them. They lost a number of their boats in September 1942 in Operation Agreement, the raid on Tobruk, largely through, they felt, a lack of understanding of the ways in which they could best be operated. The 7th Flotilla, in early Vospers, also suffered maintenance and reliability problems. But as the Eighth Army pushed the Germans westward, both flotillas moved by the end of 1942 to Malta and soon after to Bone in Algeria, now made available by the First Army's successful landings around Algiers in Operation Torch.

At this time, General Eisenhower was Supreme Commander in North Africa, and his main concern was to stop the reinforcement of the German Army in Tunisia by sea from Sicily. With the Luftwaffe able to use the Sicilian airfields, German control of the air and thus the sea over the Narrows, made destroyer and cruiser operations difficult by day; there was a definite need for more MTBs in the area. The major port of Bizerta needed to be blockaded until it could be taken and in the longer term, the destruction of any German forces seeking to evacuate North Africa would become a major requirement. That would inevitably lead on to an attack on Sicily and Italy, with a clear need for the sort of inshore patrols that only Coastal Forces could provide.

So it was that the Admiralty was pressed to make available several flotillas of both MTBs and MGBs to the Mediterranean, and the decision was taken to send four Dog Boat flotillas as they came off the stocks in their boat yards around the coasts of Britain.

The boats destined for the Mediterranean were the next four flotillas numbered successively 32nd MTB Flotilla, 19th MGB Flotilla, 33rd MTB Flotilla and 20th MGB Flotilla, which were completed during the

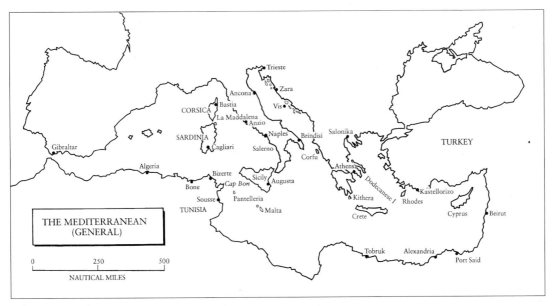

Mediterranean (general).

period November 1942 to May 1943. They were allocated to four Senior Officers of proven leadership and experience in Coastal Forces, whose first task was to attempt to influence the appointment of COs to their boats, then to inject as much urgency as possible into their completion, manning and preparation to move to Milford Haven. There they were to gather to sail in small convoys to Gibraltar as soon as they were ready.

In practice, such was the urgency that very few of the boats had any time to work up at HMS *Bee* at Weymouth, and all the problems of the supply of suitable crews became apparent immediately. While the inexperience of the available manpower was common in almost every crew assigned to Coastal Forces boats and could to some extent be countered by intensive exercising under the vigorous routine of a very efficient working up base, this advantage was denied to the Mediterranean boats. To compound that circumstance, the boats faced a tremendous initial challenge: their first voyage other than

passage to Milford Haven from their building ports was to be a gruelling seven day slog under their own power to Gibraltar. This would have tested experienced crews in tried boats. It is a testament first to the quality of the building yards and the high standards of the base crews that all the boats survived their voyages, and second to the spirit and resolve of these untried men that each voyage actually served to knit the crews together.

In particular, where the two motor mechanics were inexperienced (however technically qualified), the problems of keeping engines and ancillary services running when enormous seas made the engine room a heaving unsteady box, often became intolerable. The heat and fumes affected already vulnerable stomachs and the incidence of seasickness was very high.

This applied equally of course to the large proportion of the upper deck crew who had never been beyond inshore waters before. Fortunately there was always a nucleus of 'old hands' – the Coxswain and Leading

Seaman and a couple of seamen – to help them through the first few days. Such is the resilience of young men that their alertness and stability returned quickly, and many of them suffered no more seasickness for the rest of the commission.

So significant was the original selection of the Senior and Commanding Officers for these thirty-two boats that their names are recorded here. There were, of course, changes in the early days and where these led to replacements who remained for a long period, these are also recorded.

The 32nd MTB Flotilla was entrusted to one of the most gallant, aggressive and experienced officers in Coastal Forces. Lt P.F.S. (Stewart) Gould DSC and bar RN had commanded one of the MTBs of the 1st Flotilla in Malta before the war, and throughout 1940, 1941 and 1942 had harried enemy shipping in the Channel in the MGB flotillas based at Dover. The boats of his flotilla were completed in November and December 1942, and the majority sailed for the Mediterranean in March 1943. The COs were:

633   Lt H.E. Butler RNVR
634   Lt A.B. Eason RNVR
635   Lt R. Perks RNVR
636   Lt F.A. Warner RNVR
637   Lt E.F. Smyth RNVR
        Lt A.P.G. Joy RCNVR
638   Lt E. Rose RNVR
639   Lt G.L. Russell RNVR
640   Lt P.F.S. Gould DSC RN
        Lt R.R. Smith DSC RNVR

The 19th MGB Flotilla was commanded by Lt E.M. (Mickey) Thorpe DSO RN, who had served with distinction in C class MGBs on the East Coast. The COs were:

641   Lt A.D. McIlwraith RNVR
642   Lt C.J.C. MacNaghton RNVR
643   Lt G.M. Hobday RNVR

644   Lt E.M. Thorpe DSO RN
645   Lt B.L. Bourne RNVR
        Lt P. Hughes SANF(V)
646   Lt R.A. Forbes RNVR
647   Lt M. Mountstephens RNVR
        Lt K.E.A. Bayley RNVR
648   Lt K.E.A. Bayley RNVR
        Lt N. McLeod RNVR

The Senior Officer of the 33rd MTB Flotilla was Lt Cdr R.R.W. Ashby DSC RNVR. Ron Ashby had been a CO in the 2nd MTB Flotilla in Hong Kong when the Japanese invaded in December 1941, and had won his DSC in those operations. The COs were:

649   Lt J.D. Archer RNVR
651   Lt K.M. Horlock RNVR
654   Lt T.G. Fuller DSC RCNVR
655   Lt E.T. Greene-Kelly RNR
656   Lt D.G. Tate RNVR
        Lt P. Hughes SANF(V)
        Lt W.H. Masson RNVR
665   Lt P. Thompson DSC RCNVR
667   Lt C.J. Jerram DSC RNVR
670   Lt Cdr R. Ashby DSC RNVR

Lastly came the 20th MGB Flotilla whose Senior Officer on formation was Lt Cdr N.H. Hughes RNVR. He had been the Senior Officer of a C class MGB Flotilla and was a veteran of the Dieppe Raid. The COs were:

657   Lt J.D. Maitland RCNVR
658   Lt C. Burke RCNVR
659   Lt R.C. Davidson RNVR
660   Lt B.G.P. de Mattas RNVR
        Lt A.H. Moore RNVR
661   Lt L.H. Ennis RNVR
662   Lt Cdr N.H. Hughes RNVR
        Lt T.J. Bligh RNVR
663   Lt T.E. Ladner RCNVR
674   Lt P.J. Kay RNVR

All these boats, as they completed trials, sailed to Milford Haven and up river into Pembroke Dock, which served as a gathering point where the boats were made ready for their voyage to Gibraltar. Perhaps the most significant operation was to fit upper deck tanks which held 3,000 gallons of 100 octane petrol and thus increased the total full capacity to 8,000 gallons. Two side effects of these additions soon became apparent: first, that movement around the upper deck was even more difficult than normal, and second, that arrester bars had to be fitted to each of the guns to make sure that they could not be fired into the tanks.

Dominating the approach to the lock beyond which the boats lined the basin was the hulk of HMS *Warrior*, the Navy's first ironclad. It was sad to see her reduced to the role of a fuel jetty, her hull filled with concrete and backed by fuel tanks.

The boats sailed in groups, usually in company with other small craft and particularly with MLs, which were also building up to impressive numbers in the Mediterranean to carry out their great variety of tasks – largely unsung but of tremendous value. Each convoy was escorted by two trawlers whose main task was that of navigation and transmission of signals.

The months of March, April and May 1943 were later recognized as the peak of activity by U-boat packs in the Atlantic, and as a precaution the convoy route was taken westward to 13° west, then south to the latitude of Gibraltar before turning east into the Mediterranean. Almost all the convoys were shadowed by the Luftwaffe's reconnaissance aircraft but only one was attacked. The total distance was over a thousand nautical miles, and the boats maintained a speed of 8 to 10 knots. For the Dog Boats this was uncomfortably slow, and

The grave of Stewart Gould in the Commonwealth War Graves Cemetery at Sousse, Tunisia. (Courtesy, A. Falconer)

meant running on one engine at a time. Such was the weather invariably encountered, that huge seas not dreamed of in most Coastal Forces operations were the norm, and problems such as props racing as they lifted clear of the water required constant attention. Most boats had fuel supply difficulties when tanks were switched over, and more than one broke down completely in mid-ocean, hoisting the dreaded signal flags 'Harry Four' to indicate 'four engines out of action'. Another boat had then to attempt a tow or at least to stand by the crippled craft.

At night, when the boats showed only a shaded stern light, the officer of the watch and the helmsman had an unenviable task to keep station on the boat one cable ahead, and on the neighbouring columns of boats one cable to port and starboard.

These major problems were, in the minds of the crews, overshadowed by the enormous difficulty of maintaining any cooking facilities when the going was really rough, even when the generators could be kept running, which was not always the case. In addition each boat had only 125 gallons of fresh water: that had to last thirty-five men for seven days for all purposes and sailors, who are traditionally very clean well-scrubbed mortals, had to be content with minimal facilities.

The first Dog Boat to sail was MTB 635 of the 32nd Flotilla. She was so far in advance of the others that she sailed as the only 'Dog' with MLs, on 4 March 1943. She was followed by a group of six boats on 16 March, with Stewart Gould's 640 as the leading boat. As they arrived in Gibraltar on 23 March, five boats left Milford Haven, this time with Mickey Thorpe's 644 almost completing his 19th MGB Flotilla. Five more left on 6 April and brought the 32nd MTB Flotilla up to full strength. The largest group was of eight boats leaving on 30 April, with Ron Ashby, SO of the 33rd MTBs, leading the starboard column and four MGBs, including the three Canadians (Maitland, Burke and Ladner), to port.

It was this convoy that had the most dramatic passage. Two smoky trawlers, ahead and astern, were the escort, and the two wing columns of Dog Boats were separated by two central columns each of four MLs. The weather was poor and the following seas huge for the first three days, and it was even less comfortable when the convoy turned south having reached 13° west longitude. On that day too a long-range Focke Wulf Condor appeared and continued to circle for several hours.

That night, soon after midnight, a stream of tracer suddenly erupted from the port bow of the convoy's port column, and MGB 657 in the lead was hit and fire spurted from an upper deck fuel tank. The attack only lasted a very short time but was clearly from a surfaced U-boat, which must have dived almost at once as no trace of her could be found. Maitland in 657, with masterly seamanship, extinguished the fire by turning 'head to sea', allowing the waves to douse it before resuming station. Without doubt, had the fire taken hold, there would have been little chance of saving 657 or her crew, given the heavy sea running at the time. In retrospect, it was impossible not to admire the skill of the U-boat commander in pinpointing this group of small targets and attacking so accurately with his first burst of gunfire, in such weather conditions, so deep into the Atlantic.

At 0030, on the other side of the convoy, the sequel to this attack unfolded. The leading boats of the starboard column suddenly noticed a strong smell of diesel oil and then ran into clouds of oil smoke under which men were swimming among corpses floating in the water. Tom Fuller in 654 picked up ten of them, and Charles Jerram in 667 a further two. One of these was an engineer who turned out to be an excellent baker, and spent the next three days supplying 667's crew with a hugely unexpected and welcome supply of fresh bread. But the astonishing discovery was that the twelve survivors came from two different U-boats! Naturally there was great speculation on the cause of this double sinking, and indeed, the signal to Admiralty from Gibraltar on arrival surmised that the escort trawler *Coverley* may have unknowingly rammed one when she turned towards the U-boat which had opened fire, and that possibly the other had been sunk in an attack by a Sunderland aircraft.

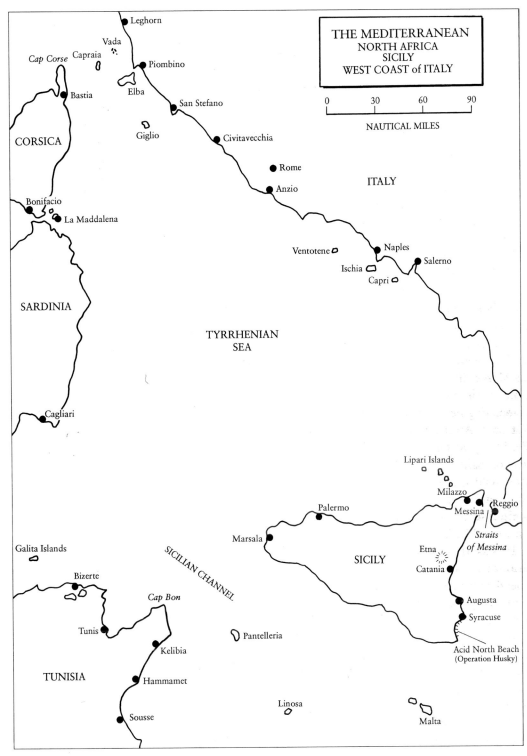

North Africa, Sicily, and the west coast of Italy.

A fuller story emerged when German records could be examined later. It seems that this was the only occasion when U-boats and aircraft were working together in this area in May 1943. U-639 and U-439 of the 1st Flotilla based at Brest were known to have been tracking this Coastal Forces convoy, and had collided after one of them had surfaced to attack MGB 657. Both the U-boat commanders had distinguished records, and U-639 (Kapitanleutnant Hans Stock) had a particularly proud list of successes, having sunk many British ships during 1942. (Appendix 1, Note 10)

Apart from two individual boats completed many weeks later, the last convoy of Dog Boats to sail left Milford Haven on 4 June and brought the 33rd MTB and the 20th MGB Flotillas up to complement.

The months of April and May 1943 are now acknowledged as marking the turning point of the war. Certainly this was true of Coastal Forces where in every sphere, at last, more reliable and powerful boats of every class were joining the operational units. In the Mediterranean, this was especially the case.

As the boats in each convoy reached Gibraltar, no time was wasted. The upper deck petrol tanks were unbolted and lifted off, and the now unnecessary arrester rails limiting the arcs of fire of each gun were removed. Within forty-eight hours, boats were refuelled and re-stored and prepared to sail on towards the focus of the Mediterranean war, in Algeria and Tunisia.

Following the landing of the First Army in Algeria in November 1942, Operation Torch, both Algiers and Bone had become available as bases, and Gould's 32nd MTB Flotilla arrived at Bone to begin operations early in April. The Coastal Forces Advanced Base at Bone had been set up shortly before by Lt Cdr R.A. Allan RNVR, a very able and experienced MTB officer, who had been a CO in the 10th Flotilla since 1941. 'Bobby' Allan, as he became universally known in Coastal Forces Mediterranean, was to play an ever-increasing role both as a base commander and in an operational capacity throughout the next eighteen months.

At this early stage, his base was primitive and desperately short of spares and equipment, but his staff performed miracles of improvisation to keep boats running. Even so, the Dog Boats of the 19th MGB Flotilla were particularly affected by lack of spares and several of them had also suffered from broken frames on the passage to Gibraltar.

But Lt P.F.S. (Stewart) Gould, leading his 32nd MTB Flotilla, was by 14 April setting out for the first time to patrol past Bizerta to the vitally important coast of Tunisia where, as the Allied armies applied the squeeze from east and west, the Germans needed to reinforce their troops and to prepare for an evacuation of their armies when the end came. He embarked in 634 (Lt A.S. Eason, known as 'Shortie') and had with him 638 (Lt E. Rose) and MGB 643 (Lt G.M. Hobday). The night's activities were typical examples of Gould's aggressive spirit. They began by finding a stranded 4–5,000-ton ship. 634 sank her with her second torpedo and followed up with a gun attack. Next they sighted two U-boats on the surface. 638 missed close ahead with her two torpedoes but Gould in 634 and Hobday in 643 charged in to make a depth charge and gun attack. The U-boat escaped by crash diving but close by were two more targets, this time escort ships or torpedo boats. Gould attacked with guns but met heavy calibre gunfire, fortunately not very accurate, and superior speed enabled the targets to escape. Even then Gould was not satisfied but took the unit on to bombard an enemy coastal position east of Ras-el-Dukara.[1]

He was out again four nights later in his own boat (MTB 640) with MGB 644 to patrol off Bizerta. He found three E-boats, attacked and damaged one badly, forcing it to retire under a smoke screen, and scored hits on the other two. Enemy night-fighters joined in the battle and although they did not hit his boats, Gould felt they did well against the E-boats!

Again on 17 April, 634 with 656 scored another torpedo hit, this time on a 4,000-ton merchant ship: escorting destroyers opened fire but didn't hang around, presumably anxious not to suffer the same fate.[2]

The sea lanes from Tunis to Sicily were so important to the enemy that it was vital for the Allied forces to make every effort to control them. The difficulty was the air superiority of the Luftwaffe, flying from nearby airfields, that prevented the destroyers from operating in daylight hours.

It seems that C-in-C was contemplating the experiment of operating MTBs during the day. This was a most unusual step, especially with a lack of air support, and the decision was made to send a group of Dog Boats to the Tunisian port of Sousse. Inevitably, it was Stewart Gould and his 32nd MTB Flotilla who were available and were selected for the task. He sailed on 25 April from Bone to gather four boats of his 32nd MTB Flotilla at Sousse.

But Gould attracted action wherever he went, and even on his passage from Bone to Sousse, as he crossed Bizerta Bay, he found two troop transports bound for Bizerta from Sicily in a last ditch attempt to bolster the beleaguered German forces there. He only had two boats, MTB 639 (Lt G.L. Russell with Gould aboard) and MTB 635 (Lt R.

Perks), and without any delay he attacked fiercely. 639 got off two torpedoes and one eye witness is sure they both hit but in any case Gould immediately followed through with a close range gun attack which was devastating. Soon the transports were on fire and sinking. 639 picked up a number of survivors who, it seems, had thought the Dog Boats were E-boats sent out to escort them into Bizerta. (Appendix 1, Note 11)

As dawn broke on 26 April the boats arrived safely in Sousse, handed over their prisoners, and awaited orders. Sousse had fallen on 12 April and had only minimal facilities but it had been chosen for this operation because it would enable Gould's unit to be in place at daybreak for a daylight patrol without the drawback of a long passage from Bone.

For reasons which will become apparent, it is very difficult to piece together accurately the sequence of events over the following hours. The author has the benefit of two accounts which throw light on some aspects, by the wireless operators in MTBs 639 and 635. Telegraphists have a unique advantage in being able to grasp a wider view of events, as on wireless watch they receive signals and hear commands from on high, as well as the constant exchange of orders between those involved in a battle.

Andy Falconer, who was the telegraphist in 635, tells how he received the signal from C-in-C Mediterranean which begins the story.

The three Sparkers available went into watch-keeping on the appropriate frequency, four hours on and eight hours off. I drew the 'middle watch' (midnight to 4 a.m.) that night. At around 2 a.m. I heard the call sign for the SO 32nd MTB Flotilla, and started recording the signal which was in code and went on and on – I felt for a whole hour. As soon as it

[1] MO7731; ROP at PRO in ADM 199/541.
[2] Mediterranean War Diary.

finished, I started to decode: it was from C-in-C [Admiral Cunningham] and after about twenty groups I called the skipper, Lt Perks, because I couldn't believe what I read in the decoded version.

Obviously after all these years I cannot repeat the message word for word, but I vividly recall the significant parts of it. 'The German evacuation of Tunisia will be attempted within the next two weeks, and it is urgently necessary to have intelligence information on the situation along the coast: gun positions, troops, harbour information and naval elements, as the RAF have not been able to gain this information. As the D class boats are new to the Germans, you are to sail and carry out this reconnaissance, closing Cap Bon and other harbours. Suggest you fly German ensigns. In addition, do all you can to clear the sea lanes.' The message was passed to the SO, and on each boat there began feverish activity by the First Lieutenants, Coxswains and Sparkers to create flags bearing the infamous swastika from bunting cut from other signal flags.

Falconer then records how 635 was unable to sail on the operation because of a serious engine defect: Gould decided he could not risk a boat with only three engines.

It then falls to John Hargreaves, the telegraphist on 639 in which Gould was leading, to take up the story. (Gould did have command of 640 in the flotilla, but at this time she was not available, so he needed to sail with one of the other COs, this time with Lt Russell in 639, with 637 and 633 in company.)

Soon after we sailed out of Sousse, I went up on deck and it was a very strange feeling to see that swastika fluttering at the masthead. Beside it, furled, was the White Ensign ready to be broken out should we go into action. At 0300 I picked up another signal for us on 'O' [higher] priority, from Malta, broadcast so that I did not have to acknowledge receipt. The gist of it was that Lt Gould should ignore the order to 'clear the sea lanes in that area' and concentrate on the gathering of information. I handed him the signal and saw the expression on his face: I reckoned there wasn't much doubt that if he sighted enemy ships he would have a go at them.

The telegraphist, of course, spent almost all his time below in the radio/radar cabin, and was cut off from what was happening on the upper deck. Others reported that the three boats, very close inshore, cruised slowly past Hammamet, past Nabeul, and examined every cove, noting all they saw. As they closed on Kelibia Point, the probable centre of any evacuation, piers were being constructed. There were huge gun emplacements and their positions were carefully entered on the chart.

The official report says that they passed a wrecked destroyer on Ras-el-Mirh Point, a grounded Siebel Ferry, and enemy fighters on the beach, apparently unharmed. They rounded Cap Bon, still in perfect visibility, and still no shots were fired. Obviously the ruse had succeeded and they were being mistaken for German E-boats or patrol vessels. It was then that Gould (known to his men as 'Nat' since Dover days) decided he must act. He sighted two Italian motor minesweepers, then two 300-ton coasters, then an R-boat and finally several Ju 52 transport planes on the beach. He decided to attack.

John Hargreaves, down in his cabin, recalls,

At 0930 I was ordered to make the signal 'Preparative Flag 5' [stand by to open fire] and soon after, 'Flag 5'. I then nipped up on deck and first saw the familiar old White Ensign streaming out above the bridge. I looked around and was astonished to see how close inshore we were: there were ships on fire, a building on the beach ablaze, and the guns were firing at some grounded aircraft.

In fact, five ships, including two minesweepers and an R-boat, were destroyed, and several aircraft on the ground and one which was just landing were disabled. Gould then sighted a large merchant ship out in the Gulf of Tunis, and decided to move offshore for a time. He investigated a German hospital ship and finally moved in towards Kelibia Point where enemy fighters were clearly protecting a convoy consisting of a merchant ship escorted by at least one destroyer. Gould closed to attack, and as he had already used his torpedoes, took on the escort.

The Italian report, which identifies the merchant ship as the *Teranio* and the destroyer as the *Sagittario*, states that 'near Ras Idda the convoy was attacked by three MTBs which were repulsed by the escort's fire and by the fighter escort – one of the MTBs was set on fire and a second damaged. . . .'

Gould closed the range and opened fire on the destroyer. 633 and 637 fired their torpedoes, but due to smoke and gunfire no hits were observed. It was clearly at this time that 639 came under the combined fire of the escort and the cannon fire of waves of attacking aircraft, and suffered terrible damage.

John Hargreaves, below at his wireless set, dramatically describes the next stage:

Down in the W/T office, it was obvious we were getting badly battered up top: it was like being in a shed with a tin roof in a hailstorm! I was ordered to call up Sousse and ask urgently for aircraft support, giving our position. I got no answer but kept belting it out. Whilst still doing that, I heard 'abandon ship' ordered and remembered a list of things I had to do. First, activate the detonators in the IFF (Friend or Foe apparatus) then shove the CBs [confidential books, codes, etc.] in the safe, carry it up on deck and drop it overboard, and then press the button in the charthouse to explode the detonators. I was horrified for a moment because the safe didn't sink at once – then it bobbed astern and went down.

It was a very unusual fact that my brother Frank was serving (as an A/B) on 639, and I knew his action station was on the bridge. I climbed up there, and found absolute chaos – everything was smashed. Frank was lying dead by his .303 machine-guns, Lt Russell the skipper dead by the telegraphs, and Lt Gould very badly wounded lying there with a gaping hole from a cannon shell. I looked round and saw our Carley Floats about 100 yards away with figures aboard them, and one of the hands trying to lower the dinghy on his own. Then I saw Midshipman Youatt, the Pilot, just abaft the bridge: half his left hand was missing and he had blood streaming from the back of his head. I was blowing up his life-jacket when he prodded me and weakly pointed over my shoulder – he couldn't talk. There were 633 and 637 moving towards us. I found the semaphore flags under the skipper's body (the Aldis lamp was smashed) and I signalled 'come alongside now'.

637 nosed her starboard bow alongside, and an officer and leading

MTB 655 on completion, fitted with six deck tanks to provide an additional 3,000 gallons of petrol for the passage to Gibraltar. (Courtesy, Peter Sergeant)

hand jumped aboard. We were soon getting the wounded over to her. Meanwhile 633 had been collecting our men from the Carley Floats. I dashed down to 633's W/T office to discover whether our call to Sousse for air support had been answered – but no, it hadn't been. Soon, 633 and 637 opened fire on 639 with their pom-poms to deny the enemy the chance of salvaging her hull: she sank quite quickly – what a sad end!

But we weren't out of the wood yet: enemy fighters were still attacking fiercely but 633's pom-pom shot one down and almost at once our air support arrived. We discovered later that my signal had been picked up in Sousse by Andy Falconer in 635 (he'd been keeping watch on my frequency all day). His skipper Lt Perks had been right beside him and decided that direct action was required. He had rushed to the anti-aircraft unit on the quay and somehow got through to a US fighter squadron based just south of Sousse, and that's how we got our cover – at last!

637 and 633 got back to Sousse without further mishap and were able to pass on the valuable information they had gathered all morning. But Stewart Gould had died of his wounds on the way, and 639's First Lieutenant, Lt A.G.D. Heybyrne, died in the Field Hospital.

There is no doubt that this gallant action established the Mediterranean Dog Boats as a potent force, and totally altered Admiral Cunningham's original view of them. It was a tragedy that it had to be at the expense of the leader who would undoubtedly have led the 32nd Flotilla on to further great victories. Stewart Gould had already proved himself in the Dover short gunboats to be a fearless attacker with a long list of

successful actions behind him. He had already been awarded the DSC and bar. For this action, because he died, there was only the choice of a posthumous VC or 'mention in despatches' and it was the latter that was eventually promulgated. His shipmates could never understand why. (Appendix 1, Note 12)

Despite this setback, operations continued and patrols from Bone intensified. Several boats of the 19th MGBs had been out night after night along the coast to Bizerta and beyond but had not found any targets. Mixed patrols with the 32nd MTB Flotilla boats were common, to enable units to be available most nights. On 4 May, one such group (MTBs 634 and 635 and MGBs 646 and 643) had to withstand an attack soon after dusk from light Luftwaffe fighter bombers off Cap Serrat. It was an intense battle and three of the boats sustained minor damage, but eight men were seriously wounded and eleven slightly. On the credit side, one aircraft was claimed as brought down and three damaged.

On 8 May two Dog Boats were involved in an incident that illustrated the unpredictability of war. Suddenly, the message was received in Bone that the great port of Bizerta had been taken by the Army. A naval 'port party' was lying ready to sail from Bone to make it possible to operate the port, and Commodore Oliver set out in MTB 637 (Lt E.F. Smyth) with MGB 643 (Lt G.M. Hobday) to get there first to prepare for their arrival.

Lt Smyth's report begins, 'Commodore Oliver hoisted his Broad Pendant at 0300 and the unit left Bone . . .'. They reached Bizerta at 0930, and watched an artillery battle raging ashore; there was no way of telling which side held the harbour. Having discovered that the western entrance to the outer harbour was blocked, the unit entered by the eastern entrance and closed the inner breakwaters. As they reached the very confined area just inside the inner harbour, a burst of 40-mm fire came suddenly from an unobserved shore defence position followed by machine-gun fire at very close range. One of the first shells hit a halyard above the bridge and both the CO and the First Lieutenant were wounded. Ted Smyth, a big man both physically and in personality, disregarded his wounds and soon discovered that the engine room had also been hit, and that the Chief MM had been mortally wounded. Smyth turned 'short round to starboard' (i.e., using what engines he had) and made for the outer entrance, making smoke, closely followed by 643. They were followed by an intense barrage of shelling from the 88-mm guns above the port, followed by salvo after salvo from the Cape Zebib heavy battery until the boats were 8 miles out. Fortunately it was not very accurate gunfire, although 643 was hit by splinters from near misses and small calibre shells from the initial surprise attack, and had two men wounded.

Commodore Oliver's report makes it clear that Ted Smyth behaved very gallantly. In the first burst, he was wounded in three places, yet 'stuck to his post apparently unconcerned until his condition became apparent to me and I ordered him below'.

With both CO and First Lieutenant wounded, Sub-Lt Bruce Arrandale, the young and very inexperienced Pilot, took over command and took 637 back to Bone in worsening weather. Even then he coped very competently with the formidable challenge of berthing her with only one engine in bad light in a crowded harbour, and was commended (and later mentioned in despatches) by his CO.

The two Dog Boats and Commodore

Oliver had had a very close shave. The port was taken only a few hours later, but faulty intelligence had nearly caused a disaster. (Appendix 1, Note 13)

The fall of Bizerta led very rapidly to the defeat of the German army trapped in the Cap Bon peninsula and thus to a very significant turning point in the war. In fact, on the day that 637 and 643 had attempted to enter Bizerta, on 8 May, Admiral Sir Andrew Cunningham made the signal to his ships, 'Sink burn and destroy. Let nothing pass.' Operation Retribution had begun.

With improved air cover now that the North African airfields were available to both RAF and United States fighters, the destroyers were able to play the major part in the blockade, but both the Dog Boats and the short MTBs of the 7th and 10th Flotillas were involved. In all some 10,000 prisoners were taken afloat.

By 13 May the Cap Bon peninsula had been cleared, and the C-in-C was able to send a message to all his ships that confirmed that he now had a very different view of Coastal Forces.

The campaign in North Africa has concluded with the surrender or destruction of all Axis Forces. It is a tribute to the work of our light forces that even in the desperate circumstances in which the enemy found themselves, no real attempt was made to evacuate by sea. . . . I have watched with satisfaction the progressively good work performed in harassing the enemy at sea during the last weeks, and in particular the good work in the last phase which has enabled a large number of craft of different types to work by day and by night in close proximity to an enemy coast without confusion and with a high degree of success. I congratulate you all on a difficult and arduous job well performed.

It soon became clear that although there was to be a short and valuable lull in major operations, during which the boats that had been heavily and continuously involved in the 'arduous job' could relax and have time to prepare for the next phase, there was still much to be done.

By this time, the boats of the 19th MGB Flotilla which had suffered structural damage and shortage of spares, were being brought to operational level. Half the boats of the 20th MGB Flotilla and half of the 33rd MTB Flotilla had arrived in Bone and were trying to make up for lost time in working together. But Bone was still subject to intensive air raids every night as the Luftwaffe from Sicily tried to disrupt the build up of shipping and supplies pouring in there daily.

There were changes in the leadership of the Dog Boats, too. The SO of the 19th MGBs, Lt Mickey Thorpe, was given command of the frigate *Bickerton* and his successor was Alan McIlwraith of 641, who was promoted to Lieutenant Commander. 'Mac', as he was universally known, was a popular, calm, pipe-smoking officer whose introduction to Dog Boats, in his first operation in 609 in August 1942, had been a testing baptism of fire. In a successful battle described in chapter two he and several of his crew had been wounded and his boat considerably damaged.

Shortly after his arrival in the Mediterranean, Lt Cdr Ron Ashby, SO of the 33rd MTBs, was required elsewhere and was replaced by Lt Greene-Kelly RNR of MTB 655. And of course, with the sad loss of Stewart Gould, the 32nd MTBs needed a new SO, and Lt Rose of 638 was promoted and temporarily took over the flotilla.

The four boats of the 20th MGB Flotilla, three of which were commanded by Canadians, were the first to move on to Malta on 1 June. At about the same time, a heavy assault began on Pantelleria, the island that had the potential to command the Sicilian Narrows because of its geographical position, and which had been fortified by Mussolini in an attempt to realize this potential. As a fighter base it had certainly been a thorn in the side of the Allies throughout the closing stages of the African campaign. Shelling and bombing of the island, and of the other two islands in the Narrows, Lampedusa and Linosa, were intensified and for a fortnight it was hoped that they would surrender, but by 11 June it was necessary to launch an invasion force. The Italian garrison surrendered almost at once, and when attention was turned to Lampedusa and Linosa they too capitulated very quickly, leaving a large number of prisoners to be dealt with. The Luftwaffe soon showed the determination of the Germans to make things as difficult as possible by sending waves of bombers to attack the ships of the landing forces soon after the surrenders.

This had an immediate consequence for the Dog Boats. Late on 13 June, MTB 656 (Lt D.G. Tate) and MGB 648 (Lt K.E.A. Bayley) had sailed to Pantelleria carrying a senior officer. Petty Officer Patrick O'Hare, the coxswain of 648, tells what happened next.

We had arrived at first light and an hour or two later we were in the harbour and preparing to move on to Lampedusa when we were attacked by FW 190s. We were alongside a water tanker which had already been hit and abandoned. During the raid a bomb exploded in the water

The hull of MGB 648 after being sunk by bombing at Pantelleria. (Courtesy, Harold Pickles)

right under the boat approximately abaft the 6 pounder gun, blowing out the boat's bottom.

656 came alongside and pushed us into shallow water, and then sailed with the Admiral to Lampedusa. Luckily no one aboard 648 had been injured. Every one of us was absolutely drenched by the water thrown up, and – surprisingly – black from the blast.

That, of course, was the end of 648, which was paid off and written off as a 'constructive total loss' (an insurance term heard too often in the next two and a half years). The crew was shipped to Sousse and then on to Bone, and remained together later to take over first 642 and then 659.[3]

[3] Letter from Petty Officer Patrick O'Hare DSM, the coxswain of MGB 648.

The North African experiences of this first handful of Dog Boats, thrown in at the deep end so soon after their Atlantic voyage, had been unlike anything their experienced COs and coxswains had ever met before. The majority of the crew members had no previous yardsticks by which to measure the dramatic and ever-changing pattern. But without doubt they would be better prepared for any of the challenges that lay ahead – and these were not long in coming.

Clearly, everyone now anticipated a landing to enable the Allied armies to drive into Europe from the south and to relieve the pressure on the Russians in the tremendous battle raging within their heartland. But where would the point of impact be? There were obvious possibilities but the High Command were at pains to prevent too great a build up of Axis defences by displaying their hand too early. This was the situation of June 1940 reversed. Then, after Dunkirk, Britain stood alone and faced the enemy across the Channel, expecting the victorious might of the German army to test its shaky defences in southern Britain. Now after a defeat of not dissimilar proportions, it was the enemy's turn to wait to see if it would be aimed at Sicily or direct to Italy, the south of France, Yugoslavia or Greece.

In the short period before the plan was revealed, the Dog Boats regrouped and the veteran boats of the last six weeks were joined by those not yet tested in action. The latest arrivals (a convoy of five boats that left Milford Haven on 4 June) saw MGBs 662, 659 and 661 sail into Malta by the end of June. This brought the 20th MGB Flotilla up to six, with two boats still to come. The arrival of MTBs 649 and 665 made the 33rd MTB Flotilla up to full strength. Those two

flotillas joined the hundreds of other small craft gathering in Malta.

The 32nd, which had borne the brunt of the fiercest action thus far, had already been reduced to six boats as 639 had been sunk on 28 April, and 638 had had to return to Gibraltar for long-term structural repairs. She was not to return to operations till the summer of 1944. That flotilla, too, moved up to Malta from North Africa at the beginning of July.

Finally, the 19th MGBs, which had suffered most from hull strain and engine defects, were based temporarily at Bizerta and held in reserve.

During June, there were a number of indications to the Dog Boats that Sicily was the front runner in any invasion plans. They were sent on nightly patrols, mainly along the east coast of Sicily, to search for inshore shipping and to report back on searchlight positions as far north as

The floating dock in Msida Creek, Malta.

Syracuse. Very little of note took place, but the boats with their raw crews found these patrols valuable training experience for what was to come.

Attention on 25/26 June switched to the port of Marsala, on the south-western coast of Sicily. A unit was sent from Bizerta, MGBs 643 (Hobday), 644 (McLeod) and MTB 651 (Horlock), with orders to penetrate the outer harbour defences and bombard the airfield there. Before they even reached Marsala, they found themselves surrounded by floating mines, and 644 was struck by one, suffering serious damage, with the engine room on fire and a number of missing and wounded. There was no hope for her, so the other boats did all they could to pick up survivors and then had the unpleasant task of sinking their sister ship. They escaped further damage by mines but were attacked by aircraft on the way back to base.[4]

Meanwhile, back in Bone, there was yet another blow to the strength of the Dog Boat fleet. 654, already out of action with structural problems, had an engine room explosion which lifted off the hatch and ended any possibility of her being able to operate again.

With all these vicissitudes, perhaps it was just as well that at a briefing in the first week of July, the boats learned that Operation Husky, the invasion of Sicily, was to begin on 9 July and that every serviceable Dog Boat was to be involved. So indeed were four short boat flotillas of MTBs and thousands of other ships of every size and description; this was the greatest invasion armada gathered so far in the war. Some would sail direct from ports in the UK and the USA, gathering like well-ordered chess pieces in their allotted positions, in

order to put ashore a vast army and then to supply it until the island was won. (Appendix 1, Note 14)

The main task initially allocated to the Dog Boats was to maintain anti-E-boat patrols off the invasion beaches in order to defend the huge array of anchored ships from attack, especially from the north. It had been expected that E-boats would be sent through the Straits of Messina at once. The landings are chiefly remembered for the appalling weather which met the invasion force as it ploughed towards the main beaches. It was bad for the Dog Boats, even worse for the 'shorts' and absolutely terrible for the small landing craft and their cargoes of seasick soldiers.

Dawn on 10 July saw an improvement in the weather, and the sight of line after line of supply ships safely anchored left the rigours of the passage forgotten. Air attacks in the first few hours were continuous, vicious and effective, and called for constant vigilance. Boats were at action stations for hours on end. The 20th Flotilla, complete except for 674 (which was still in the UK), but operating together for the first time and now with their SO, Lt Cdr Norman Hughes, bore the brunt of these attacks off the British beaches south of Cape Murro di Porco. In mid-afternoon Lt Maitland's 657 had a very near miss and suffered four casualties, which were put aboard the hospital ship *Talamba*. That raid continued for several hours, and the boats of the 20th Flotilla were pleased then to be ordered to patrol northward off Catania. In fact they saw nothing but were attacked again at first light by Junkers 88s and Dornier 217s at regular intervals and brought down two aircraft. By 1000 on 11 July they were back to Acid North beach, but there was no escaping the air attacks although the amount of fighter cover increased during the

4 Summary of Actions; *In Harm's Way*, G.M. Hobday.

day. Fuelling from tankers during air raids is not an experience to be enjoyed but was essential after thirty-six hours running, as was the scrounging of bread and water from any willing donor!

Now that the initial landings were over, plans were under way for the reinforcement of the patrols to enable relays of cover by both Dog Boats and the short boats of the 24th, 7th and 10th MTB Flotillas. Orders were given for all the boats in Bone and Bizerta to sail to Malta ready to move up to Augusta, where the plan was to establish Commander Allan's Advanced Coastal Force Base, which was moving from Bone, as soon as the port was cleared. Syracuse had fallen on the first day.

At the end of a turbulent day punctuated by air attacks (which always seemed to be aimed specifically at them) the boats of the 20th Flotilla had brought down two more aircraft and had then been ordered by Admiral Troubridge to patrol around the anchorage. At 1945, MGBs 662 and 659 were detailed to accompany the *Ulster Monarch* and the *Tetcott* while they landed a special raiding force inside the huge harbour at Augusta, so vital to the build up of troops and supplies.

Further north, a unit of Dog Boats that had sailed from Malta to patrol off Catania was involved in the first surface action of the campaign. MTBs 640 (Lt R.R. Smith), 651 (Lt K. Horlock) and 670 (Lt I.A. Quarrie) met a southbound U-boat on the surface, and attacked with torpedoes, gunfire and depth charges. The U-boat replied, causing a number of casualties aboard the boats. The Dog Boats believed they had damaged the target, and certainly there was no submarine attack on the anchorage that night.

But MGBs 662 and 659 were having a torrid time after entering Augusta harbour.

They came under fire, and 659 grounded on an obstruction and was stranded only yards from an enemy shore. 662, now commanded by Lt T.J. Bligh (as the SO had moved to take over 660), was sent to Syracuse at midnight and was dive-bombed ten times on that short but perilous passage, bringing down one of her attackers.

At first light, HMS *Newfoundland* signalled the SO to pass on a report of 659's plight, informing him that parts of Augusta were still in enemy hands and ordering him to enter the harbour to render assistance. The boats crept in, finding the boom open and no defences manned, but every effort to shift 659 was unsuccessful. But by 1100 the flotilla's energies were transferred to other duties, as HMS *Antwerp* (a headquarters ship containing the Port Party that had been standing by, specifically trained to swing into action to make the port operational) entered the harbour, and the boats were required to ferry men and equipment ashore. All this was punctuated by air raids but kept the flotilla busy all day. 659 was eventually towed off by a destroyer, and late in the afternoon 658 brought down a FW 190 to add to one that 659 had claimed. This meant her lonely vigil while stranded had at least had one positive result.

At 1030, the newly arrived NOIC Augusta was informed that his party and ships were at risk as an enemy counter-attack was having some success, so the port was evacuated temporarily, leaving 658 to maintain communication, feeling very lonely. 660 and 663, wallowing dangerously, were sent to Syracuse loaded to the gunwales with 200 extra men between them.

14 July dawned with no counter-attack, and ships flooded back in, among them Commander Allan with the LST bearing the vehicles, men and equipment of his Advanced Coastal Forces base that was in

Operation Husky: a tiny Dog Boat ferries men ashore in Augusta from the LSI HMS *Antwerp*, July 1943.

action repairing boats next day. 658 stayed in the harbour ferrying and leading in LSTs past the wrecks to their berths and anchorages, while the rest of the flotilla fuelled and provisioned from ships in Acid North anchorage.

But while all this essential activity to bring Augusta into action was proceeding, other Dog Boats of the 33rd MTB Flotilla had been engaged in surface actions during which they had encountered three separate groups of enemy craft. These were all bound for the landing area and therefore of considerable concern to the safety of the anchorage. This unit was led by Lt Greene-Kelly, the new SO of the 33rd, in 655 (Lt Tom Fuller) with 656 (Lt Tate) and 633 (Lt Joy); they had just come up from Malta and were on their first patrol. Their designated area was well to the north, and they were working in the next 'box' to a unit of the 24th MTBs (Vospers) led by Lt Christopher Dreyer RN, which was

patrolling right to the north of the Messina Straits in the narrowest part between Messina itself and Reggio on the Italian side. Dreyer had met and attacked two U-boats bound southward on patrol, and had sunk U-561. Shortly afterwards, he had sighted two E-boats moving fast down the Calabrian coast, towards the area in which Greene-Kelly was waiting. His enemy report brought the Dog Boats into an intercepting position. The E-boats were sighted at 2340 and taken completely by surprise when the attack began. The fearsome broadside of the three Dogs set both targets on fire almost at once and very quickly reduced return fire to minimal proportions. With both the enemy craft blazing and drifting towards the Sicilian shore, Greene-Kelly set course southward, pursued by probing searchlights and shells from the high calibre shore batteries. Off Cape Alessio, the unit made contact first with two fast boats moving north (probably Italian MTBs known as MAS-boats) and then with a further six or seven. They were engaged but they were too fast and were able to get away northward. However, the successful confrontation with the two E-boats was very heartwarming so early in the campaign.

The 20th Flotilla, released from their duties in Augusta, were still required to patrol in area 'C' off Catania, but were beginning to feel the strain of lack of sleep and constant attacks by aircraft. However, all seven boats were still running, which was a great tribute to the companies, especially to the engine room crews. Indeed the fact that most of the crews had not set foot on shore from 9 to 15 July, remaining for many hours at action stations, exemplified the

value of the Dog Boats in this sort of operation. Their comparative self-sufficiency was a new asset in Coastal Forces operations.

The boats that had been sent up from Bone and Bizerta began to enter the fray on 14 July. Three boats of the 19th MGB flotilla left Malta for their first patrol, and were allocated the same sector near the Calabrian shore in which Greene-Kelly had met the E-boats two nights before. Alan McIlwraith, the new SO, led the unit in MGB 643 (Lt G.M. Hobday), followed by 646 (Lt J.A. 'Tufty' Forbes) and 641 (Lt P. Hughes SANF[V]).

Almost as soon as they arrived in their patrol area, and two miles from the Calabrian shore, they sighted a U-boat on

The power-operated twin Oerlikon.

the surface. They sped towards her (as gunboats they had no torpedoes so had to close the range) and managed to rake her with gunfire before she crash-dived and disappeared. But the noise and the tracer revealed their precise position to the enemy shore batteries and at once the nearest one began to get the range and bearing all too accurately. With its third salvo it secured a direct hit amidships on 641, and it was obvious that there was no hope for her. As the possibility of hits by the shore batteries had been foreseen, the express orders were that boats should not stop to take off survivors, for fear that a battery with an established range and bearing would soon be able to pick off the rescue boats. But this went against the grain and 643 and 646 returned a little later when darkness had intensified, laid smoke and discovered to their astonishment that 641 had had no casualties: all were safely recovered.

With a base established at Augusta, it was no longer necessary for boats to return to Malta so frequently. It became policy to maintain at least twenty-four boats of all types (long and short) at Augusta, allowing others to return to Malta for maintenance and relaxation in rotation. There was certainly little relaxation for those in Sicily, working at least one night on patrol up the Straits of Messina and the next in Augusta, which was bombed continuously till the end of the month. In fact, there were few surface actions as the blockade seemed effective in preventing the E-boats from moving south with any freedom. On 15/16 July, MTBs of the 32nd and 33rd Flotillas working together under Lt Greene-Kelly (634, 670, 640 and 651) intercepted five E-boats that had been mauled by the Vospers of the 7th Flotilla in the narrowest northern section

of the Straits, and ensured that they retreated northward.

Some of the MGBs of the 20th Flotilla were employed on several nights in bombardments of coastal ports, especially those with railways and sidings: the ancient 6-pdr gun, well aimed, could inflict considerable damage at close range. One such target was Taormina, the elegant holiday resort, but there was no room for sentiment if communications could be disrupted.

The appointment of a new Captain Coastal Forces (Mediterranean) on 28 July would not at first sight have been very significant to the men of the boats as they ran the nightly gauntlet of the shore batteries on either side of the narrow straits. But the name of Captain J.F. Stevens RN was one they very quickly learned to respect. Until well into 1945 he was their leader in every way, frequently visiting the advanced bases, and fighting the behind-the-scenes battles for supplies and facilities. He recognized very quickly the extraordinary efforts of the boats and the crews that had maintained themselves in such testing conditions in full operational state, and sent personal commendations that were greatly appreciated and did much for morale. The first of these went to MGB 658 after three weeks of continuous operations: her engines had logged 300 hours and she was still in fine order. This was truly an example of the resilience of an offensive craft that could operate almost independently for long periods of time. The Dog Boat concept had once again, as in Norwegian Waters, proved its value.

Operations continued well into August and the boats were involved in covering landings behind the lines as well as very hazardous patrols almost to Messina. The purpose of these was, now, to prevent the escape of men and equipment across the narrow channel to

A Packard engine is lowered through the engine room hatch.

Italy as the fate of Sicily became ever more certain.

On the night of 15/16 August three MTBs (665, 640 and 670) were caught relentlessly in cross searchlights from either shore just half a mile south of Messina. 665, commanded by a Canadian, Lt P.A.R. Thompson DSC RCNVR, who had already shown himself as a gallant and inspiring CO during two years in a short MGB flotilla on the East Coast, received several direct hits. 665 quickly became a blazing wreck and, with heavy shelling continuing, there was no chance of a rescue operation, and there was great concern for any survivors from her crew.

Much later Peter Thompson described what actually happened.

It was an 88-mm battery from the Reggio [Italian] side which first got our range, in the blinding glare of the searchlights, and we took several hits knocking out our steering cables, wrecking the engine room and setting ablaze the main fuel tanks behind the bridge. We got a couple of Carley floats over the side, and the First Lieutenant, Drummond, did a fine job getting the wounded off. We got them on to one raft, and the rest of us took turns on the other, hanging on the ropes along the sides for the rest of the time. 'Abandon Ship' was at about midnight, and it was 0730 before we were picked up by a German flak lighter: a fully dressed young German sailor jumped over the side to help us on board. We were taken into Reggio, and saw to our chagrin the Messina ferry (which we had been told to seek and torpedo if possible as it had to run at night because of air attack) was steaming into port as large as life. So much for military intelligence!

His story of treatment and interrogation is of interest:

We soon found that it was true that treatment was best near the front line. At first, we were prisoners of the Herman Goering Division – elite troops camped on a hillside in an olive grove above Reggio. They gave us good food and cigarettes. But from then on, things were much worse in the train northward, through Rome and the Brenner Pass to Munich and in my case to Berlin to an Interrogation Centre. There, I was astonished to see a set of drawings of a Dog Boat on the wall – apparently taken from the one captured in Norway. They wanted to know more and they said, 'How was the U-boat sunk in the Messina Straits?' I hadn't any idea myself, so they couldn't get anything out of me. I spent the rest of the war in Marlag O and Milag Nord not far from Bremen.

To his experiences were added those of 665's Telegraphist, Ronald Harrison.

I found I didn't have any power to send our 'Abandon Ship' signal, but ditched the CBs [confidential books] in their weighted sack, and followed them in. The Navigating Officer directed us to the Carley float. I believe only two of the crew were 'missing, believed killed' but several were wounded. We were taken north by train, but at a camp near Naples the officers were separated from us and taken elsewhere. We were somewhere in northern Italy when the

train was in a siding and we heard church bells. We saw Italians dancing in the street and some of them came as near to us as they dared and announced that the war was over and we would soon be free. Sadly we soon found that though the Italians had capitulated, the Germans had not – so on we went northward. I was ill and left in hospital near the Austrian border, and when I came out the rest of the crew had been moved on.[5]

Two nights after 665 was sunk on 17 August, all organized resistance in Sicily stopped, thirty-eight days after the initial landings. Almost at once, boats were despatched to penetrate the narrow channel at the head of the Straits in preparation for steps still to come. MTB 667 (Lt C. Jerram) claims to have been the first Dog Boat to slip through, on a special operation to take a party to the island of Lipari, that the German garrison had just left and which surrendered shortly after. Patrols soon followed off Vibo Valentia, and the reasons became clear later.

The next major step into Europe was to be the invasion of Italy that began on 3 September when thousands of Allied troops were ferried over to Reggio with no opposition, and this was followed on 8 September by a second landing 40 miles further north, at Vibo Valentia.

At about this time, 657 (Lt J.D. Maitland) and 663 (Lt T.E. Ladner) were ordered to Bizerta and given the first of a series of missions that proved to be rather more diplomatic than military. They sailed to accept the surrender of the Galita Islands, off the Tunisian coast, and spent several days

[5] War History Case 8620; letter from Lt P.A.R. Thompson DSC RCNVR and Tel R. Harrison.

there, patrolling to Sardinian waters further north.

But although the frenzied activity of July and August necessitated a brief respite for the boats of Coastal Forces, during which the majority had to undergo repairs and maintenance in Malta, things quickly hotted up again. The Dog Boats, so new to Mediterranean operations, had met their baptism of fire with credit; they had also enjoyed close contact with the short MTB flotillas, the long serving 10th and the 7th and 24th, which they were to meet many times in later operations.

The month of September was most notable for the Dog Boats through some extraordinary events, unique even in the proud record of Coastal Forces throughout the war. Many of them flowed from the political situation in Italy which led first to the fall of Mussolini on 25 July and then, on 8 September, to the surrender of Italian forces and in particular the Italian fleet.

The timing of the announcement by the Italian government created some confusion for the armada of ships heading for the Italian coast and the landings at Salerno early on the 9th. There were Dog Boats among the

600 ships of the Allied fleet, and several were employed off the beaches on anti-E-boat patrols and ferrying senior officers. The landings were violently opposed by German artillery and armour. The Allied fleet suffered too from a new weapon, the German radio-controlled bomb, that was used with devastating effect until countermeasures were devised.

The boats of the 20th MGB and the 33rd MTB Flotillas were attached to a Task Group (80.4) under Captain Andrews USN in the American destroyer *Knight*, with the objective of securing the surrender of the islands of Ventotene, Capri, Ischia and Procida off the Gulf of Naples.

No resistance was encountered in any of these operations, in fact, in each the boats were welcomed and fêted and this was a most rewarding interlude in a campaign that had, until then, been characterized by relentless air attacks and hazardous patrols. Ventotene, the most distant island, was taken on 9 September (the day the Salerno invasion began) followed by Capri on the 12th, Procida on the 15th and Ischia on the 16th.

It fell to few officers in the lowly rank of

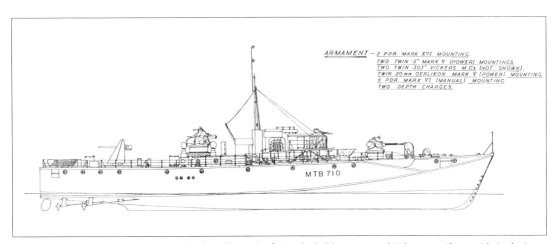

MTB 710 in October 1943. Now more heavily armed with Hotchkiss 6-pdrs aft. Served in both home waters and Mediterranean. (Courtesy, John Lambert)

lieutenant to formally receive an enemy surrender, especially of such a prestigious island as Capri. But the document exists and the Commandante of the island addressed his surrender to Lt E.T. Greene-Kelly RNR (acting SO of the 33rd) and Lt F.A. Warner (CO of MTB 636 and much later our Ambassador to Japan) and to Lt D. Fairbanks USNR. Douglas Fairbanks Jr, now far removed from Hollywood, was Liaison Officer to Captain Andrews, and was not new to operations with Coastal Forces boats. He had been at the Dieppe landings and already had a British DSC.

Capri became in due course a leave centre for US forces, and Ischia a British Coastal Forces Base, mainly for MLs.

An even more significant island surrendered to two MGBs of the 20th Flotilla on 18 September. Tim Bligh in 662 and Steve Moore in 660 were summoned from Messina to Bizerta on the 16th, received their orders from C-in-C's Chief of Staff, embarked Brigadier General Theodore Roosevelt of the US Army and an Italian colonel, and sailed for Cagliari. Their orders were to 'absorb Sardinia'. Considering the relative sizes of Sardinia and tiny Pantelleria which had taken many days of bombing and bombardment to subdue, the force of two Dog Boats and a handful of senior officers seemed pretty small. But there was no resistance and the surrender was handled without fuss or ceremony. Perhaps this first essay into diplomacy and great affairs was an indication of Bligh's future: within twenty years he was to be private secretary to a prime minister, and knighted. (Appendix 1, Note 15)

The time had come to shift the centre of Coastal Forces operations further north, and the decision was made to move the Advanced Base (well named) first to the Italian naval port of La Maddalena, an island off the north coast of Sardinia, and not long after to Bastia on the east coast of Corsica. A convoy unique in Coastal Forces' history set out from Messina on 21 September: a tanker, three LCTs carrying the workshop lorries and the Base Staff, minesweeping MLs and escorting Dog Boats. After very bad weather and stops at Milazzo and Palermo, the force arrived safely and at once began to prepare for operations off the west coast of Italy between Leghorn in the north and Civitavecchia in the south, not far from Rome. The patrol area was a minimum of 120 miles away, and involved a long slog each way with many hours on patrol. But the importance of attacking the German coastal traffic reinforcing their embattled armies north of Salerno demanded the effort, and for several weeks both Dog Boats and the Vospers of the 7th Flotilla made the long patrols north-eastward.

The move to Bastia, precipitated by the evacuation of the German garrison in Corsica shortly before, coincided with a significant action on 14/15 October in the Piombino Channel, between the island of Elba and the Italian mainland.[6]

Three Dog Boats set out from Maddalena at 1500 on 14 October: MTB 633 (Lt A. Joy RCNVR, with the newly promoted SO of the 33rd, Lt Cdr E.T. Greene-Kelly RNR on board), MTB 636 (Lt F.A. Warner) and MGB 658 (Lt C. Burke RCNVR). On the nine-hour passage, 633 had engine trouble, so Greene-Kelly sent her back to Maddalena and transferred to 636.

At 0116, two enemy ships were sighted and soon after 636 fired her torpedoes singly with no apparent result and the first target opened fire. Greene-Kelly disengaged, and in the resulting lull, 658 went alongside 636 for

---

6 MO55497; ROP by CO MGB 658; *Gunboat 658*, L.C. Reynolds.

a shouted conference. The plan was to attack individually while one boat diverted the target's attention from the other. 658 approached stealthily down the track of the moon, but was sighted and the enemy opened fire with a variety of weapons. Cornelius Burke, a very experienced CO with two years on the British east coast in short MGBs behind him, held his fire and tried the old ruse of flashing a recognition signal that had earlier been seen as the first enquiry from the enemy. It seemed to succeed as the firing stopped, and he closed the range until the gunners could not miss with their broadside. In no time, the target was ablaze from stem to stern, and was revealed as some sort of flak ship.

Almost at once, the lookouts reported another ship approaching, and clearly this was either the other enemy vessel previously sighted, or 636 coming to rejoin. 658 flashed the challenge and continued to do so until a hail of tracer came streaming past the bridge. She opened fire and it seemed that the 6-pdr scored a vital hit at once, as the target spouted fire and was pounded by all guns. The blaze lit up the superstructure and to the horror of all, it was revealed as 636. Stunned for a moment into inaction, Burke soon recovered and moved in to pick up survivors, some swimming and others in a Carley float. No sooner had that begun than the other enemy vessel approached, opening fire almost at once. Knowing this menace had to be beaten off before 658 could finish the rescue, Burke steered straight for the enemy, which was up moon, and once again opened fire at close range. The return fire was heavier and more accurate this time, and 658 suffered damage and casualties, but soon gained the upper hand and could see the second flakship listing heavily to starboard and burning fiercely. When her firing ceased, Burke returned to 636, found

more survivors and began to help them aboard. But by now searchlights and shore batteries had picked out 658 and clearly had the range. After one or two near misses, 658 broke off yet again, dropped flares and threw the batteries off target. This time she was able to finish the job, although they later discovered that Greene-Kelly, 636's First Lieutenant and seven ratings were missing. Freddie Warner, the CO, was among those rescued, and there were several wounded, together with one of 658's crew who died next day.

The Naval Historical Branch later established from enemy records that the two German vessels were 'battle ferries' numbered K169 and K176. One drifted and foundered on the rocks near Porto Ferraio on Elba, and the other was towed into Piombino Harbour but capsized at the pier.

In normal circumstances, for a gunboat to singlehandedly sink two enemy ships, each larger and more heavily armed than herself, would have been recognized as extraordinary, especially as it was 658's first surface action. But there was no elation, only horror at the fate of 636, even though Freddie Warner acknowledged that 658 had had no alternative.

This action, the first success in this new sphere of operations, had one other outcome. 658, unable to return to Maddalena, received a signal to return due westward to Bastia, only 30 miles distant. When she had left Maddalena, she had no idea that Bastia was to be available but at first light, arriving off the harbour, she found 662 nosing into the old harbour, checking facilities for Commander Allan. The port had been badly damaged in the German retreat, and the hospital to which the wounded were taken was in a terrible state.

In many ways, this action and the consequent establishment of the base at Bastia

Lt C. Burke, CO of MGB 658, over the bridge controls.

was a watershed. Shortly after this, CCF (Captain Stevens) reorganized the Dog Boat flotillas and their dispositions, partly in response to the policy decision in the UK where almost all MGBs were refitted as MTBs, but also to enable the flotillas to be distributed to cover the new challenges in the Adriatic and the Aegean. Mediterranean operations were about to enter on an even more significant and successful phase but chronology demands a return to the events in home waters.

CHAPTER 5

HOME WATERS

MAY 1943 TO MAY 1944

It will have been clear from the descriptions of the early operations of the Dog Boats in the Channel and the North Sea that those areas posed very different challenges from those in the Mediterranean, with its ever-changing fluid pattern of warfare and generally more hospitable weather.

By May 1943, the 17th MGB and the 31st MTB Flotillas based at Yarmouth, and the 18th MGBs now operating out of Newhaven, were entering a new era in the evolution of Coastal Forces operations. Ashore, with the rapidly expanding force calling for a bigger and more sophisticated organizational structure, there had been major changes. The rather independent set up of the early days when Coastal Forces were feeling their way with poorly armed boats and no past experience had given way to two Admiralty departments concerned respectively with 'material' and 'overall development and personnel'. Although flotillas were still operated by the C-in-C of each command, he had a 'Captain Coastal Forces' to implement those operations and to see that the boats were used with a full understanding of their capabilities. Training had also become more and more organized and equipment more reliable.

On the east coast, the loss of the legendary short MGB leader Robert Hichens in an action in April had marked the end of an era. But his legacy of tactics and strategies had lived on, and were now inherited to some extent by the Dog Boats. They lacked the speed of the 'shorts' but had the additional fire-power to succeed if they could get into attack positions, or even better, achieve surprise when approaching targets and escorts.

However, the enemy were also strengthening their defensive techniques. Lacking the availability and quantity of conventional ships of the same mould as British Hunt class destroyers or frigates, they adapted trawlers, minesweepers and ferries by adding 88-mm guns and a multitude of cannons to create 'flak ships' or 'gun coasters'. These became formidable opponents and had a good deal of success at preventing British boats from closing range on worthwhile targets, especially in the moon period.

Perhaps the most famous of these were four such armed trawlers which operated out of Ymuiden and which were so frequently met and so difficult to subdue that they received the grudging respect of COs who dubbed them the 'Four Horsemen of the Apocalypse'. But respect did not diminish the will to take them on, and the Dog Boats used

German armed trawlers. (Courtesy, S.C. Minette)

their considerable fire-power to share in that. The enemy's large M class minesweepers, too, were heavily armed with guns similar to the 4-in armament of British destroyers, and were doughty opponents.

It was not only in the North Sea that British boats met such escorts. The Dog Boats of the 18th MGB Flotilla, now working mainly from Newhaven with the steam gunboat flotilla, were meeting similar opposition. Indeed, the Channel boats in general, including the short boats based at Dover and Ramsgate, found that the number of enemy ships being routed along the Normandy coast between the Channel ports and Cherbourg in both directions had decreased, and those that did venture out were even more heavily defended. That, added to increasingly efficient radar controlled shore batteries, meant that there

was little point in hanging about waiting for ships and escorts to return to port, a tactic successfully used by the short boats in the previous year. There was one further development: increasingly, the enemy was moving supplies by converted landing craft similar to British TLCs (tank landing craft) but armed with 88-mm guns. These presented a low silhouette and their shallow draft made them difficult torpedo targets. These were the 'F-Lighters' which at much the same time were beginning to appear in great numbers in the Mediterranean.

Against this background of additional problems, the three flotillas of Dog Boats were kept busy but spent more and more nights on fruitless and often very unpleasant patrols in bad weather. Mixed in with these were the highly necessary but comparatively boring 'Z' line patrols to protect coastal convoys from E-boat attack, and the summer and autumn of 1943 were in many ways dispiriting to men who were anxious to get to grips with the enemy and put their training to the test.

There were, however, some successes and gallant battles in this period, and all the time new flotillas were beginning to form and move to HMS *Bee* to work up before being allocated to their new areas. The end of May, in particular, saw a flurry of contacts. On two consecutive nights, combined units of the 17th MGB and 31st MTB Flotillas found the enemy off the Dutch coast. The first, on 26/27 May, led to a spirited gun attack on four enemy trawlers off Terschelling.

The boats concerned were MTBs 632 (Lt P. Berthon), 629 (Lt C.A. Law RCNVR) and 628 (Lt R. Cunningham) together with MGB 607 (Lt R.M. Marshall). All were experienced and aggressive COs and on this occasion they made two attacks on the trawlers, and despite very heavy return fire (which led to slight damage to one of the boats and one man killed), they mauled one trawler in particular very severely. Such claims always tended to be regarded with a degree of scepticism – it was very difficult to know just how badly a target was damaged – but in this case the result was confirmed much later as accurately assessed by the intelligence reports from enemy records.[1]

On the following night, four boats of the 17th MGB Flotilla (605, 612, 610 and 609) had a harrowing encounter with heavily armed patrols. Having been shadowed by aircraft, they were unable to get close enough to attack effectively and were driven off, frustrated by the experience but without damage or casualties.

In the Channel, the very next night (28/29 May) was really most significant. A typically heroic action occurred, involving four short

MGBs of the 9th MGB Flotilla in which the SO, Lt G.D.K.('Dickie') Richards DSO DSC RN was killed when his boat, MGB 110, was sunk after it had tackled first three armed trawlers and then six E-boats off Dunkirk. Further down the coast, off the Isle of Wight, SGB 4 (Lt T. Boyd DSO), MGB 614 (Lt P.E. Mason) and MGB 615 (Lt R. Ball) had been called out from Newhaven with reports of eight E-boats approaching the convoy route. By the time the unit sighted the E-boats they had already been attacked by Albacore aircraft, which claimed to have sunk one. There was certainly a fierce exchange of gunfire before the E-boats made off. 614 was hit and set on fire in the after crew space, and her C.S.A. smoke canister was hit. This apparatus, set right astern on the transom, was a strong cylinder containing chloro-sulphonic acid which, mixed with air through the jet when the valve was opened, made dense white smoke. This could be a huge asset in action, but as the acid was highly corrosive, it was disliked universally by crews and treated with respect and apprehension.

June saw nightly patrols but no enemy contacts, and it was not till the end of July that a series of actions brought some long awaited success to the Dog Boats against the old adversaries, the armed trawlers and M class minesweepers.

There was great relief in Yarmouth when, on 22/23 July, a combined unit of the 31st and the 17th, each led by its new Senior Officer, Lt L.J.H. Gamble RN and Lt Cdr D.G.E. Probert, met the enemy. However, the battle was inconclusive despite being fierce while it lasted. Hilary Gamble, who was one of the most experienced of the RN MTB commanders, met early fire from shore batteries near Ymuiden and then engaged four trawlers (possibly the 'Horsemen'), but could not close them in bright moonlight and suffered some superficial damage to two of

[1] MO6885; ROP at PRO in ADM 199/537; intelligence report in NID/OD5048/45.

his boats. The MGBs went further north to Texel and they too took on four trawlers and two R-boats but could claim no certain hits.

Two nights later, on 24/25 July two different units from the two flotillas had greater success off Terschelling. The MTBs were led by Lt W.S. Strang, the 'half-leader' of the 31st, and the MGBs by Lt R.M. Marshall also acting as SO for the night. Two of the newer boats that had replaced those lost or under repair also took part in the patrol and had their first taste of action.

The Admiralty communiqué reads:

During the night of 24/25 July, Light Coastal Forces under the command of Lt W.S. Strang RNVR encountered a heavily escorted enemy convoy off Texel. The attack was pressed home through the escort screen and one enemy ship was torpedoed and probably sunk.

While this was taking place, another force under the command of Lt R.M. Marshall RNVR engaged the escorting vessels consisting of trawlers, M class minesweepers and R-boats and a very vigorous close range action ensued. A number of enemy craft were damaged and in the final stages of the action it was noticeable that the enemy's return fire was considerably reduced.

At one period of the action, a brisk interchange of fire between the enemy's escort craft was observed.

On many occasions war correspondents were asked to accompany the boats on operations and on this night, an American reporter took passage in MTB 628, commanded by Lt Ronald Cunningham. The reporter's article, filed for an American services newspaper, was couched in colourful language but strikingly conveys the spirit of the battle. He tells his readers that Cunningham was known as 'Coffin Nail' to his crew, and that 628 was nicknamed 'Deadbeat' in that self-deprecatory style typical of the British matelot.

There was a full moon that night. It burst, lemon-yellow and bright, from the last layer of clouds. The moon, the convoy and the intruding flotilla all met at the same time. Through a rift in the clouds, the skipper picked out four flak trawlers and 'something big' – the convoy had been sighted. . . . Suddenly night became day. 500 feet above the mast a star-shell had burst and was drifting slowly down shedding its eerie light over the boats – then another, and another, and another.

Jerry opened fire. Red tracers – 20 mm cannon – slithered slowly at the boats, whistled overhead in a burst of speed. Heavier guns opened up, sending green and white shells in with the red. The SO ordered smoke. A white plume poured from the fantail of the leading boat.

Slowly the boats headed south to reach the lower end of the escort screen, and then turned into line . . . up the yellow path of the moon they moved, through the smoke and out into the open. Undeterred they slid past the escorts until they were between the enemy and the Dutch coast . . . then Jerry opened up again and a multitude of shells whizzed by. A sudden dull crump rocked the boat. Heavy spray rained on the deck and over the bridge. A 4-in shell had struck a few yards off the port bow.

The skipper rattled the telegraphs and Deadbeat roared away . . . outnumbered but seeking an opening. A dark silhouette loomed up to the south and the bow swung round towards it. 'Pom-pom open fire! Short bursts!' We could see the hits: one flash was larger than most – 'must have been an ammo locker'. Now to use

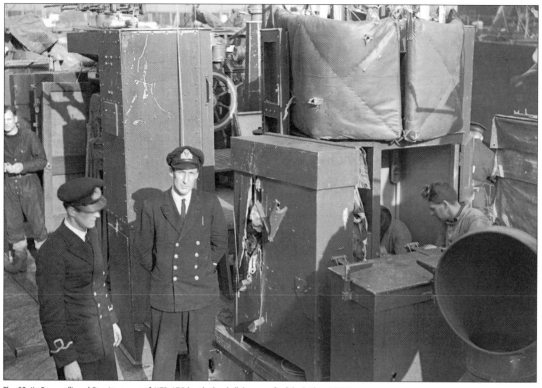

The CO (Lt Bramwell) and First Lieutenant of MTB 675 beside the shell damage aft of the bridge. (IWM)

the torpedoes. 'Tubes to the ready . . .', 'Stand by . . .' the Captain raised his head from the sights and jerked back on the firing handles. 'Both!' he shouted.

The boat lunged back, sinking its stern in its own wake. A loud swishing noise came from each side of the bridge. Swift white tracks sped from each side of the boat . . . the starboard one straight and true, but the wake on the port side was erratic, twisting from side to side.

The skipper agonized . . . 'I think we've missed!' but then there was a puff of black smoke. . . . Other battles still raged around us, but soon we were heading east and joining the others. Number One [the First Lieutenant] made a check for damage: the port torpedo tube had been hit – that must have caused the erratic behaviour. The

engine room reported two holes on the water line. That was all. No serious damage, no casualties. . . .

Four torpedoes had been fired, and everyone believed there had been one hit. This was confirmed in a post-war Naval intelligence report, 'one trawler sunk', but it was not a larger target.

The MGBs had done their stuff, too, harrying the escorts and damaging one severely. Two of the gunboats were slightly damaged, and the Motor Mechanic of 612 (PO MM Archie Morrison) was awarded the DSM for his sterling work when the boat was hit.[2]

2 MO8995; ROP at PRO in ADM 199/537; Article by US war correspondent; intelligence report in NID/OD5048/45.

Twice more in the next few days similar patrols led to brushes with the enemy trawlers off Terschelling, so July had indeed broken the famine of contact with the enemy.

August, too, proved lively for the Yarmouth flotillas, though there were all too frequent reports that the boats had been unable to close sufficiently to make their attacks successful. A combination of extreme visibility, accurate star-shell from the enemy and very heavy firing, was keeping them at bay.

On 3/4 August, the first two boats in an MGB unit were in collision during an action. Both took many weeks in dock at Oulton Broad before they could rejoin the flotilla. It is perhaps not surprising that such collisions took place: attention focused on targets, sudden orders to stop or to alter course, hits in the engine room causing checks to speed, damage to steering, the glare of star-shell or the confusing patterns of movement on pitch-black nights, all played their part in creating situations totally unlike normal expectations. And the boats prided themselves on close station-keeping when attacking, to present as tight a broadside as possible when 'Flag 5' (open fire) was ordered.

The 18th MGB Flotilla, meanwhile, based in Newhaven, had not been as fortunate in finding targets, and indeed had spent night after night on convoy protection in mid-Channel. When they approached the far coast, as they often did, they experienced heavy bombardment from the massive shore batteries and developed techniques of dodging, not much to the liking of the crew! One AB described the method as 'Come Dancing' – 'slow, slow, quick, quick, slow . . . side, side'.

But on 27/28 July, the SO (Lt Cdr I.D. Lyle – known as 'Spud' to all) in his own 611 and with only one other boat, 616 (Lt G.N. Johnstone), was sent to patrol off Dieppe: the purpose of this is not clear. The chief motor mechanic, CPO R.M. Mackintosh, describes his view of the event graphically:

After several uneventful weeks patrolling the Varne Bank we were sent on a raid to the other side, and as was quite common, we ran into a fog bank. But this time, on emerging, we found ourselves running straight into the enemy. There were only two of us and we found ourselves facing three E-boats and two larger vessels and at once there was a very heavy exchange of fire and we took some very serious hits. . . .

In fact, the two larger vessels were TLCs (or F-Lighters) with 88-mm armament, and later intelligence confirmed that one E-boat and one TLC were considerably damaged. But so were the British boats. Mackintosh continues:

The first indication we had in the engine room was the appearance of holes in the ship's side, severe damage to the main engines and a fire. I managed to put the fire out and worked like mad to keep three engines running. We could hear the guns hammering away on deck. I remember well that the engine speed indicator [the mechanically worked gadget connected by teleflex wires to an equivalent board on the bridge – the Captain turned a handle to show the revs he wanted] went crazy. It shot right up the board and out of its case! I thought to myself that if he's winding it as hard as that the situation must be desperate and he wants every rev I can give him on the engines we've got! In fact he was wanting to disengage and take stock of casualties and damage: we had one dead and five wounded and holes all over the place.[3]

[3] M08783; ROP at PRO in ADM 199/536; intelligence report in NID OD5048/45.

Lt D.G. Bradford and S/Lt F.L. Hewitt, then in MGB 333 and later in MTB 617. (IWM)

There is no doubt that during this phase of operations in the Channel all types of boats had to put up with very heavy defensive tactics by the enemy, and throughout July, August and most of September the war diary records time after time that patrols were fired on by accurate shore batteries at long range.

It was not until the night of 19/20 September that the Dog Boats from Yarmouth scored a major success after this lean period. It is significant in that it marked the appearance on the scene of Lt Donald Gould Bradford RNR who had just arrived as SO of the 31st MTB Flotilla and had taken over MTB 617. He had already made his name as an aggressive CO in C class boats, especially when he first sank one E-boat by gunfire and then rammed another which later sank. That exploit had earned him his first DSC.

On this occasion, Bradford led one of the customary combined units from the 31st and 17th Flotillas, comprising MTBs 617 (his own boat), 624 (which returned to base with engine trouble), 621 (Lt J.A.H. Whitby), 652 (Lt G.W. Claydon), and MGBs 606 (Lt D.G. Dowling, the 'half leader' of the 17th), 612 (Lt P.C. Wilkinson) and 610 (Lt W. Harrop).

As this action was not only successful but of special interest for a number of reasons, it is described here fully, with detail taken from the Action Report submitted by Bradford, together with the comments of Commander Brind RN, the CO of HMS *Midge* (the Coastal Forces Base at Yarmouth), and those of Admiral Jack Tovey, C-in-C Nore. More personal accounts, by Donald Bradford himself and by Donald Dowling from the viewpoint of the MGBs, appear in Peter Scott's book, *The Battle of the Narrow Seas*.[4]

The Action Report itself is a model of careful description and analysis, and the detailed appendices headed 'Signals received and sent', 'Track Chart', 'Communications', 'Gunnery', 'Torpedoes fired', 'Smoke', 'Radar', and 'Other Technical Matters' add greatly to its value. It is perhaps not generally known that such appendices were seen and commented upon by each of the relevant command specialist officers, and formed the basis for feedback through training to establish 'best practice' in operations. There has been recent criticism in uninformed circles of the 'amateur' nature of Coastal Forces, which included comment on the quality of reports submitted, but any perusal of the hundreds of such reports in the bound copies at the Public Record Office gives the lie to such criticism.

The unit's orders were 'to carry out an offensive sweep to intercept and attack an enemy convoy off the Dutch coast, and to destroy all enemy vessels and E-boats encountered'. The weather was extraordinarily calm to start with and visibility was good with an intermittent moon.

The boats left at 1400 and arrived in the planned initial position off the Hook at 2030. They swept northward along the convoy route, at slow speed to prevent bow-wave, and thus to remain unseen from the shore. At 2300, as they approached Ymuiden, radar contact with a large ship was picked up west of Ymuiden, at about 4 miles range and clearly very close to the shore. From the radar plot, it appeared to be stationary and to have a screen of escorts round it, and when this was totally confirmed, the unit turned back

southward to approach from a more favourable attacking position, taking advantage of the moon, which was at 050 degrees. The plot showed there were two groups of escorts, the larger ones to the north and west of the main target, and four smaller echoes very close to the target, probably an E-boat or R-boat screen. Slowly the unit manoeuvred into position, closing the target. Bradford decided that as the very large ship was clearly stationary he would fire only two torpedoes, and he was delighted to see from the plot that the close screen had moved off to the west, leaving a very convenient gap for the attack. To his chagrin, having closed to 300 yards and being all set to fire his torpedoes, he discovered by echo sounder that the depth of water from this angle was only 6 fathoms, with the possibility of the torpedoes striking bottom if fired, so he abandoned the attack and crept away to a better position. His torpedoes were finally fired at 2336 at 1,000 yards range and in 7 fathoms of water. Silently the unit turned away, eyes glued to the target, and one minute later the torpedoes hit, throwing up two large columns of smoke and water, completely obscuring the ship.

Bradford then attacked the two trawlers seen during the initial approach. Leading his six boats in close order, he illuminated with 2-pdr star-shell and ordered all boats to open fire. He used the TCS (radio telephone on the bridge of each boat) that worked perfectly, and the lethal broadside of six Dog Boats very quickly reduced the nearest trawler to a blazing wreck before it was able to reply with any real effect. Fire was shifted to the second trawler, which again suffered severely from the concentrated fire. The MGBs saw two R-boats coming out of Ymuiden on the starboard quarter, and 610 and 612 dealt with them, scoring many hits and forcing them to retire.

---

[4] MO10745; ROP at PRO in ADM 199/536; narrative from Lt Ivone Kinross; *Day In, Night Out*, D.G. Bradford.

The M class minesweepers, the four larger vessels seen on the plot to the north-east, began to close, firing star-shell, and then opening fire with all guns. 610 was hit and seen to be on fire but maintained station and was still firing with all guns even while fighting the fire. As the enemy's fire became ever heavier and more accurate, so the unit withdrew under smoke to the south-west, hoping for a chance to return and finish off the second trawler. But Dowling saw four more M class heading out of Ymuiden at high speed, so the unit withdrew again to a point 8 miles from the scene of the action and stopped to assess damage and casualties.

MGB 610 had her fire under control but was making water, and 606 had two guns out of action and had only six rounds of 6-pdr ammunition left having fired eighty-eight. Bradford therefore detached them both to return to Yarmouth but was not yet satisfied that his operational orders had been carried out. The remaining four boats set course to return to the convoy channel, and moved off north-eastward to resume their search for targets. 617's radar, having previously functioned excellently, had been damaged in the action, and 652 assumed radar watch, passing information by TCS.

At 0138, 652 plotted targets at 3 miles, moving south-westerly towards the unit, and almost at once three M class sweepers and two TLCs were sighted. The unit closed but came under very intense and accurate fire, so Bradford at last decided there was no chance of approaching unobserved, and withdrew to the west. C-in-C Nore signalled at 0228, 'Return to harbour', and so they did.

Taking stock of casualties Bradford found that it was the three MGBs which had suffered most. 610 had one killed (the L/MM when the engine room was hit) and one L/Sea wounded. 612 had one A/B killed, and 606

one A/B wounded. Four of the boats had received hits, mostly from 20-mm shells, though 610 had received a 37-mm shell hit in the after petrol compartment, the shell then passing into the engine room and causing the fire and damage to the engines.

Reporting on the performance of equipment, Bradford commented especially on the value of the R/T system, the TCS set with its receiver and transmitter on each bridge, which enabled all the boats to respond promptly to changes of course during the approach. The 291 radar set proved its worth with excellent early contacts and also for torpedo firing; 2-pdr star-shell was very effective both as an illuminant and as an incendiary device; and the Holman projector firing flares to dazzle superior enemy fire seemed to prevent more hits than might have been expected from the heavy barrage from the M class sweepers. Lastly, he commented that, 'there was a great need for the provision of some fool-proof, efficient and reliable form of aural gunnery communication, as neither the sound-power telephones nor the loud hailer were completely satisfactory'.

Commander Brind, in passing the report up the chain of command, emphasized these points and added three others. He commended the highly skilled close station-keeping that had enabled such concentrated fire during the gun attacks; he remarked that the enemy's shore radar or communications could not always be as efficient as previously anticipated, as, although the unit had been within five miles of the shore for four hours, the escorts were clearly unaware of its presence, but most significantly he stressed that it was Lt Bradford's handling of the situation throughout that had led to the success achieved.

In his turn, Admiral Jack Tovey, the C-in-C, added to the praise for Bradford: 'The

Petty Officers Fred and Frank Coombes, identical twins, both coxswains of Dog Boats in the 55th MTB Flotilla, and both awarded the DSM. (Courtesy, Coombes family)

operation was carried out with excellent judgment and determination by Lt Bradford. It is evident that his force had been well drilled and that the Commanding Officers had a good understanding of their SO's ideas and intentions.' He also confirmed that the torpedoed ship was the *Strasbourg*, commended the good communications maintained, and singled out MGB 610 for special praise for maintaining close station and continuing the action even when on fire and damaged.

The ultimate results of this splendid action were threefold. The *Strasbourg* was detailed as a 17,000-ton liner that had gone aground but was now so damaged that although she could not 'sink below the waves', she remained a wreck. Bradford had established himself as a great Dog Boat SO who was to lead his flotilla with flair and considerable success for a further year and, in due course, awards were announced. A bar to his DSC for Bradford, a DSC for Lt W. ('Bob') Harrop, the CO of 610, and a 'mention' for Lt Don Dowling, the CO of 606 and leader of the MGBs. Among the six boats, the crews were not forgotten. There were five DSMs including one for the coxswain of MTB 621,

81

PO Fred Coombes (Appendix 1, Note 16), and ten then were mentioned in dispatches. One of these was posthumous, and hides a gallant and sad occurrence. L/MM Eric Robson in 610 volunteered to try to plug the hole in the ship's side after she had been hit. Air was being sucked into the engine room and making it difficult to put the fire out, and at his own suggestion, he was held by his ankles over the side to stuff the hole with rags. He succeeded, but as he finished was struck by an Oerlikon shell and killed.[5]

The intention of renumbering flotillas and converting all MGBs (including the Dog Boats) to MTBs by fitting torpedo tubes had been mentioned months earlier. The process began in late September 1943 and within a few weeks the newly numbered flotillas were operating, often with a group of new boats that either replaced those sunk or damaged, or increased the size of the flotillas to ensure that there were always enough boats available to make up units, even when some vessels were under repair or refit.

Strangely, the officers and men of the boats converted knew little of this, and indeed the whole business of re-forming and renumbering of flotillas has not remained strongly in the minds of those affected by it. Understandably, the business of getting boats to sea on operations was more important than organizational tinkering!

But in fact, if one accepts that loyalty to an established outfit is a very important aspect of motivation and pride in any military organization (as in regiments and RAF squadrons), the new flotillas were indeed very important agents in the burgeoning of *esprit de corps* at a time when more boats were joining the Dog Boat force and new flotillas were being formed. This was, of course, not unrelated to the unfolding plans for the 'Second Front' even though the date and place were mere conjecture in the autumn of 1943. Rather than list all the very numerous new formations in the detailed way used in earlier chapters, it is perhaps only necessary to give a broad picture of the changes. More detail will become clear as the description of operations continues.

The MGB flotillas in home waters were re-numbered as follows. The 17th MGB Flotilla became the 50th Flotilla, still based at Yarmouth, and from August 1943 its SO was Lt Cdr G.L. Cotton. He took over 605, which had always been the SO's boat.

The 18th MGB Flotilla became the 51st MTB Flotilla, still based at Newhaven although deployed elsewhere in the Channel ports as required from time to time. Lt Cdr Ian ('Spud') Lyle carried on as SO and as CO of 611 and indeed his continuous service in that post from early in 1943 to December 1944 was probably the longest of all Dog Boat flotilla SOs. He received almost a full complement of new COs who remained with him in most cases for many months. Of the 'old' MTB flotillas, the 31st became the 55th under the leadership of Lt D.G. Bradford RNR. Although it was normal for the SO of a Dog Boat flotilla to be promoted to Lieutenant Commander, Donald Gould Bradford, because he was an RNR (i.e., ex-Merchant Navy) officer, had to wait for confirmation of his rank, and was not promoted till the following March – a strange matter. The 55th continued at Yarmouth until April 1944, and the flotilla was enlarged to twelve boats. Most of the COs continued in command for long periods, with Lt W.S. ('Biscuits') Strang as the half leader in 668.

Other newly formed flotillas were working up as their allocated boats left the boatyards. HMS *Bee*, the training base now at Holyhead, was extremely busy and ensuring a

[5] Awards from *Seedies' List of Coastal Forces Awards*.

high state of efficiency even though the crews were still mainly very young and straight from training. A large proportion of the new COs were carefully selected experienced C class MGB or ML captains, with two years of operations behind them. Their seamanship alone, after month on month of enduring poor weather and heavy sea conditions, made them valuable assets to the Dog Boat ranks.

Two of the new flotillas had originally been planned as MGBs but began life as the new style MTB flotillas with increasingly enhanced armament and equipment. These were the 21st MGBs that became the 52nd MTB Flotilla, and the 22nd that was renamed as the 53rd MTBs.

The 52nd was allocated to Dartmouth and had Lt Cdr T.N. Cartwright as SO. Its operations in the western Channel were to have the usual mix of offensive patrols (off the Brittany coast and the Channel Islands) and convoy protection, with the additional and rather specialized duty of minelaying as required.

The 53rd were sent to Lowestoft to reinforce the hard-worked east coast flotillas, and were led by Lt Cdr D.G.E. McCowen.

The next 'purpose-built' MTB flotilla was the 58th, and its SO was the battle-hardened Ken Gemmell, now promoted to Lieutenant Commander. Its task was to back up the Norwegian flotilla at Lerwick in the Shetland Islands, although it was not long before it returned to the east coast to meet the demand for its services there. In addition, the strategic aspects of operations in the northern seas cut down the opportunities of safe passage and fruitful night patrols off the Norwegian coast because of the longer days and the shorter nights.

Following on these flotillas were the 59th, 63rd and 64th all being built and taking the Dog Boat allocated numbers well into the 700s. Except for one or two early boats they were not to be ready until the spring of 1944.

It was, perhaps, Lt Donald Gould Bradford's flotilla, the 55th, that reacted most vigorously to the boost of increased numbers of boats and the challenge of their new leader. Only appointed in September, the sinking of the *Strasbourg* within two weeks had given him a flying start, and the flotilla was immediately hard at work on offensive patrols and the highly necessary and demanding, if dull, 'Z' line convoy defensive operations that saw most boats at sea very frequently.

But the next major operation from a Dog Boat viewpoint, on 24/25 October, fell to the 50th Flotilla. It developed from a defensive patrol into a full-scale battle with E-boats. A month earlier, the German High Command had begun a new tactic of sending large forces of E-boats against British North Sea convoys, and one unit that had just torpedoed a trawler had been taken on gallantly by two MLs that surprised it on their way home. In that action, the two MLs each in turn rammed the second boat in line and sank it before it could escape.

On this repeat operation, no fewer than thirty E-boats were despatched to attack the large northbound convoy. They came in a large number of small units and were engaged by a great variety of British naval forces, including five destroyers, Dog Boats, C class MGBs, MLs and RMLs, short MGBs and MTBs, some of which were summoned by signal from Lowestoft into intercepting positions.

It was a most unusual circumstance, and indicative of the importance of this action, that the dispatch of Admiral of the Fleet Jack Tovey, the C-in-C Nore, describing it to 'the Lords Commissioners of the Admiralty' on 18 November 1943, was chosen as one of four Coastal Forces actions to be published in a supplement to the *London Gazette* on 15 October 1948. The report is so complex and

Lt R.M. Marshall at the controls of his C class MGB, before taking command of MGB 607. (Courtesy, G.M. Hudson)

Lt R.M. Marshall (CO), S/Lt Lloyd Bott RANVR (First Lieutenant) and coxswain PO Merriman on the bridge of MGB 607. (Courtesy, J. Arkell)

The bow of MGB 607 after ramming and sinking an E-boat. (Courtesy, J. Arkell)

comprehensive that the section which deals with the Dog Boats is repeated in full. The dispatch indicates that the two units from the 50th Flotilla were MGB 607 (Lt R.M. Marshall), and MGB 603 (Lt F.R. Lightoller), comprising Unit Y; and MGB 609 (Lt P.G.N. Edge) with MGB 610 (Lt W. Harrop) as Unit R.

Each of the five destroyers and the eight units of Coastal Forces craft had been allocated 'waiting' positions or patrols to seaward of the most vulnerable area for attack on the convoy, which was around Smith's Knoll. Early warning of large numbers of attacking craft was given by RAF bombers which were dropping parachute mines off the Dutch coast, and at 2318 HMS *Pytchley* obtained a radar contact on E-boats well to the north. She not only drove them off but also damaged one, and even more importantly she was able to alert the Nore Command Operations Plot so that new dispositions could be made. In particular, 607 and 603 were sent north-eastward to 'cover the inferred line of retirement to Ymuiden', and 609 and 610 north-westward to cover the most northerly track of the convoy. It was very fortunate that almost all the sixteen groups of E-boats arrived in the attack area astern of the tail of the convoy, and the cleverly disposed defensive units prevented any attacks on it apart from one, when the trawler HMS *William Stephen* was sunk, having become a 'straggler' from the convoy escort.

Both Unit R and Unit Y were involved in the action at about 0140, and both played distinguished parts. C-in-C's dispatch reads:

Unit R – MGBs 609 and 610 – moved up to their northerly position at about 0100, and obtained hydrophone contact and then radar contact even before they were alerted by shore radar. From 0100 to 0141 Unit R stalked the enemy, keeping between him and the convoy. As soon as the enemy showed signs of closing the convoy, Unit R attacked, twice forcing him to withdraw to the eastward, the second time for good. The second boat in the line, on which 609 and 610 concentrated their fire, was undoubtedly hit hard and forced to leave the line. This group of E-boats was the only one to operate north of 57F buoy (east of Sheringham).

Unit Y – MGBs 607 and 603 – were by 0030 in position to intercept returning E-boats, and

at 0206 they engaged a group of E-boats steering an easterly course about 22 miles northeast of Smith's Knoll buoy. The unit pressed home its attack with great vigour and set two E-boats on fire. These E-boats were seen to blow up. MGB 607 (Lt. R.M. Marshall) also rammed and sank a third E-boat.

At 0400 MGB 603 with 607 in tow obtained radar contact to the northward. Tow was slipped and at 0418 MGB 603 went into action with six E-boats at a range of under 800 yards. As the result of being first to open fire MGB 603 obtained many hits on one boat and probably damaged it severely. After a running fight the enemy made off at high speed at about 0445. MGB 603 then rejoined 607.

The dispatch comments specifically on the actions of each unit involved, and is very generous in its praise for the Dog Boats and indeed for the part Coastal Forces in general played.

Unit R (MGB 609 and 610): the Senior Officer of this unit, Lt. P. Edge, showed a quick and sound appreciation of the C-in-C's object in fleeting the unit, i.e., the defence of the northbound convoy, and throughout handled his unit with tactical ability of a high order. Skilful use of radar gave him an exact picture of the enemy's movements and enabled him to go into action at a moment of his own choosing. The moment he chose was entirely correct and there is no doubt that this well fought action saved the convoy from being located and attacked. The unit was unfortunate in not obtaining a kill, especially as a probable one had to be sacrificed in achieving the object.

Unit Y (MGBs 607 and 603): Lieutenants Marshall and Lightoller showed admirable judgement and a magnificent fighting spirit in this, the most successful action of the night. It is considered that the claim to have destroyed three E-boats is substantiated. Once again the value of 2-pdr star-shell both as illuminants and as incendiary ammunition was demonstrated.

This action also shows the devastating effect of the gun-power of the D class MGBs in an attack which is pressed well home. The results obtained give clear proof of the very high fighting efficiency of these two boats.

The gallant action fought single-handed by MGB 603 against six E-boats not only showed determination to lose no chance of engaging the enemy but may well have saved 607 from destruction.

To these resounding plaudits, the C-in-C added a more general commendation that showed what a long way Coastal Forces had come, after early doubts, in official recognition.

An E-boat (S112, sunk in September 1944 by 724 and 728). (IWM)

This action gives general proof of a great improvement in the efficiency of the Coastal Forces, particularly as regards communications and the use of radar. The small number of material breakdowns also indicates a higher standard of interest and handling by the COs and crews of boats and reflects great credit on the maintenance officers and staffs of the bases. Furthermore, it clearly demonstrates the value and essential need of constant training and practice.

The sequels to these gallant actions were satisfying. 603 picked up nineteen survivors from S88, one of the E-boats definitely sunk by the unit. 607, despite severe bow damage from the ramming that sank another E-boat, was safely towed back to Yarmouth by 603. Edge, Marshall and Lightoller all received DSCs, as did Sub-Lt J.N. Arkell, the Pilot of 607. A further eight DSMs and seven MIDs were awarded to the crews. (Appendix 1, Note 17)

Nine days later, on 3/4 November, a combined unit of the 55th and 50th Flotillas from Yarmouth had another bruising battle. In September, Donald Bradford had had a very successful action but this time, although considerable damage was inflicted on the enemy, British boats and their crews suffered grievously. It all began quietly enough, with Bradford leading in 617, his own boat, followed by 630, 671 and 632 in one division; a second division was led by Lt Donald Dowling of the 50th Flotilla, with 621 and 650. The first objective of the operation was to land a party of commandos on the Dutch coast in a dhory. This was the repeat of an unsuccessful landing attempt a week before, when a mine detector in the dhory had so distorted the compass that the party had never reached the fog-shrouded beach after the launch.

As the unit approached the coast, they literally 'ran into' the group of four E-boats obviously positioned to intercept them. There was a short range engagement in which two of the E-boats were hit and damaged (later confirmed by intelligence reports) and retreated towards the coast. But 617 was also hit and the Oerlikon turret put out of action and the gunner killed. Bradford decided that the landing was clearly compromised, and sent 617 back to base with the commandos, transferring to 606 which became the lead boat.

Bradford then set out in poor visibility on an offensive sweep northward from the Hook. Very shortly after, he sighted a convoy and went in straight away to attack the escorts with the hope of penetrating the screen. No sooner had he fired star-shell than a large merchant ship was seen and he pressed home his attack. It later transpired that this was a large buoy-laying ship *Main*, screened by Vp 1401 and Vp 1419 and the flak vessel FJ23, all heavily armed and well prepared.

The first three boats in line took on the escorts and the last three the merchant ship, and all recorded hits but Vp 1419, firing 88-mm shells, concentrated on 606 and almost at once hit her bridge, penetrating the armour plating and bursting inside, killing the Vickers gunner, wrecking the controls, voice pipes and steering gear, and depositing all the bridge personnel in a confused and dazed heap in one corner. As they picked themselves up (both Bradford and Dowling had received shrapnel wounds) the boat received four more heavy blows, two in the engine room, one in a petrol space and the fourth in the tiller flat. The helm jammed over and 606 careered round in a circle until the engines could be stopped. As Bradford took stock, he realized that 606 was in the centre of a battle, with John Whitby in 621

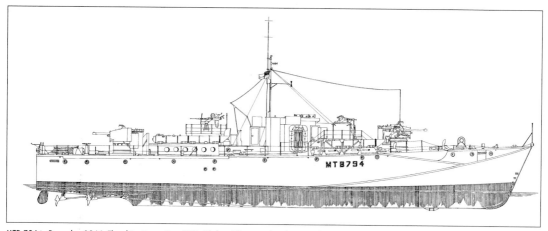

MTB 794 in December 1944. The ultimate wartime MTB with four 18-in torpedo tubes, two QF power-operated 6-pdrs and twin 20-mm Oerlikon. (Courtesy, John Lambert)

now leading the rest of the unit in heavy exchanges of fire with all the enemy ships. There were now several more of them, some on fire but all still firing. One escort ominously headed straight for the disabled 606 but was clearly not fully under control and missed narrowly astern. 621 received more hits and withdrew westward. Dowling and the First Lieutenant, 'Tubby' Hewitt, had rigged the after steering position, the Leading Motor Mechanic had got two engines going spasmodically (the Chief MM had been killed) and 606 broke out of the circle. She was on fire, had been hit on the waterline and was still under attack.

The Navigating Officer, Sub-Lt Ivone Kinross, in a very graphic description, wrote:

I realized they needed a compass aft, so I wrenched the main compass off its stand and carried it aft. Don Bradford stayed on the bridge trying to direct the boat, and I went down into the engine room to see what was happening. I went down the for'd ladder and found visibility cut to about three feet by a steamy smoky fog. I tried to move aft along the centre gangway but was

horrified to see a long blue flame horizontally barring the way. It came from the starboard inner engine. I couldn't get by, so shot up the for'd ladder and made my way back aft and down the after hatch. There was smoke and fire everywhere and strong exhaust fumes. I was worried that the methyl-bromide automatic extinguishers might either be inadvertently set off or activated from the bridge. I knew they were lethal, so I turned all four ignition switches to 'off' and rushed up to report the shambles to the SO, who had seen the abortive efforts of 630 to rig a tow and decided 606 was too far gone to save. Lt Jim Kirkpatrick laid 630 alongside and all the wounded were passed over. Don Dowling organized the destruction of the secret gear and the safety of the confidential books, and Tubby Hewitt was sent to set demolition charges in the engine room.

Hewitt himself describes his plight at this stage rather plaintively:

While I was setting the charges, I suddenly realized 630 had departed – and I was left behind in the burning boat! I felt very lonely. Fortunately, Alan Yates, the First Lieutenant of 630, realized I was not among those present, and 'Kirk' reversed 630 back to collect me. All the time we were lit up by star-shell and still being shelled.

The toll of casualties indicated just how fierce the battle had been. One officer (Sub-Lt E. Wood-Hatch, the Pilot of 621) and nine ratings were killed, and no fewer than twenty-one were wounded, many seriously. Bradford admits to being very depressed after this action but upon analysing it with Commander Brind, the base CO, he reflected that the method of approaching targets in line ahead to attempt to breach the escort screen was bound to put the leading boat at greatest risk. As the imperative was constantly to attack any ships providing a supply line to support the German offensive in Russia, this was a risk that had to be accepted.[6]

For all the flotillas this was a quiet period from the point of view of successful offensive patrols, although every night when weather permitted units were out in the Channel and beyond the east coast convoy line in the demanding defensive role.

It is perhaps necessary to emphasize here the significance of the convoy protection patrols that fell, not alone, but very heavily on the Dog Boat flotillas. At this time, the safety of the supply convoys was perceived by those planning the build up for the invasion of France to be so vital that for a period of several months, the 'Z' line patrols were given Priority One, even taking precedence over the attacks on the enemy's shipping lines. This was driven home to the reluctant

COs by a series of VIPs who visited the bases to make sure it was understood.

This meant that SOs had to accept that their boats would be out every other night when they were in operational state, but on at least three out of four of those nights they would be wallowing in a 'Z' position near Smith's Knoll rather than aiming for the Dutch coast.

The destroyers that could be spared from the Atlantic were stationed along the convoy route with a 10-mile beat. The actions to repulse the attack by thirty E-boats on 3/4 November described earlier in this chapter show how shore radar and communications in all the boats had improved. This enabled early notice of enemy movements and consequent deployment to be given. Training was intense and the experience of the COs and the radar in the boats played a big part. Danger did not only come from the maurauding E-boats (in fact they tried to avoid contact, seeking ships of the convoy to torpedo) but from mistakes of identification by the larger elements of the British screening force, especially when they were newly appointed to the area and not used to distinguishing Dog Boats from E-boats.

Records show that November and December 1943 were illuminated for the Dog Boats by just one action, and that is only significant because it involved the first two boats of the 59th Flotilla to be completed, MTBs 700 and 705. They had recently arrived in Dover, where one division of the 59th was to be based (the other would be at Yarmouth) and they were summoned to take part in a special operation on 23/24 December. 705 was temporarily commanded on this night by Lt Cdr D. Wilkie, because her CO, Lt A.H. Lewis, had gone sick two days earlier. David Wilkie had been appointed SO of the 64th Flotilla, but none of his boats was completed and he had come to Dover to

---

[6] *Day In, Night Out*, D.G. Bradford; MO13169; ROP at PRO in ADM 199/537; accounts from F. Hewitt and I. Kinross.

become acquainted with Dog Boats. It was to prove an effective way of learning the ropes. He was an experienced officer and took it in his stride. 700 was commanded by Lt O.B. Mabee RCNVR.

A large 400-ft enemy merchant vessel, escorted by a large force of R-boats and M class minesweepers, left Boulogne and was immediately tracked by British shore radar and engaged by coastal batteries. A unit of the 13th Flotilla of short MTBs was sent from Dover but missed the convoy because of bad visibility. MLs and other MTBs laid a minefield, which the merchant ship crossed safely, but the mines sank one M class escort. Another unit of 'shorts' from the 9th Flotilla also failed to find the convoy, but 705 and 700 made contact with the escort off Gravelines and took on several R-boats. It was a fierce battle, and 700 was severely damaged, but only after two R-boats had first been mauled by the formidable Dog Boat broadside. Two other short boat units made another attack, meeting seven R-boats, but the merchant ship got through.[7]

At last, the boats could return to enjoy a peaceful Christmas, with all the release of tension associated with the traditions of the service at the festive season. In this as in many other aspects, the officers and men of the boats showed their respect for Naval customs. Just as they would be meticulous in 'falling in on the foc's'le' when entering harbour, even after a long, wet, and bloody patrol, and 'piping the still' when passing a larger ship or the base, so the boats sought to demonstrate that being small did not mean being casual! The Naval Christmas dinner routine was carefully followed, with the CO or First Lieutenant changing places with the youngest rating and the officers serving the men the most lavish meal that the tiny galley could provide.

That Christmas 1943 was no exception in all Coastal Forces bases, although Donald Bradford recalls that the 55th in Yarmouth were unlucky that day. The whole crew had just finished their meal, the tot followed by extra rations of beer had left everybody happily singing or subsiding in sleepy corners, when an urgent message arrived: C-in-C Nore required a strike patrol of four boats as an important enemy convoy was expected to leave the Hook at nightfall. For a very short time spirits were high, but the weather turned foul from the east, and the patrol soon became a nightmare. It was obviously too rough for any gun action, but in the hope that it would be possible to make a torpedo attack, Bradford pressed on to the convoy route. When he turned south to sweep towards the Hook, the full blast of the wind and sea on the beam rolled the boats so severely that the torpedo tubes were nearly under the water. It was time to call off the patrol and race for home with a following wind. Bradford described his crew as a 'sodden, cold and heartily fed-up crowd of men who would now have to wait another twelve months for the fleshpots of a Christmas night'. But as the messdeck quip went, 'it's no good dripping – you shouldn't have joined!'

Rather like the previous November and early December, January and most of February 1944 brought little contact with the enemy. However, there were many more opportunities for crews to be 'sodden and cold' on convoy protection patrols and forays to the far coast whenever a let up in the foul weather permitted.

Lt R.W.V. (Robin) Board, the CO of 610, recorded several 'jottings' in highly descriptive prose at this time, and two of them seem very appropriate to include here to

[7] MO1687/44; NID in OD5084; *A Caul and Some Wartime Experiences*, A.H. Lewis.

illustrate the human aspects of life in the North Sea in mid-winter.

The first is entitled, 'Shore batteries on the Dutch coast – impressive shooting.'

Eight MTBs are stealthily approaching the Dutch coast, looking for a convoy. It is a dark night and the long passage across has been tiring; keeping station in line ahead at speed, without lights, requires the highest concentration.

Approaching the convoy route, they reduce speed to 10 knots and move into line abreast. The CO can just make out his neighbours 50 yards on either beam – the pale streak of their wakes behind the darker blur of their hulls. The slow approach seems interminable, the darkness ahead like a wall. Suspense is high.

There's a sudden crash in the sky, followed by three more, and four brilliant white star-shells burst high behind them, silhouetting the wide line of prowlers: it is brighter than day and the whole world has turned black and white. There is no colour: everything is drawn in darkest contrast. There is no place to hide. It is very beautiful.

The star-shells are followed by a salvo of four huge splashes which silently rear up from the sea behind the boats, four times as high as their masts, where they seem to hang like pale poplars in a field before slowly collapsing. When another salvo bursts slightly to the west, the SO thinks of discretion and orders 'Blue One Eight'. The flotilla turns together 180 degrees to starboard in a copybook manoeuvre, perfectly illuminated by the star-shells once more slowly floating down.

'George Two Five' (speed 25 knots) follows, and each boat's four motors roar

into life in a smother of spray bursting white against a black sea. The last salvo falls ahead of them, and the CO and Cox'n are soaked as they try to avoid steaming right into one as it rears up in their path. The stars burn out one by one and blessed all-enveloping night returns.

The Cox'n grudgingly remarks 'seven miles off the coast and straddled by 8" salvoes – not bad shooting'. They set course for home, thoroughly discomforted and frustrated.

The second 'jotting', entitled 'The power of food as a stimulus – comforts well earned', follows naturally on the other side of the North Sea several hours later.

In His Majesty's small warships, interest in food is intense. A sensible Admiralty permits a modicum of choice in the rations drawn from the Base Victualling Office, and the messdeck, by majority vote, instructs the messman accordingly.

In addition, a system called 'Sea Comforts' is in operation. This depends on the actual time spent at sea, in what are – after all – extremely uncomfortable boats. The longer the patrols, the more 'Comforts' at the weekend.

The MTB is returning from a long winter's night patrol in the North Sea. It started at mid-afternoon yesterday, and the boat is now wallowing in a nasty quartering sea in the chilly dawn as she approaches the welcoming arms of the harbour. Everyone is tired and wet and chilled to the bone. The entrance seems a long time coming. At last it is close enough for No. One to think of calling 'Harbour Stations', but before he can, the Cox'n leans conspiratorially towards the CO and whispers 'Four and a half minutes, sir – Comforts!' The CO wearily orders 'Hard a'port' and the boat slowly swings back to seaward, dives angrily and throws spray over the bridge. As she turns again towards the harbour lights, the Cox'n checks his watch and grins; 'OK sir!' and they gratefully slide into the smooth water between the arms.

The crew are much appreciative, and grin broadly as they secure alongside. That little circuit has put them into the next bracket for 'Comforts' – they'll get sixteen more units! The CO knows they will be expended entirely on tinned damsons – an American delicacy recently discovered in the Victualling Store and to which they seem exclusively addicted.

As winter drew towards spring, the talk in the flotillas turned occasionally towards the probability of the 'Second Front' being launched in the summer. But where and when? It is now a matter of record that behind the scenes, staff planners were already busy with dispositions and preparations in Coastal Forces. More and more Dog Boats were joining new flotillas with boat numbers creeping up towards 750. Some flotillas were prepared for minelaying. But the east coast flotillas were to continue in their relentless battles with the elements for some time to come, and in the Channel the great priority was shortly to become the protection of the south coast ports against maurauding E-boats intent on laying mines in the swept channels.

On 22/23 February, those old warriors 609 and 610 of the 50th Flotilla were involved with the destroyer HMS *Garth* in repelling an attack by fifteen E-boats in the convoy route near Smith's Knoll. *Garth* sank one E-boat (S94) and the Dog Boats had a

brief action which had, apparently, no result other than to turn the E-boats back without contacting the convoy. Two nights later, 617, 621 and 629 of the 55th with *Eglinton* and *Vivien* had a similar brush, but this time Bradford moved across to Ymuiden and caught the E-boats returning. They intercepted two groups, one of four and then one of six, and secured hits on at least four of them: the return fire was spasmodic, but the unit suffered one fatal casualty. It is, of course, futile to generalize on such matters, but the crews of the Dog Boats always considered that once they were within range of E-boats, they could get the upper hand in gunnery quite quickly, and that the fire from E-boats was often high and wide. Such confidence was a great help when pressing home an attack, however tenuously it was based!

March was the beginning of a hectic and successful period for the Dog Boat flotillas, and indeed for all the Coastal Forces MTBs. Because this narrative, by definition, is concerned with the Dog Boats, little is said of the work of the short boats. But apart from the fact that in the winter months the 'shorts' were unable to operate as constantly as the Dogs in poor weather, they were being very successful in many attacks, led as ever by inspiring SOs such as MacDonald, Arnold-Forster and Trelawny – worthy successors to Hichens, Dickens, Richards and Horne. More were to emerge in the heady days ahead.

On 6/7 March, it was the turn of the newly formed 53rd Flotilla of Dog Boats, under their SO, Lt Cdr D.H.E. McCowen, to fight a spirited battle in their first opportunity of contact with the enemy.

McCowen's flotilla had three boats still with their MGB armament and no tubes: his own 693, 695 (Lt D.L.W. Macfarlane) and 689 (Lt W. Messenger). The other two boats were true MTBs: 694 (Lt J. Colvill) and 690 (Lt R.D.F. Marlow). The unit's orders were to patrol along the Dutch coast from Egmond southward to the Hook. As they approached Ymuiden, in arrowhead formation and at 10 knots, they sighted three trawlers at 4 miles range. Visibility was extreme and without some subterfuge, surprise was going to be impossible. McCowen decided to close Ymuiden and if possible to pass his unit off as E-boats.

When they were very close to the entrance, they found that there was a cluster of about twelve enemy vessels to seaward (trawlers, R-boats and a gun coaster) and two merchant vessels. It seemed that a convoy was forming up. Showing great coolness, McCowen led his three gun boats closer in (they were by now only 500 yd from shore batteries at Ymuiden); he then

sent the two MTBs to attack the merchantmen.

With the aid of some imaginary E-boat call signs and some deliberately bad morse from an ill-trained lamp, the range was reduced to a mere 200 yd and enabled the first broadside, with complete surprise, to devastate the gun coaster and also to damage two of the R-boats before they even opened fire in reply. To confuse the enemy even further, several small enemy craft came out of Ymuiden. After attacking the R-boats and receiving some damage, McCowen's inshore group opened fire on the trawlers and secured hits before they disengaged; they could hardly miss at such short range.

The two MTBs fired their torpedoes, and considered that the smaller of the merchant vessels was hit and seemed to be sinking. They

Lt R.F. Marlow, Lt W. Messenger, Lt Cdr D.H.E. McCowen and J. Colville after the 53rd Flotilla's action off Ymuiden in 1944. (Courtesy, D. McGrath)

went on and engaged the trawlers and R-boats before 690 received a hit in the engine room from a shore battery: only prompt action by the engine room crew extinguished the resulting fire and enabled a withdrawal. The enemy, still thoroughly confused, continued firing at each other with increasing success for some time – all a by-product of the daring and totally unexpected in-shore attack so close to the port.

Five of the six Dog Boats were damaged, but only 695 received significant casualties when early in the action she was hit on the bridge, and both the Pilot (Sub-Lt J.W.G. Morrish) and CCF Nore's newly appointed Gunnery Officer (Lt D.T. Wickham RN) were killed. The same shell wounded the CO, First Lieutenant and Cox'n and in the trauma 695 rammed 693, but fortunately neither boat was disabled. The CO, Douglas Macfarlane, ignored his wounds and brought 695 back to harbour five hours later before collapsing. Not surprisingly, he was awarded a DSC and his Cox'n, Petty Officer S.J. Mears, a DSM.

It had been an astonishingly successful first action for the 53rd Flotilla, displaying great team work, and McCowen's DSO was richly deserved.[8]

Only three nights later, on 9/10 March, the 55th fought another successful action off Terschelling. Donald Bradford considered there might be more chance of finding targets with less alert escorts in an area where no patrols had been deployed for many months, beyond Den Holder towards Borkum, off Terschelling and Ameland. Bradford had a unit of six boats, each commanded by his most experienced COs, in 617, 621, 629, 668, 624 and 652.

They left Yarmouth early in the day and

8 MO3608; summary of recorded actions; War Intelligence Report (WIR) 220.

were in position at midnight, steering south-west along the convoy route. Almost at once they detected a convoy of twenty ships steering north-east at 7 knots. It took over two hours to shadow and get into position for a zone attack (a spread of torpedoes from four boats) with the main target a 'three island type' tanker about 400 ft in length. 668 and 624 were told to withhold their torpedoes and to make a gun attack on the escorts. During the run in, the unit of four came under heavy fire, and had to cross the bows of a flak trawler. This allowed each boat to attack, and she was eventually silenced, stopped and left blazing. Seven torpedoes were fired, the tanker was seen to be hit under the foremast and her bows broke off.

The unit disengaged and stopped about 5 miles north of the convoy to take stock. 617, the SO's boat, had been hit in the after fuel tank by a 37-mm incendiary shell that penetrated the engine room and damaged the starboard inner engine. Bradford sent her back to base and transferred to John Whitby's 621. His next decision was to send 668 ('Biscuits' Strang) and 624 to make a second torpedo attack, while the three others moved in to create a diversion with gunfire. Strang was at the expected position by 0415 but found that the convoy had dispersed and he had to search further before two radar echoes were investigated and found to be a large tug and an escorting trawler. 624's torpedo attack missed, but the tug was soon silenced by gunfire, and 668 went alongside. The tug was flying the German ensign and 668 was greeted by nine crew who claimed to be Dutchmen, who said that, of the twenty-seven crew including a German armed guard, the remainder had jumped overboard – no trace of them could be found. The tug was sunk by gunfire, and 668 and 624 set off to rendezvous with the SO. Because of the delay, they did not find the other unit, and returned independently to Yarmouth, arriving at 1645.

It had been a long and exhausting patrol, but with two ships sunk including a tanker, and a trawler well mauled, a successful one. It was especially so as there were no casualties and only 617 suffered serious damage.[9]

March continued in a very active fashion. On 14/15th and 23rd/24th, the division of the 59th Flotilla at Dover had two engagements in the Dover Strait, providing diversions for attacks by short MTBs. Their other incomplete division at Yarmouth joined in with boats of the 50th Flotilla and the 55th in two actions on 24/25th and 28/29th, with some limited success and very little damage to the boats.

March ended on 28/29th with a very different experience for Ian Lyle's 51st Flotilla in their first action after their reorganization: they had originally been the very early 18th MGB Flotilla. They were now based at Newhaven, and although labelled MTBs, still had their MGB armament and no tubes. Their six-boat patrol that night (611, 602, 614, 613, 608, 615) was later labelled 'whisker-singeing' as it took them right to the harbour mouth of Dieppe. As soon as they arrived, they met two groups of R-boats and a corvette or torpedo boat and engaged them at very close range. The shore batteries joined in and illuminated the whole scene with star-shell. One R-boat was seen to explode and others were hit, but all the 51st's boats suffered severely, particularly from the shore batteries, and the resulting casualty list made grim reading: twelve killed, eleven seriously wounded and eighteen with minor wounds. All the boats got back to Newhaven, but

repairs put them out of action for some time.[10]

It was during April that the first effects of the longer term plans leading to Operation Neptune, the naval aspects of the invasion of Normandy, began to become apparent.

The flotilla switches began with the return of Lt Cdr Ken Gemmell to Yarmouth, after his great successes on the east coast in 1943. But now he was SO of the 58th Flotilla, and his boats had spent from September to March in the very different operations off Norway from their base at Lerwick in the Shetland Islands. Soon after their arrival on the east coast, they were joined by their Norwegian partners, the 54th Flotilla, who for the first time came down to operate in British home waters. They came with a tremendous reputation for their aggressive and determined spirit, and were acknowledged as fine seamen.

The strategic reasons for the switch of these two flotillas were twofold. The first was clearly to reinforce the Dog Boat strength available for the invasion, as Bradford's 55th and McCowen's 53rd were both destined for the Channel area to play important roles in Operation Neptune, leaving gaps at Yarmouth. The second was the fact that Norwegian operations became hazardous with the very long daylight hours through the summer.

At much the same time, the 64th Flotilla, specially adapted for minelaying and led by Lt Cdr David Wilkie, were about to begin their very significant contribution to the success of Neptune, switching base from Dover to Portsmouth. Two flotillas were based in the West Country – the newly formed 65th (all Canadian) Flotilla led by

---

[9] MO3828; ROP at PRO in ADM 199/265; signal HMS *Midge*.

[10] MO4302; ROP at PRO in ADM 199/261; letters from crew members.

Lt Cdr J. Kirkpatrick at Dartmouth, and the 52nd (SO Lt Cdr T.N. Cartwright) that had been well established there since October 1943. Both these flotillas were to play an important part in the western Channel in the months to come.

Much of the effort of the Coastal Forces bases and their associated repair yards was devoted to a steady increase in the percentage of boats in full operational state, together with all available design improvements that were being steadily implemented. With the vast increase in the number of flotillas and indeed the MLs that were to play their considerable part throughout, Coastal Forces were almost ready to take on their allotted tasks in Operation Neptune. It had been necessary, too, to move the working-up base HMS *Bee*, which had done such a magnificent job at Weymouth in preparing boats for operations, as the Portland area was

to become chock-a-block with every type of craft for the invasion. *Bee* was now at Holyhead, well removed from that congestion.

One very popular aspect of the flotilla moves was the fact that the teams of Wren specialists, particularly the Ordnance Artificers who took great pride in maintaining and repairing the guns of the flotilla they were assigned to, moved with the boats. They were such a part of the flotilla team that they were regarded as essential to its success and their continuing service was a great boost to flotilla spirit.

But during April and May it became clear that the enemy too was preparing, although everyone was kept guessing as to the point of attack. The number of E-boats concentrated in the Channel ports, particularly in pens at Le Havre and

MTB 707 sinking after a collision with the French frigate *L'Escaramouche*, April 1944. (Courtesy, W. Last)

Cherbourg, increased enormously, and their minelaying sorties became more and more frequent. This kept all the flotillas busy, especially as the build up of supplies in the south coast ports required even more convoy activity.

All these factors explain why April and early May 1944 saw hundreds of patrols but only three major offensive successes for the Dog Boats.

The first, on 10/11 April, fell to the Norwegian 54th Flotilla now operating from Yarmouth. The flotilla had a new SO; Lt Cdr Christian Monsen had taken over from Lt Tamber who had led them with such distinction for the first seventeen months of their existence. The COs clearly found it difficult to adapt to the different conditions on the east coast, but had lost none of their aggression.

On this night, they had to operate in bright moonlight, and having found a convoy between Egmond and Ymuiden, made three attempts to get through the very strong screen. Each time they were repulsed by a heavy barrage of fire under star-shell. They attacked one group of E- or R-boats and claimed to have damaged two of them. They themselves sustained some light damage but had no casualties.

The second successful engagement, on 23/24 April, was in the western Channel, off Cherbourg. It involved nine boats drawn from three flotillas in three separate units: 617, 632 and 671 of Bradford's 55th, now based at HMS *Dolphin*, the submarine base at Gosport, as an overflow from *Hornet*; 707, 721, 702 and 701 of the 63rd from Portland led by Lt Cdr G.C. Fanner, and 680 and 608 of the 51st from Newhaven.

The 55th, on their arrival at *Dolphin*, had adopted a unique and innovative flotilla symbol. Each boat had a vivid red slash of paint at the bow beneath the flare, with shark's teeth painted on. Its whole purpose was to strengthen flotilla *esprit de corps* and however much some scoffed and murmured 'showmen', there is no doubt that it worked! This night they were sent to patrol off Pointe de Barfleur, east of Cherbourg. It was a beautifully calm night – very different from the majority of nights the 55th had experienced in the North Sea for so long. Except for signals that indicated that 608 and 680 had chased E-boats returning from a minelaying exercise off Dungeness but had only had a brief long-range contact, there seemed little happening.

Jeff Fanner, with his four boats, was just off Cherbourg lying in wait for returning E-boats, when at 0100 three Möwe class torpedo boats (not dissimilar to British Hunt class destroyers) steamed out of the harbour, followed by a large group of R-boats.

Fanner's boats stood little chance: the enemy found the range immediately and began a fierce barrage, some of which struck home. The SO ordered smoke and beat a hasty retreat with one boat heavily damaged but just able to keep up.

Bradford could see the tracer and hear some of the R/T, and guessed that the 'Möwes' might move along the coast eastward if shore radar had detected his unit. But it was not until 0346 that his own radar picked up echoes of the three torpedo boats moving along the coast towards him. He was disposed ready in arrowhead formation to seaward of the enemy's line of advance, and prepared to make a torpedo attack, each of his three boats poised to fire her two torpedoes at each designated target as they passed ahead.

The waiting seemed interminable, but when two of the torpedo boats had passed

One of the boats of the 55th Flotilla, identified by their symbol – the shark's teeth on the bow. (IWM)

by and just as he was about to order 'Flag Four' (fire torpedoes), the three targets turned simultaneously towards the Dog Boats and star-shell burst overhead, followed by a barrage from all their forward guns. From then on, it was a matter of getting out as fast as possible, firing furiously to inflict damage as they went, and then making smoke and even dropping depth charges in front of the charging enemy ships. Some damage was unquestionably caused, and fire spurted from one of the targets, but the third MTB in line, Larry Toogood's 671, was hit first in the charthouse and then in the engine room by big shells, and Bradford heard an explosion and saw 671 had stopped. He was desperate to help if he could and decided to try another depth charge although he knew it would expose both his boats to further shell fire. He saw one torpedo boat move towards the blazing 671 and then knew there was no way he could help. He just hoped they were picking up survivors.

Surprisingly, the charge Bradford had made seemed to deter the 'Möwes', and one after the other they broke off the attack and departed towards Cherbourg, one of them clearly reduced in speed.

With heavy hearts 617 and 632 made their way back to Portsmouth, each with one engine out of action, and both with many holes and casualties. Bradford signalled C-in-C and a destroyer and a frigate were sent to try to contact the 'Möwes', and also search for any signs of survivors from 671. The frigate found one mattress floating amid the wreckage of 671, with two men clinging to it. One was the Pilot, Sub-Lt Colin Morley, and he told the sad story of the end of 671. Apparently the 'Möwe' had made no attempt to pick up survivors – she had

continued to fire more shells into the blazing wreck. Twenty had survived the horrific attack, but several more were lost, including the First Lieutenant, when the petrol tanks blew up. The rafts had all been destroyed so the handful who were left clung to mattresses and bits of wood. But many hours later when the frigate found them, only two were left. The rating, A/B Alfred Day, was awarded a DSM for his bravery and efforts to help the survivors. He had been the twin Oerlikon gunner of 671.[11]

As a final run up to Operation Neptune, when the effort to have all flotillas at a high state of readiness for the huge demands that were to be made on them was at its height, the month of May was something of a disaster. In three separate incidents, three Dog Boats were sunk and another badly damaged. What was even worse was the fact that two of the incidents resulted from errors of recognition and what is euphemistically labelled 'friendly fire'.

The first was on 4 May, when 708 and 720 of the 63rd Flotilla were returning to Portland from a long and uneventful patrol in the Cherbourg area. It was a glorious morning, with excellent visibility. Suddenly out of the blue came a flight of Beaufighters and despite the White Ensigns, they attacked with lethal rocket fire. The results were devastating: 708, particularly, received hits in every part of the hull during three attacks, the engine room was ablaze and many were seriously wounded. Lt Cdr Fanner, the SO and CO of 708, had to order 'abandon ship', and the casualties and crew were taken aboard a frigate and the wounded given first class treatment by a Surgeon-Lieutenant. 708 had to be sunk by

[11] *Day In, Night Out*, D.G. Bradford; WIR 217; Portsmouth signal.

a Hunt class destroyer. 720 had also been hit many times and suffered casualties, but did not catch fire so was towed back to Portland. She was paid off, and recommissioned on 6 June 1944 with a new crew.[12]

Next came another sad loss – the sinking of 732 by the Free French Hunt class destroyer *La Combattante* on 28 May. This time the terrible mistake did at least have an understandable background. 732 (Lt A.H. Randell) and 739 (Lt W.L. Fesq DSC RANVR) of the 64th Flotilla had already begun their minelaying activities in the previous weeks, with torpedo tubes removed and replaced with rails for carrying and laying spherical horned mines. It was ironic that during a period of nightly minelaying expeditions off Cherbourg, David Wilkie's 64th Flotilla would return to *Dolphin* where they were now based, to discover that E-boats had been engaged on similar operations off the south coast ports, so that their return was often delayed while channels were swept.

On the night of 27/28 May, however, 732 and 739 were not minelaying but were called out to intercept E-boats on their way to the south coast. They were sent to Beachy Head, and *La Combattante* to Selsey Bill. Obviously something went wrong with identification: a cryptic note in the battle summary says, 'neither *La Combattante* nor the MTBs had activated their IFF equipment ['identification friend or foe'] specially designed to prevent such occurrences'. *La Combattante* opened fire on 732 believing she was an E-boat laying mines, and secured two 4-in hits almost at once, causing her to blow up and sink. The sad result was a long casualty list: one officer and twelve ratings missing, and

five wounded, and of course the loss of one valuable minelaying boat at this crucial time.[13]

And if that was not enough, on the next day, 672 of Tom Cartwright's 52nd Flotilla was mined returning from patrol just off her home port of Dartmouth. She was commanded by J.N. Wise, the half-leader of the flotilla, and although he managed to beach her, she was written off and Wise went almost at once to recommission 720 when her repairs were completed after the Beaufighter attack.

Apart from these three incidents, the month in the Channel was full of unremitting E-boat raids and concerted action by frigate and MTB defensive patrols. Earlier in the month there was one success for Tom Cartwright's 52nd Flotilla, on 6/7 May. It was an unusual operation and was most remarkable for the careful navigation and seamanship required. Cartwright's flotilla was particularly suited for their task this night, as they were sent to destroy a German Elbing class destroyer that had been driven on to the rocks near St Tregarec on the north Brittany coast by the Canadian Tribal class destroyer HMCS *Haida*. Intelligence revealed that a salvage operation was shortly to be attempted, and even though it was the full moon period, the urgency of the matter meant that risks were to be taken.

Operations in and around the Channel Islands and the Brittany coast, with their myriad rocks and tiny islands and ripping tides, called for high skills, but the experience gained on many patrols stood the 52nd in good stead. Cartwright, an experienced sailor, made the remark that in peacetime it would have been regarded as

---

[12] MO6144; ROP in PRO in ADM 199/267; personal account by Frank Loy, Cox'n of 708.

[13] MO6603; ROP in PRO in ADM 199/267; notes from Charles Burford of 732.

MTB 696 passes Albert Bridge after repairs and refit at Teddington. (Courtesy, T. Alexander)

the height of folly for anyone to play around the Minquiers at night unless he was a native, but that is just what they frequently had to do in the course of duty. They were by this time aided by the new navigational device called QH, which enabled a very precise approach to be made, and Cartwright considered that without it his task would have been twice as difficult.

His report is a masterpiece of under-statement. He describes how he sailed in 673 (his own boat) with 677 and 717, and had three short boats of the 1st MTB Flotilla as backup in case a diversion was required.

He stopped the unit 3 miles from the target and the short boats remained ready to act if enemy ships approached. The three Dog Boats closed at 8 knots, and the target

was soon sighted in the bright moonlight. At first they thought they were watching the wash of fast boats, but soon realized they were breakers against the rocks surrounding the destroyer. When about 4 cables away, they could see that the target had shifted even more since an aerial picture had been taken a few hours earlier; instead of having a slight list to port and her hull mostly exposed, she was now awash with a 25° list to starboard. Coolly, despite being about half a mile from the beach, Cartwright nudged in to 2 cables from the target 'to have a better look at her' and then decided that one torpedo was all that would be needed. After manoeuvring to get a clear run for his torpedo, he fired, it ran true, struck under the bridge and sent debris high into the air. When the water column subsided, the bridge, foremast and funnels had disappeared and the stern had settled down more deeply.

As the boats quietly left the scene, a searchlight suddenly picked them up and the coastal batteries opened fire. The unit increased speed to 23 knots and zig-zagged until the threat was over.

As the CO of HMS *Cicala* (the Coastal Forces base at Dartmouth) commented in forwarding the report, 'this difficult operation was brilliantly carried out, great care and forethought having been shown in overcoming the navigational problems on this dangerous coast'. C-in-C in his turn remarked that the MTB had achieved what several sorties by aircraft had failed to do, and that air reconnaissance had now reported that the destruction of the target was complete.[14]

A new and very important phase of operations in home waters was now imminent, but attention should first be given to the activities in Norwegian waters, left at the end of chapter three as the winter of 1943/4 loomed with its longer nights.

[14] MO5805; ROP at PRO in ADM 199/264.

CHAPTER 6

NORWEGIAN OPERATIONS

SEPTEMBER 1943 TO MAY 1945

The general Coastal Forces reorganization of flotillas in September/October 1943 seems to have been received by the 30th MTB Flotilla with its all-Norwegian crews based in Lerwick, in just the same way as it had been in the bases both on the south coast and on the east coast. No mention at all is made of it in contemporary reports and apparently the change of name to the 54th Flotilla was of little significance. The SO, Lt Tamber, continued his aggressive and much respected leadership. There were great hopes that the blows to flotilla morale by the loss of 345 and the murder of her crew in July 1943, and the mauling some of the boats had taken at much the same time in attempting risky operations during the virtually 'no night' period, could be set aside in September. (Appendix 1, Note 18)

The flotilla tried several times to mount operations, but the boats were invariably detected by aircraft and suffered from cannon attacks. It was decided, as a start to the new season, to try something new – a patrol to a more distant area off Kristiansund, just south of Trondheim.

On 9 September MTBs 618 (Lt Per Danielsen) and 627 (Lt H. Henriksen) were towed north from Lerwick by two patrol craft. When the approaches to Kristiansund were reached, the tows were cast off and the patrol craft returned to Lerwick. The two boats crept into the Inner Leads and soon after found the German SS *Anke*, attacked her with a full spread of torpedoes and secured three hits, sinking her. On this occasion, there was no attempt to disguise the fact that she had been attacked by MTBs; in fact the boats followed up with a gun attack. It was considered that there might be more strategic advantage in causing the German authorities alarm that shipping so far north and in the protection of the Inner Leads could be attacked. In fact, this was successful: thereafter the Germans ceased further seaborne movements at night in the Trondheim area.[1]

Per Danielsen had long been recognized as a skilled and fearless commander. Two years before, in October 1941, he had set the tone for Norwegian operations when, in his Thornycroft MTB 56, he had been towed all the way from Scapa Flow to Bergen, torpedoed a tanker, and returned safely to

[1] MO54410; War History Case (WHC) 7942; intelligence in NIDOD5084; V-Adm Gundersen.

add a bar to the DSC he had won in MTB 54 even earlier, as described in chapter three.

This success was greeted with great joy at Lerwick, but bad weather restricted operations considerably for much of September and October.

As the winter season began, however, there was great delight as the hard-pressed boats of the 54th Flotilla in Lerwick were joined by a new British flotilla, the 58th, led by the redoubtable Ken Gemmell. He was now a Lieutenant Commander and raring to go in a different and even more challenging sphere of operations from those in which he had made his considerable mark, in the 31st Flotilla on the east coast, earlier in 1943.

His new flotilla consisted of MTBs 666, 669, 681, 683, 684, 685, 686 and 687, and they arrived at Lerwick in several batches over the period from October to December 1943. It was not long before they were brutally introduced to the dangers and rigours of northern long-range operations.

A decision was made to follow up Per Danielsen's Trondheim success with another daylight patrol, and this time a boat from the 58th Flotilla (669) was chosen to go, together with 688 (Lt A.W. Prebensen) of the Norwegian flotilla. It became a feature of the next three months that the two flotillas worked in great harmony, both ashore and afloat. More often than not, units sent to sea were a mixture of the two. The CO of 669 was Lt John Fletcher, and 25 October was his first Norwegian patrol. The two boats made the long passage north to the Trondheim area during the dark hours, and at 0725 they sighted two coasters off Bessaker, and immediately attacked with gunfire. One target, the *Kylstraum*, laden with 170 tons of cement, was crippled and driven ashore. A German report reveals that this attack drew the attention of a defensive patrol vessel from Trondheim to the scene, the ND16 (*Möwe*). She opened heavy fire and, as it was daylight, the MTBs retired under cover of a smoke screen. ND16 raised the alarm, and from 0815 onwards, aircraft were alerted to find the boats.

At 0930, a flight of three fighters located and attacked, and were met with a fierce anti-aircraft barrage, which damaged one of the aircraft. Both boats were, however, hit and damaged, 688 having one engine put out of action and 669 losing her port 0.5-in turret, each with some casualties. Ten minutes after the first attack another three fighters appeared to make a second pass.

688, the leading boat, was able to take avoiding action, despite which her 2-pdr pom-pom gun for'd was put out of action. 669, on the other hand, was badly holed on both sides and fire broke out in the for'd petrol tanks. The methyl-bromide automatic extinguishers could not function as the pipe had been fractured. Even worse, the mixture had escaped into the engine room. By this time only one engine was still running, and the fire was out of hand, so 669 had to be abandoned. 688 took off her crew and fired into the stricken 669, which was last seen heeling over to port with smoke pouring from her. Fortunately, the fighters did not pursue 688, presumably being at the limit of their range, but she was shadowed by a BV 138 and attacked at both 1053 and then by a relief aircraft at 1600, each time unsuccessfully. 688 got back to Lerwick early next morning.[2]

On 20 November, 625 and 627 had made a Welman run to Bergen. The two davits on each boat enabled them to launch four of these tiny craft, on this occasion controlled by two British and two Norwegian 'drivers'. When practically inside the port, one of the

---

[2] MO54937; V-Adm Gundersen.

MTB 683 of the 58th Flotilla with her after deck covered by 4-gallon patrol cans on a long-range operation in Norwegian waters. (Courtesy, J. Perkins)

craft surfaced and was promptly attacked by Germans. The Norwegian driver was taken prisoner, while the three other drivers had to abandon their craft and swim ashore.

Two days later, on 22 November, 686 was alongside at Lerwick with 626 outside her. 686 was commanded by Lt A. McDougall and had been the first of Gemmell's 58th Flotilla to arrive at Lerwick. The boats were loaded with their extra fuel in petrol cans on the upper deck and the crews were making their final checks. Somehow or other, an Oerlikon gun on 686 was accidentally fired, the petrol cans ignited, and fire spread like lightning to both boats. There were massive explosions as ammunition and the main petrol tanks went up, and both boats were destroyed. There was understandably near panic in Lerwick, but no other boats were caught up in the disaster,

which left 686 with four of her crew dead, and 626 with one. It was the sort of accident that was always in the minds of all Coastal Forces crews, vulnerable as they were at all times. The training and the strict standing orders should have prevented such disasters, but considering the numbers of boats they were rare.

The two boats had actually been preparing to leave to attempt the rescue of the Welman drivers left behind the night before, but this mission was no longer possible to mount. It is a small epic of the Second World War that these three men, hunted by the Germans, managed to avoid capture for more than two months. They joined up with fourteen refugees and were taken back to Lerwick by MTB 653 on 6 February 1944.

Another type of special operation up to the end of 1943 was the laying of mines in the Inner Leads, often carried out by the Dog Boats before they took up their lurking positions. Up to forty mines could be carried by each boat. They were R-mines detonated by contact, and were about twice the size of a football. Each mine was suspended from the surface by a small float, and they were interconnected by rope with an anchor each end.

They had some success. A coaster was sunk, and several German ships damaged but the main benefit was the psychological effect on the German operators who never knew what type of hazard to expect next, and were therefore committed to use more and more resources to protect their shipping.

But the crossing of the North Sea with both mines and petrol cans on deck never became a popular pastime, and when 625 suffered considerable damage from the explosion of a mine on deck, these operations were gradually phased out.

Another of the 58th Flotilla boats to arrive early in Lerwick was MTB 666, commanded by Lt D.N. Buller. On 13 December, there was an urgent call for a boat to carry out a clandestine operation (known in the boats as 'cloak and dagger'), and as no other boat was available, Buller found himself plunged in at the deep end on his first patrol in these waters. One-boat operations were, in fact, rare. It was a complete success: he landed fuel and radio equipment to agents, and brought back ten refugees.

By January, Gemmell had the bulk of his flotilla at Lerwick, but the weather had closed in and patrols were not often possible. Even when they were possible for both flotillas, they found that the Germans had greatly increased their countermeasures. They had, to a great extent, discontinued their coastal traffic during the dark hours, so there were few of the significant targets (large merchant vessels and tankers) that had brought such success in the early patrols in 1942/3.

The weather and the winter seas were still the greatest threats in the minds of the crews. One morning in February 1944, MTB 666 (still Lt Buller) had been on patrol with MTB 625 of the Norwegian flotilla. They left the coast after an uneventful night in the Inner Leads, but were met by an appalling north-easterly gale and the boats were separated. A few miles off the Norwegian coast, 625's keel was broken, and her forward compartments began to flood. Torpedoes were fired and ammunition thrown overboard to lighten the boat. During the night that followed the RAF station at Sumburgh Head (the most southerly point of Shetland) recorded the amazing wind velocity of 130 m.p.h. 625 struggled on westward and, kept afloat by the partially empty fuel tanks, hardly manoeuvrable and with only one engine running, she was beached in Shetland. She was wrecked in a salvage attempt some days later.

Meanwhile 666, leaking very badly, had managed to make Shetland and had found shelter in a tiny sheltered anchorage north of Lerwick; next day she was helped back to base. Her return passage had taken twenty-four hours longer than usual.

Soon after this, on 13 February, 627 (Lt Henriksen) and 653 (Lt Marthinsen) of the 54th Flotilla carried out a long-range patrol off Trondheim which had, in the words of the Norwegian report, 'one tragic and one amusing aspect'. The CO of 653, Lt Matland, was the owner in peacetime of a 600-ton coaster that had been taken over by the Germans and was now sailing on the Norwegian coast. Jokingly, to everybody who would listen, he gave the following warning, 'whatever you do on the other side, keep away from my *Henry*'. Just prior to

Lt Marthinsen, Lt Cdr Monsen and Lt Herlofsen. (R. Nor. Navy)

13 February operation, 653 was taken over from Lt Matland by his First Lieutenant, Lt Marthinsen, who was given the customary warning about *Henry*.

The boats were towed north towards the Trondheim area, and entered the Inner Leads without difficulty. Almost at once they encountered a convoy consisting of two escorted merchant vessels. They sank both with torpedoes and returned safely to base. The following day it was announced by the German-controlled Norwegian radio that 'British pirates' had sunk a Norwegian coastal passenger steamer SS *Irma* with great loss of life. As a rule, the coastal passenger steamers sailed independently and with lights burning. In the case of the *Irma*, she had been darkened and in convoy. Nevertheless, the propaganda effect of the fact that Norwegians had been killed by Norwegians could have been disastrous. It was therefore with admiration and gratitude that the flotilla could listen to a BBC announcement

saying that British Coastal Forces had sunk the *Irma*.

For Lt Marthinsen, there was the additional embarrassment that he had to confess to his former CO that the other ship, the one that he had sunk, had been the *Henry*.[3]

The news came at the beginning of March that both flotillas based at Lerwick were to be moved to the east coast bases. This was all part of the strategic plan for the forthcoming invasion, when several flotillas at Yarmouth would move to the south coast, and as it was intended to keep up the pressure on the Dutch coast shipping, reinforcement would be necessary to take their places. In any case, the light nights were about to make Norwegian operations very hazardous.

The transfers began early in March, with the 54th Flotilla bound for Yarmouth, and Gemmell's 58th for Lowestoft. On their way,

[3] ACOS signal 151124; V-Adm Gundersen.

a special operation was planned from Aberdeen, and on 5 March, one British boat (681, Lt E.S. Forman) and three Norwegian boats sailed on a long-distance patrol off Kristiansand. It was known that the Germans, believing their coastal shipping along the south coast of Norway to be immune from attack, did not provide escorts in this area. The operation was planned with a double purpose; firstly in the hope that there might be some juicy targets, but secondly that even if there were not, the Germans would know that their shipping was at risk from MTB attack along the hundreds of miles from the extreme south to the north of Trondheim. It was hoped that this would force them into more extensive counter-measures and thus indirectly slow down their flow of shipping.

In fact, the boats met no shipping and found that the low coast with few typical coastal topographical characteristics made landfall navigation difficult. They came very close inshore and were fired on by shore batteries, but without any damage.

Looking back on the winter, when there had been an increased number of boats available, both flotillas were very disappointed that the bad weather and the lack of German shipping had given them so few opportunities for successful attacks.

The 54th Flotilla looked forward to their spell at Yarmouth. The move brought a change of Senior Officer, as Lt Tamber, after his very long spell in command, gave way to Lt Cdr Christian Monsen RNorN for the period of operations on the east coast.

In fact, the flotilla was worked very hard, and in just the same way as the British flotillas, their operations were divided between offensive patrols off the Dutch coast and the ceaseless need to patrol the 'Z' line to the east of the convoy route from E-boat attack.

The Norwegian report summarizes this period as follows:

The results of the offensive operations were not anywhere near what they had previously achieved on the Norwegian coast. The Commanding Officers found firstly that lacking the ability to use tactics of 'hide and seek', as among their islands at home, meant that they had to adjust considerably. And they realized very quickly that the German convoys here were more strongly escorted, and their defensive tactics (in particular their use of star-shell and heavy calibre long-range fire) were very effective. Finally, they found that their previous training had not prepared them adequately for flotilla or unit attacks on escorted convoys, in particular in respect of the requirement for close station keeping.

The 54th Flotilla returned to Lerwick at the end of September 1944, reinforced with some new boats and brought up to a total of eleven. This number included 618, 623, 627, 653 and 688 of the older boats, and 709, 711, 712, 715, 717 and 722 of the more recently completed craft. They were joined later by 716. This second group originally appears to have been intended to form a second Norwegian flotilla, the 62nd, but in fact joined the extended 54th after working up at HMS *Bee* at Holyhead. The 62nd Flotilla was therefore never formed.

The boats numbered above 696 were built specifically strengthened for work in these northern waters. Earlier boats had frequently needed repairs to frames that often took them out of service. Now problems with frames were considerably reduced.

At this stage there was a change of leadership, with Lt Cdr Charles Herlofson RNorN becoming SO. The British 58th

Flotilla did not return with the 54th to Lerwick.

The winter months of 1944/5 proved far more productive for the flotilla than those of 1943/4. Perhaps this was mainly because the weather conditions were by no means as severe throughout, although there were, as expected, periods when operations were curtailed. But also the boats found many more targets and were extremely successful in harassing enemy shipping and causing real problems for the occupying force, which had to supply its garrisons largely by sea.

The flotilla began operations in the Inner Leads immediately, and on 7/8 October, 712 (with the new SO, Lt Cdr Herlofson, in command) and 722 (Lt Bogeberg) sighted two ships moving north, some distance apart. The COs of the boats were constantly worried by the fact that the Germans had requisitioned Norwegian ships and that some

of the seamen were Norwegians: they were naturally very concerned to avoid killing their own countrymen.

On this occasion, 722 fired her torpedoes at the leading coaster of medium size, but missed. 722 then decided to sink the coaster by gunfire, and she was soon set on fire and stopped. 722 went alongside to take off survivors, and discovered that the coaster was the Norwegian MS *Freikoll*, and that her crew were all Norwegians. Only four of the crew of nine were wounded, none of them severely, and all nine were taken aboard. The *Freikoll* drifted ashore and was a total wreck.

Meanwhile, 712 had attacked the other vessel with the 6-pdr but surprisingly had secured no hits. When on closing the target was discovered to be the Norwegian fishing vessel *Vikar*, fire was checked, and 712 went alongside. The CO apologized to his fellow countrymen for the attack, but they told him

Two boats of the 54th (Norwegian) Flotilla hidden under camouflage in a fjord. (R. Nor. Navy Museum)

he had no reason to be sorry, they would have expected to be attacked! They were delighted to meet the MTB and asked to be remembered to friends of theirs who were serving in the flotilla at Lerwick. The four wounded from the *Freikoll* were transferred to the *Vikar*, while the five who were unharmed all asked to be allowed to return to Shetland with the MTBs.

On the way back, the COs of 712 and 722 had mixed feelings. On this, their first taste of action in their new boats, the gunnery and torpedo control had frankly been very poor but at least their countrymen had not suffered as they might have done.[4]

On 1 November, 712 (Lt Cdr Herlofson) and 709 (Lt Hjellestad) had penetrated the Inner Leads near Askevold and were lying camouflaged in a good daylight lurking position. After a long wait, they sighted two German patrol vessels moving south in line ahead; they later turned out to be Vp 5531 and Vp 5525. They carried out a gun attack, closed to 200 yd and devastated the two vessels with their broadsides. Vp 5525 blew up and sank almost immediately, and Vp 5531 was set on fire, was obviously sinking and eventually drifted ashore and was wrecked. The MTBs took off all the survivors.[5]

One action not recorded in Vice-Admiral Gundersen's report is included in the list of Coastal Forces actions, and as it appears to have been very successful, it deserves a mention. MTBs 688 (Lt A. Sveen) and 627 (Lt B. Syvertsen) were patrolling in the Inner Leads north of Bergen on 13/14 November when they sighted a convoy. It was a very dark night and as they approached they were challenged but used the device of 'foxing' an

imaginary reply and challenge, and thus closed the range. With visibility poor, 688 thought she was firing at a large merchant vessel and secured two hits. 627 fired two torpedoes of the spread at the merchantman, but realized she had hit an armed trawler, one of the escorts. The two boats then went on to attack another of the escorts with gunfire, and survived heavy return fire but had some casualties. They were unsure of the results, but intelligence reports later revealed that three patrol vessels (not a merchant ship) had been sunk – an excellent return.[6]

The flotilla struck again on 27 November, when four boats operated in two units north and south of the port of Askvoll. Both units found good lurking positions, and eventually 715 (Lt P. Danielsen) and 623 (Lt O. Hoddevik) in the southerly area sighted a northbound convoy of one quite large ship escorted by Vps. 715 fired her torpedoes, but missed, and both MTBs followed up with a gun attack that brought heavy return fire, and both sides sustained damage: 623 had one of her crew killed. Two coastal batteries intervened with very accurate fire, and the boats withdrew.

About two hours later, the same convoy was attacked north of Askvoll by 717 (Lt A. Olsen) and 627 (Lt B. Syvertsen). This time, 717 hit the large merchant vessel with one torpedo and she sank. She turned out to be the German SS *Welheim* of 5,500 tons. 627 also fired her torpedoes, and in a near miss damaged the escort Vp 5503. 627 was also hit but not severely damaged, and the boats withdrew to the west.[7]

A patrol on 7 December by 653 (Lt S. Marthinsen) and 717 (Lt A. Olsen) on a very dark night south of Bergen turned out to be very eventful. The two boats sighted a convoy

---

4 MO81543; V-Adm Gundersen.

5 MO58344; results from intelligence, NID6397/45.

6 MO58396; results in NID24/T 85/45.

7 MO58466; signal NOIC Lerwick 282256; V-Adm Gundersen.

A shouted consultation on passage to patrol. (R. Nor. Navy Museum)

with one particularly large target, and tried to get into a good position for a torpedo attack. In doing so, 653 ran aground and despite frantic efforts, could not be backed off. By sheer good fortune, as she lay there stuck, the German SS *Ditmar Koel* (12,000 tons) sailed into her line of sight. 653 fired both torpedoes and not only hit with both, but also was sufficiently lightened to get her off the shoal! The *Ditmar Koel* had stopped, and 717 fired two more torpedoes, one of which hit and caused her to sink. Reports later indicated that the Germans never knew what had hit them and concluded that the sinking was a result of sabotage.

653 had suffered damage to her hull from the grounding, and was taking on water quite fast. At first the crew baled like mad with buckets to enable the engines to continue to run, but when the engine room flooded, 717 took her in tow and after a long slow passage reached Lerwick safely.[8]

Despite the traditional Norwegian love of Christmas, on 23 December six boats were dispatched from Lerwick to patrol in pairs in three separate areas. The intention was to launch simultaneous attacks against German shipping, causing maximum confusion and delay in the coastal traffic.

The first pair to strike were 712 (Lt A.F. Sveen) and 722 (Lt K. Bogeberg) who found an M class minesweeper (M489) and torpedoed her. Having used their torpedoes, they prepared to return to base for Christmas, but created a bit more confusion

[8] MO13284; signal NOIC Lerwick 082011; V-Adm Gundersen.

by closing a lookout station with a garrison barrack alongside. They bombarded it with 6-pdr shells, setting the buildings on fire.

711 (Lt J. Borresen) and 716 (Lt A.B. Gundersen) were not so lucky. They had been assigned to an exposed operational area, and found that a very heavy and increasing swell prevented them from finding any safe lurking position where they could lie camouflaged. They were forced to return (in time for Christmas festivities).

But the third pair, 717 (Lt A. Olsen) and 627 (Lt B. Syvertsen), having met similar adverse weather conditions, found a suitable camouflage location on the morning of 24 December, and settled down to wait. By the evening, the COs made the decision to 'take the night off' as it was Christmas Eve and they were in such a well-concealed position. They found Christmas trees ashore, cut them down, and decorated the mess decks as best they could. The cooks made a great effort, and a happy gesture was to invite a family from a remote farm nearby to come aboard to celebrate Christmas with them. They all spent the evening singing the traditional Christmas carols.

But the patrol was not only notable for this happy and unusual way of celebrating, right under the enemy's nose. On the evening of Christmas Day, the boats moved to a lurking position, and they were rewarded with the approach of a convoy. 717 fired her torpedoes at an escort, but missed; 627 had one hit on a coastal tanker, MT *Buvi*, which grounded and sank. There was an exchange of gunfire with the escorts, and then the boats withdrew, arriving back at Lerwick on the afternoon of Boxing Day.[9]

The flotilla entered 1945 confident that,

[9] For 23/24 December: MO368; NOIC Lerwick 241422; for 25/26 December: MO434; NOIC Lerwick 262001.

with the progress of the Allied armies through Europe, the liberation of their beloved homeland from occupation could not be far off. But the first task was to continue their attacks on German shipping and thus exert as much pressure as possible on the enemy's resources.

The 'triple unit' strategy had proved sufficiently productive for it to be repeated on 6 January, once again each unit having two boats. The northern group off Stavfjord, 722 (Lt K. Bogeberg) and 709 (Lt K. Hjellestad), attacked a convoy of two merchant ships escorted by an M class minesweeper and two other patrol boats. In great jubilation, 722 secured two torpedo hits on a large iron ore carrier, SS *Dora Fritzen*. She sank in a few seconds with a cargo of nearly 12,000 tons of iron ore – a real blow to German industry. 709 fired her torpedoes at the second merchant ship, SS *Nikolaifleet*, but although they thought they had secured one hit, she did not stop or sink. The boats continued with a gun attack on the M class mine-sweeper but after a heavy response, they withdrew to the west. SS *Nikolaifleet* (6,000 tons) did not escape for long. On the following night, 8/9 January, with a heavy escort now increased from three to nine units, she ran into the second unit further to the south, off Sognesjon. 711 (Lt A. Sveen) hit her with both torpedoes and she sank very quickly, again with a full cargo of iron ore. This time 711 and 623 (Lt O. Hoddevik) had to fight their way out past the escorts, but accomplished this without significant damage and with no casualties.

The third unit (712 and 716), even further to the south off Bommelofjord, made it a hat trick, intercepting a lone merchant ship steaming south with an armed trawler as escort. 712 (Lt Cdr C. Herlofson) hit SS *Viola* (2,000 tons) with one torpedo. She blew up and sank with a valuable cargo of 1,000 tons

Lt Stenersen (715), Lt Kvinge (SOO), Lt Cdr Herlofsen (SO 54th), Lt Gundersen (716) and Cdr Monsen (SNNO) at a briefing for an operation. (R. Nor. Navy)

of chrome and zinc. The boats then took on the escort and damaged her after a heavy exchange of fire.

It had been a remarkable two days, with the Germans suffering loss after loss of precious ships and cargoes in three different locations. It was later discovered that the German Admiral of the Norwegian West Coast Command attributed these sinkings to enemy intelligence (*feindliche Spionendienst*) and prohibited henceforth all telephone communications dealing with the sailing and escort of shipping. He was probably not far wrong, but perhaps decoded signals may have been the main source of intelligence, and totally unsuspected.[10]

[10] Three actions: MO830; MO1414; MO831; with detail from German sources.

The next patrol of interest took place on 25 January. 709, 716 and 715 found their designated area of operations occupied by a large herring fishing fleet. As it would have been impossible to remain undetected, it was decided to return to base. But on leaving the coast, to everyone's amazement, a large Norwegian trawler, the SS *Nordholmen*, was encountered. The German fishing regulations absolutely prohibited any ship from straying outside the Inner Leads, but this trawler was taking a short cut from one fishing ground to another, defying the regulation in typical Norwegian fashion. The unit's leader sent 716 to put a boarding party aboard her, and they had no difficulty, particularly as they took with them a liberal amount of Navy rum, tins of Spam and corned beef. The crew of twenty-seven aboard the *Nordholmen*

Boats in northern waters (location uncertain). (Courtesy, A. Phipps)

seemed delighted with the proceedings, and the unit began escorting her back to Lerwick – a very useful prize! In the morning, however, when the rum had worn off and their radio reported very good fishing on the Norwegian coast, they demanded to be returned. Needless to say, their request could not be accommodated.

January continued the story of successes when, on the 31 January/1 February, 717 (Lt A. Olsen) and 715 (Lt P. Danielsen) left Lerwick for an operation off Ravnefjord south of Trondheim. Arriving in the Inner Leads, they spent the day under camouflage, but during the night they encountered two M class minesweepers proceeding north towards Trondheim. 717 attempted to fire her torpedoes at M381 but had two misfires. 715 hit M382, the second in line, with both torpedoes and she broke in two and sank.

There was a fascinating sequel to this story, one of the remarkable coincidences of war. Twelve days later 717, now with Lt Cdr Herlofsen in command, and this time with 716 (Lt. H.B. Gundersen) was patrolling in precisely the same area, and again sighted an M class minesweeper on a southerly course. 717, smarting over her previous miss, fired her torpedoes, hit, and watched the ship go down. She turned out to be the very M381 that 717 had missed twelve days before![11]

In mid-March, C-in-C Home Fleet arranged for the RAF to mine an inshore coastal passage, with the intention of forcing

[11] Two actions: MO1540; MO2020; with detail from V-Adm Gundersen and German reports.

One of the 54th Flotilla with the special camouflage painting designed to blend in with the background of the Norwegian coast. (R. Nor. Navy)

the enemy shipping to use channels further west, which were more advantageous for MTB attack. The strategy was successful; on 12 March, 717 (Lt Cdr Herlofson) and 711 (Lt A. Sveen) left Lerwick and took up a lurking position near Rovaer where German shipping could now be expected. Early the next evening, a northbound convoy was sighted. 717 made the first attack on a merchant ship, but missed, and then 711 scored two hits on a large target that sank after a violent explosion. The flotilla heard later that the ship they had sunk was in fact the ex-Norwegian passenger liner *Paris*, which had been converted to become an anti-aircraft auxiliary cruiser MRS 4. Even more satisfying to these patriots was the news that she was manned partly by members of the 'Quisling Navy',

understandably despised by the Royal Norwegian Navy.[12]

March ended with the redoubtable 717 (Lt Cdr Herlofson), again with 716 (Lt H.B. Gundersen), involved in another successful operation, on 29 March. Four days earlier the same unit had attacked a convoy in the same area but later admitted angrily that their approach had been compromised by the accidental failure to 'darken ship' completely – a cardinal error in Coastal Forces operations. It had led to damage and casualties, although they believed they had secured one hit on a merchant vessel.

This time they were in an ideal lurking position in the deep shadow of the land. In

[12] MO3727; Home Fleet signals 130817 and 292333.

bright moonlight, two German patrol vessels were seen approaching. Both were taken completely by surprise and engaged relentlessly at very close range. The leading boat, Vp 5532, almost immediately caught fire and drifted ashore, but the other, hit repeatedly by 6-pdr shells, managed to get within the protective range of a coastal battery. As they withdrew, the boats, as they often did, continued their policy of harassment by bombarding a lookout station. But this time, alerted by the earlier signs of battle at sea, the fire was returned accurately, and 717 was hit and her Cox'n killed.[13]

As April drew towards its close, it seemed that the end of the war must be very near. But operations continued, to allow no respite to the enemy, and on 24 April, 711 and 723 left Lerwick for a patrol to the Inner Leads near Stavanger.

On 23 April, the German U-boat, U-637, had left Stavanger for operations in the Atlantic. Two days later, her CO decided to return to base due to a fault in the U-boat's main switchboard. In the early morning of 26 April, on a lovely sunny day close to the shore, the CO observed through his periscope what he believed to be two R-boats waiting to escort him back to base. He surfaced happily, and was faced by 711 (Lt A. Sveen) and 723 (Lt E. Kristiansen) who, after an uneventful night in the Inner Leads, had just started on their way back to Lerwick. Both the MTBs fired their torpedoes, but by good ship-handling, U-637 turned and 'combed the tracks'. Why the CO decided to remain on the surface to fight it out, rather than dive, is not known, because Kapitanleutnant Wolfgang Rickberg was killed shortly after. A running gun battle followed, at ranges all below 500 yd and mostly much closer. The

MTBs tried to get ahead of the U-boat to drop depth charges, while the U-boat countered by trying to ram. After a while, the gun crews of the U-boat were literally swept off their platforms in a hail of shells at close range, and replacements were killed or wounded as they scrambled up on the deck. The conning tower was shot to pieces, and the boats saw an explosion aft, and signs of an internal fire. The U-boat slowed right down, and 711 managed to drop four depth charges ahead of her. She was obviously crippled and out of control in shallow water, and as nearby coastal batteries had opened fire, and conscious that the nearest major German base was very close, the boats withdrew and set course for Lerwick.

They heard later that U-637, by supreme efforts of the surviving crew, just made it to harbour but clearly she took no further part in the war! The MTBs had expended practically all of their 6-pdr ammunition (362 rounds), and almost all the ammunition for their lighter guns, so they would have been very vulnerable to air attack. 711 had one man killed. They reached Lerwick in the late afternoon. It had been an astonishing climax to the operations of the Norwegian 54th Flotilla.[14]

As this completes the story of the Norwegian flotillas, an attempt should be made to assess the significance of the work of the MTBs in this demanding area of operations.

Careful study of German post-war sources (confirmed accurate from the provision of names and tonnages of ships sunk) reveals the following list of definite sinkings:

Eighteen merchant vessels
One U-boat
One auxiliary AA cruiser

---

[13] For actions 25/26 and 29/30 March: MO3863; MO4135; results in NID 6397/45.

[14] MO4771; ROP held by author.

Three M class minesweepers
Three armed trawlers

Damage to many other ships through gunfire and mining has not been recorded. Four enemy aircraft were shot down.

The losses by the flotillas were as follows:

MTB 345 captured.
MTB 631 and 712 after grounding.
MTB 626 by fire and explosion in harbour.
MTB 625 by shipwreck.

The loss of life:

Seven (six Norwegians and one British) executed by the Germans after the capture of 345.
Six killed in action.
Six killed in fire and explosion.

Strategically, the operations of the flotillas tied down considerable German resources, requiring escorts for convoys even in areas that were not frequently attacked, but where occasional patrols alarmed the sailing authorities and forced additional use of escorts. The uplifting effects on morale in the fiercely proud Norwegian civilian population, smarting under the yoke of occupation, is hard to quantify sufficiently. To hear of the exploits of their own sailors on their own doorstep was surely a constant support as they listened to news broadcasts on their well-hidden radios.

Perhaps the factor beyond all others that impressed seafaring men, and certainly impressed all other Coastal Forces personnel when they heard of the achievements of these boats, was the realization that their operations were always afflicted by distance from base and the threat of bad weather. The enemy and retaliatory fire often paled before the might of the sea; it was the inherent seamanship of the Norwegians that saw them through, and their determination to give the enemy no rest that brought so much success.

The recognition by the Admiralty of the sterling work of the Norwegian flotillas is to some extent shown by the number of British awards made to officers and men. It is by no means a clear picture, as it seems that parameters changed at some stage of the war. There is also no statement of criteria for the occasions on which British or Norwegian awards (or for a time, both) were made. But it is a fitting conclusion to the story of Norwegian Coastal Forces to record the British awards made. They were all 'ungazetted' but that was protocol rather than estimate of worth.

Rear Admiral (then Commander) T. Horve RNorN: Hon CBE
Lt Cdr C.A. Monsen RNorN (SO 54th MTB Flotilla): Hon OBE
Lt P. Danielsen RNorN: DSC and bar to DSC
Lt A.F. Sveen RNorN: DSC and bar to DSC
Lt R.A. Tamber RNorN (SO 30/54th MTB Flotilla): DSC
Lt C.O. Herlofson RNorN (SO 54th MTB Flotilla): DSC
Lt B. Christiansen RNorN (MTB 619): DSC
Lt F.N. Stenersen RNorN (MTB 715): DSC
Lt K. Bogeberg RNorN: DSC
Lt S. Marthinsen RNorN: DSC
Lt B. Syvertsen RNorN: DSC
PO S. Gjelsten (MTB 619): DSM
POEng F. Solberg (MTB 619): DSM
L/Sea J. Johansen (MTB 711): DSM
A/B H.F. Olsen (MTB 711): DSM
PO K.J. Wahlgren (MTB 715): DSM
PO O. Hovden (HMS *Fox*, CFB Lerwick): DSM

AWARDS TO BRITISH PERSONNEL SERVING WITH THE NORWEGIANS
L/Sig R.V.F. Collins (MTB 619): DSM

Tel E.J.W. Slater (MTB 620): DSM
There were numerous awards of 'Mention in Dispatches'.[15]

There is no clear record of Norwegian awards but Vice-Admiral Gundersen in his report explains the status of the awards.

The War Cross (W.Cr): the highest Norwegian wartime decoration. Its unofficial status was probably slightly less than that of the DSO.
The Saint Olav's Medal (St.O.Med.): a status approximately equivalent to the DSC.
The War Medal (WM): was awarded after eighteen months of sea duty. It was also awarded for achievements where the British equivalent would have been 'MID'.

Many of these awards were made to the officers and men of the Norwegian Coastal Forces, and were richly deserved.

In May 1945, the boats of the 54th MTB Flotilla sailed from Lerwick to Norway for the last time, to operate (in peacetime) for the next few years from their homeland, having written a distinguished page in the record of the Norwegian Navy's contribution to the Allied cause in the Second World War.

[15] British decorations conferred on Norwegian personnel. From *Seedie's List of Coastal Forces Awards*.

CHAPTER 7

MEDITERRANEAN OPERATIONS

In chapter four, the point was made that the operations of the Coastal Forces flotillas in the Mediterranean were very different from those in home waters. Quite apart from differences in climate and sea conditions, the war in the Mediterranean was fluid, and naval forces operated wherever the overall strategic and tactical necessities dictated. In the western Mediterranean, for instance, the MTBs and MGBs, after the German evacuation of North Africa and the conquest of Sicily, operated entirely off the west coast of Italy and in the Adriatic. HMS *Gregale* at Malta was their 'back base' but their main repair bases were two old Italian naval ports, La Maddalena on an island in the Straits of Bonifaccio between Sardinia and Corsica, and Brindisi on the east coast of Italy, recently liberated as the Allied armies fought their way northward up the Italian peninsula.

The months of October and November 1943, to some extent a breathing space after the rigours of the invasion of Sicily, were significant mainly for a major reorganization of the dispositions of the boats to these new areas of operations. Just as in home waters the decision had been taken to arm almost all the MGBs (both 'short' and 'long') with torpedoes, and to renumber the flotillas accordingly, so Captain Coastal Forces

(Mediterranean) was assessing the needs of a reorganization in his area.

Captain John Felgate Stevens RN had already made his mark and had very rapidly established himself as a highly respected leader and first-class administrator. He reviewed the operational needs in the light of his available forces, the nature of enemy shipping, the type of waters in which they operated, and the distances between the main areas of conflict. His conclusion was that a different solution was required in this theatre of war.

He had four flotillas of 'short' MTBs, all at this time being upgraded with new boats, and two flotillas of Dog Boat MTBs, both reduced in number by the ravages of their activities in the past six months. (Appendix 1, Note 17) He reasoned that, bearing in mind the fact that the enemy had very few large ships either as cargo carriers or escorts, those MTBs could cover all the needs of torpedo attack. It would be a far more flexible arrangement to keep his Dog Boat MGBs, with their additional fire-power, and use them in mixed units. In fact, he had already been operating them in this way for months.

His solution, agreed by C-in-C, was to reform the four Dog Boat flotillas into new groups known as MTB/MGB flotillas,

Painting the ship's side in dry dock.

composed of more or less equal numbers of each configuration. He could then dispose them with flexibility in the three areas at present demanding their presence: the west coast of Italy, the Adriatic and the Aegean. Results eventually justified Captain Stevens's conclusions completely.

It took two months to reorganize the flotillas, largely because so many boats were undergoing repairs and refits, and they were widely scattered over a sizeable area. The majority of those in full operational state tended to be in Maddalena, but throughout November and December they were being moved up to Bastia where Commander R.A. (Bobby) Allan was building up the capacity of the Advanced Coastal Force base. The operations during this period were largely

exploratory, as intelligence was being gathered on the pattern of enemy convoys along the west coast of Italy.

One factor made the task of Coastal Forces here even more significant. Increased Allied air power in the region was denying the enemy the use of road and rail and sea transport during daylight hours, forcing them to rely on the movement of supplies during the hours of darkness. Thus from Genoa to their line north of Naples, there was likely to be an ever-increasing number of targets.

It soon became clear that a high proportion of the cargoes were being transported in F-Lighters, converted tank landing craft bristling with guns protected by armoured emplacements around the gunwale. There were many escorts – converted ferries

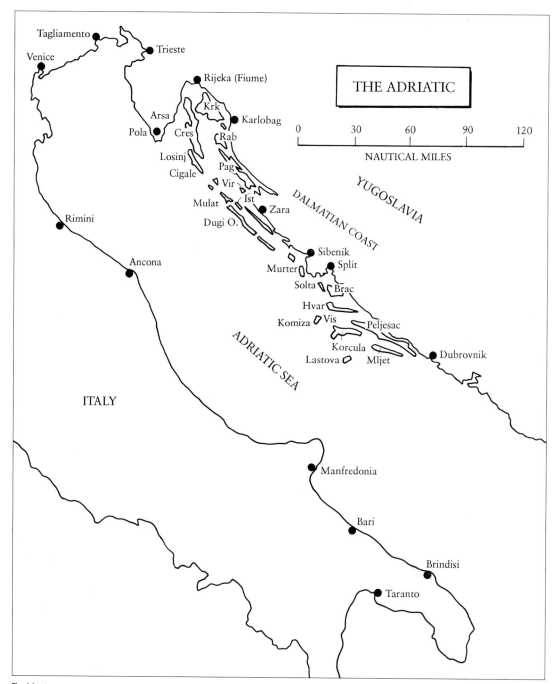

The Adriatic.

and patrol craft in great variety – and the German Command was building up the number of E-boats and R-boats in this theatre. They were being sent down into the Mediterranean through the French canal/river system in just the same way that the Royal Navy's 1st MTB Flotilla had returned home from Malta in November 1939. Bases were being established in Spezia, Leghorn and San Stefano/Porto Ercole further down the coast.

The Germans also had some light destroyers, mainly of Italian origin, that had been seized after the capitulation of the Italian government. Not all the ships of the Reggia Marina had managed to sail to Allied ports or be scuttled, and they became very useful additions to the scanty force of major vessels available to the Germans.

The port of Bastia had two harbours: the 'ancient port' to the south, into which 662 and 658 had sailed on 15 October, had changed little since the Middle Ages. As was so often the case, it had been well chosen by the early merchants and sailors, and was protected from the winds and swell of the Corsican coast. However, it was small, had limited jetty construction and could not take the numbers of boats envisaged for a major base. The New Harbour was very extensive, had a huge newly constructed outer wall and a long stretch of excellent quays with buildings alongside, which quickly became home to the Advanced Coastal Force base. Unfortunately, any south-easterly wind brought a swell that made life uncomfortable for boats alongside. There were wrecks in the harbour of rusty merchantmen bombed earlier in the year that were still to be cleared.

Very quickly, the old harbour became the base for the 7th MTB Flotilla, then comprising 70-ft Vospers, and for the newly arrived 'Ron Fifteen' (more properly the 15th PT Squadron of the US Navy) that had been operating from Bizerta and Bone for several months. This flotilla's boats were of Higgins construction, and to the Dog Boats their most significant contribution to operations was their highly effective radar equipment. This was far in advance of anything available to the British Coastal Forces at this time. Through a revolving aerial within a dome mounted on a squat mast, it provided a continuous and easily read signal on a 'PPI' screen, with its constantly sweeping beam illuminating a circular plot that highlighted echoes. The display showed coast, rocks and ships at ranges that totally transformed the work of lookouts and made it possible to assess a target's course and speed often long before it could be seen with the naked eye.

Close and friendly relationships were rapidly established, and Commander Allan (and the Dog Boat COs) quickly saw that, used together, the 'eyes' of the PT boats could be allied to the fire-power of the Dog Boats to enhance the effectiveness of both. Over the next year, this was to lead to the development of a unique and highly successful method of attack on German shipping.

The Senior Officer of 'Ron 15' was Lt Cdr Stanley Barnes USN, and he proved to be a huge asset, happy to work in close cooperation with the Royal Navy under whose operational command he was placed.

The weather was poor during these months, but there are five or six recorded actions on the west coast of Italy during November and December. These predate the formation of the new flotillas and set the scene for what was to come.

From Maddalena, MTB 670 and MGB 660 sank a 300-ton schooner by torpedo off the Tiber on 15/16 October. CCF Mediterranean's monthly summary of operations indicates that weather and sea-state made operations possible on only six nights between 4 November and 2 December. However, the first recorded joint operation of a patrol of Dog Boats with a PT as 'radar boat' took place on 5 November, but no targets were found. On 11/12 November, 670 with PT boats attacked a convoy off Civitavecchia, inflicting damage but with no definite results.

At this stage, the German naval command clearly became concerned about the new threat posed by Coastal Forces patrols from Bastia, and on 29/30 November sent E-boats to lay mines off the harbour entrance in an attempt to seal in the boats. There were four Dog Boats in Bastia at the time, but they received no alert from the port authorities. In a (retrospectively) amusing incident, however, several PT boats were out of their Old Harbour berths, having received an only partly understood message in French to 'clear the harbour' and, coming across the E-boats and mistaking them for Dog Boats entering harbour, tagged along behind. One even

collided with the transom of an E-boat, and was cursed in German for the collision. The E-boats left hurriedly and were rapidly out of range. MLs quickly cleared the mines.

Early in December a new threat became apparent, when Italian destroyers, now part of the German 10th Destroyer Flotilla, made forays to the Corsican coast. PTs first made radar contact with them in the Piombino Channel on 11 December but on 17 December the destroyers got closer to Bastia than at any other time, and shelled the town with no significant result.

It was two nights later that the Dog Boats met these heavier enemy vessels for the first time, and at least prevented their close approach to Bastia. The SO of Ron 15, Lt Cdr Barnes USN, gave the details in his report as the action (which developed in three phases) began with unsuccessful torpedo attacks by two units of PTs south of Cap Corse.

Lt Cdr S.M. Barnes USN (SO, 15th PT Squadron) and Lt Cdr J.D. Maitland RCNVR. (Courtesy, A.T. Robinson)

At this time, MGB 659 (Lt K.E.A. Bayley, SO of the unit) and 663 (Lt T.E. Ladner) with MTB 655 (Lt H.M. Pickard RCNVR) were patrolling the Piombino Channel with PT 209 as radar boat.

Ken Bayley had been able to pick up all the signals of enemy positions being sent to the PTs from Senior Officer Inshore Squadron (SOIS) in Bastia,[1] and made speed westward in an attempt to intercept the destroyers east of Elba. PT 209 gave them good range and bearing information and when they had closed sufficiently, 655 and PT 209 turned south to make their torpedo attack. The two MGBs maintained their course to close even more and attacked the destroyers with 6-pdr and pom-pom, coming under fire from the destroyers' main armament and 40-mm guns. No torpedo hits were secured, and only long-range gunnery hits considered possible, but the effect was to turn the destroyers north-eastward and away from Bastia. (Appendix 1, Note 20)

Before addressing the detail of the new flotillas, chronologically it is helpful to describe the activities of the Dog Boats in the other two operational areas before the reorganization.

In October the four currently operational boats of the 19th MGB Flotilla had been allocated to operate in the Aegean. They were 645, commanded by Lt B.L. Bourne and with the SO, Lt Cdr A. McIlwraith aboard; 643 (Lt G.M. Hobday), 647 (Lt M. Mountstephens) and 646 (Lt B.L. Knight-Lachlan). Knight-Lachlan had taken over from the original CO, 'Tufty' Forbes, who had been recalled to the UK.

Geoffrey Hobday amplifies the brief statement in CCF's report which simply indicates, 'four boats of the 19th MGB

Flotilla sailed to Alexandria'. He makes the point in his book, *In Harm's Way*, that the distance from Gibraltar to Alexandria is as far as the distance from Southampton to Gibraltar. This was another example of the differences between Mediterranean operations and those in home waters. But the passage in October 1943 was very different indeed from what it would have been even six months earlier, with the whole African coast now in Allied hands and the air threat from Sicilian airfields removed. The boats fuelled at Benghazi and Tobruk and enjoyed the passage immensely. At Alexandria, they berthed at the Royal Egyptian Yacht Club at Ras-el-Tin but very rapidly the realities of war surfaced again. 643 and 646 were dispatched urgently to the Dodecanese area, with McIlwraith aboard 643. This involved first a 400-mile passage to Beirut, and an essential stopover to fuel and stock up with provisions that would be unobtainable in the area they were bound for. They also received training in camouflage techniques as without doubt they would be required to hide in coves and rocky coasts during daylight when the Luftwaffe would be searching for any enemy activity.

From Beirut, the two boats sailed yet another 400 miles for the islands, their first destination being Kastellorizo, an island close to the (neutral) Turkish coast, stopping briefly at Paphos on the south-west corner of Cyprus for yet another top-up with fuel. It was by now about the second week in November, and strangely it seems that the two Dog Boats had not been given very specific orders or briefed in any detail on the strategic situation. In fact, they had been deployed at a time when the Germans had sent very large forces into the area and increased their air power considerably, to ensure that the islands could neither be held nor recaptured by the Allies.

---

[1] In 1944, Captain N.V. Dickinson RN. An ancient title for an operational command, held at Bastia by Nelson.

The island of Rhodes, only 70 miles west of Kastellorizo, was held by the Germans and regarded as the key to the control of the area. There had been plans for the Allies to take it, but the High Command had decided that sufficient forces could not be spared for the assault and gradually, over the months of September and October, the situation had deteriorated. Those islands that had been held by light Allied forces began to fall, the first major one being Kos on 3 October, and the enemy had total command of the air. Naval units, including destroyers and cruisers, had to be dispatched to attempt evacuations and to attack German transports in their assaults. Several British destroyers were sunk, and cruisers were damaged in air attacks, and the islands continued to fall one after the other like dominoes. An attempt was made to hold Leros, but it was taken on 16 November.

During all this time, MLs had been doing sterling service in their usual unsung way. The 10th MTB Flotilla of short boats (Elcos), the longest serving flotilla in the Mediterranean, under their SO Lt Cdr C.P. Evensen DSC, had been attacking shipping and attempting first to run troop reinforcements into Leros, and later to evacuate them.

The two Dog Boats arrived in the middle of this fluid and deteriorating situation. At first they patrolled around the southern islands and particularly Rhodes. They could not berth in Kastellorizo, which by day was under constant air attack, but instead

MGB 643 in Vathi Bay, Turkey, close to Kastellorizo. (Courtesy, J. Hargreaves)

MGB 643's boarding party in the Aegean. (Courtesy, J. Hargreaves)

sheltered in an inlet on the Turkish coast where, so long as they did not attempt to venture ashore, they seemed safe. As darkness fell they would creep across to Kastellorizo to fuel and then set off on patrol.

Surprisingly, they found no targets and under the stress of lying up under constant threat of air attack, and with food and water shortages, began to be very depressed with the futile nature of these operations. But when Leros fell on 16 November, they were ordered north to that area, and left at once to make the hazardous passage to Mandalya Gulf, an inlet on the Turkish coast that was in use by the MLs and the 10th Flotilla MTBs. It was a tonic to join up with kindred spirits, including Lt Tom Fuller who had

brought MTB 654 out to the Mediterranean, but then moved to a short boat when 654 had been written off in an explosion at Bone.

The boats were then sent north to reconnoitre Samos but found that there too the island had just fallen after a heavy air assault.

At the end of November, the boats were ordered to return to Kastellorizo to assist in the evacuation. Their first duty was to ferry out troops to destroyers that would make the dash for Alexandria. The whole process had to be done quickly and in pitch darkness, to give the destroyers time to get away sufficiently early to be as far as possible out of aircraft range by first light. There were 500 troops to be moved, and each boat was crammed full on each of several trips.

Hobday describes how this difficult task was accomplished and that by 0100 they themselves set off southward to Alexandria carrying many passengers, arriving on 29 November. They had found their five weeks in the islands frustrating and exhausting, but another example of the extraordinary demands on Coastal Forces craft in the Mediterranean.

For the SO, Alan McIlwraith, there was no respite in the fleshpots of Alexandria. Almost immediately he left with the other two boats,

MGBs 645 and 647, on a special mission in the Dodecanese.

The objective on this occasion was to assist the Greek destroyer *Adrias* to return to Alexandria for repairs. On 22 October she had struck a mine off Calino and lost her bows. Despite this, she managed to beach herself on the Turkish coast. Even though British forces had by now evacuated the whole area, apart from raiding expeditions, it was decided to attempt to recover the *Adrias*, and her ship's company were working furiously to ensure

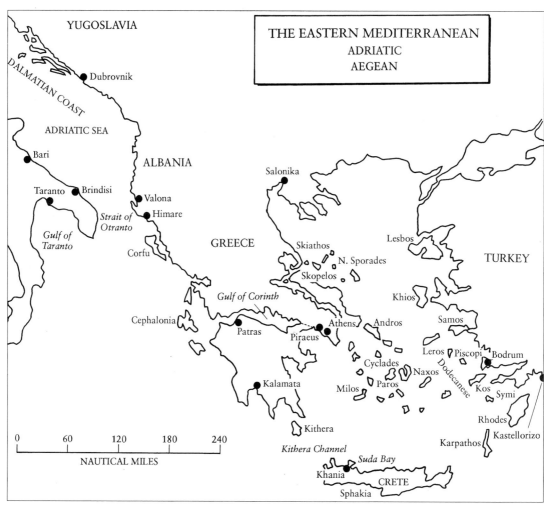

Eastern Mediterranean — Aegean and Greece.

enough engine power and to shore up the damaged destroyer. 645 and 647 located the *Adrias*, rendered every assistance (including helping with cutting down trees to complete the shoring up process), and finally escorted her in what seemed an endless passage south that led to her safe return to Alexandria on 6 December. The *Adrias* and her tiny escorts entered harbour to a remarkable demonstration, as ships all around sounded their sirens to celebrate this feat of determination and seamanship.

The Greek government showed its appreciation in no uncertain terms. Alan McIlwraith, Basil Bourne and Maurice Mountstephens were each awarded the Greek War Cross and granted permission to wear this decoration.

The official history of the war at sea sums up the sad story of the Dodecanese Campaign in terms that precisely echo the feelings of the men involved in it at the time.

So ended a series of fruitless operations the cost of which was not light. The British and Greek navies had four cruisers damaged, six destroyers sunk and four others damaged. Two submarines and ten coastal craft were also lost. The RAF lost 115 aircraft and the Army suffered nearly 5,000 casualties. We had learned in many campaigns from Norway in 1940 to Malaya in 1942 that to attempt to maintain garrisons in theatres where the enemy held command of the air was bound to end in costly failure. Yet these were the conditions in the Aegean in 1943.[2]

The other area still to be covered in this account of the period from October to December 1943 is the Adriatic.

[2] *The War at Sea 1939–1945*, Volume 3, Part 1, SW Roskill.

The only deployment of MTBs in this region after the fall of Sicily had been the positioning of the 20th and 24th MTB Flotillas of 'short' boats at Taranto, and they had, in September, carried out an audacious attack on shipping in Valona Bay in Albania.

However, Churchill was pressing for greater naval involvement in the Adriatic, and particularly in the Dalmatian Islands, and was considering throwing the weight of the Allies behind Tito's Partisan forces.

As a first move, HMS *Vienna* was moved to Brindisi, and Commander A.E.P. Welman DSO DSC RN, who had recently been appointed as Commander Coastal Forces Western Mediterranean (CFW), set up a base there. The 20th and 24th Flotillas moved there, and shortly afterwards CFW sailed HMS *Vienna* to Bari. Almost every RNVR officer in Coastal Forces knew Commander Welman, a veteran of the First World War CMBs, as he had commanded the training base at Fort William from its formation. At the same time, Lt Cdr M.C. Morgan-Giles RN had been appointed to supervise the operation to supply arms and equipment to Tito, to enable his 'National Army of Liberation' to begin the task of driving the German army out of Yugoslavia. At this stage, the Germans held the majority of the Dalmatian coast, although in practice they only did this through the establishment of garrisons on the principal islands and at strategic points on the mainland. In effect, several divisions of German troops were being held down by the Partisan forces.

Liaison officers were sent to meet Partisan commanders, and gradually trust was established, especially reinforced when the supplies began to arrive, carried by several 'gun-running' MLs.

The first positive move towards the establishment of an MTB base in the islands came on 16 October when Commander

Welman himself, with three boats of the 24th MTB Flotilla, entered the port of Vis on the island of the same name, lying about 40 miles off Split on the mainland. He and the boats were warmly received, and a decision was made to establish a base at Komiza, at the western end of the island. Other small ports in various islands also served as temporary setting-out points for operations, including Hvar with its excellent berths for small boats.

It was mid-November before Dog Boats first moved across to the islands to join the short boats of the 24th and 20th Flotillas. Only a small number of boats could be accommodated at first, and usually these included no more than two Dog Boats. There seemed to be few targets, and occasionally the boats indulged in some bombardment of German garrisons.

It has already been noted that all available serviceable boats of all flotillas had, after Sicily, sailed to Maddalena to operate on the west coast of Italy. As there was no obvious pattern to the redistribution of boats until the reorganization was confirmed at the end of December, it seems that the first Dog Boats to be sent to Bari and then on 'to the Islands' (as the Dalmatian operations were always called) were those completing repairs and refits.

Two MTBs, 637 of the 32nd, and 649 of the 33rd Flotilla, were involved in the first successful operations of the new campaign. 637 was commanded by Lt Robert C. Davidson, a Scot who had been first CO of MGB 659 in the 20th Flotilla, and 649 by Lt Peter Hughes of the South African Navy. Hughes was also a Scot, but at the start of the war he had been a District Commissioner in the Colonial Service. He had been CO of MGB 641 when she had been sunk by a shore battery in the Straits of Messina during Operation Husky.

649 was reported as carrying out a bombardment close to the Peljesac peninsula

on 12 December and, on completion, she sighted a two-funnelled ex-Austrian steam torpedo boat leaving the Neretva Channel. She attacked immediately and damaged the much larger ship severely. It escaped to the island of Lagosta and was later bombed by the RAF.[3]

A few days later, 637 was operating with MTB 297 (CO and SO Lt Lancaster) in support of a major Partisan raid from the north coast of Brac to land several hundred troops near the garrison at Omis, just south of Split. Having completed this task, 637 was carrying out a diversionary bombardment when she sighted a group of ships approaching – at first she took them to be a Partisan force. When they did not respond to the challenge, Davidson closed and saw that the largest vessel was a Siebel Ferry carrying troops and drums of petrol, and that there were two other small landing craft. Siebel Ferries were slow, heavily armed, very 'beamy' craft capable of carrying a large quantity of stores, and were used extensively in the Mediterranean. Davidson attacked, inflicted some damage, but received several hits including one in the engine room and one that caused casualties on the bridge. After moving away to get inshore, he attacked again and this time his broadside set fire to the petrol in the ferry and she blew up. He had also fired one torpedo, but captured enemy documents revealed that it was the gun barrage which caused the damage. The ferry was 'SF 193'. The two other small boats were also destroyed.[4]

Peter Hughes in 649 had another success on 19 December, when he intercepted two schooners off Hvar, stopped and boarded them, took twelve prisoners and returned with the vessels as prizes back to Bari. Later,

---

[3] CCF Med's monthly letter.
[4] MO750/44 and MO1442/44; ROP at PRO in ADM 199/258.

MGB 663 at speed off Bastia. (Courtesy, P.J. O'Hare)

this was to become a frequent occurrence in these waters, but the operation is notable as the first of its kind, and raised great interest.[5]

It was at this stage that CCF implemented his plan to re-form the flotillas, and decided upon their distribution between the west coast of Italy and the Adriatic. There was no longer any call for Dog Boats in the Aegean.

All four flotillas received new Senior Officers, who were promoted to Lieutenant Commander, and they each contained roughly equal numbers of MTBs and MGBs. Captain Stevens was proved, in retrospect many months later, to have been a shrewd judge of character, as all the flotillas prospered under their new leadership.

One bold and unconventional stroke was to put together six boats all commanded by

Canadian officers, place them under the command of Lt Cdr J. Douglas Maitland RCNVR, and make them the main strike force at Bastia. The nucleus of this flotilla was a group of three very experienced MGB COs from Vancouver, close friends since before the war. They had all come to the UK in 1940 and commanded short MGBs on the east coast.

After two years, the COs had been granted home leave to Canada but before they left had arranged their new appointments which they would take up on return in January 1943. They had quite deliberately engineered that they would be given commands in the 20th MGB Flotilla of Dog Boats, knowing that it was earmarked for Mediterranean service. Douglas Maitland, CO of MGB 657, was the accepted senior of the three, hard and uncompromising, calm and fearless in action. Cornelius Burke in MGB 658 was probably the most colourful: dashing and aggressive

[5] MO750/44; ROP in PRO in ADM 199/258; the first recorded incident of prizes being taken in this campaign.

Commander Robert Allan DSO, OBE, RNVR. (Courtesy, A.T. Robinson)

and an unconventional and inspiring CO. Tom Ladner in MGB 663 had already distinguished himself in Hichens's 8th MGB Flotilla. He was a lawyer (later to be QC and head a huge practice in Vancouver), and displayed meticulous attention to detail, bringing extreme efficiency to his boat, that had an unrivalled reputation for operational availability. These three developed an almost uncanny, instinctive communication in action and earned the soubriquet of the 'Three Musketeers'. The other three boats were commanded by younger Canadians who had begun as First Lieutenants. Campbell MacLachlan in MTB 640 had been Stewart Gould's 'Number One' in this same boat before Gould was killed: he was a renowned sportsman from Ontario. Herb Pickard in

MTB 655 had come to the Mediterranean in 658 under 'Corny' Burke, and was another lawyer and a leading Canadian golfer from Winnipeg. Willie Keefer, from Ontario, was an experienced short boat CO who was given command of 633, but before long he was replaced by Steve Rendell, another Vancouverite, who had started as Douglas Maitland's First Lieutenant in 657.

The base commander at Bastia, Commander 'Bobby' Allan, found in the Canadian 56th Flotilla exactly the aggressive spirit he wanted. There was the additional bonus that the Canadians got on very well with the US PT commanders of 'Ron 15', and their joint operations quickly developed the very necessary rapport.

The 57th MTB/MGB Flotilla was placed in

Commander A.D. McIlwraith (CFW). (Courtesy, A.T. Robinson)

the hands of Lt Cdr T.J. Bligh, who continued to command MGB 662. Tim Bligh was a natural leader, an extrovert with a huge personality backed by the intellect of a scholar at Balliol. He was later to become a senior Treasury official, and was knighted after years as Private Secretary to Harold Macmillan. At twenty-five years of age his qualities were already emerging fast. He too had several very experienced COs. Lt W.E.A. (Walter) Blount had earned a DSC in a MASB in home waters, and had recently taken over MTB 634, one of the oldest boats with a fine record of efficiency. Lt R.C. (Bob) Davidson had also served in MASBs, and his MTB 637 has already been mentioned earlier in this chapter. Lt A.T. (Terry) Robinson in MGB 660 was an engaging Irishman. The last two boats for the 57th were MTBs 638 and 670. They were both in refit, and joined later.

The 57th was sent round to the Adriatic from Maddalena and Bastia in December. They were to return to Bastia in March for a two-month stay.

The new SO of the 60th MTB/MGB Flotilla was Lt Cdr B.L. Bourne, CO of 645. Basil Bourne, who had commanded a C class MGB in home waters, succeeded Alan McIlwraith when he was promoted Commander and appointed as CFW: he had a reputation for efficiency and was known as a true gentleman. He too had his quota of experienced COs. Lt G.M. Hobday of MGB 643, Lt Knight-Lachlan of MGB 646, and Lt M. Mountstephens of MGB 647 had been together in the 19th MGB Flotilla and had just returned from Alexandria. They were joined by Lt C.J. Jerram DSC of MTB 667 who had spent the years from 1940 to 1943 in an ML in the Channel and taken part in the raid on Dieppe, and Lt W. Masson who commanded MTB 656. As soon as this flotilla gathered, after the boats which had been in the eastern Mediterranean returned in

early January, they moved to Brindisi to begin operations 'in the Islands'.

Finally, the 61st MTB/MGB was placed in the hands of Lt Cdr T.G. Fuller DSC and Bar RCNVR. Tom Fuller was thirty-five, and was so eccentric and nonconformist that Captain Stevens seemed very bold to make this appointment. In 1939 he had been running his own large construction company in Ottawa, but had bullied his way into the RCNVR despite being in a reserved occupation. Once in the UK, he had overcome all reservations about his age, and had already commanded several short boats before bringing MTB 654 to the Mediterranean. He had won his first DSC in an MGB in the Channel, and had just added a Bar in an action in the Dodecanese when temporarily commanding an Elco MTB of the 10th Flotilla. Tom Fuller was not only piratical in appearance with a full set of facial hair, but was piratical by nature, and CCF assessed him as highly suited to the type of operations among the Dalmatian Islands. Once again he was to be proved right.

The boats available to Tom Fuller immediately were MTB 649 (Lt Peter Hughes SNAF(V)) and MTB 651 (Lt K.M. Horlock), both of whom had already proved themselves. Ken Horlock had been one of the few COs to bring an ML back from the carnage of the St Nazaire raid. The other two serviceable boats were MGB 661 (Lt L. Ennis) and MGB 674 (Lt P.J. Kay). Within a month or two, Ennis would be handing over to Lt R.M. Cole, and taking over 674. Fuller decided not to command his own boat, but to remain independent and ride in the boat of his choice on each operation.

In practice, the three flotillas allocated to Brindisi for the Dalmatian operations worked without particular reference to flotilla allegiance. Planning was more influenced by

MGB 674 on the slip at Brindisi. (Courtesy, H. Moran)

Base staff at CFB Bastia. Lt(E) H. Coatalen is on the right. (Courtesy, W.G. West)

availability as boats returned to the mainland for repairs, servicing and rest after continuous patrols in the islands.

In Bastia, the new 56th Flotilla soon settled down and began to become very familiar with the landmarks for the patrols in the various sectors from Spezia southward. The island of Elba stood outlined 30 miles due east from Bastia, normally visible at long range even at night. The islands of Gorgona, Capraia, Pianosa, Montecristo and Giglio were great navigational aids, and the two main groups of rocks at Vada and Grossetto soon became useful reference points.

Just as important were the personalities among the base staff: outstanding among them was the Base Engineer Officer, Lt (E) Hervé Coatalen, who was a peer among 'plumbers', able to work miracles despite the problems created by distance from sources of spares and supplies in general. His workshops were housed in the lorries that had been the

basis of the 'Advanced CFB', already veterans of Bone, Augusta, Messina and Maddalena as the war had advanced.

For some reason, CCF decided to leave MGB 659 at Bastia, although she had been allocated to the 57th Flotilla – perhaps this was done to increase the availability of fire-power, given the probable targets on the west coast. It was indeed 659 with two PTs that had the first brush with the enemy on 17/18 January 1944, when at the northern end of the region, off Spezia, several F-Lighters were sighted, attacked unsuccessfully by the torpedoes of the PTs, and taken on single-handed by 659 in a gun attack. She inflicted some damage, and for her pains received a small shell in her engine room. The following night, 655 with PT 209 sighted two enemy destroyers believed to be minelaying north of Elba. Several torpedoes were fired but no hits obtained. The PTs were experiencing problems with their torpedoes which were unreliable, too slow and inaccurate. The Dog Boat MTBs also found it difficult to secure hits, as most of their targets were of very shallow draft. It was some months before the availability of more modern torpedoes with CCR pistols was to bring a rapid increase in success.

It was not until 20 January that the main core of the 56th gathered at Bastia, on the return of two of the boats from major repairs. At once the new flotilla swung into action with three consecutive nights of successful enemy engagements.

It began on 21/22 January, the night of the vitally important but heavily resisted landings at Anzio, designed to speed the northward progress of the Allied armies and to enable Rome to be cut off. Coastal Forces from Maddalena and Bastia were allotted a special task in an operation named 'Lurcher One', which was a simulated landing designed to confuse the enemy, off Civitavecchia, 55 miles north of Anzio. The PTs of 'Ron 15' (the USN 15th PT Squadron), carrying units of the US Psychological Warfare Service, were to project amplified sounds of a major landing being launched, and HMS *Dido* was to bombard Civitavecchia at the same time. The 56th were there to escort the PTs, to join in with fireworks to simulate gun flashes, and had in their orders the additional invitation to 'create as much alarm and despondency as possible in the neighbourhood'.

The Dog Boats reached their patrol area between the islands of Giglio and Giannutri by 2109, made rendezvous with the PTs as planned at 2341, and moved southward in

A cheerful crew at 'stand easy' in working rig.

Possibly water-contaminated fuel being filtered through chamois leather – a laborious process.

two columns towards the 'phony release' position. It was at this stage that events parted company with the script. At 0147, only a few minutes before the 'noises off' were to begin, Lt Cdr Barnes USN, the SO of the PT boats, called up Maitland on R/T. His radar showed possible targets at 2,800 yd on the port bow, moving on a similar course to the Dog Boats and PTs at about 7 knots.

Maitland led off his five boats to attack, and rapidly closed the range until he had visual sighting of what appeared to be an F-Lighter escorted by two E-boats, one on each beam. The attack when it came took the enemy completely by surprise and at 200 yd range the five Dog Boats poured their broadsides into the F-Lighter. After a short

pause the F-Lighter began to respond and 658 was hit several times, and the pom-pom gun's crew was wounded. But the second run finished the main target off, and she lay stopped, burning fiercely. The port E-boat, which had received the attention of 659 and 655 in particular, was also on fire, but suddenly the starboard E-boat shot between these last two boats and disappeared. 655 had been hit, and disengaged to the west. Maitland made one more run to make sure both the targets were no longer capable of action, and exactly five minutes after the action began it was all over. Suddenly, shore batteries opened fire and seemed to have the range and bearing, so the boats broke away and went in search of the damaged 655. As they did so, the F-Lighter (which must have been carrying ammunition) blew up. Maitland's report estimated that the multi-coloured flash and smoke rose to 1,500 ft.

655, which had been hit by two quite small shells in the engine room, had holes in the exhaust pipes and until they were repaired the leaking fumes caused real problems for the motor mechanics. The unit came together at first light and returned in high spirits to Bastia. The three boats that had been hit had only superficial damage, but A/B Leslie Brayshaw, the pom-pom loading number on 658, died soon after he was handed over to the base medical officer.

As ever, Commander Allan, the base CO, struck an accurate note when he commented in forwarding the SO's report: 'This was the first time that the newly constituted 56th Flotilla operated as such. After this start it is satisfactory to note that their tails are nearly as high as the explosion they caused. The tactics were thoroughly aggressive and the results very satisfactory.'

There was also an apposite comment from the SO of the PTs, Lt Cdr Stan Barnes, who at a debriefing meeting considered that all the efforts of the Psychological Warfare unit's diversion had been surpassed by the magnitude of the explosion the Dogs had caused.

Despite the minor damage, all five boats were refuelled, repaired and ready for operations by the evening, and Maitland, hearing that another patrol was required, decided to take 657, 663 and 659, leaving 658 and 655 ready if a third patrol was called

Lt Cdr J.D. Maitland RCNVR (V56), Captain N.V. Dickinson RN (SOIS) and Commander R.A. Allan aboard MGB 657.

for on the next night. This time the patrol area was much further north, only just south of Leghorn, and again the boats found a convoy, this time detected by their own radar as they did not have a PT with them as 'radar scout'. It was picked up at 4,200 yd.

As Maitland and his three Dog Boats closed, within twenty minutes visual sighting confirmed six F-Lighters in two columns of three, with E-boats on each side of the starboard column. He manoeuvred round the rear of the convoy and prepared to attack at close range down the starboard side, realizing simultaneously that the leading ship in each column was much larger and might well be a destroyer or torpedo boat. The nearer one began to challenge, so Maitland went quickly in to attack, ordering all three boats to tackle the last F-Lighter in line. The range was only 100 yd when they opened fire. Once again the target was ablaze almost at once but every ship in the convoy opened retaliatory fire, and one E-boat came hurtling past the stricken F-Lighter straight at the boats. 663 and 659 were able to switch their whole broadsides to this new menace, and she too burst into flames after an internal explosion. 659 had been hit and turned out of line, and the fire from the F-Lighters and the larger escorts intensified, including many 88-mm shells. Maitland decided that with only two boats, surprise lost and vastly superior odds against him, he would withdraw and return to base.

Next night, the third in a row, 23/24 January, it was the turn of 658, with 'Corny' Burke as SO, and 655. This time, PT 217 completed the unit to act as radar scout. The original patrol area was inshore of Capraia Island, but at almost midnight, after four hours of searching for targets, a signal was received from SOIS (Senior Officer Inshore Squadron – Captain Dickinson, at Bastia) ordering the unit to move as rapidly as possible much further north to the area of the

Vada Rocks. It was not at this time known to the boats that the excellent intelligence available to the operating authority was due to the ability to decode enemy signals: they simply believed that the information must come from spies or clandestine observers.

It was 0400 before PT 217's radar picked up an enemy convoy at 4 miles range, travelling north at 12 knots. It was a very dark night, and Burke decided to increase speed and gain bearing on the convoy, if possible from inshore to take maximum advantage of the deepest blackness to the north-east.

Once again, the convoy seemed to consist of two columns of three F-Lighters, but with only one escort astern, probably an E-boat. Burke ordered a torpedo attack, and PT 217 fired one which seemed to run true but missed. Believing that the F-Lighters were riding light, he decided not to waste more torpedoes: 217 sped off to the south-east, and was seen by the E-boat, which opened fire. This was just the diversion that Burke hoped for. He was able to come up on the blind side of the E-boat and the last F-Lighter in the line, and the two Dog Boats had the opportunity of an unobserved attack. Within half a minute, the E-boat was on fire and stopped, and 658 and 655 were in among the convoy which seemed to have scattered in a confused state. Now using 658's own radar, Burke attacked another E-boat, the next F-Lighter, and finally a much larger target which, from the barrage coming from it (fortunately not very accurately), seemed to be some form of armed trawler.

Burke noted with great satisfaction that quite apart from the damage his unit had inflicted, the confusion had led to the enemy ships firing at each other. But both 658 and 655 had received some damage – in 658's case several 20-mm shell holes near the water line – so he withdrew, met up with PT 217 whose help had been invaluable, and returned to Bastia. There had been no casualties, but as so often was the case, the weather had the last say. A howling gale blew up, which whipped up high seas, and it took a further four hours to gain the shelter of the base.

Next day, an intelligence report reached SOIS from the RAF and other sources that one F-Lighter and one E-boat had been sunk, three others damaged, and a 900-ton minelayer was aground near Vada Rocks, inshore of the position of the action.

The 56th had begun its existence with a most emphatic expression of the aggression and efficiency of its boats. Word spread around Mediterranean Coastal Forces with news of this hat trick of successes, and the flotilla's reputation was established. (Appendix 1, Note 21)

The weather remained bad for several days, and February came in with hopes of a continuation of the run of success. On 7/8 February the first opportunity arose. 658, with Maitland in command as 'Corny' Burke was ill, 659 and 640 met a convoy 10 miles off Giglio Island. It had almost exactly the same formation as those seen two weeks before, but with large 'flak ships' ahead and astern. It was a bright moonlit night, and every one of the targets was armed with 88-mm as well as the usual 40-mm and 20-mm guns. With no chance whatsoever of achieving surprise, the Dog Boats tried twice to approach from inshore, using the darker background of the land, but the convoy seemed to have no difficulty in keeping track of them. They lobbed 88-mm shells in their direction, outside the range of even the 6-pdr gun on the MGBs. When even heavier shells from the shore batteries began to arrive, Maitland turned away and watched the convoy enter San Stefano harbour. He returned to Bastia to discuss with Captain Dickinson (SOIS) and Commander Allan

A Packard engine, airborne and ready to be fitted. (Courtesy, W.G. West)

possible tactical answers to this problem of attacking the heavily armed convoys in the 'moon' period. The same dilemma was facing the offensive patrols off the Dutch and the Channel coasts in home waters and is described in chapter five.[6]

One idea was to try out a device using depth charges suspended from oil drums and linked by a grass line: a sort of specific mining trap which could be laid in lines across the path of a convoy. The boats experimented off Bastia but did not have sufficient confidence to try it out in practice.

Reports were being received that the Germans were reacting to the successful gun attacks on their F-Lighters by converting a

6 MO3983; ROP in PRO in ADM 199/268.

LCG 19 – one of Commander Allan's battle squadron for Operations Gun and Newt. (Courtesy, A.T. Robinson)

number of their cargo carrying lighters to a purely defensive role and arming them with a number of 88-mm guns. At this stage they were dubbed 'flak ships'.

On 13/14 February, 658 (Burke, with Maitland as SO) and 659 (Barlow), with PT 203 as radar scout (and the only torpedo boat), met a similar convoy off Leghorn, once again in bright moonlight and flat calm conditions. It was detected early by the PT's radar, but was visible with the naked eye up-moon at more than a mile. The PT fired two torpedoes that missed astern, but a new enemy tactic manifested itself. Two of the F-Lighters (soon obvious as the more heavily armed type) moved out of the convoy line and placed themselves meticulously between the convoy and the Dog Boats. Maitland closed in to attack them but was met with a fierce barrage of heavy shells and was forced to turn away.

His action report reflected the flotilla's frustration, but Commander Allan, in forwarding it through SOIS to the Command, gave a hint as to plans being made when he commented: 'The fact that these aggressively designed boats manned by remarkably aggressively minded officers and men cannot get to grips with the enemy, is giving rise to a sense of frustration. It is, however, believed that the situation is fully appreciated and you are aware of the various tactics and devices with which we are hoping to discomfort the enemy.'[7]

The PTs had one 'device' which had just arrived, a rocket firing projector, but it proved so dangerous, so inaccurate in trials, and so unreliable that it was never used in action.

But what Commander Allan knew was that just as the Germans were using specially adapted F-Lighter 'gun ships', the Royal Navy had developed LCTs armed with two 4.7-in guns, called LCGs, manned by expert Royal Marine crews. He reasoned that with the advantage of the magnificent SO radar in the PT boats, it would be possible to deploy LCGs to attack convoys at long range, and to use the MTBs and MGBs both as escorts and as 'sweepers-up' and 'finishers-off'. Once he had secured the services of three LCGs (14, 19 and 20) training exercises began.

[7] MO4108; ROP in PRO in ADM 199/268.

A PT boat of 'Ron 15' acting as radar plotter. (Courtesy, A.T. Robinson)

Commander Allan, himself an experienced MTB CO, decided to take command of the force and to deploy it like a battle fleet with himself as controller ('Admiral') stationed at the plot aboard one of the PTs, and able to move his forces around by passing ranges and bearings and courses of the enemy, together with directions as to course and speed to be used to make interceptions. The LCGs, of course, were much slower than the PTs and Dog Boats and everything depended on early detection of a convoy and the ability to position the LCGs to attack it.

Commander Allan had asked for reinforcement of the Dog Boats at Bastia and late in March, the 57th Flotilla, led by Lt Cdr Tim Bligh, arrived to bring the number of boats up to twelve, of which eight or nine were usually available for operations.

After a long period of bad weather, the first LCG action (Operation Gun) took place on 27/28 March off Leghorn and was a complete success. The three LCGs were

vectored into position, south of Vada Rocks, and at just the right time, a convoy of six F-Lighters appeared, escorted by two ex-Italian destroyers (or more likely torpedo boats). Allan, directing events from his PT boat radar screen, sent in PT boats to fire torpedoes at the escorts, and they were driven off. Given precise ranges and bearings, and using flashless ammunition, the LCGs fired star-shell, one or two sighting shots, and then, with incredible accuracy, sank each of the six F-Lighters in turn. The main attack force was not seen at all by the enemy, who just did not know what had hit them. Bobby Allan did not send in the four Dog Boats (MGBs 662, 659, 660 and MTB 634 of Tim Bligh's 57th Flotilla) as he wanted the enemy to continue being in their mystified state.[8]

The 56th and 57th Flotillas continued their patrols, often in mixed units, frequently meeting

8 MO6163; ROP in PRO in ADM 199/268; War intelligence Report, 21 July 1944.

the same problems of penetrating the screen of specially armed F-Lighters, which by now were being described in reports as LCGs! The Dogs were glad that these were not manned by expert Royal Marine gunners equipped with very precise sighting mechanisms.

On 7/8 April, Tim Bligh led a mixed unit of 57th and 56th Flotilla boats with two PTs for the first time, but it was not long before his own 662 had developed a serious engine defect, so he dispatched her back to Bastia and transferred to 658 ('Corny' Burke), which with 640 (Cam MacLachlan) made the unit once again all 56th. It was bright moonlight, but the PTs came up with a long-range radar echo close inshore (nearly 8 miles away). The enemy was sighted at about 3 miles, sailing north towards Vada Rocks,

and the target seemed to be just two vessels, a large armed trawler and an E-boat, with no LCGs to contend with. Bligh attempted to get well ahead and then inshore of the enemy, and suddenly the PTs alerted him to new echoes – another group of ships were coming southward from Vada Rocks.

At Burke's suggestion, these crossing convoys were used to make possible the exchange of 'foxing' recognition signals. This enabled 658 to get very close to the E-boat. When 640 and the PTs had fired their torpedoes at the spread of ships, 658 opened fire and very quickly the E-boat was burning from stem to stern down to the waterline, and was, unkindly, under fire from the trawler. 658 had been hit and had two engines out of action, so made smoke and

Lt Cdr T.J. Bligh (V57) and Capt J.F. Stevens (CCF Med) on the bridge of MGB 662. (Courtesy, A.T. Robinson)

A swastika for every enemy ship sunk.

watched the enemy ships of both convoys, now thoroughly confused, all firing at each other. They were joined in this by shore batteries whose shells were uncomfortably close to 658. The trawler (later considered to be a KT ship – a heavily armed transport) had been hit. But 658, by now only creeping along at 11 knots behind a smoke screen, rejoined 640 and returned to Bastia, where she nearly sank alongside with shell holes on the waterline. Several months later, Tim Bligh was awarded the first decoration of his illustrious career for this action (a DSC) which was later to be followed by an OBE, DSO and a bar to the DSC.[9]

[9] MO6881; ROP at PRO in ADM 199/268; detail in *Gunboat 658*; *Seedie's List of CF Awards*.

Tim Bligh again led one of the mixed units (his own MGB 662, with MTBs 633 and 640 of the 56th) on 9/10 April. 633, now commanded by Lt A.S. (Steve) Rendell RCNVR, was making her first appearance after repairs. Bligh found precisely the same difficulties as Maitland had experienced, meeting three 'probable LCGs' off San Vincenzo and being outranged after a brief attempt at a gun attack.

The same unit, with three PTs, had another brush with an F-Lighter convoy on 13/14 April in the same area. This time, on SOIS's orders, the tactic of a spread of torpedoes at shallow settings was tried: ten were fired, but they all missed, either below or ahead of the targets. The PTs were still having difficulties with their torpedoes, and those of the Dog Boats did not yet have the technical improvements that were to lead very shortly afterwards to a rapid increase in successful firings.[10]

The second LCG action was mounted on 24/25 April and was named Operation Newt. It was more complex and even more effective than Operation Gun a month before, and was once again a huge personal success for Commander Bobby Allan, acting as 'Admiral' of his 'battle squadron' of small ships. The same three LCGs (14, 19 and 20) were involved, together with Maitland as SO MGBs in 657 with 662 and 660, and Bligh as SO MTBs in 640 with 633 and 655. Commander Allan was embarked in PT 218, and his intention was to direct the whole operation from the radar screen by R/T. There were six other PTs involved, one group in particular (202, 212 and 213) acting as a 'scouting force'.

Over a period of five hours, the 'battle squadron' encountered three different groups of targets spread over 50 miles of the coast. German records show that one convoy of three F-Lighters (F515, F423 and F621) and the tug *Tebessa* sailed from Leghorn southward at 2000. Already in the area were three 'armed F-Lighters', F610, F350 and F589. In addition, two patrol vessels (M7607 and Vp 7013) each towing a barge sailed northward from Porto Ferraio (on the north coast of Elba) towards Leghorn.

Commander Allan had the complex task of deploying his various groups as the enemy units converged on each other north of the Piombino Channel. By 0005, he was able to order the LCGs to open fire at 3,000 yd. After firing star-shell, they began picking off their targets, with great effect. It is unusual that a Senior Officer's report of claimed sinkings is clearly borne out by enemy records, but in all but one aspect this is the case in this action.

[10] MO6481; ROP at PRO in ADM 199/268.

The enemy clearly had no idea that their main adversaries were LCGs. Their report stated: 'The three ferry barges [F-Lighters] and the tug *Tebessa* [of the southbound convoy] were attacked off San Vincenzo by MTBs and destroyers or torpedo boats. All four were sunk.' In fact, the third of these F-Lighters was finally destroyed by Maitland and his MGB unit, who found it entirely undamaged, abandoned by all but a few hands. She was destroyed, blowing up with a great explosion. The MGBs went in to pick up any survivors, and found twelve, of whom six were Dutchmen from the *Tebessa*. The enemy report continues:

> The escort group of three armed barges saw this attack and proceeded to join the battle. They were immediately engaged by the Allied force, and two were sunk, with loud explosions. The third (F589) tried to escape behind a smoke screen, but she was hit and severely damaged and two of her guns put out of action. In panic, some of the men jumped overboard as ammunition began to explode. . . . The enemy remained, illuminating with star-shell, and after twenty minutes attacked again and inflicted further damage. The barge did not sink but was beached south of San Vincenzo.

The last attack was by the MTB group, which Commander Allan sent in to finish off the engagement. The final tally was six vessels sunk and one disabled.

There is some confusion over the results of the next attack, which was on the northbound convoy that had reached the Vada Rocks area. The Germans admit that Vp 7013 blew up and immediately sank, concluding she had been hit by a mine or torpedo. This was at 0120. Whether she was sunk by an LCG or a PT of the scouting force is not clear.

633's mascot, Lady, the only female aboard this Dog! (Courtesy, H. Moran)

There was a sequel to this extraordinarily successful action, which in other circumstances could have significantly affected its outcome. At 0400 Bastia signalled that their radar plot showed an unknown enemy force that was stopped 3 miles west of Capraia, an island 30 miles out from the mainland, well outside the scene of all the other engagements. Allan detached his scouting force and the MTBs to attack, having realized the enemy were large units – possibly the destroyers or torpedo boats which had made occasional forays towards Bastia in the past. The PTs were heavily engaged but secured no hits and the one Dog Boat with torpedoes left failed to intercept.

It transpired later from enemy documents that the enemy force was a group of three German torpedo boats, the TA26, TA23 and TA29, laying mines off Capraia. At 0145 TA23 hit a mine in a field which had been laid by British forces a few days earlier. She was torpedoed and sunk by TA29 at 0645.

What is not clear is the astonishing fact that these three powerfully armed vessels, which were certainly in the area between midnight and 0130 and must therefore have seen and heard all the evidence of a major engagement, made no move to intervene. Even the fact that they were carrying mines at the start is surely insufficient explanation for such apparent indifference.

Months later, there was great satisfaction among the officers and men of the Bastia base and all the boats that had operated there, when Commander Allan was awarded the DSO for his brilliant direction of the LCG operations.[11]

Patrols continued throughout May and

[11] MO57612; ROP at PRO in ADM 199/268; *Seedie's List of CF Awards.*

into June without significant success. There were clear indications that the Dog Boats were to be concentrated in the Adriatic, where results had begun to be spectacular, and Tim Bligh took the 57th Flotilla back to Brindisi at the end of May. The 56th were involved in trials which clearly related in some way to a projected landing force, as they towed LCAs (assault landing craft) at various speeds. Soon after came the answer.

A large force of coastal craft gathered in Bastia, together with landing craft, and the LCGs were joined by their counterparts, the Rocket LCTs. Appropriately for this bastion of military activity on the only free area of French soil, Free French troops arrived and the boats were briefed for Operation Brassard, the invasion of Elba on 17 June.

The landings, although ultimately successful, were bitterly opposed, but the 56th were used only as a shield for the landing force and were not in action. But on the day after the landings, 655 (Pickard with Doug Maitland, the SO on board), 633 (Rendell), 663 (Ladner) and 658 (with W.O.J. Bate in temporary command) were sent to cover a possible evacuation of German troops, and after firing torpedoes, were attacked heavily by an Italian destroyer. Both 658 and 655 suffered serious damage and casualties, but intelligence later reported that the operation had interrupted and prevented the only major attempt at evacuation, and also that one loaded F-Lighter had been sunk in the torpedo attack.

There was one more blow for the 56th Flotilla before they departed from Bastia to move round to the Adriatic. MTB 640 (Lt Campbell MacLachlan RCNVR) struck a mine returning from a patrol north of Elba. Her bow disintegrated right back to the bridge, and five men were lost. There was no chance of towing her back to Bastia, and 658 sank her. This was the first of a series of

minings which was to tear the heart out of the 56th Flotilla – but not for several months yet.

Within two days, the 56th left for Malta and the last Dog Boats left Bastia. Commander Allan reported to CCF:

> Having been in Coastal Forces for four and a half years, I am inclined to think that the last six months have in every respect been the happiest that have ever been known, not only to me personally, but to Coastal Forces in general. I attribute this largely to the magnificent spirit in the flotillas attached. The 56th Flotilla under its all Canadian leadership infected us all with a spirit of New World camaraderie and almost embarrassing keenness . . . .

So ended the Dog Boat operations on the west coast of Italy, which had begun a year earlier with the invasion of Sicily. It is now appropriate to return to describe the very different conditions under which the other three Dog Boat flotillas had operated since January in the Adriatic.

The plans to strengthen the Coastal Forces presence in the Adriatic had received a notable set-back when, in December, a totally unprecedented and surprise Luffwaffe air raid on Bari dealt a triple blow. Firstly, HMS *Vienna*, the Coastal Forces depot ship, was severely damaged and put out of action. Secondly, among the seventeen ships sunk in the raid was a cargo ship carrying sixteen Packard engines destined for the MTBs. And thirdly, several short MTBs were damaged by blast, and a number of officers and ratings suffered injuries. Among these were some who, in rescuing survivors from the merchant ships, found themselves burned painfully by mustard gas. One of the sunken ships had been carrying a contingency cargo of shells containing this deadly chemical, which spread rapidly over the surface of the harbour. There were many acts of heroism: Lt Cdr Morgan-Giles RN, about to take over as the Senior Naval Officer, Vis (SNOVIS) particularly distinguished himself and was awarded the George Medal.

Within a week or two, Morgan-Giles had established himself in Komiza on the island of Vis, and had begun his new role of directing Coastal Forces operations, responsible to FOTALI (Flag Officer, Taranto and Liaison, Italy). He had first to build a relationship with the Partisan staff (not an easy task) and to liaise with the considerable military presence of Army and Royal Marine commandos who had arrived at much the same time.

On the mainland, Brindisi was shortly to receive the Italian seaplane tender *Miraglia* as a replacement for *Vienna* as Coastal Forces depot ship. In addition the small port of Manfredonia, 120 miles north of Brindisi and within 70 miles of Vis, was being developed as a secondary repair base.

Komiza itself, with limited berthing space, was at this time not able to hold a great number of boats, and frequently units were made up of a mixture of Dog Boats and Vospers – the short boats of the 20th and 24th Flotillas. The 57th, commanded by Tim Bligh, had just arrived from Bastia and soon began to make its presence felt.

A report by CCF (Captain Stevens) at this time illustrates the problems of this primitive operational base.

The operations among the islands off the Dalmatian coast have been unique. Experienced observers who have seen service in home waters before coming to the Mediterranean recall with amusement that at home they thought they were hard-worked if they were out three nights a week, from an established base, at which, on their return, they retired to comfortable shore accommodation while base staff overhauled their boats.

During recent weeks, boats spent sixteen days in the islands, during which they carried out patrols on thirteen nights,

An F-Lighter.

spent two of the other nights refuelling by hand, and been called to action stations at least five times each day by air alarms.

There have been sudden storms of great violence. Broken frames have been patched with iron slabs from the local blacksmith and any boat returning to the mainland has been robbed of parts.

Indeed, those 'sudden storms', particularly in the winter months, added considerably to the strains of operating in small boats. The Bora, sweeping southward without warning as it funnelled down the Adriatic, sometimes lasted for a week or more. Its intensity was such that it whipped the comparatively shallow waters into the very short, steep seas that the hulls of the Dog Boats were most vulnerable to. And on several occasions, boats sheltering in coves and otherwise protected anchorages were driven helplessly aground.

At this stage, the majority of the vessels carrying German supplies were schooners, although gradually more and more well-armed escorts were provided, and F-Lighters appeared in ever-increasing numbers. Clearly, the most important task of the boats at Komiza was to sink as high a proportion as possible of these supply vessels, in order to cut off much needed stores from the often isolated garrisons which had only just been re-established. During December the majority of the islands had been retaken and reinforced by German troops, so that havens such as those on Hvar, Korcula and Brac, which had been used by British craft when they first arrived, were no longer available.

January 1944 saw a period of very bad weather in the islands. Patrols were mounted whenever possible, but the enemy's small craft were similarly affected, so few targets were found. There were other types of operations, often requested in support of

Partisan or commando raids to harry the enemy. On 13/14 January, it was reported that German troops were mounting a further landing on Brac, and MTB 651 (Lt K.M. Horlock) was sent with MTB 226 (Lt P. Hyslop) to attempt an interception. They chased a small merchant ship into a tiny harbour east of Sumartin and torpedoed it, and then attacked a Siebel Ferry. It was clearly heavily damaged although they could not be sure that it had been destroyed.[12]

At the end of the month, on 29/30 January, Lt Cdr Tim Bligh in MGB 662, with MTB 97 (Lt M. Bowyer) set out on his first patrol in the Adriatic, and indeed one of his first as the new SO of the 57th Flotilla. They found a small tanker and a schooner at the eastern end of Brac and made a gun attack, as neither was a suitable target for 97's torpedoes. Both were sunk, after eight Italian prisoners had been taken. Interrogation by the Italian speaking British Liaison Officer in Vis revealed that there had been a German presence aboard each vessel, as guns' crews, but all had been killed in the engagement. The schooner was the 350-ton *Folgore*, just returning from use as a supply ship and on her way from Durazzo (in Albania), bound for Sibenik, north-west of Split.[13]

Bligh was out again in his 662 on 2/3 February, this time with MTB 649 (Hughes). Their patrol was northward to the Zara Channel, and after questioning some fishermen, they sighted a three-masted schooner situated very satisfactorily up-moon. Despite some spirited return fire, she was rapidly set on fire at very short range. Survivors began to jump overboard, and twelve of them were picked up. After a

12 MO2016; ROP at PRO in ADM 199/268; *Our Lady of the Pirates*, Kenneth Horlock.
13 MO2874, MO3983 and MO3261; ROP at PRO in ADM 199/268–9.

colourful firework display as ammunition and signal flares ignited, the schooner blew up with an enormous explosion. It was not surprising to Bligh that after interrogation of the prisoners, it was discovered that the 350-ton *Francesca di Rimini* was carrying 320 tons of ammunition. Below decks had been twenty-five German soldiers as passengers, who were all thought to have perished.[14]

There were two more Dog Boat actions in the next few days involving Bligh in 662, Hobday in 643 and Jerram in 667, but the rest of February saw Vis in defensive mode as intelligence reports led to a belief that the German command was planning to launch an attack on the island, realizing that it was truly a thorn in its side. Anti-invasion patrols were mounted, which involved Hunt class destroyers as well as Coastal Forces craft.

It was March before a regular pattern of contact with the enemy was resumed, and the Dog Boats had a series of successful actions, normally with very light opposition. On four nights in the ten days between the 8th and 18th, they sank three schooners, all carrying valuable supplies, and took twenty-eight prisoners with the consequent advantages to intelligence gathering. Sadly, there was also an incident in which, after challenging a target and receiving an incorrect reply, 649 sank the vessel and later discovered that it was a Partisan patrol boat (known as a 'Tiger'). Luckily, 649 was carrying a Partisan liaison officer whose report totally absolved 649 from blame, and thus maintained the mutual trust which had grown between the Yugoslavs and British boats. Most of the Dog Boats involved were the 'veterans' of the Adriatic operations – particularly Ken Horlock in 651, Peter Hughes in 649 and Bob Davidson, now temporarily in command of 674 while his 637 was under repair.

14 MO3986; ROP at PRO in ADM 199/268–9.

But there were new faces too, such as Lt Cdr Basil Bourne, SO of the 60th Flotilla, and the colourful Canadian Lt Cdr Tom Fuller who had just been made SO of the 61st. It was Fuller who was about to spark off an astonishing period, for most of April, when night after night his boats were to set a new pattern of warfare, unique in the Second World War and purely the result of a combination of his piratical nature and the type of enemy targets he met.

It began on 2 April when he was embarked in Horlock's 651, followed by 647 (Mountstephens). Ken Horlock, in his privately published and charmingly written memoirs, describes precisely how it came about.

On this night, we carried out various tasks entailing visits to Mljet and then to the Peljesac Peninsula, from which we lifted four Americans with a prisoner.

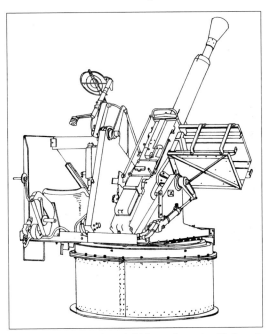

The 2-pdr Mark VIII gun on the Mark XVI (powered) mounting. (The forward gun in most boats of the class until the introduction of the QF 6 pdr.) Rate of fire: automatic; 115 r.p.m.: controlled; 96 r.p.m. (Courtesy, John Lambert)

Having time in hand, we worked along the coast of Peljesac, where the mountain falls steeply into the sea, and we went close in.

Even then, it was by accident that I looked at the cliff . . . something didn't seem quite right . . . it was worth turning for another look. There was a vertical line among the lines etched diagonally in the rock face.

It was the mast of a small schooner which was held flat against the mountain wall, holding its breath as it were. 'Hell', said Tom Fuller, 'Let's capture it'!

Horlock had explained earlier in his book that 651 had trained a boarding party led by his First Lieutenant, Frank Dowrick, for a year. At last they had come into their own!

A towing bridle was already rigged. When the men leapt on to the schooner's deck they landed on great piles of coiled barbed wire – obviously part of the cargo. Naturally this painful obstacle delayed the capture and the rigging of the tow; the fact that there were four German soldiers aboard was insignificant, as they 'sensibly realised that resistance was hopeless' and surrendered.

She was a thirty tonner, carrying also explosives, a jackhammer drill, compressor land mines, cigarettes and cigars and eight bags of delayed (Christmas!) mail for the Korcula garrison.

We took her back to turn over to the Partisans at Vis. Outside Komiza we cast off the prize and with the White Ensign and the Partisan flag hoisted superior to the Nazi swastika she had been wearing, Number One and his boarders took her in under her own power. They had a tremendous reception from the towns-people and the Partisans.

Obviously it was a splendid system and it represented a double loss to the enemy. He lost a ship, and the Partisans gained one.

Horlock goes on to describe how the same two boats – led by Fuller – were out again two nights later, and met two schooners running along the coast of Murter Island, much further north.

We each took one and ran down on them from astern. The attack was perfect, for they really knew nothing about it until our boarders were swarming across on their decks . . . .

In no time the boarders received the tow from us on the fo'c'sle and we had her secured and under tow. In twelve minutes precisely, to be exact . . . 2320 to 2332!

647 had the *Ennesta*, 90 tons, bound

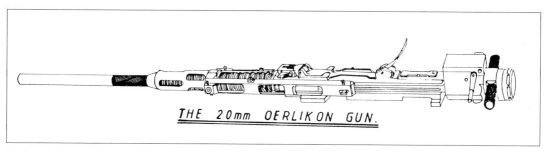

The 20-mm Oerlikon gun. Rate of fire: 470 r.p.m. (Courtesy, John Lambert)

from Zara to Sibenik, cargo firewood, crew four Italians and two Germans. Our prize was the *Dante 2*, 50 tons, cargo wheat, and with 20 mm cannons, crew three Italians and two Germans. She also carried deck cargo of brand new 20 mm Breda cannon fresh from the factory, with all spares and plenty of ammunition.

The Italian master of the *Ennesta* informed us that although the Germans were offering every inducement to the schooner masters to come south with cargoes, nevertheless in Zara vessels were lining up with engine trouble! But he did mention that his cousin, master of the *Svetj Nicola*, was thinking of coming down next evening!

Horlock describes how he received permission to return to the same area off Murter Island on the following night, this time as SO himself and with MGB 661 (Lt R.M. Cole) in company, to try for his hat trick against the *Svetj Nicola*. By now, 651 (and indeed many of the boats at Komiza) had been given small boarding parties from No. 2 (Army) and 40 (RM) commando. When the schooner appeared, and 651 was suddenly alongside her, the surprise was so great that the Italians all put up their hands before the commandos had time to leap over! The two Germans dived overboard but they got no further than 661, and one of them was carrying the German recognition signals – a valuable find. Again the cargo was wheat. That and the boat itself were welcomed by the Partisans, who marvelled at the magic of the Dog Boat attacks.[15]

The run of success in the boarding operations continued, with Fuller present as SO on each occasion, on three more nights in April, with ever-increasing numbers of prisoners and with even more welcome supplies aboard the prizes.

On 6/7 April, he took 661 (Cole) and 647 (Mountstephens) and captured the 400-ton schooner *Libecchio* off Murter Island (a very popular prize on return to Komiza as it was full of foodstuffs). Then on 11/12th, with the same unit and in the same area, he varied the pattern by sinking a schooner and I-boat, ramming a motor boat, and capturing two more schooners. On 14/15th, again with Cole in 661 but this time with 646 (Knight-Lachlan) in support, he sank a 100-ton tug and the 400-ton tanker it was towing by gunfire, and returned to Komiza with a 250-ton lighter and thirty-five prisoners.[16]

Clearly, the message to the German authorities (which seems to have taken a long time to permeate bureaucracy), that it was pointless to send schooners laden with valuable supplies down the coast virtually unescorted, finally got through. For some time after this, there were no sightings, and when they did recommence, the escorts had been strengthened and the goods were being carried far more often in F-Lighters, many of them with reinforced armament of 88-mm, 40-mm and 20-mm guns. Fortunately, because in the islands it was often more possible to achieve surprise, they did not cause as many problems here as they did on the west coast of Italy (and indeed in home waters at much the same time) where in good visibility and with no surprise possible, attacking boats could be kept at long range.

There was a further and very important consequence of Fuller's astonishing sequence of boarding operations. As has already been mentioned, the German High Command had been vascillating over a plan to eliminate Vis

---

[15] Three actions (2/3, 4/5, 5/6 April) MO6881; *Our Lady of the Pirates*.

[16] Actions 6/7, 11/12, 14/15 April MO5954 and MO6881; ROP at PRO in ADM 199/268–9.

as a base: the Navy wanted it badly, but the Army and Air Force were opposed. Decisions to mount Operation Freischutz were postponed from February to 17 March to 4 April and then to 12/13 April. The minutes of the Fuehrer's Naval conferences in 1944 reveal that Admiral Doenitz, alarmed by the reports he was receiving of the problems being caused by the attacks by Coastal Forces craft from Vis, which had reached a crescendo in the few days before the conference, pressed hard for a positive decision.

The minutes record the conclusion:

General impression: The Fuehrer is inclined to agree with the C-in-C Navy, but concludes as follows: 'if the Army is opposed to begin with, and the inner conviction is lacking, then nothing will come of it anyway.'[17]

With boarding operations drying up and a spell of bad weather, the next major task for the Dog Boats (and indeed the short MTBs and MLs) was to support and escort two major Partisan raids later in the month. On 21 April, the raid on Mljet left the whole garrison either captured or dead, and the next night saw a similar result on Korcula, in which the Partisans claimed to have eliminated a total of 756 Germans, the majority captured.

The next sighting of enemy shipping was on 1/2 May, when Lt Cdr Basil Bourne, SO of the 60th Flotilla, embarked in MGB 645 (his old boat, now commanded by Lt P.G. Martin RNR) and, with 667 (Jerram), was patrolling north of Brac. The unit was clearly sighted from the land, and Bourne led them southeast of Brac, where two vessels – difficult to identify close in against the dark shore – were

attacked and sunk. A second engagement began shortly after, when an I-boat (generally described as a small but well-armed patrol boat but used for many purposes including troop carrying) put up spirited resistance in a gun battle, and before being sunk damaged 645 considerably on the port side, two turrets being put out of action.[18]

Another strong Partisan raid on the island of Solta took place on 13 May, with Bourne in 645 (Martin) and with 674 (now commanded by Lt M. Bowyer, an experienced short boat CO) and 649 (Hughes) as its support group.

Tom Fuller returned to the fray after a well deserved short break on the mainland. On 18/19 May in 661 (Ralph Cole) and with 667 (Charles Jerram), he encountered a large coaster escorted by an R-boat and two I-boats in the Peljesac Channel. Forced to attack before the enemy reached the shelter of the Korcula shore batteries, he found himself observed and attacked at 600 yd. Almost at once, with the Dog Boats scoring hits, 661 herself received a hit that began a bright fire on deck, which drew more fire. Fuller continued to close through a hail of shells from the R-boat, and 661's gunners excelled themselves with a devastating attack which brought the spirited resistance to a close. But then the Motor Mechanic, staggering to the bridge, reported a serious fire in the engine room which was out of control despite all his efforts. All his men had got out on deck. He then collapsed. The CO pulled the methyl-bromide extinguisher levers, but the boat was under way at 14 knots with the engines still running.

Meanwhile 667 had been attacking the I-boats and the coaster, which were no longer firing, so every effort was then made to save 661. Jerram brought 667 alongside,

[17] Notes of Führer's Naval conferences 1944.

[18] MO6509 and MO7577; ROP at PRO in ADM 199/268–9.

which at this speed was a difficult manoeuvre, and gradually reduced the speed while the fire was fought with the additional extinguishers and pumps he could provide. Leading Telegraphist L. Pegler took charge of the fire fighting and soon it was under control. 667's Motor Mechanic re-entered the engine room once it had been vented, and 661 miraculously was able to proceed rather gingerly and return to base. L/Tel Pegler and L/MM A.R. Hayter of 661 were awarded DSMs, and Sub-Lt R.S. Smith, the young and recently arrived Pilot, the DSC, for their bravery in the saving of 661.[19]

Clearly there was a dearth of schooner targets at this stage, but on 20/21 May a 250-ton oil barge in the Mljet Channel was driven ashore in flames, this time after a gun action at 100 yd range, by a unit led by Basil Bourne in 646 (Knight-Lachlan), 674 (Bowyer) and 656 (Masson).

For some time, the very aggressive commando forces in Vis had been waiting their chance for a major operation, and it came at the beginning of June in the form of a raid on the island of Brac. It was designed to take pressure off the Partisan forces in Bosnia by drawing off German units. A number of Dog Boats (as well as two destroyers) gave cover for the landings, which involved 1,000 British Commandos, 2,500 Partisans, and 100 American special troops. The enemy fought bitterly, and the mountainous terrain was even more of a problem than expected. The forces were withdrawn on 4 June, but had suffered serious casualties, totalling 70 killed and 250 wounded. Lt Col J.C. Manners DSO RM, the CO of 40 Commando Royal Marines, was killed, and Lt Col J.M.T.F.

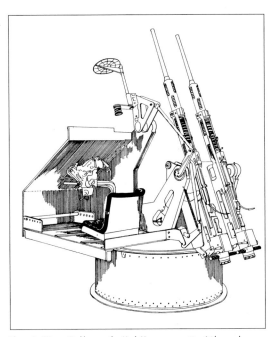

The twin 20-mm Oerlikon on the Mark V power mounting (side panel removed). As fitted either on the coach roof over the engine room, or on the stern. (Courtesy, John Lambert)

Churchill, CO of No. 2 Commando, was taken prisoner.[20]

Surprisingly, there were only two Dog Boat actions in June, the first on 9/10th when Mountstephens in 647 with 656 (Masson) met a flak lighter and an I-boat in the Mljet Channel. Both were seriously damaged, a fact confirmed by a German report, but in what Mountstephens recorded as a short but spirited close range encounter, 647 was badly damaged by very accurate fire from the flak lighter and suffered casualties. Four were killed (including a Royal Marine in the boarding party) and five wounded – a serious blow to such a well-knit crew.

Lt Cdr Tim Bligh with his 57th Flotilla returned to the Adriatic from Bastia and arrived at Vis in mid-June; his first eventful patrol was on 24/25 June. His unit was

[19] MO7580; ROP at PRO in ADM 199/268; *Seedie's List of CF Awards.*

[20] Bruce Lockhart, *The Marines Were There.*

MGBs 662 and 659 (Barlow), with MTB 670 (Hewitt). They went north to the coast of Murter Island, and were rewarded when they sighted a warship which was identified as the T7, a well-armed two-funnelled ex-Yugoslav torpedo boat of about 250 tons, one of the few really significant threats to British boats in the islands. Bligh ordered 670 to attack with torpedoes, but both missed astern and Bligh had to decide whether, with his unit now in an adverse position and probably detected, to make a gun attack. He dismissed the entreaties of his Partisan Liaison Officer to let her go, and set off in pursuit. He worked his way into an inshore position, still abaft the beam, prepared to close the range as far as possible until T7 opened fire. When she did, at 150 yd, the three Dogs, now gaining bearing every second, were able to bring all their forward and port side guns to bear, and their attack, accurately delivered, had T7 on fire with guns silenced within half a minute.

Suddenly the T7, still steaming at about 12 knots, swung to starboard across 662's bows. Whether it was an attempt to ram or the result of damage to the steering was irrelevant: she just missed 662 (Bligh estimated by 5 ft!) and steamed straight into the Murter shore. After a while, a thorough search was made of her, five prisoners taken (others escaped), her weapons examined, and she was left firmly aground, filling up and on fire above decks. An Army demolition party later ensured there was no chance of salvage.[21]

With the number of available Dog Boats greatly increased, patrols were stepped up and enemy shipping sought night after night. But targets proved scarce, and it was not until 17/18 July, on a very dark night indeed, that a unit led by Lt Peter Barlow in 659, with 649 (Hughes) and 670 (Hewitt) finally had

some success in the Mljet Channel when they found a Siebel Ferry and a small lighter escorted by I-boats. They sank the I-boats and severely damaged the Siebel Ferry. This time it was Hughes's boat that was damaged, being hit in the forward tank space. A serious fire resulted, successfully dealt with by the crew. Four men were wounded.

The next action, on 25/26 July, was particularly notable as it was Tom Fuller's last patrol as SO of the 61st Flotilla. It was also one of his most successful. He was embarked in 651 (Lt Len Ennis, who had just taken over from her long-standing CO, Ken Horlock) with 667 (Jerram) and 670 (Hewitt). He adopted the tactic of lying close into the Peljesac shore, and when an enemy convoy was sighted, the unit was in a perfect position to attack. There appeared to be a large schooner (without masts) with several E-boats ahead and to seaward, and two I-boats astern. 670 was ordered to fire star-shell as the enemy opened fire, and at once the schooner (later to be identified as the 'flak' schooner, Vega) was ablaze. Fuller attributed this, possibly from information from a prisoner, to a shell landing in a bucket of petrol. 651 quickly dealt with the I-boats, and all three Dog Boats secured prisoners and picked up survivors. The E-boats had until this time retired further to seaward, but with 667 silhouetted against the blazing Vega, they could not resist temptation and fired three torpedoes at her, and a further three at 651 and 670. All missed. The E-boats were savaged, and seemingly totally confused, fired on each other with some success. They did, however, hit 651 in the engine room, and she was left stopped and unable to use her turrets, but the E-boats departed. (The unit claimed at least two E-boats sunk, but German lists of the Mediterranean E-boat flotillas, giving the 'fate' of every boat, have no record of boats lost on this night, so possibly they were damaged rather than sunk.)

---

[21] MO9140; description by T.J. Bligh.

Despite the attentions of shore batteries on Hvar, 670 towed 651 safely back to Komiza. Sadly, the Pilot of 667, Sub-Lt John Dean, was lost when he fell between the boats on boarding the I-boat. No fewer than sixty-five prisoners were taken.[22]

On 29/30 July, it was the 57th Flotilla's turn again, and Bligh in 662 led 660 (A.T. Robinson) and 634 (W.E.A. Blount) northward to Vir Island, beyond Zara. After a four hour wait they sighted a schooner with a strange silhouette, and Bligh wondered if this was one of a new breed of armed 'Q' schooners with additional gun platforms (as in the previous action, when the *Vega* had no masts and was labelled a 'flak' schooner). But if she was, it availed her little, as a single attack by the three boats silenced her rather ineffective return fire. But she would not burn, and drifted towards the shore. Bligh ordered Walter Blount to sink her with a torpedo, and he did so expeditiously. Bligh took prisoners and established that the ship was the brand-new schooner *Tritone* (390 tons) on her maiden voyage, carrying flour and fodder.[23]

With Dog Boat operations on the west coast of Italy completed, and those in the Adriatic and Greek waters about to enter a new phase, this narrative returns to home waters to describe the very considerable part played by the Dog Boats in Operation Neptune – the invasion of Normandy.

[22] MO10089; ROP at PRO in ADM 199/268–9.

[23] MO10075; CCF's report in CFPR July 1944.

CHAPTER 8

HOME WATERS

Operation Neptune, the naval aspects of Operation Overlord, the invasion of Normandy, was the most complex and largest amphibious operation that had ever been attempted at this time. (Appendix 1, Note 22)

It was to be expected that Coastal Forces would have a very large part to play in the protection of the vast armada of ships and landing craft during the first phase. But the protection role would have to continue for as long as it was necessary. It would involve nightly patrols in tightly regulated areas to ensure that the assault area would not be attacked by the E-boats and other craft the enemy was expected to throw against the anchorage and the supply route. In particular, the threat from the E-boat bases at Cherbourg in the west and Le Havre in the east would necessitate constant offensive patrols to intercept any attacking craft.

As in all operations in the 'Narrow Seas', the destroyers and frigates would play a large part in this, but in the inshore areas, within the range of coastal batteries, it was the more expendable MTBs which were to bear the brunt. That there was air supremacy was one huge advantage to the Allied ships but this meant that attacks when they came would be by night, and so within the normal province of Coastal Forces.

The RAF, of course, did all they could to destroy facilities in the enemy ports in huge bombing raids, and ultimately succeeded in reducing the number of E- and R-boats which could operate.

Although this narrative must clearly attempt to describe the Dog Boats' part in Operation Neptune, it is important that this is not interpreted as an indication that they played a lone, or even the major, role among the MTBs employed. The total force involved in the Channel from the Dover Strait westward to the Channel Islands was twenty-two flotillas: eleven of 'short' boats, eight of Dog Boats, two of C class MGBs, and the SGBs. And of course there were many flotillas of MLs and of HDMLs which once again totally belied their name by remaining off the beachhead in significant roles for many days.

From the operational control point of view, D-Day saw a totally new and untried system of 'control frigates' coming into play. It had been recognized that the direction of many separate units of MTBs, each in well defined sectors, would require very careful and precise information about targets if confusion was to be avoided. The frigates, with high quality radar and using experienced Coastal Forces ex-COs as Control Officers, were able to 'vector' units to the enemy, and to keep other ships informed of their movements. This was invaluable, as the boats could work in close proximity to the destroyers without fear of a failure of identification. The COs of the MTBs, many of them old friends of the Control Officers, had great confidence in them: their well-known voices on the R/T made them close allies in the complex movements they had to make.

The preparations for the operation, from a Coastal Forces point of view, began with the appointment of Captain Coastal Forces (Channel) Captain P.V. McLaughlin and his staff on 8 March 1944. Apart from his Specialist Officers, he had two very experienced Coastal Forces men as his Operating Staff Officers, Lt C.W.S. Dreyer DSO DSC RN and Lt Cdr P.M. Scott MBE DSC RNVR.

As described briefly in chapter five, the most obvious sign of what was to come was the gradual redistribution of flotillas. Only one Dog Boat flotilla had previously been based at *Hornet* at Gosport in 1943, but by 14 April 1944 there were three there: the 51st (Lt Cdr I. Lyle), the 53rd (Lt Cdr D.H.E. McCowen) and the 55th (Lt Cdr D.G. Bradford RNR). *Hornet* would have been hard-pressed to fit in an additional twenty-eight boats (there were twelve in the 55th), but HMS *Dolphin*, the submarine base close by, offered the use of jetties, workshops and accommodation which were invaluable.

Training in Frigate Control began, but it had to be fitted in with the increasing demands of convoy protection, as the Channel convoys rapidly increased in frequency and size.

The first operational deployment of the Dog Boats related to 'Neptune' fell to the

The ship's company of MTB 749 of the 64th Flotilla (CO J.G. Fletcher) in 1944. The flotilla was minelaying nightly prior to the invasion of Normandy. (Courtesy, A.J. Simmonds)

MTB 728 as a minelayer in 1944. (Courtesy, A.R. Birrell)

specially adapted minelaying flotilla, the 64th, led by Lt Cdr D. Wilkie. The codename for the minelaying plan was Operation Maple, and it began on 19 April. Apart from the 64th Flotilla, which was to lay moored mines, two 70-ft MTB flotillas – the 13th and 14th – were to lay ground mines. The lays were in three fields, off Le Havre (Scallops Area), Cherbourg (Greengage Area) and east of Cap d'Antifer (Peach Area). All three were in some degree anti-E-boat minefields, but their main function was against destroyers, torpedo boats and larger ships.

The laying of these three fields involved the carrying and sowing of a total of 562 mines. In all, thirty sorties were made, often in bad weather and virtually always within range of the shore batteries. Accurate navigation was essential, and undoubtedly this was among the most stressful of all assignments carried out by the boats of Coastal Forces.

The Dog Boats of the 64th normally carried nine mines each on a sortie, and they carried out the laying of a total of 334 mines over eleven nights. Their worst experience, on 20/21 May off Cherbourg, when they had to lay forty-four mines in a north-westerly wind of Force 6 to 7, was applauded as a remarkable feat. When their minelaying role was completed, they reverted to normal operations.[1]

The Dog Boat flotillas involved in Operation Neptune were moved about over the next two to three months as the demands changed, but the dispositions from east to west were broadly as follows. At Dover (advanced base Newhaven): the 59th Flotilla (Lt Cdr D.H. Mason RN); attached to the Eastern Task Force, from Portsmouth: the

[1] CCF (Channel)'s Report on Op. Overlord, App. 3 (mining operations).

55th Flotilla (Lt Cdr D.G. Bradford RNR), and a little later, the 51st (Lt Cdr I.D. Lyle); attached to the Western Task Force, from Portsmouth: the 53rd Flotilla (Lt Cdr D.H.E. McCowen, replaced as SO in July by Lt Cdr S.D. Marshall) and the 63rd (Lt Cdr G.C. Fanner); at Plymouth for operations off Brittany and the Channel Islands: the 65th Flotilla (Lt Cdr J.H.R. Kirkpatrick), which was entirely manned by officers and men of the Royal Canadian Navy, the 64th (Lt Cdr D. Wilkie) after their minelaying commitment, and the 52nd (Lt Cdr T.N. Cartwright).

On the night of D-Day – 5/6 June – the weather was so bad that the boats, carrying out a multiplicity of tasks as the great armada moved towards the Normandy coast, had a very uncomfortable passage. But the one major advantage arising from the decision to launch the attack in such bad sea state, was

that surprise was total. The first opposition to the landings came from the German land forces. In fact, on the first morning, the Möwe class torpedo boats made a brief sortie from Le Havre but were soon repelled by Allied destroyers, although they first managed to torpedo a Norwegian destroyer. No E-boats came from Le Havre, and those that ventured out from Cherbourg made no contact with any of British ships.

Even on the first night after the landings (6/7 June), when a major assault might have been expected, the attacks were not pressed home urgently. The list of Coastal Forces actions records four enemy contacts that night. Only one involved Dog Boats when Bradford as SO in 624 (Stewart Marshall) with 682 (Bill Beynon) of the 55th, together with four of the 29th, engaged six to eight R-boats leaving Le Havre. One was seen to blow up (possibly in Wilkie's minefield) and

Officers at Dover: Lt A.H. Lewis (59th), Lt Cdr Howard Bradford (SO 59th Flotilla), Lt Dempster, Lt P. Best (59th). (Courtesy, A.H. Lewis)

two others were badly mauled. The other brushes were to the west, where one LCT was torpedoed by an E-boat.

On the next night there were seven contacts, two of which were by Dog Boats, both on the eastern flank. Once again Bradford and his 55th flotilla featured. In the same position as the previous night, a few miles west of Le Havre, Bradford sighted an Elbing class destroyer followed by two 'Möwes', and it seemed they were stalking yet another ship to the north. When star-shell was fired this turned out to be a British corvette escorting a convoy, and Bradford saw his chance while the enemy's attention was diverted and went in to attack. One torpedo hit on a 'Möwe' was seen (and confirmed later by intelligence reports) and the other enemy ships returned to Le Havre towing it back.[2]

Further east, in mid-Channel, five boats of the 59th Flotilla from Dover, led by Denis Mason, were vectored to a group of four E-boats from Boulogne. They attacked and claimed to have damaged one: they were sent on to another group, and fought a brief action. Reports indicate that later Typhoon aircraft sank one E-boat and damaged others.[3]

The level of activity, and the importance attached to the maintenance of the constant patrols on each side of the main supply route, is graphically illustrated in the following quotation from the privately published memoirs of Lt A.H. Lewis. Arthur Lewis was CO of 705 in the 59th Flotilla at Dover, operating at this time out of Newhaven, and from the first night was allocated a patrol area within a 20-mile grid square on the chart, to the north of Cap d'Antifer.

He writes that, very early in the period immediately following D-Day,

MTB 705 sustained quite serious damage and casualties in a conflict with E-boats. The casualties were transferred to a frigate with a medical team aboard. On return to Newhaven, I expected the repairs to take several days, but as soon as we got alongside, the boat was besieged by about forty shipwrights, ordnance artificers and mechanics. In no time they were putting everything to rights, including an enormous tingle[4] over a large hole in the boat's side, and the installation of a complete new 0.5 inch power turret. At the same time, replacements for the injured crew members were coming aboard with their kit bags. All the repairs were completed, the boat refuelled, and ammunition topped up by late afternoon, and by 1800 we were off again to our 'box' off the French coast.

He also comments that on the following night 705 was again in action and one of the replacements (an 18-year-old Ordinary Seaman on his first trip to sea) was wounded. Such was the pace of operations at this momentous time.

The 55th, divided into three units of four, and each given a different task, have already been mentioned as being in action on D+1 and D+2. Bradford's own unit had actually been in the van of the whole approach, screening the minesweepers as they led the cruisers and destroyers of Force J into their bombardment positions on 5/6 June, and being astonished to discover they had had no surface action to fight. Thereafter, his unit had remained in the Assault Area,

---

[2] MO13001; Summary of actions; *Day In, Night Out*.

[3] MO7912; ROP at PRO in ADM 199/262.

[4] Temporary repair over hole in hull, commonly using a thin sheet of copper.

taking on supplies from HMS *Scylla*, and trying to get some opportunity for the 'watch off' to have some sleep. Their nights were spent on patrol or in action, always close to the minefields even in daytime. There was a general rule that no one stayed below whenever the boats moved (except of course the engine room crews, the telegraphists and radar operators) as the threat of mines was always present.

Bradford describes how the crews were exhausted after four continuous days and nights in this high state of tension and alertness, and how his own unit of two boats was relieved on the fourth day for return to *Dolphin* for a rest period. His third unit took over, but he stayed a further day to show the newly arrived boats the ropes.[5]

The second unit of the 55th, led by the half-leader Lt W.S. 'Biscuits' Strang, had been in action on the night of D+3, and had a harrowing patrol, compounded by the obvious problems of ship recognition in such a crowded area. Strang was ordered to sink what was believed to be a stopped E-boat, but at the crucial moment it switched on recognition lights and proved to be an ML! A little later there was more confusion between the duty destroyer division and three enemy ships – an 'Elbing' and two 'Möwes'. Athough this confusion destroyed any chance of an attack, it at least prevented any danger to the anchorage, as the enemy were turned back to Le Havre.[6]

In this vital area between Le Havre and the anchorage, there was constant activity. The 59th Flotilla from Dover, and the units of the 55th closer to the Assault Area (together with the 29th short boat flotilla), were each in action on almost every night in the first week.

[5] *Day In, Night Out.*

[6] Summary of actions; W.S. Strang's account in *Battle of the Narrow Seas.*

Their efforts were acknowledged by Admiral Sir Philip Vian, the Naval Commander, who signalled:

The Coastal Forces operating in the Eastern Task Force Area are doing fine work. MTBs have intercepted each night. It is largely due to them that the Assault Area has been enjoying immunity from surface attack. The MLs have performed an essential if less spectacular task. The 55th MTB Flotilla, under Lt. Cdr. Bradford have particularly distinguished themselves.

Similarly, on the western flank, McCowen's 53rd Flotilla was in action on many nights off Barfleur (often with the 35th Flotilla of short boats), preventing attacks from Cherbourg. In particular, on 10/11 June, a combined unit of the 53rd and the 35th Flotillas was vectored by HMS *Duff* to intercept five E-boats in two stages. The 'shorts' – 448 and 453 – arrived first and had a close-range action, cutting through the E-boats' line and dropping a depth charge. 448 was badly hit and began to sink, but the E-boats were diverted back to the westward, where McCowen in 693 and 691 found them. As was so often the case, the E-boats were able to use their speed to get away, but on their return they were intercepted: one of them was lagging astern and was cut off, set on fire and stopped. Six survivors were rescued.[7]

Units of the 63rd Flotilla were in action on each of the next three nights to the north of Cherbourg, either against E-boats or M class minesweepers, which were heavily armed. On each night, too, the shore batteries kept up heavy and accurate fire whenever British boats were detected. On 13/14 June, for

[7] MO7417; CCF (Channel's) Report, App. 1.

The wreckage of the bombed E-boat pens at Le Havre with boats of the 66th Flotilla tied up outside. (Courtesy, J.Y. Ferguson)

MTB 755 drops a depth charge. (Courtesy, B.L. Bazeley)

instance, 704 (with Lt H.E. Ascoli as SO), together with 714, fiercely attacked three 'M's with guns and torpedoes, and secured a hit on at least one, which caught fire and stopped. The German communiqué admitted damage to one of their ships.[8]

That night was the first in a period of bad weather lasting until 23 June, which hindered operations by both sides, but reports indicate that, 'the defence of the western flank was so effective that the enemy seldom managed to break through into the American area'.

The minefield laid by Wilkie's 64th Flotilla (codenamed 'Greengage Plus'), containing 202 moored mines, turned out to be a very effective deterrent to the passage of enemy patrols from Cherbourg, and reports conclude that two E-boats were sunk by mines before it became sterile on 10/11 June. Thereafter British forces were disposed in a

closer blockade of Cherbourg, which was finally evacuated on the night of 23/24 June.

In the east, there was even more intense activity from Le Havre, so close to the Assault Area that it represented a constant threat. A major decision was made on D+8 (14 June) to mount a heavy bomber raid on the harbour, and its success made a huge impact on the balance of the naval war in the area. Peter Scott in *The Battle of the Narrow Seas* records that all the torpedo boats based there were sunk or damaged beyond repair, an Elbing class destroyer put out of action, and thirteen E-boats destroyed. An Admiralty report (M013001) records that, following this raid, there was no activity in the Assault Area for seven nights. Defensive patrols, however, kept the flotillas busy.

But the war was not only confined to the invasion area, and away from the core area of Operation Neptune, the Dog Boats operating in the far west and off the Dutch coast were,

[8] MO7417; Summary of Actions; CCF's Report.

of course, carrying on their patrols relentlessly.

From Brixham, the 65th (Canadian manned) Flotilla led by Lt Cdr J.R.H. Kirkpatrick RCNVR, began to make its mark, mainly in and around the Channel Islands and the Brittany coast, west of Cherbourg. Lt Cdr T.N. Cartwright's 52nd Flotilla worked from Dartmouth in the same area.

Kirkpatrick's maturity, calmness and logical decision-making both ashore and in action were (unknown at the time of course) a pointer to his ultimate appointment as a judge in Canada. The 65th spent the first week of Operation Neptune defending the convoys supplying the western flank of the invasion forces, but from 11 June they were mounting offensive patrols further west. On 17/18 June, off Cap de Flamanville, they found a convoy with a heavy escort of three armed trawlers and two M class mine-sweepers. The conditions were bad, and their attack was hurried and seemingly unsuccessful, with their torpedoes fired at long range. They closed and made two further gun attacks despite heavy return fire, and as they retired, watched the German ships firing on each other. They were delighted later to learn that enemy radio admitted that one ship (M133) was hit, although it managed to make harbour.[9]

A few days later, on 22/23 June, both the 52nd and the 65th attacked a convoy off the Channel Islands. The unit from the 52nd had to break off when a German patrol from the west intervened, but the 65th attacked with gunfire at close range, and succeeded in sinking a minesweeper, setting a merchant ship on fire and causing much damage. In return, 745 (Lt O.B.

Mabee) was seriously damaged in the first run. Captured German documents inter-preted by NID later confirmed the sinking of the minesweeper and that the ship left ablaze was the supply ship *Hydra* which was also sunk.[10]

To complete the picture of these 'western' flotillas in June, the 52nd, led as usual by Cartwright in 673, again met the enemy off Jersey on 26/27 June. Although no action report can be found, the summary indicates that they made two attacks: the first from astern in low visibility was completely unobserved. Cartwright decided on a gun attack at 400 yd, and claimed one trawler possibly sunk and another on fire. Astonishingly, he achieved a second unobserved approach, and 673 torpedoed an M class minesweeper (M4620) and followed up with a gun attack on the second 'M' in the patrol, severely damaging it. There was considerable return fire once the attacks began, but damage was light, although one man was killed and two wounded.[11]

Meanwhile, much further north, off the Dutch coast, targets were not found very frequently. The Germans had sent E-boats round to Le Havre (some of which were sunk in the air raid of 14 June) but kept back the heavier escorts rather than risk their destruction in further raids. These units were deployed to protect the infrequent convoys and also to guard against being taken by surprise if there were further Allied landings. Certainly the fact that Coastal Forces maintained rigorous patrols, despite several flotillas having been moved to the Channel, was a deterrent to any enemy plans to increase convoys bearing supplies to

[9] MO8119; ROP at PRO in ADM 199/262; *Chronology of War at Sea.*

[10] MO8037; Summary of actions; *Chronology of War at Sea.*

[11] MO7785; Summary of actions; sinking confirmed.

Lt J.V. Fisher, Lt Cdr K. Gemmell and Lt Cdr D.G.H. Wright. (Courtesy, Lord Fisher)

Le Havre, or to send more defensive units into the Channel.

The three Dog Boat flotillas based in the east coast ports of Yarmouth and Lowestoft were the Norwegian 54th, who spent four months between May and September at Yarmouth before returning to Lerwick; Gemmell's 58th, which had arrived in Lowestoft from Lerwick in March; and the 50th (which from mid-May had a new SO, Lt Cdr H.W. Paton), which appears to have had a roving commission in these months.

The first action in the area during this period was fought on 9/10 June off Egmond by six boats of the 58th Flotilla, and was a resounding success apart from the loss of 681. Until this time, few torpedo attacks on shallow draught targets had succeeded. But in May, at last, Coastal Forces had begun to receive torpedoes with a magnetic pistol (CCR) and this was to revolutionize the success rate. This new non-contact pistol triggered by the magnetic field of a target, enabled the torpedo to be set to run deeper, which had many advantages. The torpedo was not affected so much by surface waves, it left a less visible track and it was able to get ahead of any track it did leave. When it exploded without actually being in contact with the target's hull, it was more likely to break the back of a ship, or to damage vital regions such as engine rooms and magazines that might have been inaccessible through the sides.

So it was that Gemmell's boats, when they met a patrol of four armed trawlers and a gun coaster in very low visibility, were able to fire six torpedoes in the first attack after stalking and plotting the enemy, and to claim hits on three trawlers. In a second attack, this time without the advantage of surprise and so bringing heavy return fire, two torpedoes were fired and a hit claimed on the gun coaster. In this attack, 681 (Lt E.S. Forman) was set on fire and sank, two of her

MTB 720 of the 58th Flotilla under way with northern waters camouflage. (Courtesy, G.M. Hudson)

crew being killed and seven wounded. The claims were later substantiated by German radio, which admitted that three ships had been sunk. The combination of Gemmell's well-known aggressive leadership and the new weapon had dealt a heavy blow to the limited number of escorts available to the enemy, at this sensitive time so soon after the invasion.

Details of the enemy force and of the loss of 681 are given in a Search File from Naval Historical Branch which, with access to German records, reveals there were seven Vps minesweeping off Egmond: Vps 1314, 1315, 1317, 1419, 2020, 2021 and 2022. The initial attack was completely unobserved, and it was only when two of the Vps were hit and sank that the rest opened fire. Two more were hit in the second attack.

The CO of 681, Lt E.S. Forman, and all his crew except the two who died were picked up by 687 and 683. Forman's report reveals that 'the ship was a mass of white flames from the bridge forward below deck, and the topsides had parted from the deck' – giving him no course other than to abandon ship.[12]

The Norwegian 54th Flotilla was in action off Texel on the next night (10/11 June). Once again it was with a heavily armed escort to a convoy, including M class minesweepers. Rocket flares were fired after the enemy's course had been plotted, and then a torpedo attack was made in which 715 claimed a hit on an armed trawler. 712 was hit in the heavy enemy fire, and the unit's line was disrupted as the other boats followed her instead of pressing home the attack. The SO acknowledged that the inexperience of the Norwegians in this form of attack in close formation was their undoing on this occasion, but they did not give up, and a

long-range gun duel led to an enormous expenditure of ammunition.[13]

Only a week after his first big success, Gemmell led five boats of his 58th Flotilla on 14/15 June in another action off Texel. This time, conditions were very different. Extreme visibility necessitated the subterfuge of 'bogus' recognition signals and flashing but even so the enemy opened fire at 2,000 yd, and the torpedo attack was made at that range. All ten (armed with CCR pistols) were fired: four exploded short and were thought to have hit the bottom, but two boats reported hits. A 600-ton gun coaster was seen to sink, and a large tug was clearly in difficulties. A gun battle followed, and a large trawler was damaged.[14]

The 50th Flotilla, who spent many nights on convoy defence, had a bitter experience on 25/26 June when patrolling off the Dutch coast. 734 was attacked by British (Swordfish) aircraft, and so badly damaged that she had to be sunk – a sad task which fell to Peter Wilkinson in 612.

To complete their hat trick in June, the 58th Flotilla once again found a patrol of four trawlers, this time off Walcheren, and caught them at the entrance to Oostgat on the night of 26/27th. The torpedo attack was made at 1,200 yd under fire, and although a number of the torpedoes once again hit bottom in shallow water, 687 and 684 each scored a hit and sank a trawler. Very clearly the new torpedoes and pistols were making an enormous difference to success rates, and spirits were high.[15]

There was one more momentous action in this period for the 58th Flotilla, with a bizarre ending. Although the action report is not available, there are two personal accounts

---

12 MO6888; Summary of actions; search report at NHB.

13 MO7009; ROP at PRO in ADM 199/265.

14 MO7009; ROP at PRO in ADM 199/262.

15 MO7305; ROP at PRO in ADM 199/262.

of each phase and also a report from the Naval Historical Branch, with details compiled from access to German reports.

The boats involved on 4/5 July were Gemmell in 687, 729 (E.S. Forman and his crew from 681, sunk only three weeks before), 723 (McDougall), 666 (Buller) and 684 (Storrie) – all long-standing COs in the 58th. At 0047 they made radar contact with enemy ships, and closed in until, by 0132, they were a mile and a half from Ymuiden. At 0214, a German patrol of Vps 1411 and 1415 with AFs 41 and 47 (Schelde Gun-boats), sighted them and opened fire with their 20-mm and 37-mm armament. Gemmell fired rockets and moved in for a torpedo attack, two boats (723 and 684) claiming hits on two targets. When they retired to regroup, they realized that 666 was not with them. The account by Randall Tomlinson, an A/B on the bridge of the SO's boat, records graphically the sequence of the subsequent events.

Over the R/T, Lt Buller, the CO of 666, called up Gemmell. His plight was desperate, yet he spoke casually and seemed so unconcerned that it sounded as if he was telephoning a friend ashore. On the bridge we listened to him (the message was amplified for all to hear) reporting in his usual matter-of-fact tone, 'I'm in a bad way, with all engines disabled. I've lost some men over the side and am preparing to abandon ship. I've destroyed the CBs. I've got one of the blighters snooping around my stern, and another steaming up the starboard side.'

Gemmell picked up the microphone and quietly gave orders to Buller and to the rest of the flotilla who were stopped alongside us. 'Hold on. We're coming in. I'll draw their fire while Archie [McDougall in 723] and 'Aspic' [Storrie in 684] will come alongside to take off your crew.'

'Aspic, Roger, Out' and 'Archie, Roger, Out' were the brief acknowledgements from the two COs. He led the other four boats in towards 666 and all hell let loose. Everyone was firing everything they'd got – tracer of every colour criss-crossing as the enemy's fire intensified.

I went aft to assist the 6-pdr crew, but they needed neither help nor inspiration. Almost knee-deep in empty shell cases the lads had formed a human chain to pass up shells from the lockers below decks, as the ready-use boxes on deck had long since been emptied. As a crew we had all experienced heavy fire many times, but this was the fiercest ever, with many bigger calibre guns in addition to the

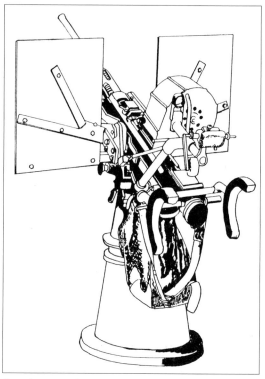

The single 20-mm Oerlikon gun on a pedestal mounting, as fitted in some MGBs in the Mediterranean in place of the 0.5-in turrets, on each side of the bridge. (Courtesy, John Lambert)

machine-guns, all now at really close range.

Reluctantly, Gemmell realized it was impossible to rescue our shipmates on the doomed 666, and even to save ourselves was now a serious problem. He grasped the microphone and called the flotilla – or rather what was left of it as only 723 and 729 were still close up in our wake astern. 'Hallo Jackals, Hallo Jackals. It's too much, too much. Follow me, follow me.' We turned away and increased to full speed. Almost at once I saw 723 just astern receive a direct hit on the bridge: a shower of red sparks burst amidships, she reeled, slowed, swung off course but regained station almost at once.

Gemmell grabbed the mike and yelled, 'Hallo Archie. Are you OK?' A dazed voice came through, 'No. We've had a direct hit on the bridge and it's a shambles. But we'll keep going.'

The sad sequel to this came as we neared Lowestoft. 723 flashed us up with the message, 'Lt McDougall has died'. Gemmell was desolated. He had lost Don Buller and Archie McDougall – two old and trusted friends – in one night, and 666, one of his most reliable boats.[16]

But what happened to 666 is an amazing story, revealed first in the search report prepared by Naval Historical Branch after access to German records. It was a 37-mm shell from Vp 1415 that hit 666 in the engine room, and set her alight. The fire was put out, but 666 was stopped and helpless with no power to the turrets and a number of wounded. Meanwhile, Vps 1401 and 1418 had arrived and, seeing 666 stopped, had opened fire on her with 88-mm. As they closed, her crew were abandoning ship.

[16] MO7991; Summary of actions.

Eventually, two Vps went alongside and one picked up survivors.

It so happened that the Staff Communications Officer for CCF (Nore) – Lt Cdr C. Macintyre RN – was out in 666 that night (a deliberate policy among staff officers to keep themselves closely in touch with operational realities). He was later taken prisoner, but compiled some notes which were submitted after the war.

In them, he recalls that he was with the CO and First Lieutenant when they jumped overboard, having first seen the crew into Carley floats and also having set the ten minute delayed action fuse for the destruction charge. They were still in the water nearby twenty minutes later, and tried to return aboard to reset the charge but found it impossible to do so. Macintyre, swimming towards the lights of Ymuiden, actually saw the tracks of torpedoes fired by the MTBs passing close by, and saw a hit on one of the Vps – which disintegrated into small wreckage. His notes go on to affirm that 666 was not sunk. She was towed into Ymuiden and the Germans managed to get her to the nearest available slipway, which happened to be next to a mine store. Next day, Kriegsmarine experts came from Berlin. He goes on, 'About 2 a.m. next morning, I was woken by an enormous explosion. I thought it must be an air raid or a homeward bomber dropping his load. When dawn came, my guard told me the boat was "Kaput".'

And that is not the end of the story! Macintyre tells that many years later, he met in the course of business a man called Kuyper who told him that his father had been the Harbour Master in Ymuiden at the time, and that his stories of the blowing up of 'the British MTB' had always intrigued him. In due course, he got his father to write an account of his memories, translated it, and sent it to Macintyre.

The former Harbour Master says that he saw, early that morning, one of the armed trawlers towing a British MTB, with the Nazi ensign at the masthead. A short time later, an explosion followed, and the ship turned over and floated with the keel topside. (This was presumably the result of the destruction charge, much delayed.) There was a very strong smell of petrol and all traffic in the harbour was forbidden.

The inspector of a salvage company came into his office and told him he had been given the order to salvage the MTB and to put her in the floating dry dock in the fishing harbour. The Germans had indicated that it was their intention to transport her to Germany and to exhibit the prize in different cities.

Knowing these facts, Mr Kuyper, aware that the salvage man was an anti-Nazi, advised him to use short slings, which led to further hull damage to the MTB. By 1900, though, after several hours on the slip, the hull was sufficiently repaired for her to be moved, and the Germans decided to berth her in the E-boat bunker. Next morning at 0700 there was a tremendous explosion, and when he arrived at the harbour, he saw that three of the six entrances to the bunker were damaged, and one totally destroyed.

He was told that the enquiry revealed the cause of the explosion to be that the fuel tanks of the MTB had leaked into the bilges, and after the heavy steel doors of the bunker were closed, the density of fumes became so high that when a light was switched on at the start of the day, it ignited with catastrophic effects. One E-boat was totally destroyed, and another heavily damaged. Half the bunker complex was out of use and was never repaired later.

So it seems that 666 had the last laugh! The explanation of the explosion seems totally acceptable: indeed it is remarkably similar to the fate of 601 at Dover three days after receiving extensive damage in action, as recorded in Chapter 2.[17]

Having described operations by the Dog Boats in the three areas (Assault Area both east and west flanks, Channel Islands and the Nore) through June 1944, the story returns first to the Assault Area at the start of July.

Early in July, the Scallops minefield off Le Havre had become safe and the important task of preventing E-boat attacks from Le Havre on the anchorage and the supply route depended on a close blockade, with patrols as near to the shore as the coastal batteries would allow, especially off Cap de la Heve. The E-boats in Le Havre were constantly being reinforced from Ostend and Boulogne and had to be intercepted if possible. Their route was often first past Cap d'Antifer.

For a further exacting sixteen days, Bradford and his 55th were out night after night, often in conjunction with Tony Law's Canadian 29th Flotilla of short boats. It was a period of constant activity and was extremely gruelling. Actions are recorded on six nights out of twelve for units of the 55th. (Appendix 1, Note 23)

4/5 July 632 (Bradford with Ford) and 650 (Fulton) met five large R-boats and four E-boats in line and in close order. Bradford decided to try torpedoes against the R-boats and was jubilant that two were hit. They were turned back to Le Havre, the object of the exercise. Later, 632 and 650 had another battle with two M class minesweepers which were damaged and turned back but 650 was so badly hit that she was paid off, and 632 had a serious fire. Both limped back to the anchorage. (MO7438 and MO10117)

[17] Search document at NHB; evidence from McIntyre and Mr Kuyper.

5/6 July 652 (Claydon), 628 (Cunningham) and 617 (Spare CO) were involved in the first attack by 26 'Neger' one-man torpedoes which sank the minesweepers *Cato* and *Magic*. The 55th joined MLs in repelling them and 617 certainly sank one. The German records say nine were lost. (MO57566)

6/7 July 617 (Bradford), 629 (R.R. Smith), 621 (Whitby) and 628 (Cunningham) with two short boats of the 14th Flotilla attacked two M class, one corvette, and six or seven E/R-boats off d'Antifer. They claimed to have sunk the corvette and one E/R-boat. (MO7609)

7/8 July 617 (Bradford), 629 (Smith), 628 (Cunningham), with a mixed unit of 'shorts', had a series of actions. They left an E/R-boat on fire, and later 629 sank a 'Neger' one-man torpedo. This time, twenty-one 'Negers' attacked the anchorage, and hit the Polish cruiser *Dragon* which was beached as a blockship in Gooseberry harbour. Many of them were sunk. (MO10117)

12/13 July 617 (Bradford), 621 (Whitby) and 624 (S. Marshall) once more met a large force of 'M's and E/R-boats and damaged several. Shore batteries intervened and 624 was badly damaged by a near miss. (MO10117)

13/14 July Two units were out: 621 (Whitby) and 652 (Claydon) in one, and 617 (Bradford) and 629 (Smith) in another. The first unit yet again met 'M's and E/R-boats but the attack was inconclusive, being beaten off by heavy fire and shore batteries. 621 was very badly damaged. (MO10117)

14/16 July 629 (Smith) and 682 (Beynon) had the last action of this phase for the 55th. They met two separate enemy units, attacked both, and inflicted heavy damage – possibly sinking one R-boat. (MO10117)

'A close shave' – a bow attack in an exercise. (Courtesy, Donal Rigg)

After this, CCF (Channel) decided that the boats of the 55th had taken such a beating, and the crews were so weary, that the flotilla was withdrawn, and its long history of success under Bradford came to an end. Most of the older boats were either paid off or recommissioned after long refits, and new boats came in to re-form the flotilla two months later under John Whitby.

Their distinguished part in the six weeks of the initial assault and the blockade of Le Havre was acknowledged not only in Coastal Forces but also at the highest level, and Bradford was awarded a richly merited DSO, and after some well deserved leave took on several very responsible shore appointments. (Appendix 1, Note 24)

Other flotillas appear in the records – particularly Ian Lyle's 51st, Geoffrey Fanner's 63rd and David Wilkie's 64th, which, after its tremendous minelaying activities, had joined the offensive patrols. The 59th led by Denis Mason in the Dover Command further east was also constantly patrolling. These and other flotillas were often positioned in areas where frequent contact with the enemy was not as probable as in the close inshore zones, but they performed a vital deterrent service and their time at sea was unrelenting.

One action fought by Wilkie's 64th very close to Le Havre on 14/15 July deserves a mention. They worked with a unit of the 29th Flotilla, which first attacked three E-boats and left one on fire as they were driven back to harbour. The Dog Boats joined in and also drove the enemy trawlers and R-boats back, but 738 was damaged and her Pilot, Midshipman Walmsley, was so badly

Two Dog Boats of the 53rd Flotilla at Kingswear on the River Dart. (Courtesy, R.E. Eifion-Jones)

wounded that he died three weeks later. (MO10117)

There were two more actions in the area before the end of July – the first on 25/26 July by Fanner's 63rd, who fired torpedoes at the M class ships as they went into Le Havre without scoring a hit. (MO10117) The other was by the 50th (led on this occasion by Peter Wilkinson) with two units of short boats in mid-Channel, from Dover on 26/27 July. Two groups of E-boats attacked British convoys, and one got through and torpedoed two ships: the other was intercepted briefly by both destroyers and Coastal Forces, who claimed some damage. (MO10727)

On the east coast, Gemmell, who was about to hand over the 58th to Lt Cdr D.G.H. ('Jake') Wright, had a last action, together with two boats of the Norwegian 54th who were shortly to return to Lerwick. In a fierce battle on 19/20 July off Terschelling, they attacked a patrol of trawlers and TLCs first with torpedoes and then at close range with gunfire. The heavy return fire and some clever avoiding action meant that there were no torpedo hits, but as the patrol retreated into harbour, one trawler was severely mauled, although at the cost of damage and casualties aboard Gemmell's boat, 687. (MO8424)

There was also an unusual and unexpected incident off Brest on 24/25 July when the 64th and 52nd were minelaying. They were attacked at long range by aircraft releasing glider bombs: 679 was near-missed but not damaged, and the lay was completed. (MO8788)

August began well in the Assault Area when on 2/3 August, a two boat unit of the 51st Flotilla, led on this occasion by Lt R. Ball in 608 with 614 (Newman), took on four E-boats, of which two (S180 and S167) were damaged. A second unit of the same flotilla,

Lt J.F. Humphreys, CO of MTB 724 of the 64th Flotilla. (Courtesy, E. Robertson)

680 (Barker) and 613, also engaged the same E-boats, and S181 was damaged. As there had also been a major air raid on Le Havre that day, and German records indicate that S39 and S114 were sunk and S79 and S91 were badly damaged, the E-boats had taken a huge blow.[18]

On the 8/9th, it was the turn of the 53rd to find the enemy off d'Antifer, in a mixed force with two SGBs and three PTs – all recently transferred from the western flank after the fall of Cherbourg. The Dog Boats were first to be vectored in, took on eight auxiliaries and R-boats, and fired six torpedoes, sinking at least one (Vp 241), although another was also thought to be hit.

Elsewhere, the West Country boats were

[18] MO57817 and MO10735; Summary of actions; *Chronology of War at Sea.*

SS *Miantin Omaha* sinks in fairway into Le Havre, victim of an oyster mine. Boats of the 66th Flotilla rescue survivors. (Courtesy, G. Hastings)

keeping a watchful eye on any German attempts to reinforce the east. On 5/6 August, Cartwright with four boats of the 52nd attacked a group of TLCs and armed trawlers off St Malo. Wise in 720 claimed to have sunk a trawler 'with a lucky torpedo shot'. And ten days later, on 15/16th, two boats of the 64th, led by Lt J. Humphreys off the Ile de Groix, Lorient, engaged and sank an armed trawler.[19]

There was one more major action on the east coast before the end of August, which again demonstrated the huge difference that the CCR pistols were making to the success rate of MTB torpedo firing. Lt Cdr D.G.H. Wright, now SO of the 58th Flotilla and in command of 687 in succession to Gemmell, made a fine start to his new appointment. This is not surprising, as he was one of the most experienced of all Coastal Forces

commanders, and had already been SO of short boat flotillas.

On 24/25 August, he led a force of five Dog Boats – 687, 684 (Storrie) and 723 (S. Stewart) of the 58th, and 769 (W.N. Dye) with 763 (M.J.R. Yeatman) of the 63rd. It will be apparent from the numbers of these boats that they were the replacements that were now reaching the flotillas in great numbers, often manned by the crews of the boats they replaced. The new boats had the advantage of the latest improvements, including armament, bridge protection and radar equipment, which had often not been available to the older boats.

The unit detected the typical patrol for this area, off the Hook of Schouwen to the north of Walcheren, and stalked it for an hour. There were four ships – an M class, an armed trawler, a gun coaster and a TLC. Wright approached very quietly and ordered his boats to take one target each, except for two

[19] Two actions (1) MO9456 and (2) MO9892; both ROPs at PRO in ADM 199/262.

who were to fire together at the largest target, the M class. When they fired at 900–1,200 yd, each target was hit: 687 hit and sank the trawler with her two torpedoes; 769 with four 18-in torpedoes hit the gun coaster with one; 763 aiming four 18-in, and 684 with two 21-in, hit and sank the M class; and 723 with her two hit the TLC. All the 21-in torpedoes had CCR pistols and were deadly. Wright returned to Lowestoft with one boat slightly damaged and no casualties.

It was on this very night, 23/24 August, that the last phase of the Channel war began. The Germans had clearly decided that the evacuation of those ships that could be spared for use further east must begin from Le Havre, even though at the same time an attempt was made to reinforce the defences of the port which was under great pressure on land. Allied plans were made to increase the patrols of destroyers, frigates and MTBs off d'Antifer, Fecamp and Dieppe, and Peter

Scott in *The Battle of the Narrow Seas* describes the week between 23 and 30 August as 'the most dramatic and the most successful period which the Coastal Forces ever had in the Narrow Seas'.

There is no doubt that the 'short' MTB flotillas carried the brunt of this blockade, and the 35th (Dudley Dixon), 13th (Mark Arnold-Forster) and 14th (David Shaw) particularly distinguished themselves, together with a flotilla of US PT boats.

The availability of Le Havre as a major supply port for the military did, however, bring about a situation where Dog Boats were required, and John Findlay's anti-submarine 66th Flotilla was summoned. It had been found that as the port was finally evacuated, the Germans had sown the approaches liberally with a new type of pressure mines – named oyster mines – which took on the character of either an acoustic or a magnetic mine according to the pressure of

The boats of the 66th Flotilla in a trot outside the wrecked E-boat pens at Le Havre. (Courtesy, G. Hastings)

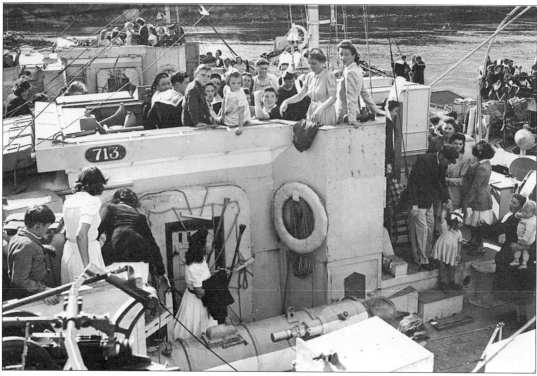

MTB 713 at L'Aber vrac'h with French civilians aboard. (Courtesy, T. Alexander)

water displaced by a ship passing over them at more than 10 knots. They were extremely difficult to sweep, and to prevent loss of supply and troop ships, the 66th were asked to attempt a method of steaming fast over the minefield and dropping a pattern of depth charges. It was a hazardous operation but one which the 66th carried out with gallantry, despite incurring considerable hull damage from near misses and sympathetic detonations.

There was an interesting aspect of the 66th Flotilla's stay in Le Havre. They were directed to berth outside the palatial E-boat pens that had been built to withstand bombing but had failed to do so. They found the pens totally destroyed, with wreckage of trapped E-boats among heaps of rubble, the result of precision bombing.

So ended the Channel war for British boats, as the remaining E-boats and all the great range of patrol craft of all sizes were forced to escape, if they could, through the Narrows to carry on the fight from first the Belgian, and then, by October, the Dutch ports.

They were, of course, followed by flotilla after flotilla of Coastal Forces boats re-allocated in the first place to the east coast bases to harry the enemy in the North Sea while the forces on land and in the air drove the enemy northward and eastward.

The Admiralty acknowledged the part played by the MTBs (and of course all Coastal Forces) in the momentous struggle of the past three months when the following signal was received:

Their Lordships are particularly impressed with the recent fine work carried out by

MTB 5009 in Portsmouth harbour, 'swinging' to check the compass. (Courtesy, D. Campbell)

Coastal Force craft off the coasts of France and the Low Countries, and congratulate not only the crews themselves but also those concerned with the direction and administration of the craft. Their efforts have contributed largely to the success of operations in France.

The story of the Dog Boat flotillas operating from the east coast bases in September 1944 and, after the fall of Ostend, often from the Coastal Forces Mobile Unit in that port, is not enlivened by as many thrilling actions as have been described in previous chapters. They tended to be fought when circumstances often unexpectedly led to encounters with the heavy escort groups on much less frequent convoy escorting duties, or to interceptions with E-boats returning from minelaying sorties or attacks on the east coast convoys. For the vast majority of the time the flotillas were back to the slog of British coastal convoy protection, or later engaged in the defence of the shipping corridor into Antwerp – the Schelde Estuary.

The period from September to December in particular was characterized by a greatly diminished level of enemy activity. This is not surprising, bearing in mind the enormous toll that had been taken of the E-boats, R-boats, trawlers, minesweepers and the multifarious auxiliary craft that had gallantly fought an unequal battle with the massed forces brought against them from June to August. Destroyers, frigates, Coastal Forces craft, aircraft and the minefields had decimated their ranks, especially in the last desperate attempts to evacuate remaining ships from Le Havre, while at the same time trying to help supply the beleaguered garrison which held out until 12 August.

One very human confirmation of the destruction comes from the mouth of an E-boat CO, Harold Garmsen, in a talk to Canadians many years later. Among many other fascinating comments – often revealing great similarities of outlook between the men of Coastal Forces of each side – he said this of the period he spent in the 2nd Schnellboot flotilla in S221.

In two months of action, only one operation was carried out without interference from MTBs, MGBs, destroyers or aircraft. Two of my flotilla's boats were sunk, and one damaged. The following month, two more were lost.

We used to listen in to the BBC because after an action when we lost a boat, if survivors were picked up, their names were given, followed by the statement, 'they belong to the few surviving E-boat men of the war'. (Appendix 1, Note 25)

But the British flotillas also needed time to regroup and to assimilate new boats into flotillas. Orders had already been given, some months before, to stop production of Dog Boats, but those coming from the boat yards with all the latest improvements could now replace the oldest boats which had taken the brunt of operations for nearly two years. What was not so easy to replace was the experience of those officers and men who had been lost or wounded, or – an increasingly common experience at this stage – were simply wearing out after years of unrelenting responsibility at a very young age. This was recognized at a high level, and a programme of rest periods and medical checks was instituted in some areas. TB was not an uncommon affliction in the cramped, damp conditions aboard the boats on continuous operations. Some Senior Officers were given responsible posts ashore where their experience and understanding of the needs and capabilities of the boats were invaluable.

Another important factor during this

MTB 772 at Lowestoft in 1945. (Courtesy, H.A. Young)

'shake down' was the continuing demand for a high quality of training that had been led in the first place by Captain H.T. Armstrong RN when he had become CCF (Nore) in 1943, and which had remained a very significant feature of the Nore command. Additional training was required for those flotillas that had not until now been required to operate under the direction of frigates. The high quality radar and communications systems and specially qualified Directing Officers of these frigates had proved their value throughout the whole period of Operation Neptune and it was decided that they would now be used in the North Sea.

The flotillas now based in the east coast ports which will be mentioned from time to time included the following. The 58th, Gemmell's old flotilla, was now commanded by Lt Cdr D.G.H. Wright (known universally in Coastal Forces as 'Jake'). The 64th, David Wilkie's flotilla which had so distinguished itself minelaying in the build up to the invasion, was moved about from

time to time, but spent most of its time in the Nore. The 50th, whose SO was Lt Cdr H.W. 'Colonel' Paton until he was relieved by Lt Cdr J.H. Hodder in November, had served for a very long period in Yarmouth, except for a short spell during 'Neptune' in the Channel. In September, they returned there briefly, but by the New Year were back in Yarmouth. The 53rd had been taken over from McCowen by Lt Cdr S.D. (Stewart) Marshall in July, and was to play a particularly significant part in the next few months.

The 63rd had for the past year been commanded by Lt Cdr G.C. Fanner, but in September 1944 was disbanded and reformed at Yarmouth with twelve new boats under a new SO, Lt Cdr P.C. Wilkinson. A very significant flotilla, new to the Nore, was Lt Cdr J.R.H. Kirkpatrick's 'all Canadian' 65th. It was a considerable wrench for them to leave Brixham on 7 September and head for Yarmouth.

All these flotillas tended to operate in units

MTB 724, the prototype 4-tube Dog Boat. Lead boat in the action on 18/19 September 1944 when three E-boats were destroyed. (Courtesy, J.F. Humphreys)

of three boats, and it became common practice (exactly as in the Mediterranean) for boats of different flotillas to make up a unit for a patrol according to availability.

To complete the general picture of the Dog Boat flotillas, which would otherwise seem to have 'disappeared', it should be mentioned that the 59th had been allocated to the Mediterranean, and was refitting and re-equipping from September to November 1944. The redoubtable 55th, after its distinguished service under Donald Gould Bradford, had paid off and was, until later in the year, re-forming under one of its former COs, John Whitby. The 51st, still under Ian Lyle, had remained in the Channel, and Tom Cartwright's 52nd was still based in the West Country, with a new SO in Lt Cdr F.D. Russell-Roberts, but was paid off in November and a new 52nd created with Lt Cdr A.R.H. Nye as SO to play a part in the New Year. His new flotilla was unique in that it was to be composed of a mixture of Dog Boats and Camper and Nicholsons boats. The other Camper and Nicholsons had featured in the Ball Bearing Runs to Sweden in 1943, and some were currently in the 15th MGB Flotilla (DDOD(-I)) on covert operations.

The first action of note in September took place on 18/19th of that month. HMS *Stayner*, accompanied by two boats of the 64th Flotilla, 724 (Lt J.F. Humphreys), SO for the night, and 728 (Lt F.N. Thomson), were patrolling between Ostend and Dunkirk. Ostend was about to fall, but Dunkirk, although virtually surrounded and bypassed by the Army, was to remain in German hands until almost the end of the war.

E-boats were at this time evading the blockade to take in much-needed material to the beseiged port. It was a very dark night, and when *Stayner* vectored the two Dog Boats to investigate the targets revealed on its radar, they were so close when they met that the three E-boats, as they tried at once to avoid action, turned too late. The Dog Boats poured their broadsides into the first E-boat which was immediately stopped and disabled. They charged on to the others, still scoring hits, and found that one had stopped and the other was making off at 40 knots. They chased, and to their relief it began to slow (clearly it had been damaged) and so they caught it, and in no time it had burst into flames.

A signal to *Stayner* brought her to the scene to destroy the first E-boat, and a return to the second found the crew abandoning ship. Altogether a total of sixty-seven prisoners were taken, and a very significant prize was that one of them was Kapitanleutnant Karl Muller, the SO of the 10th E-boat Flotilla, and one of the most experienced and successful leaders in German Coastal Forces. He revealed that after the first E-boat had been sunk, the other two had collided and that was why the Dog Boats found the second one (his own) stopped and the third unable to make good its escape.

It was not an uncommon experience for boats to collide in action: high speeds, rapid changes of course, poor visibility, sudden checks after a hit in the engine room all made it very understandable. Similarly (and not for the first time in these pages) the two Dog Boats also fell victim to another hazard in the midst of the confusion of battle: they mistook each other for the third E-boat and exchanged fire, scoring hits on each other. Fortunately none were serious.

But the result was gratifying. A victory for two Dog Boats over three E-boats (S183, S200 and S702) when these were already in short supply, and the capture of Muller, were indeed heavy blows to German morale. Both Humphreys and Thomson were awarded thoroughly well deserved DSCs, and their

Two of the 53rd Flotilla laying an effective smoke screen. (Courtesy, Donal Rigg)

crews, old campaigners and highly efficient gunners, a batch of awards.[20]

The Canadian 65th had begun patrolling immediately on their arrival in Great Yarmouth, and from 10 to 21 September provided one unit on every night without seeing the enemy. Then came a week of storms, and frustration was setting in. But on 30 September, with five boats, Kirkpatrick at last met some enemy ships off Terschelling. It was his ill fortune to discover that there were no merchant ships to torpedo, but only a patrol of heavily armed M class mine-sweepers which opened accurate fire at 8,000 yd – far beyond the range of the 6-pdrs. Lt Mabee's 745 received a hit in the engine room which knocked out two engines and cut off fuel and cooling water to the others. The two Motor Mechanics performed miracles of improvisation to get the undamaged

engines running, and 745 limped back to Yarmouth.[21]

It was early in October when, following the taking of Ostend by the Army and its clearance, Commander Brind arrived there with 'CFMU1' – the Mobile Unit base that had first been set up at Arromanches within the Assault Area. There, it had simply enabled boats to receive supplies and immediate repairs and servicing, but now in Ostend it had a well appointed port, good berthing facilities, and the opportunity of reducing 'passage to operations' time dramatically, compared with the long flog across the North Sea. At first, it catered for a small number of boats, which returned to the east coast ports after a few days, but gradually it became the main operating base for many boats.

Throughout the invasion period, the Germans had attempted to attack the anchorages with their new 'secret weapons',

[20] MO10879; War Diary; *Battle of the Narrow Seas*; *Chronology of War at Sea*.

[21] War Diary; *Champagne Navy*.

The Coastal Forces weatherproof suit designed to withstand bad weather in the North Sea. (Courtesy, Donal Rigg)

the human torpedoes and the explosive motor boats, with comparatively little success after the initial surprise attacks. Both the MLs and the MTBs had sunk many of them. On 5/6 October, a strong force of the 'Linsen' (explosive motor boats) set out from the Schelde to attack British minesweepers off the Belgian coast. A German document reveals that 'unfavourable weather conditions and strong defence made the operation a fiasco. Thirty-six "Linsen" were lost or had to be abandoned.'

On 29/30 October, Stewart Marshall led seven boats of his 53rd Flotilla on a patrol off Ymuiden after British aircraft reported the presence of E-boats. An hour later, the unit sighted nine E-boats and being in an advantageous position, closed to 300 yd, attacking fiercely as the enemy sought to enter Ymuiden. One or more E-boats were certainly damaged but they all managed to get into port. On the same night, the frigate *Retalick* detected an enemy force off Schouwen. Three boats of the 63rd were directed there, and sighted twelve ships, apparently trawlers, TLCs and R-boats, that were almost certainly minelaying. They attempted to close to attack, but in extreme visibility were kept at arm's length under heavy fire, and had to withdraw. 769 was damaged, but not seriously. In a very similar way, two nights later, off the Hook, two units of the 53rd attempted to get close enough to fire torpedoes at a group of M class ships and trawlers, and first tried a zone attack but were beaten off. Individual attacks at 2,000 yd were then attempted, and a possible hit on an M class was observed but never confirmed.

This minelaying immediately preceded the vitally important assault codenamed 'Infatuate' on Walcheren. The island dominated the Schelde Estuary and had to be cleared of German troops to enable the safe passage of convoys into Antwerp, impatiently awaited by the Army as a main supply port. The assault was launched on 1 November, supported by Dog Boats (particularly the 65th), to prevent attacks by E-boats.

Despite a very heavy landing force of infantry and Army and Royal Marine commandos, with the LCGs and LCRs (Rocket Craft), which were now standard for all landings, the enemy were so well prepared in defensive positions that it took a week of bitter fighting to subdue them. After all, they knew the attack had to come and had had months to get ready. But by 8 November the German garrison surrendered, at the cost of twenty-six landing craft and very heavy casualties to the Army and Marines.

The way to Antwerp was now clear, and the first convoy entered the port on 28 November. For Coastal Forces, this created a vital new priority. As well as ensuring the defence of the main east coast convoys, which continued throughout the war, they now had to guard the Schelde against attack. It was a new perspective to have their own base at Ostend, with the main focus of activity 50 miles to the north, and the E-boat bases in Dutch ports such as Ymuiden, a more or less equal distance away on the other side.

Throughout November, the Walcheren operation and then the protection of the minesweepers clearing the approaches to Antwerp had given the Dog Boats an enormous work load. Kirkpatrick, in his monthly summary of the 65th's activities, claims to have carried out seventy-two patrols, although his method of calculating this is not clear.

On 15/16 November Kirkpatrick in his own boat, 748, was called upon by HMS *Retalick* (unusually as a single boat) to investigate a group of targets in the mouth of the Schelde. It was very dark and he suddenly came upon them, six E-boats

The Vickers G.O. 0.303-inch on a twin Mark V mounting, fitted in all the class, and mounted in the sponsons on each side of the bridge. (Courtesy, John Lambert)

moving slowly along; he guessed they were preparing to lay mines. Taking his chance, he roared down the line firing at each one as he rushed past. It was all over in a few seconds: they had been caught napping and their reactions were not quick enough to fire effectively at him.[22]

It was on 22/23 December that E-boats were next out in force. It seems that one group of five was sent to lay a mine barrage north of Dunkirk. They were attacked by a frigate and MTBs, and S185 was sunk. Another group of six was engaged by short boats of the 30th Flotilla off the Hook of Holland and S192 was sunk. A third group of five reached the shipping channel and laid

mines, but 755, 694, 693 and 772 of the 53rd, with the destroyer *Walpole* and the frigate *Curzon*, sank at least S182 and possibly more. And finally, a fourth group tried to attack a convoy but was beaten off by frigate patrols. This mass attack after a long period of limited operations by the E-boats seems to have been the first of a series that reached a new level of intensity in January.[23]

The year ended sadly for the 63rd when 782 was mined, and sank in the Schelde. Three men were missing but the rest were picked up, two of them wounded.

[22] Summary of actions; *Champagne Navy.*

[23] MO1910; Summary of actions; *Chronology of War at Sea.*

It was on 13/14 January that a new phase of mass E-boat attacks began, with many flotillas contributing to extremely determined forays in considerable numbers. By using their speed and aiming at many different areas they seemed to have avoided most of the destroyer and Coastal Forces patrols on the first night, laying mines which claimed victims off Cromer, and further south too. The German reports indicate that no fewer than six of the fifteen E-boats had to return with engine trouble. On the second night, six E-boat flotillas provided a total of twenty-five boats, for raids into different areas as far apart as the Humber Estuary, the mouth of the Thames, off Margate, in the Schelde Estuary and west of it, and off the Dutch coast. Some laid mines and others attempted torpedo attacks on convoys. Most were intercepted by British patrols, but several claimed hits, especially on an LST.

They tried again on 23/24 January, this time with seventeen boats in four groups. Each was intercepted by MTBs and attacked, and driven off with some damage. Most of the MTBs concerned were short boats, but a unit of the 63rd (776 and 775) was successful in joining HMS *Torrington* to damage one E-boat off Walcheren. On this night, too, S199 was sunk and S701 was later written off, the E-boat having collided with MTB 495 in an action near Tongue Sand Fort.

It was on 14 February that the worst disaster to hit Coastal Forces in the whole war occurred at Ostend. At 1602, in the crowded corner of the harbour known as the 'Crique' (at least to the Canadian flotilla), there was a sudden shout of 'Fire!' Flames carried by petrol in the water immediately began to engulf the boats, leaping from one trot to the next, and spreading to seventeen boats within less than a minute. It was at 1605, three minutes later, that the first explosion came. Witnesses say it was heard

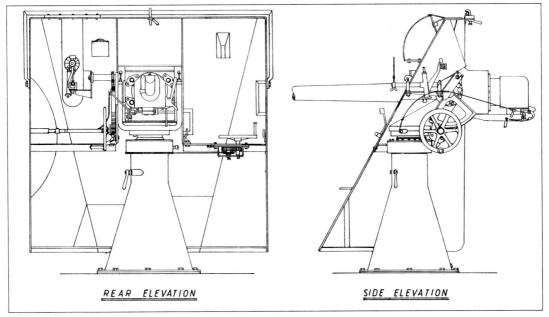

REAR ELEVATION   SIDE ELEVATION

The 6-pdr Hotchkiss QF gun on a HA/LA Mark VI mounting. Manually controlled, and mainly used on the stern of the MGBs of the class. The gun itself was originally designed in 1885! It was highly regarded for accuracy, reliability and effectiveness. (Courtesy, John Lambert)

across the North Sea in England. In Ostend it shattered windows and shook the ground and brought everyone into the streets. In the harbour there was chaos: logical thought seemed impossible as a second huge explosion rent the air. Ammunition, depth charges and torpedoes all added to the horror. Boat after boat blew up and clearly many men had been trapped below decks, especially in the four Dog Boats berthed in the rear trot behind the two rows of four short boats at the heart of the conflagration. The quick thinking of one man in the first minute of the catastrophe saved the first trot of three boats: a stoker leapt down to the engine room of 485, started up, and went full ahead, parting the shore lines and dragging the other two boats with her to put a gap between them and the centre of the fire. She was alight astern, but willing hands put out the fire and those three boats were saved.

The terrible results were indeed a blow to morale and effectiveness. The human cost was staggering: sixty-four killed and sixty-five wounded among naval personnel and more among the civilians in the harbour area. The Canadian 29th Flotilla lost five boats and the flotilla was paid off: three other 'shorts' were destroyed. The four Dog Boats caught astern of the seat of the fire were all destroyed: 776 of the 63rd, 789 of the 64th, and two boats of the newly formed 52nd Flotilla, 791 and 798.[24]

There was a sequel three days later to add to the sense of loss. 605, one of the oldest Dog Boats still in commission, visited Ostend on 17 February and as she left, she struck an underwater obstruction. The shafts snapped and a propeller carved a hole in the ship's bottom. All aboard were safe, but she turned turtle under tow and sank outside Ostend harbour. It seems, from a letter to the author from A/B George Lesslie, a member of CFVA, that 605 was being used in Dover to run VIPs to Ostend, and clearly they had been there on this occasion to assess the results or the causes of the explosion.

But the work of the flotillas had to go on and patrols began again almost at once. These were very necessary as the E-boat activity continued unabated and there were some successes, despite suffering losses almost every time they went out. Boats of the 63rd, the 65th and the 58th were involved in brushes with E-boats on several nights. As always, they knew they would be too slow to catch them in a straight chase, and bemoaned the lack of high speed diesels!

The 65th had five boats out, working with the frigates on 24/25 February. In a series of actions, together they prevented four groups from gaining any position to attack the convoys or indeed to carry out minelaying. In the process, S167 was crippled in one brush and scuttled herself. Twenty-three survivors were picked up. Almost exactly the same scenario was repeated on the last night of the month, in bad weather, with similar results. However hard the E-boats probed, fled, and returned (in an extraordinarily resolute manner), they were diverted by very well organized defences: five frigates and three groups of MTBs including 795 of the 64th and 779 of the 63rd were involved. Once again one S-boat (S220) was sunk.

In similar E-boat attacks on the Schelde shipping route on 9/10 and 17/18 March, boats of the 65th and 53rd were involved and it was noted in both reports that the E-boat gunnery (which had often been regarded as ineffective by the crews of the MTBs) had apparently improved and more hits were being sustained in the rapid brushes as E-boats attempted to evade and return elsewhere.

Knowing how difficult it must have been for the E-boat flotillas to sustain so many

[24] List of boats in Summary of actions; J.P. Perkins, *Champagne Navy*.

MTB 5003 at Rotterdam soon after VE day. Crew members demonstrate the 2-in rocket flares. (Courtesy, R.E. Eifion-Jones)

gallant operations when supplies were short, as they were at this stage of the war, it is impossible not to feel admiration for the crews' resilience and determination.

In the period 17–25 March, despite the usual highly trained frigate and well organized MTB defences, the following operations were carried out. The results are taken from German records of the S-boat flotillas, recorded in *Chronology of War at Sea*.

17/18 March: 2nd Flotilla lay mines off Smith's Knoll.

18/19 March: 6th Flotilla (Lt Cdr Matzen) lay mines on east coast and attack convoy FS 1759 off Lowestoft. Seven hits claimed, freighters *Creighton* and *Rogate* sunk.

2nd, 4th, 6th and 9th mine the Schelde route. LST 80, freighters *Samselbu*, *Empire Blessing*, and a trawler sunk and a Liberty Ship damaged. 8th Flotilla out of action following an air attack on its base at Ymuiden on 14 March.

21/22 March: 2nd and 5th Flotillas attack convoy on Schelde route, but break off with engine trouble. S181 sunk by Mosquito on return, off Texel, and SO of 2nd Flotilla, Cdr Opdenhoff, killed. In total, seven boats damaged.

22/23 March: 4th, 9th, 6th Flotillas try again, only 9th lay mines. Two freighters, trawler, ML 466 and LCP 840 sunk by mines. 4th and 6th boats driven off. 5th and 8th Flotillas transferred to Baltic and Norway.

Even the very newly formed Dog Boat flotillas such as the 67th (with Lt Cdr J.H.

Hodder in command) were entering the fray as more and more boats joined the defensive patrols: 5005, 767 and 796 all met the enemy on 18/19 March (see above) off the Humber Estuary as part of the whole force of destroyers, frigates and Dog Boats deployed that night.

As the last few weeks of the war brought ever increasing pressure, so the E-boat losses continued, and this attempt to delay the end, at least at sea, by virtually the only striking force left to the enemy, began to succumb to the constant attacks. There were three more sallies in April, in each of which the E-boats were intercepted and could claim successes only as a result of the mines they managed to lay. They also lost boats in close actions when they were detected in positions where they were unable to use their speed to escape. The Dog Boats shared these interceptions with short boats, and all of them suffered in inflicting damage. It was a bruising contest to the end.

Briefly, 6/7 April saw the last sortie by the 2nd S-boat Flotilla (SO, Lt Cdr Wendler) when six boats laid mines in the Humber Estuary. As they withdrew, they were intercepted by 781 and 5001 of the 68th Flotilla (the last few Dog Boats built, all the 600 and 700 numbers having been used up, were in a series starting at 5001). HMS *Cubitt* had already attacked and sunk one of the E-boats, but in a very close and hard hitting action, 5001 herself caught fire and blew up with many casualties. Shortly after, aircraft vectored on a unit of short boats of the 22nd Flotilla, and once again the two leading MTBs each rammed an E-boat, resulting in the sinking of S176 and S177. Sadly the boat of the SO of the MTBs was sunk with the loss of most of her crew and the other, after first colliding with the wreck, was so badly damaged that it returned to base stern first. But the 2nd S-boat Flotilla

had suffered so severely that it never operated again.[25]

On 7/8 April, the next night, the 4th and 6th S-boat Flotillas, mustering thirteen boats, set out to lay mines off the Schelde, but did not reach the shipping channel. Each of their units was intercepted, first by short boats which sank S202 and S703, and then by 745 and 736 of Kirkpatrick's Canadian 65th, still in the fray after continuous patrols over eight months of gruelling operations, which repelled them and inflicted damage. S223 hit a mine off Ostend and sank. A third S-boat unit trying to transport EMBs to the Schelde was turned back by bad weather. (MO4432)

But incredibly, the very last reported operation by the E-boats – on 12/13 April – was still in strength, with twelve boats from three flotillas setting out to lay mines in the Schelde. They were successful to some extent (one tanker was sunk and others damaged) but in the last Coastal Forces engagement with E-boats in this sector of the war, the 65th (797 and 746) severely damaged two of them, suffering slight damage and casualties themselves.

So ended the 'Battle of the Narrow Seas', in the Channel and the North Sea, in which Coastal Forces had played a very significant role.

On 13 May 1945 came a single small ceremony, amid countless other similar tokens of the end of the war at sea in the west, to symbolically mark the end of that battle.

For many of those who were present either at sea or gathered at Felixstowe to see its culmination, the atmosphere was deeply moving as memories of six years of relentless conflict flooded back.

The event was, in fact, the passage of a senior German naval officer, Admiral

25 MO4597; detail from John Lake; ROP held by author.

Brauning, bringing to C-in-C Nore the charts of the enemy minefields. The actual surrender of German naval forces, including the E-boats, had taken place a few days earlier, as part of the 'unconditional surrender' terms.

But to everyone's delight, the Admiral made his passage in two E-boats, and with him was the Senior Officer of the 4th E-boat Flotilla, Korvetten-Kapitan Fimmen. And that was not all. An understanding C-in-C Nore had arranged that the two E-boats should be met and escorted over the last 50 miles into Felixstowe by a representative force of ten MTBs. Those ten boats, which included Dog Boats, Vospers, 71-ft 6-in British Power Boats and others, carried Senior Officers of many of the flotillas which had fought the enemy in these waters.

They met the E-boats at about 1400 on a sunny peacetime Sunday afternoon off the South Falls buoy. Leading the Allied boats was the senior of the flotilla SOs present, Lt Cdr J.H. Hodder, and with him travelled Lt Cdrs D.G.H. Wright and P.M. Scott, both of whom went aboard the E-boat carrying the Admiral. The escort formed up on either side of the E-boats, which were wearing the white flags of surrender, to the great satisfaction of the men in the MTBs.

Together they set course for Felixstowe at 20 knots. Peter Scott observed that although the Dog Boats were wetter than the E-boats, with spray bursting over their bridges in a freshening westerly, 'the E-boats rolled much more, and would certainly have provided a much less steady platform for gunnery'.

When they entered the small basin at Felixstowe, the men from the base and the flotillas there crowded the jetties to watch the E-boat COs demonstrate their boat-handling expertise, 'by going alongside at a spectacular speed, assisted by the effect of their large screws and considerable astern power'.

At last the teams of technical experts from the Admiralty could inspect these beautifully designed boats, which had carried on their aggressive patrols even when the odds against them had increased steadily.

For the men of Coastal Forces, their very presence alongside in a British base was the confirmation that at last the war of the MTBs in home waters was truly over.[26]

There is one further aspect of the work of Coastal Forces in home and Norwegian waters that deserves examination, and chapter nine is devoted to the exploits of one Dog Boat, MTB 718. In this book she represents the clandestine operations of the 15th MGB Flotilla, specializing (unlike all others) in avoiding contact with enemy ships, but in even more hazardous ways getting closer to the enemy and the occupied coastline than any whose exploits have featured thus far.

[26] Peter Scott, *Battle of the Narrow Seas*.

CHAPTER 9

MTB 718

CLANDESTINE OPERATIONS TO THE SHORES OF BRITTANY AND NORWAY

There is every justification for including the clandestine work of MTB 718 in a history of the operations of the Dog Boats, as it illustrates sharply the tremendous variety of tasks that fell to the boats, and their versatility. (Appendix 1, Note 26)

Mention was made briefly in chapter two of Captain Frank Slocum RN whose department in Admiralty was known as DDOD(I): Deputy Director, Operations Division (Irregular). Back in 1941, the boats at his disposal, many of which came from Coastal Forces and were largely C class MGBs, were assigned from time to time to clandestine operations. As the demands for the expertise of his department increased, the decision was made to form a flotilla specifically at his disposal, and it was designated the 15th MGB Flotilla.

Three coxswains of the 15th MGB Flotilla: PO F.S. Smith DSM (502), PO H.E. Mould DSM* (318), PO W.H. Webb DSM (503). (Courtesy, W.H. Webb)

The early plans for the composition of the flotilla included the C class MGB 314 commanded by Lt Dunstan Curtis, but before she could take up her place, she became the headquarters ship for the St Nazaire raid, and although she got out of the inferno of that raid, albeit severely damaged, she had to be sunk by a destroyer on the return voyage. Her place in the flotilla was taken by a sister ship, MGB 318, which had a distinguished record right through to the end of the war.

The next boats to be chosen were three Camper and Nicholson boats: MGBs 501, 502 and 503. Eight of this class had been ordered pre-war by the Turkish Navy and taken over before completion, and the other five have already been mentioned as being involved in blockade-running to Sweden under mercantile flags. They were beautifully finished boats, of similar size to Dog Boats, and well armed. Once again fate intervened, and 501 blew up after a galley fire on an exercise near the Longships Lighthouse. She alone of the three had Packard petrol engines: 502 and 503, both nearing completion, had three Davey Paxman diesel engines, giving a top speed of 27 knots. When they commissioned, they joined 318 and MA/SB 36 to form the 15th MGB Flotilla at Dartmouth.

CO of 502, and Senior Officer of the flotilla, was Lt Cdr Peter Williams, who featured in Chapter 2 as a CO in 1942 in both C class boats and in Dog Boats, even then involved in clandestine operations.

Captain Slocum also had another sea-going unit, of non-Coastal Forces boats, fishing vessels, which were based in the Helford River. The two groups worked independently.

MTB 718 in Flekkfjord, July 1945. (Courtesy, C. Milner)

Captain Slocum's headquarters were in London, but his Operations Officer, Commander E.S. ('Ted') Davis DSO RNR was based in an office in the Royal Naval College at Dartmouth, and his duties included very close liaison with C-in-C Plymouth and with the RAF – particularly Coastal Command and the Beaufighters at St Eval. Ted Davis had himself been on countless DDOD(I) missions to the enemy coasts, and his experience was invaluable. He had been the Navigating Officer of the *Queen Mary* in peacetime, and his attention to navigational detail was vital to the success of the operations.

In short, these were mainly concerned with landing of agents, and the picking up of both agents and Allied personnel who had evaded capture or who had escaped from prisoner of war camps. The 'pin-points' (chosen beaches) were invariably difficult to access, in order to make the risk of sighting or detection as small as possible. This automatically meant that navigation and seamanship had to be of the highest standard.

MTB 718 joined the flotilla in Dartmouth on 26 March 1944, having been built at Robertson's Yard at Sandbank in Holy Loch, and she made her way southward, fitting in a few days 'working up' *en route* at HMS *Bee* at Holyhead.

Her CO was Lt R.F. (Ronald) Seddon, a fine seaman with a proven record in Coastal Forces. He had commanded an ML working from Lowestoft and distinguished himself when, in September 1943, his ML, with another, had rammed and sunk an E-boat (S96). The First Lieutenant was Sub-Lt M.I.G. (Guy) Hamilton and the Navigator, Sub-Lt J.S. (John) Townend. The crew was to become a very close-knit and competent unit,

The ship's company of MTB 718. (Courtesy, C. Milner)

but at this stage needed training in the special tasks which lay ahead.

They soon discovered that a great deal of research and the lessons of many past operations had refined both the equipment and the techniques which were required. In particular, the art of successful landings, which invariably involved the mother ship lying a short distance offshore while a boat party rowed in to the chosen beach, had been thoroughly investigated. Most essential of all was a specially designed and purpose-built 'surf boat'. It was clinker-built, with a straight bow and stern to allow rapid turn-round, specially designed oars and long rubber-covered crutches, and it was steered by a long sweep oar and equipped with a sea anchor to help stability in breakers.

The boat's crew of three was normally, and in the case of 718, always, commanded by the First Lieutenant, and remained as consistent as possible to enable experience to be gained, but all the seamen received training in case they were required to substitute. The boat could carry five passengers in addition to the crew.

Of course, the navigation to bring the boat to the right landfall had to be meticulous. It

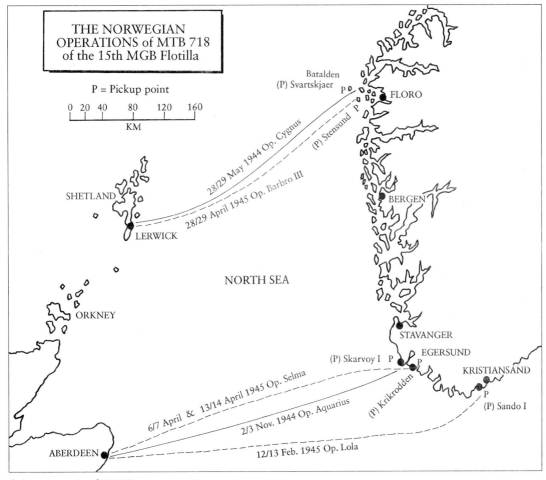

The Norwegian missions of MTB 718.

was greatly assisted by the installation of 'QH', a radio position-finding system using a gridded chart, and by the use of specialist Navigation Officers who were embarked on every operation.

There was one overriding standing order which placed a very heavy responsibility on the shoulders of every CO in the flotilla, and strangely it was an important factor in 718's first operation. The COs were expressly ordered, 'you are not to open fire except in extreme circumstances of self defence, and even then only if you have no other alternative'. The rationale was clear. If a boat should be sunk in an engagement with the enemy, the survivors among her crew would become prisoners of war but any passengers other than escaping service men would be executed as spies. And of course it was possible that they would, under torture, betray the shore organization whose members would be rounded up and shot.

718's first mission was to accompany MGB 502 to Beg-an-Fry near Morlaix, and it was codenamed 'Scaramouche' ('Scarf'). The orders from C-in-C Plymouth were specific:

Object
To rescue ten escaped POWs from a sandy beach about half a mile SE from Pointe de Plestem.

Intention
Operation to be carried out by MGB 502 and MTB 718 from Dartmouth on the night of 15/16 April 1944, or on one of the two following nights.

Method
Arrive off the beach at 0130/16 and leave the vicinity not later than 0300.
Boats are to proceed inshore to embark the prisoners with special care regarding

SILENCE and the RECOGNITION of the prisoners before grounding or landing.
Every precaution is to be taken to avoid falling into a trap. A careful watch is to be kept for suspicious movement ashore. W/T SILENCE is to be maintained except in emergency.
Note is to be taken of any enemy lights visible or other activity that may be observed.
Lt Cdr A.H. Smith RNR and Lt M.P. Salmond RNR will be borne additional on board 502 and 718 for navigational duties.

ACKNOWLEDGEMENT and DESTRUCTION
These orders are to be acknowledged on the attached form and are to be burnt on completion of the operation.

Operation Scaramouche was meant to be a 'training run' for 718: MGB 502 had often visited Beg-an-Fry before, and given normal conditions this should have been a straightforward mission. But in this sort of operation there are so many factors that nothing can be straightforward – and so it proved. There is no doubt that the tension of approaching very close to an enemy coast, and actually being in touch with the people there, was tremendous. That applied every time, but certainly the crew of 718 and especially those who would row in the surf boat, felt it deeply on this first occasion.

But all went well. Guy Hamilton, with the chosen surf boat's crew who were destined to become the first choice crew from then on, disappeared towards the beach, lost in the darkness very quickly. Twenty minutes later, a blob of extra blackness transformed itself into the returning surf boat, gliding silently towards 718. The scene is well described by 718's Telegraphist, Charles Milner:

There were half a dozen people in the boat. One was a well-dressed man in civilian clothes carrying a briefcase just as though he was catching his commuter train. Next came an attractive girl who, in reply to my pointed directing hand and my 'Ici, mademoiselle' (the first chance I'd had to use my Grammar School French since leaving school four years earlier), replied, 'It's OK, Jack. I've been on these boats before!' We discovered later that she and the other girl were SOE agents who had escaped from the hostage prison at Castres.

As soon as the surf boat had been hauled inboard, the two boats crept away from the pick-up point and began to thread their way on silenced engines through the rocks and shoals. Suddenly, about 5 miles out, the totally unexpected happened. There, on a parallel but reciprocal course, three German patrol boats were sighted, closing rapidly. It seemed there was no way in which an encounter could be avoided. Peter Williams, the CO of 502 and the SO of the unit, was faced with the responsibility of making an instant decision on the action to be taken. Almost at once, the leading enemy ship challenged, and Williams ordered his signalman to make any reply, as clumsily as possible, to delay any response. By now, the two boats were only 150 yd apart, rapidly passing with guns trained on each other. Suddenly, the second enemy boat opened fire and sent a burst of 20-mm shells at 502 just abaft the bridge.

The signalman turned his Aldis lamp skyward and flashed a series of 'i's to indicate (he hoped), 'Stop! you are firing on friends'. Miraculously, the firing stopped, and in no time the enemy boats were past and 502 and 718 increased speed and set course for Dartmouth.

502 discovered that A/B Sandalls of the Oerlikon gun's crew had been hit and killed:

718 was hit right aft but without any significant damage. Strangely, 718's first operation was the occasion of the only fatal casualty throughout all the flotilla's clandestine work.

Williams later agonized over his decision not to open fire, knowing that his unit could almost certainly have sunk the enemy patrol boats. But reasoned thought brought the conclusion that he had been right. His main worry, that future use of the Beg-an-Fry area might be compromised, was dispelled when intelligence reported that the German naval authorities in St Malo had reprimanded the captain of the enemy patrol boat for firing on one of his own ships![1]

718's next operation, and the first on her own, was to break new ground. Ron Seddon discovered later that it resulted from an emergency request from the Norwegian authorities that as a matter of 'life and death' a specialist boat in clandestine operations should be sent north. So, on 24 May, 718 left Dartmouth and sailed up the west coast, staging at Holyhead and Fort William (both well known to the crew) for fuel, and negotiating the Caledonian Canal to Inverness before arriving at Lerwick early on 27 May after a passage of 850 miles. They were suprised and honoured to find that Captain Slocum had travelled north to see this new centre of operations and to brief Seddon on Operation Cygnus.

They sailed next day at 1511. This was a token of the urgent need for haste in this operation, as really they should have changed their fuel. There was a suspicion that they had taken on some water-contaminated petrol at Holyhead, but the risk was taken. On board were one of Slocum's specialist navigators (Lt M.P.

[1] *The Secret Navies*; Operation orders from CO 718.

Salmond RNR), a Norwegian Pilot (a Petty Officer) with local knowledge of the landing area, a Norwegian officer as interpreter, and a Norwegian boat's crew to back up 718's own stalwarts. They also had an additional 1,000 gallons of fuel on deck in cans, each holding 4½ gallons.

Their orders ('Top Secret') were 'to rescue Norwegian agents and civilians from Batalden Island'. A study of their charts revealed that Batalden was about 80 miles north of Bergen, and offshore of Floro and Nordfjord.

The passage was slowed by the need to top up the fuel tanks. This was a laborious process while under way on two engines, but by 0126 the ship was eighteen miles from the pin-point, speed was reduced to 14 knots and engines silenced. 718 always considered herself a lucky ship, and to Seddon's delight, visibility was down to below 5 miles due to fog – a valuable asset for secrecy, if not as helpful for navigation.

It was not known to Seddon and the crew until later that this approach to a well-defended enemy coast in daylight and with enemy air supremacy was regarded as extremely hazardous, and was only sanctioned because the agents and their civilian helpers were known to be in imminent danger of capture. So the fog was indeed miraculous.

The landfall was made accurately and with visibility then down to half a mile, Batalden Island was sighted, and the pin-point identified on the port bow. The Pilot took 718 in through rocks, and after an exchange of the correct identification signals – a great relief – a motor boat with a dinghy in tow was seen setting off towards the MTB. (This had been suggested in the operation orders, as to send in a boat would entail leaving behind evidence of the departure point.)

Soon the boat was alongside, the occupants helped aboard, and the motor boat scuttled. Once again the human aspect is best described by Charles Milner.

The party consisted of two Norwegian agents and a family of nine civilians who had been sheltering them and were fleeing to Lerwick as many other Norwegians had done. There were some young children and a couple of them were given bunks on the forward mess deck in view of the overcrowding in the wardroom. We were all touched by their helplessness and we looked after them as best we could: they would face exile from their homeland for an unknown period.

He adds that he has since met one of the agents and the five sons of the family in Norway, and knows that they returned home safely after VE Day. He discovered later that the family was that of the postmaster at Fario, on Batalden, and that their fate might indeed have been terrible had they not escaped.

718 was back in Lerwick by 1400 on 29 May. Congratulatory messages were received from ACOS (Admiral Commanding Orkney and Shetland) and from Captain Slocum. Seddon was fascinated to hear (fortunately after the operation) that it had been regarded as so hazardous that there had been a considerable expectation that 718 would not return!

What interested him even more – as a pointer to future operations – was that the agents told him that being to windward they did not hear the MTB's engines in the approach until she was within a quarter of a mile.[2]

718 returned a few days later to Dartmouth after her round trip of 2,500

[2] ROP from CO 718; material from Charles Milner.

miles, having been virtually isolated from the momentous events of D-Day. In fact, they were passing through Holyhead on 6 June, and arrived in Dartmouth during the afternoon of 7 June. They had expected a big welcome from the other boats of the flotilla after carrying out the first Norwegian operation, but (understandably) interest was focused elsewhere, and their return was an anticlimax for the crew!

At first they wondered whether the massive landings would make the flotilla redundant but that idea was soon dispelled. It was made clear that the 'escape line' from Brittany would be even more important with the huge increase in air strikes and the military operations ensuring an escalation in the number of possible evaders.

718's next expedition was on 15/16 June 1944 and was codenamed Operation Reflexion. This time, the objective was to land three agents at pin-point on a beach at Anse Cochet, known as 'Bonaparte', near the village of Plouha, about 12 miles north-west of St Brieuc. Once again it was tucked away among rocks and islands and it needed very exact navigation to find it. The night was dark, with an overcast sky, but sea conditions were good – unusual for this period of the fateful month of June 1944.

Seddon reached the distance off the pin-point at which he wanted to anchor at 0200, about three-quarters of a mile from the beach, and the surf boat party prepared to leave. The boat's party was Guy Hamilton, with Leading Seaman Albert Dellow and Able Seaman Hayward Rockwood, two strong and capable oarsmen. Hamilton carried a walkie-talkie radio and an RAF compass, and was told that his course for the beach was 215 degrees true. Five minutes after leaving at 0215, he tested communications and went out of sight heading on the right bearing. Then silence.

Those aboard 718 peered after them and settled down to wait, expecting a return in about thirty minutes. Seddon's report describes how very bad interference on the radio made it impossible to decipher a message at 0240, but he sent out 'homing' signals from 0230 to help Hamilton's return. In the intervening period, 718's anchor had begun to drag appreciably (not a good thing in such a tight anchorage), and more grass line had been veered, but it still would not hold. At 0245 it became necessary to start up, and expecting the boat's return at any moment, Seddon remained in position until he felt it necessary to ease slowly in towards the pin-point to help Hamilton's return. By this time, he was beginning to get really concerned – the boat was well overdue, and no radio messages were getting through. He wondered whether Hamilton had come to grief in some way, although as there had been no sounds or signs of trouble from the bearing of the pin-point, it was almost certainly not from the enemy. So taking a considerable risk, he eased silently and very slowly in to a mere four cables from the pin-point – but still no sign. Could the boat have missed them, and be further out to sea? Seddon risked a signal to seaward but there was no response. Next he tried a search further out, and signalled inshore, all to no avail.

Sick at heart, Seddon considered all his options. There was now not enough time to send another boat away, nor to go in again. He cursed the faulty radio. At 0350, mindful of the danger to his ship in a daylight return from so deep in enemy territory, he reluctantly abandoned the search and set out for Dartmouth.

Meanwhile, (as was learned later from Hamilton), the landing of the agents had actually gone very smoothly, in exactly the right place. Now all Hamilton had to do was to return to 718. He wrote later:

We rowed out for the right period of time, on the reciprocal course. No sign of the boat. Strange . . . either we weren't there, or the boat wasn't! Dellow and Rockwood sat listlessly over their oars, breathing heavily and eyeing me as if to say 'up to you now, chum!' Suddenly the silence was broken by the soft hum of engine noises well inshore of us – it had to be our 718. 'What the hell! Why inshore? Damn this . . . walkie-talkie!'

When we heard the engines inshore of us we just sat where we were – anyone who has tried to chase an MTB in a rowing boat will appreciate the point.

I flashed around . . . the engines gradually faded away . . . they had missed us, or we had missed them. Dellow knew it. Rocky knew it. I knew it. . . . We'd had it!

We headed for the nearest rocks, reaching them after a grim display of tired rowing and frayed tempers. I threw the walkie-talkie overboard in disgust. Dellow unloaded the gear and hid it. Rockwood filled the boat with rocks. I dug holes in the bottom with a jack knife, and broke one of my fingers doing it. I watched the boat sink.

From a naval point of view, the story seemed to have finished there. But it did not. Seven days later, Seddon was handed a signal which had come through from the Resistance: 'SAFE. BEACH CLEAR FOR FUTURE OPERATIONS. HAMILTON.'

And a further three weeks later, Seddon was a passenger in MGB 503 for a pick up from Plouha. He had heard that his three 'lost sheep' were to be among the group of 'evaders' to be brought off. His feelings when he welcomed them aboard were difficult to analyse. He said afterwards that he hoped he would never have a month like it again in all his life.

It is beyond the scope of this book to describe in detail what befell Hamilton and his two seamen even though it is a fascinating and most unusual story. But briefly, after avoiding a minefield, they made contact with the Resistance through a young girl, Marie Therese Le Calvez, and after some mistrust, were fed and sheltered and eventually added to those in the 'pipeline' of escaping prisoners of war. The fact that Guy Hamilton had fluent French was of great assistance.[3]

The period between the ill-fated, although actually successful, Operation Reflexion in mid-June and the next major clandestine mission in September was by no means idle. 718 was frequently sent over to France for minor tasks, including a visit to Courseuilles shortly after a base was established. There were exercises with MGB 502 from the Helford River, and a spell in Gillingham for a refit at the end of July. There followed, on 8/9 August, the last visit to Bonaparte Beach: the Germans had withdrawn from Plouha on the 4th. Guy Hamilton took a party ashore at first light, and was greeted by an excited French reception party who had been able to see the silhouette of 718 for the first time – a wonderful moment for them.

Operation Haven on 23 August saw 718 entering Lannion Bay in daylight, unsure if the enemy had left the area. They had, and the jubilant Resistance group were celebrating the liberation of Paris. An SAS party of twenty-seven were embarked for return to the UK. They had parachuted into Brittany on 4 August to join General Patten for the breakthrough at Avranches, and had coordinated the movements of the French Resistance with those of the US Army advancing towards Brest.

On 12 September, Operation Korda took

---

[3] ROP and additional material from CO 718; detail from Guy Hamilton in 1946.

A rare photograph in occupied France, June 1944. S/Lt Hamilton, L/Sea Dellow and A/B Rockwood of MTB 718 in a Brittany cornfield with the Ropers sisters. (Courtesy, C. Milner)

718 to L'Aber vrac'h, much further west, to photograph the coast. This area was now clear of enemy troops, and as preparations were being made for an assault on the island of Ushant, they took stores and equipment to the FFI (the French Forces of the Interior) who were busy mopping up pockets of resistance through western Brittany. The enemy garrisons in the ports of Brest, Lorient, and St Nazaire were holding on tenaciously. After a week in and around L'Aber vrac'h, 718 was sent round on 17 September to south-west Brittany with supplies to be landed at Benodet.

This operation was codenamed 'Knockout', and had both a lighter and darker side. 718 was welcomed in Benodet by the civilians and the Resistance forces who were delighted to receive the arms she brought. On the way round the coast, she was fired on by German forces in the area of Audierne. Lt Seddon was persuaded by the Resistance commanders, who were due shortly to attack the garrison there, to sail close to Audierne on the return voyage to Dartmouth, and to bombard it 'to soften up the opposition for them'. This he did to good effect after carrying out photographic reconnaissance. 718 was hit by several shells, one of which penetrated a petrol tank (fortunately full and self-sealing, therefore not causing an explosion) while another made a mess of the CO's cabin. The return was delayed to ensure there was no danger from the fumes, and 718 sailed safely to Dartmouth. Shortly after, the news that Audierne had been cleared of its garrison was received.[4]

4 ROP from CO 718.

October was spent on detached duty at Newhaven, and 718 did a number of runs to Dieppe and Ostend, both recently liberated.

At the end of the month there was another call to return to Scotland and Norway for an operation more suited to their specialized role. This was carried out from Aberdeen, and was codenamed Operation Aquarius 2. The objective was to bring four Norwegian agents back to UK from a pin-point near Egersund, on Skarvoy Island, not far south of Stavanger, a passage of nearly 300 miles for which additional fuel was carried in jerry cans. After Operation Cygnus, Seddon had applied his mind to find a more efficient method of topping up the tanks. On that long haul he had found that spillage had been wasteful and potentially dangerous, and the system of emptying individual cans very slow. He had recommended that using a cutaway 40-gallon drum with a fuelling pipe would speed up the process and be more efficient. So it proved to his entire satisfaction. For this operation, a Norwegian 'Pilot' was carried, but the navigation was in the hands of 718's Navigator, Sub-Lt John Townend.

718 left Aberdeen at 0700 on 2 November, and Seddon's comment was that the weather was lovely for the Norwegian sea in November – but not for clandestine operations. The visibility was extreme and the coast was sighted at a distance of 32 miles. The sky had cleared, and with the dusk, the moon shone brightly.

Seddon's report reveals just what a fine seaman and tactical thinker he was. He took every precaution for a silent approach, records meticulous awareness of distances and landmarks, and when the unexpected happened, he dealt with the situation calmly and with great skill. He was aware that not only would his course take him across the main coastal convoy route, but also that aircraft regularly patrolled the area from Stavanger, and that E-boats were based at Egersund.

So when he sighted a convoy at Green 20°, crossing his course some 8 miles ahead, he was prepared. He stopped and lay bows on to the convoy to present a minimum silhouette. Much would depend on the alertness of the escort, which appeared to be an M class minesweeper and a trawler ahead, and two trawlers astern.

At 2224, the two trawlers turned towards 718 and challenged with the letter 'L' – at 7 miles range! Quietly Seddon started outer engines on underwater silencers and eased away westward. When he found that the trawlers were moving with him, he increased speed and opened the range still further. At 2250, the 'M' fired star-shell. Seddon remarks rather caustically that they were very ineffective, bursting a long way astern: 'the moon was a far better illuminant!'

He watched the trawlers rejoin the convoy and it began to move away from his destination area. He stopped and waited, reasoning that if aircraft were called out it would be within forty minutes. He was desperately anxious not to give any indication of his aiming point, which could easily compromise the beach, so was prepared to move further out and wait patiently.

The expected Dornier flying boat arrived at 2350, and flew inshore up and down three times. 718 was stopped, in order not to display any wake, but had power so that anti-aircraft fire could be opened if she was attacked. By 0115 it seemed safe to proceed, but as an additional precaution, Seddon set a course to the southward of the pin-point to disguise his objective, and to keep out of range of the radar station at Obrestad.

From then on, all went well. The Norwegian Pilot confirmed Townend's navigation, and they moved towards the

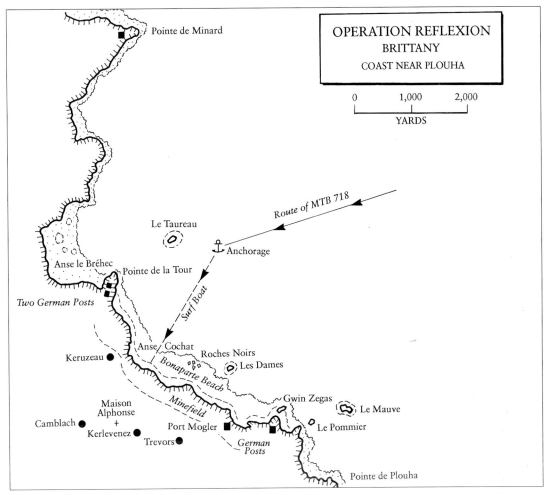

MTB 718 – Operation Reflexion, Brittany.

beach. Hestnes Light, three-quarters of a mile to the south, provided efficient floodlighting, and there were the four men on the beach, responding correctly to the identification challenge. Hamilton and his crew moved in to pick them up, and by 0415 they were aboard and 718 was away.

They still had to negotiate the busy shipping route, and there, sure enough, was another convoy. Seddon increased speed to 25 knots well ahead of it, and they showed no signs of being interested. He wondered whether they thought 718 was a E-boat from Egersund.

The weather deteriorated badly by midday, but Aberdeen was reached at 1830. There were three subsequent points of interest. First, Seddon learned from the agents that shortly before 718 arrived, an E-boat passed the pin-point and they only just refrained in time from signalling to it! Then, having made a number of very acute observations about equipment in his report, he was delighted to receive specific assurances from DDOD(I) that they had been noted, and that orders had been issued. And lastly, there was a signal from Captain

Slocum congratulating Seddon and 718 on 'your completion of "Aquarius", which appears to have been a copy-book example of a faultlessly executed operation'.[5]

There followed three months of mundane duties from Newhaven, mainly passages for a variety of purposes to Dieppe and Ostend. It was not until the beginning of February that 718 was summoned again to resume operations in Norway, and directed in the first place to Lerwick. This proved to have been a very misguided order as, on arrival, she was sent to Aberdeen for two reasons: firstly, because the agents who were to be involved in the next operation were there, and secondly, because the sea voyage involved was far shorter from Aberdeen than from Lerwick.

Unfortunately, on the passage south, 718 met terrible weather. Two Force 8 gales, which had not been forecast, made this one of the worst voyages she had ever had to endure. Most of the crew were very sick, and the boat suffered considerable damage to the watertight hatches, hull and electrical gear. Most, but not all of the damage was made good at Aberdeen, and it was certainly not a good preparation for Operation Lola, which was planned for 12 February 1945.

The object of this operation was to land two Norwegian agents and 1½ tons of stores on the island of Sando, along the southern coast of Norway a few miles west of Kristiansand, with the intention that they would set up an observation post and W/T station. It was to be the longest operation ever carried out by 718, and in addition to the agents, she carried a Norwegian Pilot (an officer from the Norwegian 54th Flotilla at Lerwick), and 2,000 gallons of petrol in jerry cans, together with an extra Norwegian surf boat.

5 ROP from CO 718; letters from Captain Slocum.

Charles Milner, the Telegraphist, brings a very human touch to a description of the hazards of this operation:

Before we left, Lt Seddon called the crew together to brief us. He said this was to be a very long and hazardous trip, that the weather forecast was not favourable, and that our pin-point was again on the 'wrong side' of a busy convoy route. We had to be prepared for the fact that there was a chance that the ship might not get back; if we were left ashore, we should try to make for neutral Sweden. We were issued with printed notices in Norwegian and English to help us make contact with Allied sympathisers. One had to select a likely looking native, point to the Norwegian translation, e.g., 'I am English' and 'Are there any Germans or Quislings anywhere near?' and 'I must sleep, where can I find a place to rest?' . . . and then hope for the best!

The CO split us up into 'escape groups' of three, to make sure we didn't travel in large numbers.

It is, I think, an indication of his sureness of touch with the crew that he raised a laugh when he added, 'However, all is not black. There is a shortage of young men in this particular part of Norway, and I have it on excellent authority that the girls are definitely sex-starved!'

I wondered just how this priceless piece of Naval intelligence had been researched, and I suppose we all contemplated our prospective overland journey to the Swedish border, waving our pieces of paper at potential helpers and passing from the arms of one eager Nordic maiden anxious to serve the Allied cause in a practical way, to the arms of the next!

MTB 718 in a Norwegian fjord. (Courtesy, C. Milner)

The operation, if it did not conclude in that particular way, turned out to be as hazardous as predicted, but mainly through that old worst enemy, the sea.

Seddon's report reveals both the problems that arose and his meticulous care over navigation and every aspect of the execution of the operation. He notes each landmark as sighted, the reduction of speed and the change to underwater silencers. He describes the horrors of fuelling under way in a gale – a process which lasted two and a half hours. The landfall after 200 miles was confirmed by a fix on lighthouses revealing the position to be very close to planned track. Snow squalls began to complicate navigation and rock dodging. Conditions were so bad that the Norwegian Pilot recommended abandoning the operation and returning to Aberdeen: many of the crew, and the two agents suffering badly from seasickness,

would readily have agreed, but not Seddon. They identified the island of Sando, and felt their way gingerly up the east coast until they believed they had arrived at the pin-point (twenty-six hours after they had left Aberdeen).

They anchored 50 yd off shore, and Seddon sent Hamilton in with one of the agents to see if landing was possible. However, they thought the swell made it too hazardous. They raised anchor, and felt their way again, using the leadline, to the north-west of the island, protected from the swell. Hamilton and the agent found a suitable beach, and the redoubtable Hayward Rockwood (the Newfoundlander who had once been left behind in Brittany) suffered total immersion in the ice-cold sea, leaping ashore to drag the surf boat in.

The unloading of stores took two hours, and they left the agents in poor shape from seasickness and lack of sleep, but finally departed at 0400 to repeat the navigational nightmare through the rocks and islands in snow squalls until they were out over the convoy route and away. In his report, the CO paid tribute to the skilled navigation of his young Navigator, Sub-Lt O'Brien. In the deeper waters of the Skaggerak the sea and swell were only slight, but once in the North Sea conditions deteriorated rapidly, and they were ploughing into a westerly gale and rough seas at a maximum speed of 6–8 knots all day. The W/T was out of action from sea water, the forward bilges were filling up as the pounding opened seams, and the rising water in the engine room covered the 24-volt batteries. It was a dreadful night, but eventually, at 0710, they sighted land, and entered Aberdeen at 0830 on 15 February. They had been at sea for fifty-eight hours in very harrowing conditions.

It was typical of Captain Slocum that soon after, he wrote two personal letters to Seddon, the first to congratulate him on his success in a very difficult operation, and the second to tell him that the potentially very important W/T station was now operating and likely to be completely successful.[6]

718 spent some time in dock and under repair in Frazerburgh after this gruelling expedition, and the crew had a short spell of leave for each watch.

It was 6 April before their next operation was planned, and once again it was from Aberdeen, this time to the pin-point at Skarvoy Island near Egersund, which had been used for Operation Aquarius 2 in November. The codename was 'Selma', and the objective was to land two agents and a ton of stores.

When 718 approached the Norwegian coast, there was thick fog, and considerable difficulties with navigation, but it soon became apparent that the enemy were very much on the alert in the area. 718 was only 200 yd from Egeroy Light (very close to the pin-point), when it was suddenly switched on, giving everyone on board a great shock. Shortly after, searchlights began sweeping the area. Seddon did not feel any danger to his boat, as the fog was preventing any visual sighting, but he became convinced that the enemy was aware of their presence. He consulted the agents, and alternative plans were discussed, but all agreed that to land the agents in such circumstances would place them at considerable risk. The operation was therefore abandoned, and postponed.

It was rearranged for 13 April. This time weather conditions were much more favourable, and navigation proved trouble free, with numerous sightings of recognizable landmarks, identified by the Norwegian Pilot, a Leading Seaman from the 54th Flotilla who came from the area.

The two agents, who had in fact operated in this area before (they were two of the four who had been taken off in November), suddenly suggested a slight alteration in the pin-point, and Guy Hamilton took them in to check the practicalities of landing. After rowing round to another beach, the decision was made and the landing of men and stores promptly and quietly made in flat calm. The agents waved them farewell in excellent spirits.

Even on such an uneventful mission, the sea had the last laugh. In the last five hours of the passage home, the wind increased dramatically, eventually to a Force 7 south-easterly, and gave 718 a very uncomfortable quartering sea to take her back to Aberdeen by 1600.[7]

---

6 ROP from CO 718; notes from Charles Milner.

7 ROP from CO 718.

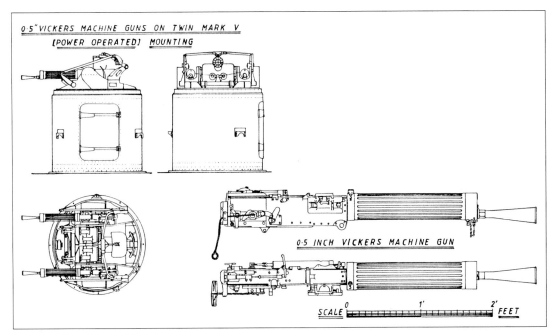

0·5" VICKERS MACHINE GUNS ON TWIN MARK V [POWER OPERATED] MOUNTING

0·5 INCH VICKERS MACHINE GUN

SCALE 0 1' 2' FEET

Rear elevation of gun. (Courtesy, John Lambert)

718's last clandestine mission was named Operation Barbro 3 on 28 April 1945, only a few days before VE Day. There was an urgent request for stores and W/T equipment to be landed at a watch post near Stokkevaag on the island of Stensundo, very close to Batalden where Operation Cygnus had been mounted in May 1944. The Report of Proceedings is not available, but clearly the expedition was successful. Charles Milner remembers the agents who received the stores coming on board to thank the CO and crew, and shaking hands all round, cheerfully adding, 'see you again in a week or two when it's all over!'

He also recalls that in Lerwick when it was announced that the following day, 8 May, would be 'VE Day', there was much celebrating with the Norwegians, and that 718 then set off for Aberdeen. As luck would have it they met very bad weather and as usual, seasickness laid many low but the arrival of the signal 'Splice the Mainbrace' at about midday had a magic effect![8]

The story of 718 in the last year of the war is quite different from that of most of the Dog Boats, but without doubt has deserved a place in this history of the class. Their distinguished achievements were quite properly recognized by the list of awards announced in the *London Gazette* on 11 December 1945.

DSC: Lt Ronald Franklin Seddon.
DSC: Lt Mervyn Ian Guy Hamilton.
DSM: POMM William Robert Cartwright.
DSM: L/Sea Albert Edward Dellow.
DSM: L/Tel Charles William Milner.
DSM: L/Sea Cyril Albert Stanley.

There is a sad postscript to the story of the 15th MGB Flotilla, which although it does not

[8] Notes from R. Seddon and C. Milner.

directly concern a Dog Boat, does relate to a distinguished former CO of MGB 607, Lt R.M. Marshall DSC, the pre-war rugby international, who had later commanded 503 in the 15th Flotilla in many clandestine missions.

When 718 returned to Aberdeen on VE Day, the crew discovered to their astonishment that several of the flotilla (the Camper and Nicholsons 502, 503 and 509) had just arrived there with the expectation of being used for numerous intelligence tasks on the Norwegian coast, and even to Sweden. They had just been renumbered as 2002, 2003 and 2009, and, very shortly, 2002 was dispatched to visit Gothenburg. By a stroke of fate, Lt Mike Marshall took temporary command of 2002 although he was actually the CO of 2009 and had recently become SO of the flotilla, and promoted Lieutenant Commander. The other boats of the flotilla began to get worried when after two days no signals were received from 2002.

Seddon in 718 requested permission to go to search for her. This was granted, and he set off following the course she would have taken. 718 found herself in an area where mines, which had been cut adrift by the Germans, were all around. They searched for two days to no avail.

On 16 May, the news came through that two survivors had been picked up after four days on a raft. PO/MM T. Sheehan and A/B N.T.J. Hine DSM were in a bad way, suffering from exposure, but they were able to confirm that 2002 had been sunk by a mine on 12 May at the entrance to the Skagerrak, and the gallant Mike Marshall and the rest of the crew had perished tragically five days after the end of the war. (Appendix 1, Note 27)

The wreckage of 2002 was subsequently found by a Norwegian fishing boat.

This history of Dog Boat operations now concludes with the final section of Mediterranean activities, largely concentrated in the Adriatic. There, too, the tragedy of boats lost, like 2002, to mines, rather than in direct action with the enemy, was to become all too familiar.

CHAPTER 10

MEDITERRANEAN OPERATIONS

The Dog Boat flotillas in the Mediterranean in July 1944 were at the beginning of a new phase. With the transfer of the 56th Flotilla to the Adriatic, all the boats were now concentrated there.

In practice, the losses over the previous fifteen months had reduced the total number of available Dog Boats from the original thirty-two to only twenty-three, and CCF Mediterranean took advantage of an opportunity created by the departure of Lt Cdr Tom Fuller, the SO of the 61st Flotilla (who had returned to Canada), to disband the 61st Flotilla and over the next few weeks to redistribute the boats to the other three flotillas, which were all under strength.

MGB 658 at the base at Manfredonia.

This was not as drastic a step as it might seem, as the boats had been operating in mixed units without particular reference to flotilla allegiance for some time. In any case the ravages of action and continuous operations were necessitating the withdrawal of boats from time to time to Malta, Brindisi or Manfredonia for repairs, and for a planned programme of major improvements.

So although some of the dispositions were delayed until boats returned from such refits, the new flotillas were eventually as below.

56th MTB/MGB Flotilla (SO: Lt Cdr J.D. Maitland DSC RCNVR, no longer all-Canadian COs): MTB 633 (Lt A.S. Rendell RCNVR), MGB 642 (Lt. E.F. Smyth DSC), MGB 649 (Lt P. Hughes SANFV), MTB 655 (Lt C. MacLachlan RCNVR), MGB 657 (Lt Cdr J.D. Maitland DSC RCNVR), MGB 658 (Lt C. Burke DSC RCNVR), MGB 663 (Lt T.E. Ladner DSC RCNVR).

57th MTB/MGB Flotilla (SO: Lt Cdr T.J. Bligh DSC): MTB 634 (Lt W.E.A. Blount DSC), MTB 637 (Lt R.C. Davidson DSC), MTB 638 (Lt D.H. Lummis), MGB 659 (Lt P.D. Barlow), MGB 660 (Lt A.T. Robinson), MGB 662 (Lt Cdr T.J. Bligh DSC), MTB 670 (Lt E. Hewitt), MGB 674 (Lt M.G. Bowyer).

60th MTB/MGB Flotilla (SO: Lt Cdr B.L. Bourne): MGB 643 (Lt D.G.E. Bird RNZNVR), MGB 645 (Lt P.G. Martin RNR), MGB 646 (Lt B.L. Knight-Lachlan), MGB 647 (Lt M. Mountstephens DSC) MTB 651 (Lt L.H. Ennis), MTB 656 (Lt W.H. Masson), MGB 661 (Lt R.M. Cole), MTB 667 (Lt C.J. Jerram DSC).

In August, operations were all based on Komiza, although it was not long before they were to move on further north. More

MGB 658 alongside at Komiza, Vis, in August 1944.

berthing space was made, and boats not alongside would lie to buoys in the harbour under the cliffs. The pace of operations was therefore able to be stepped up, and there were notable successes throughout the month for the Dog Boats.

The first unit of the 56th to arrive in Komiza on 30 July was immediately involved in a complex combined operation that took 657 (Maitland), 667 (Jerram), 663 (Ladner) and 658 (Reynolds, the First Lieutenant, in temporary command) for three consecutive nights as a covering force for Operation Decomposed Two. The object was to cause damage and casualities to the enemy positions and garrison at Korcula, and in the town of Orebic on the mainland of the Peljesac Peninsula, less than a mile away across the narrow strait from Korcula itself.

In common with most garrisons in Dalmatia, the Germans had been forced to retire inside a heavily defended and wired perimeter. From this they sent out strong patrols at frequent intervals to keep control over the surrounding areas, and to prevent concentration of Partisan forces.

In Orebic there was a coast defence battery with a number of 105-mm guns, and Korcula Harbour was a busy port of call for the German coastal convoys. These moved only at night and waited by day in ports under the protection of shore anti-aircraft guns. The area had been well surveyed by a reconnaissance team of two Royal Artillery officers who disguised themselves as peasant girls and moved into the area picking grapes in the vineyards. They had confirmed that excellent targets were available.

The naval part of the operation involved covering the landing of the observation officers on the first night, then escorting landing craft to a cove on the island of Lagosta on the second, and then shepherding the landing of a battery of eight 25-pdrs on

the south coast of Korcula before dawn. The actual bombardment went like clockwork, with the enemy totally unaware of the source of the fire, being confused by the decoy run of an LCI sporting a canvas funnel to simulate a destroyer just beyond the range of the Orebic battery. To complete a truly tri-service operation, the bombardment was followed by a strike from the Hurricanes based on Vis. None of the Dog Boats were called upon to take any aggressive action, but they were continuously at sea for each of the three consecutive days.[1]

The real significance of this comparatively small attack was that it was later known to have been the first of a series which led, a few weeks later, to a gradual withdrawal northward of the enemy.

On 7/8 August, Tim Bligh in his own boat MGB 662 led MTBs 667 (Jerram) and 670 (Hewitt) northward to their patrol area off Vir Island, north of Zara. It was a fine calm night, with visibility at about 1½ miles. Soon after 2200, a convoy of three ships was sighted approaching from the south. As they got nearer, Bligh identified them as a small escort and two F-Lighters. Remembering how little success the Dog Boats had previously had when using torpedoes against F-Lighters, he decided to attack first with guns. He opened fire at 2216 at 350 yd range, but even as his first salvo hit the leading F-Lighter, she opened fire very accurately and scored immediate hits, putting one of 662's engines out of action and damaging another, starting a fire and causing ten casualties straight away. But 662's gunners did not waver. With those of 667, in close station, they poured a concentrated and accurate return fire on the F-Lighter, which presently burst into flames with guns silenced.

Events followed each other with almost lightning rapidity. At 2218, the second

---

[1] Report by SNOVIS (Lt Cdr Morgan Giles).

F-Lighter seemed to be trying to escape, and Bligh ordered 670 to attack her with torpedoes. Hewitt found that he had a real problem, as the target turned right round to the southward and started to steal away without firing any guns. He hastily manoeuvred, turning short round, adjusted his torpedo sight and at 2226 sank the target with one torpedo, becoming (according to Bligh later), the first Mediterranean Dog Boat to sink a moving F-Lighter with a Mark IV torpedo.

662 was in real trouble. Phosphorous fires were spreading in pockets all over the boat, and the engine room fire had been so severe that the methyl-bromide extinguishers had to be used, requiring evacuation of the engine room. The motor mechanics went below again rather earlier than they should have done, and started one engine to allow 662 to hobble away to avoid the shore batteries which had opened up. The two MTBs used their three remaining torpedoes trying to sink the first burning F-Lighter but failed to hit. However, by midnight, gunfire finished the task and she sank.

They took seventeen prisoners, and later interrogation revealed that the boats had sunk F963, armed with one 88-mm, a quadruple 20-mm, twin 20-mm, and two singles, even more heavily armed than a Dog MGB, and F968, also with an 88-mm but without the quadruple and twin 20-mm. Bligh commented later that in his view the crews of the F-Lighters (perfectly capable of outgunning Dog Boats with their lethal 88-mm) sometimes seemed to lose confidence and fail to press home their advantage. Perhaps the fact that their gun positions were heavily protected with armour and reinforced concrete led too strongly to a sense of self-preservation and affected the gunnery.[2]

[2] Summary of actions; CFPR July/August 1944; Information from T.J. Bligh.

It was not long after this that, after nine fruitless patrols, the boats of the 56th Flotilla met the enemy. By this time, the three boats available were the long standing partnership of 657, 658 and 663 – all still gunboats, and commanded by the three old friends from Vancouver. After something like twenty actions together over eighteen months, Maitland, Burke and Ladner had built up an uncanny understanding.

The action of 17/18 August was later called the 'Battle of the Mljet Channel', and the story has been told many times. In particular, the author in his book, *Gunboat 658*, was able to give a very detailed personal account of the six stages of an action which lasted over five hours. Since that was written, and through the good offices of the distinguished naval commander and historian, Vice-Admiral Sir Peter Gretton KCB CB DSO OBE DSC MA, it has been possible to secure a great deal more information from German sources, and to have a far clearer picture of the events of that long night.

It began with the task of landing two Royal Marine commandos on the north-west corner of Mljet Island. This was soon followed by the detection of a unit of four or five fast targets moving north-westward. From their speed they could only have been E-boats, which had rarely been encountered for many months in the Adriatic. This detection was possible because 657 was now equipped with an American radar set. This had a constantly revolving aerial within a dome on a short mast, feeding to a PPI screen on which echoes were displayed at astonishing ranges with pin-points of light. These in turn gave precise bearings and enabled accurate assessments of course and speed. 657 had been the first Dog Boat to secure one of these sets; this was entirely due to the very close relationships between the 56th Flotilla and the PT boats in

The twin Oerlikon, SO Radar, port single Oerlikon and the bridge .303 guns.

Bastia. After months of subtle negotiations, lubricated somewhat by a transfer of a quantity of Scotch whisky, the USN had agreed to this loan, which was later to lead to more and more boats being similarly provided on a far more official basis. But at this time 657 was the only boat in the Adriatic to be so well equipped, and the set proved its worth on this night.

Maitland gave chase, hoping for a chance to do battle with E-boats, but was hopelessly outstripped for speed. But by 2300, the unit was well placed, stopped close under the Peljesac cliffs not far from the narrow entrance to the Mljet Channel through which any convoy from Split would have to move south-eastward towards Dubrovnik. Within minutes, the radar detected a convoy moving towards them from the north-east at about 3 miles range. As it closed, it appeared to consist of three larger ships and a number of smaller craft.

Maitland allowed the convoy to close to 300 yd, confident that his unit was invisible against the wooded cliff. And so it proved. Total surprise was achieved as 663 was ordered to fire star-shell, and the three gunboats moved out to attack, running slowly along the line and opening fire on each target in turn. As ever, the close station-keeping allowed the broadside of three 40-mm, ten 20-mm and three 6-pdrs to have immediate effect. But the two largest vessels, apparently mastless schooners with raised gun platforms and quite heavily armed, soon replied effectively, and although the last boat in line, an I-boat (small escort vessel) was clearly sunk, when the Dogs checked at the end of the run to reload, both 657 and 658 had been hit. 657 had a small fire on deck, which was quickly extinguished, but 658 had been hit in the engine room by a 37-mm shell; there was a large hole in the ship's side and three engines stopped. 658's veteran Motor Mechanic Bill Last worked like a demon and although clearly the two port engines were out for the night, he got the starboard inner going, and Burke was able to report to the SO that he could continue on two engines.

The initial run had revealed that the convoy consisted of at least six ships, two of which were clearly schooners adapted as gun coasters, two barges and two I-boats. Maitland at first thought there were two more, and believed one of the barges was an F-Lighter, but the enemy report reveals that the schooners were the *Jota* and the *Dora*, armed with several 37-mm and 20-mm guns; the *Helga* and *Peter*, both tanker barges; and two I-boats (I68 and I48). The E-boats previously detected were indeed four of the 3rd E-boat Flotilla S58, 57, 60 and 30, and they were there as 'remote escorts'. It is very strange that soon after they left Dubrovnik, the SO's boat S33 had engine trouble, and returned to base. Instead of transferring to another boat, the SO went back with her and handed over the unit to the CO of S60, for which he was later very understandably sharply criticized by 'Group South' (Admiral Fricke). More will be heard of this flotilla later.

The second attack run began just before midnight, and was from seaward of the convoy on a parallel course. This left the enemy boats silhouetted against the bush fires that their own gunfire had caused during the first run. The schooners opened heavy fire but fortunately most of it was high and only inflicted slight damage. The smaller vessels in

the rear were again hit hard, and one was almost certainly sunk.

Once more the gunboats got well ahead, reloaded, and attacked again at 0035, and this time the second schooner (the *Dora*) was set on fire and soon after blew up. The first schooner (the *Jota*) turned sharply in towards the cliffs.

At this stage, the convoy, or what was left of it, had scattered, and Maitland hunted the ships for the next three and a half hours, circling and illuminating the coastline. At about 0150 the schooner *Jota* was found and set on fire, finally exploding at 0325. Hampered by false radar echoes so close to the shore, it took time to find the missing oil tanker, but at 0250 she was found and sunk. The unit could find no evidence of any movement in the original direction of the convoy, so retraced its steps until it reached the position of the first attack, where the bush fire was still burning fiercely. At 0400, although no target could be seen, heavy fire was opened from the shore which was, and remained, a mystery. By this time ammu-nition was very low, and the fire ashore was putting the unit in a vulnerable position, so Maitland withdrew. Both 657 and 658 had sustained a number of 37-mm and 20-mm hits.

The claims that Maitland, after discussion with Burke and Ladner, made in his report turned out to be accurate except in one respect: they all believed that an E-boat had been involved in the second attack and sunk. The German report confirms that both the *Jota* and the *Dora* and I48 of the close escort were sunk, and the oil tanker *Peter* left burnt out, to be finished off by Hurricanes next morning. The oil tanker *Helga* and I68 were damaged but hid right inshore and did eventually get back to Korcula.

The activities of the four E-boats are shrouded in mystery, but clearly the boats were so lacking in aggression that the

Lt T.E. Ladner, Lt Cdr J.D. Maitland (first V56) and Lt Cdr C. Burke (Second V56) return to Vancouver. (Courtesy, C. Burke)

German report says, 'strong criticism was levelled at them, as they failed to provide any effective protection for the convoy . . . they were unable to locate the convoy until the action was observed to commence, some 6,500 yards away at about 2335, and they then stood off for virtually the whole of the engagement because they were unable to distinguish friend from foe!'

Whether 'virtually' implies one sally is uncertain. The report unsatisfactorily concludes, 'the E-boats suffered no losses' – an unnecessary statement if they were never close enough to become involved, so perhaps they were, and Maitland was right.

This action has been given close attention for three reasons. Firstly, the availability of the detailed enemy report reveals much about the morale of the 3rd E-boat Flotilla at the time, and the enhanced state of the makeshift escorts. Secondly, there was no doubt that both Morgan-Giles (SNOVIS) and CCF saw this success as very significant. In forwarding the report, Captain Stevens commented:

This action may well be described as a peak performance by the 56th Flotilla with its all-Canadian COs under the magnificent leadership of Lt Cdr J.D. Maitland DSC RCNVR. That he was faultlessly followed by Lt C. Burke DSC and Lt T.E. Ladner is clear from the Report, and to one who knows them is almost to state the obvious . . . this was teamwork of the highest order.

In conclusion, it is thought that this action may be described as the shrewdest blow that the enemy has suffered on the Dalmatian Coast and may well have speeded his evacuation of the islands.

In fact, that evacuation was to begin in earnest very shortly after.

The third – and very poignant – reason is that with the advantage of hindsight, the action turned out to be the last time the 'Three Musketeers' operated together, as both 657 and 663 were sunk by mines shortly afterwards.[3]

For Ladner and 663, there was no respite. A unit was required on the next night, 18/19 August, and they were out again in the same area: clearly intelligence predicted another convoy. The unit of three MGBs was led by Peter Barlow in 659, with Tom Ladner in 663, and 643 (with a New Zealander Lt D.G.E. Bird newly in command), and sure enough they intercepted five E-boats in the Mljet Channel, and were able to attack before the E-boats could escape. They caught one and sank it. Once again, the German report explains the circumstances.

S33, 58, 57, 60 and 30 sailed from Dubrovnik as escorts to a group of I-boats which had been sent to search for survivors of the previous night's attack, and were once again intercepted by MGBs. S57 (Lt Buschmann) received at least twenty 40-mm hits in her engine room and was quickly reduced to a flaming shambles, and was scuttled to prevent capture.[4]

As had been predicted, September saw the beginning of the withdrawal of German garrisons not only from the southern Dalmatian Islands, but also from Greece and the Aegean islands.

There were at this time sufficient Dog Boats to spread them more widely in view of

3 MO11267; ROP at PRO in ADM 199/268 and 269; enemy report from NHB; personal description from author (present in 658).

4 MO11260; ROP at PRO in ADM 199/268 and 269; *German Coastal Forces in WW2*.

the ever-changing situation, and a decision was made to send two units from Brindisi into the Corfu Channel – a move obviously prompted by intelligence reports. One unit was from the 57th Flotilla, led by Tim Bligh (662, 674, 637 and 634), and the other from the 56th, but in the absence of Maitland chasing spares for his SO radar, it was led by Basil Bourne, the SO of the 60th, who travelled with Burke in 658.

For both units, these operations involved a long passage by daylight, a long patrol with its probability of action, and then a long return. In fact, the 56th did not meet the enemy, but the 57th did, and they were in the more distant area off Cephalonia.

The boats, which left on 3 September, met a convoy of small schooners and lighters and expended a very large amount of ammunition in sinking seven boats and taking eighteen

prisoners. In all when they got back to Brindisi they had been under way for a total of 47 hours and covered 535 miles.

There was, at this time, a new development in the Adriatic. For the first time a base was established in the north of Italy. Following up the Army advance a new mobile base was able to reach Ancona, and it brought immediate benefits, especially as shortly after this, Komiza on Vis began to be too far behind the main centres of action as the Germans were driven north. Ancona was a big port with good facilities, and it put the head of the Adriatic (Venice, Trieste, and the west coast of the Istrian Peninsula) within range of operations. Several Dog Boats of the 56th were dispatched there straight away after the Corfu operations, and were launched into anti-E-boat patrols along the swept channel off the coast towards Venice.

MGB 657 showing the deck curled upwards after a mine blew the stern off.

The Eighth Army were held up about 50 miles north of Ancona, and fleet destroyers were sent up to assist the bombardment behind enemy lines. E-boats and aircraft had the nasty habit of laying mines after the channel had been swept.

It was on the fourth night of these patrols, on 11/12 September, that 657 was mined. Her stern was blown off and the deck peeled back as though a giant smoothing plane had taken a large shaving against the grain. The after bulkhead held and it was possible for 633 (Rendell) and 658 (Reynolds) to tow her back to Ancona and deposit her in an ever-growing 'graveyard' of damaged boats. She was declared 'CTL' (constructive total loss) and her very distinguished commission had ended with cruel abruptness. Maitland, who had not been aboard, was devastated, and mourned the loss of five missing members of his crew. He handed over the flotilla to 'Corny' Burke, who was promoted, and was himself appointed Staff Officer (Operations) to the SNO Northern Adriatic (SNONA), Captain N. Vincent Dickinson, who had been SOIS in Bastia.

Meanwhile, the enemy evacuation of the islands was proceeding apace, assisted by commando and Partisan landings. Korcula, Mljet and Hvar had all been taken, and Brac was on the way. Burke's first success as V56 (the signal form of 'SO 56th Flotilla') came on the night of 22/23 September when he embarked in 655 (now commanded by Campbell MacLachlan) with 633 (Rendell). It was a 'flap' patrol and the orders were to prevent the evacuation of the island of Sulet (also known as Solta), which had an important strategic position not far off Split. They arrived at exactly the right moment, as three I-boats emerged from Rogac Cove, and immediately engaged them and sank all three. They were carrying equipment and guns from the garrison, and about 200 men.

Next day, Burke received a signal from SNOVIS which read:

The Royal Marine Commandos today occupied Rogac and Grohote. They have sent the following message for you: 'Complete Combined Op. Royal Navy and Army in the right place at the right time. Well done the Navy – thanks and congratulations from all ranks. CO 43rd RM Commando.' It appears that the three I-boats you sank last night contained the whole garrison of Solta. Well done indeed.[5]

Operations continued both in the more northerly islands of Dalmatia, and northward from Ancona towards Venice. On 8/9 October, 642 (E.F. Smyth, SO for the night) and 655 (MacLachlan) were patrolling off Maestra Point just south of Venice. They met two schooners and attacked at 150 yd range, and left one sinking (its keel out of the water) and the other on fire. After two runs, two more schooners were seen approaching from the north, and both were attacked. When the enemy's fire had completely ceased, one was boarded and found to be abandoned, and the other was clearly badly damaged. At this stage, 655's radar operator (whose 291 set had performed very well all night) reported two large echoes to the NNE at 7,000 yd, and almost immediately, star-shell broke overhead and two large ships, presumed to be destroyers, were seen approaching at high speed, firing heavy calibre shells which were close to hitting. 642 had suffered casualties and three of her guns were out of action, so the unit withdrew southward and returned to Ancona.

It had been a successful patrol and was particularly pleasing as Ted Smyth, the CO of

5 MO12829; ROP at PRO in ADM 199/268 and 269; signal from SNOVIS.

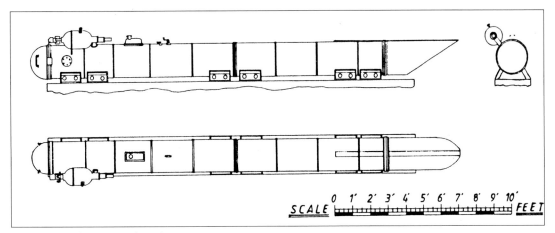

SCALE 0 1' 2' 3' 4' 5' 6' 7' 8' 9' 10' FEET

The 21-in torpedo tube. (Courtesy, John Lambert)

MGB 642, had not long returned to the fray, joining the 56th Flotilla after many months recovering from wounds. He had had a distinguished record in short gunboats on the east coast in 1941–2, and had, as CO of 637, been involved with Stewart Gould in his last and classic action off Cap Bon in April 1943, and shortly after had been wounded when taking SOIS into Bizerta.[6]

On the next night (9/10 October) a unit returned to the same area, led by Basil Bourne with 649 and 663. It was 663's first patrol ever without Tom Ladner in command, and by a quirk of fate was to be her last. The boats were returning at 18 knots from the area of Venice, having had a fruitless night, when a mine exploded midships beneath 663. There was no way in which she could be saved, and three of her crew were killed and eight wounded.

So, only four weeks after the mining of 657, the 56th had lost 663 as well, and the legend of the 'Three Musketeers', boats and COs, who had operated together countless times through the Sicily campaign and from

Maddalena and Bastia, was no more. Tom Ladner had just been appointed as SOO (Staff Officer, Operations) to CCF in Malta and he felt the loss of 663 very keenly. She had been renowned as a highly efficient boat, always ready for operations, and with a record second to none in action.

But war continued relentlessly, and only two days later, on 11/12 October, Tim Bligh took four boats of his 57th Flotilla into an action off Vir Island, north of Zara, which by its results and by the significance of the challenge it presented to the heavily armed F-Lighters, has frequently been referred to as the finest Coastal Forces action of the war.

It has been described in detail in both *Flag 4* and *The Battle of the Torpedo Boats*, and each had the advantage of a beautifully written report by Bligh. Indeed, that report was published in the *London Gazette* of 15 October 1948 as one of a selection of the great Coastal Forces actions of 1939–45.

The true significance of the action was that this was a battle between four Dog Boats and at least seven F-Lighters and four Pi-L Boats (smaller lighters with a high bow and stern which made them difficult to distinguish from F-Lighters except from a beam view). In many

---

[6] MO134408; ROP at PRO in ADM 199/268 and 269.

circumstances (frequently described earlier in these pages) these would have been daunting odds, as the German craft, some with 88-mm and quadruple 20-mm guns, could defend themselves well and prevent a short-range attack. But close inshore, in low visibility, with uncertainty of identification, 'absurdly close ranges' (Bligh's words) and 'excellent gunnery and admirable coolness on the part of the Dog Boats' COs', all these possible hazards were nullified, although early on in the action damage and casualties were suffered.

The operation had begun unusually, as this was a period in the Dalmatian campaign when the islands were being rapidly evacuated by the enemy, and SNOVIS was probing northward with a view to using anchorages close to the action, Vis now being rather too far south. Partisans and covert forces (the LRDG especially) were feeding back information. Tim Bligh's most senior CO (Walter Blount), who had already visited the island of Ist, well north of Zara, was sent on ahead of the unit to discover the latest intelligence. Bligh's orders were to be prepared to lie up at Ist for one night, to patrol the mainland route on the second, and return to Vis on the third, depending on what was found.

His unit was his own MGB 662, followed by MTBs 634 (Blount), 637 (Davidson) and 638 (Lummis). Blount and Davidson were immensely experienced, and Lummis, although less so, was to perform very well.

In fact, they patrolled with no enemy contact on 10/11 October, but armed with more information, were in position off Vir Island, some 20 miles north of Zara, by 2220 on the evening of the 11th. 634 had some engine trouble, with fumes affecting the engine room crew, but seems to have been ready enough when Bligh in 662 sighted enemy ships on the port bow at about 400 yd range. He eased his unit close inshore, and

identified the targets as four F-Lighters, one of which was ominously heading straight for 662, and one that looked in silhouette to have the higher profile of a 'flak lighter'. As the unit moved forward to attack, this ship opened fire and with its first salvo killed one of 662's pom-pom loading numbers. All four Dog Boats opened fire. The smoke and the low visibility made accurate observation from the SO's boat impossible, and in his report he uses the device of giving each CO's account separately. Briefly, before she drew ahead, 662 saw two Pi-L boats blow up, two F-Lighters heavily damaged and an E-boat disabled.

Blount in 634 decided he was too close to attempt a torpedo attack as ordered; the pom-pom's ready use locker was hit and went up in flames, but the flak lighter at 50 yd range was hit time after time and burst into flames, with her bridge collapsed. He then saw another group of F-Lighters steering southward (the first indication that there may have been two convoys crossing), and engaged them, damaging two before they moved into 637's field of fire. Lastly, what Blount thought was an E-boat appeared, and he saw it explode and sink.

Davidson in 637 then had his turn. Faced with less enemy fire and at point-blank range his gunners were relentlessly hitting all three targets presented to them, one of which became a blazing wreck. He also saw two large objects to port which turned out to be upturned vessels.

Lummis in 638 further damaged two of 637's F-Lighters and a Pi-L boat and fired on another E-boat.

Bligh, of course, did not have the benefit of all this information at first, but by now all his boats were to the north of the action. He felt sure no enemy ships would be moving on northward, so decided to make a wide sweep westward, southward and then back into the shore about a mile south of Vir Light. By now it was 2346 and he moved quietly up the coast. He sighted the wrecks of two lighters, and was well up towards Vir Point when he saw targets on the port bow, close inshore. 637 illuminated with star-shell, and the unit engaged three craft: an F-Lighter was seen to sink and the others were hit. Heavy fire came suddenly from hidden sources further south, but ceased after the boats fired at the flashes.

It was just on midnight, and knowing the moon was due to rise at 0114, Bligh decided to wait in order to gain the advantage of more light to help his unit finish off any remaining vessels by torpedo. He had great confidence in his radar operator and believed it unlikely that he would allow any craft to creep southward and escape close inshore. So he moved westward again and took up a waiting position about 2 miles off Vir Light until 0151, when he illuminated with star-shell, but was chagrined to find no evidence of any targets. He had two more pauses, and finally moved into the coastline at 0251, and searched southward. Almost at once he found a very large F-Lighter bow-on to the beach – a perfect torpedo target. 634 duly obliged with hits by both torpedoes. Soon after, he found another group of two beached 'Fs' and some small craft. They were all subjected to heavy fire, and 637 sank the only one not blazing with one torpedo at 0337.

Bligh felt that no vessels remained to be dispatched, and decided to return to Vis. In discussion with his COs, he analysed the results of the action. He comments, very wisely, '. . . great difficulty was experienced in this task. The natural desire to claim what one believes to have been sunk has been curbed!' His conservative and considered estimates were:

Six F-Lighters sunk.
One F-Lighter probably sunk.
Four Pi-L boats sunk.

One E-boat sunk, one possibly sunk, and two damaged.

It has not been possible to find an enemy report to confirm these results. All these experienced COs identified the E-boats. But research into German records of the E-boat flotillas indicates that at this time, the two flotillas active in the area (the 3rd and 7th) were so depleted that they had been combined as the new 3rd Flotilla on 9 October, and were now based at Venice, Trieste and Pola well to the north. There is also a statement that 'the first sortie under this new organization took place on 3rd December 1944'. In addition, the definitive list of 'fates' of E-boats reveals no sinking of an E-boat on the night of 11/12 October 1944. It seems unlikely, therefore, that these targets were E-boats, but they may have been some other form of similar profile craft.[7]

Whatever was the case, this was a very impressive performance by Bligh and his boats, at a cost of one man killed (at the very start of the action), two seriously and one slightly wounded, and only superficial damage to the boats.

C-in-C Mediterranean (Admiral J.H.D. Cunningham) strongly concurred with CCF's comments in forwarding the report, which concluded:

. . . victory was made possible by brilliant and inspiring leadership. I have on several previous occasions remarked on Lieutenant Commander T.J. Bligh's splendid leadership of his 57th Flotilla in action. On this occasion he set a seal on his previous performances.

In my letter dated 3rd October 1944 I remarked on the brilliant success of three boats of the 56th Flotilla in a prolonged

[7] *German Coastal Forces in WW2.*

Rear Admiral Morgan with Lt Cdr Morgan Giles (SNOVIS) inspecting partisans at Vis. (Courtesy, A.T. Robinson)

night action. It is a matter of great personal satisfaction to me, knowing all the officers of both flotillas and having watched the happy mixture of close co-operation and friendly rivalry existing between them, that the 57th Flotilla has now crowned its career with an equally, and possibly even more brilliant success.

Quite properly, awards for this action followed later. Bligh received a DSO, each of the other COs a DSC and there was a total of seven DSMs for members of the four crews, with many others 'Mentioned in Dispatches'.[8]

[8] MO13105; ROP at PRO in ADM 199/268 and 269; *London Gazette* 15 October 1948; *Seedie's List of CF Awards.*

It is interesting to note that far from resting on their laurels, the 57th are recorded as being involved on 21 October in a very unusual daylight operation off Dugi, on passage to join Morgan-Giles who had moved with LCH 282 as his headquarters ship to Ist the day before.

Bligh in 662 with 637 and 638, and also 674 (Bowyer) and 659 (Barlow) intercepted a group of enemy craft. They forced the enemy to scuttle two I-boats and a Siebel Ferry, and captured two further I-boats, taking ninety-two prisoners of war. They discovered later that the men being carried had earlier been evacuated from Dubrovnik.

As November was largely a quiet month for the Dog Boats in the northern Adriatic, the

MGB 660 landing troops on the island of Kithera south of the Greek mainland. (Courtesy, A.T. Robinsong)

opportunity is taken now to piece together the rather fragmented story of the activities of the Dog Boats – largely from the 60th Flotilla – in the southern Adriatic, off Greece and in the Aegean in the autumn of 1944.

Just as the southern Dalmatian Islands were being evacuated, so the German army was withdrawing from the southern islands of the Greek peninsula, and clearly the two long patrols to the Corfu Channel and to Cephalonia at the beginning of September had been early indications of this activity. In mid-September, a decision was made to establish a base for small craft, MLs and minesweepers in particular, on Kithera, an island off the southern point of the Peloponnesian Peninsula. Basil Bourne sailed southward from Brindisi on 14 September in 667 (Jerram) with 647 (Mountstephens), 645 (Martin) and 659 (Barlow) and landed troops on the island to

establish the base. For two weeks, under very primitive conditions, they carried out patrols from Kithera off the islands and the mainland, landing agents, and assisting the SBS in their operations. There was a lighter side to their 'occupation', as the natives proved friendly, and there was much haggling over provision of food to supplement the rather dull rations aboard the boats – one of the advantages of operating in remote Mediterranean regions.

Although the four boats Bourne commanded in these early operations remained, and were occasionally replaced, several other boats were employed individually on special operations, and 661, 646 and 651 were to join later. 660 (Terry Robinson of the 57th Flotilla) was detached for special operations with units of the LRDG (Long Range Desert Group) first in Albania, and later in the Aegean. Having established a reputation for clandestine operations, she was then assigned to a group known as the RSR (Raiding Support Regiment) who were regarded as the most aggressive troops the boat ever carried.

It fell later to 660 to take the King of the Hellenes, with his staff, back to his homeland, picking him up from HMS *Ajax* and taking him into Piraeus soon after Athens was fully liberated.

Of Basil Bourne's original group, 667 was relieved by 651 (Ennis) fairly early on but she returned later, commanded by Douglas Goodfellow, a New Zealander. Charles Jerram had been promoted Lieutenant Commander and appointed SO of a new flotilla of US-built Vospers (the 28th MTBs), which were to achieve astonishing results in the northern Adriatic for the last five months of the war.

On 30 September the boats moved up to Poros, 30 miles south of Athens, and an impressive build up of ships began, filling Poros Bay and clearly presaging the taking of Piraeus, the great port serving Athens. Several cruisers arrived – among them *Orion*, *Ajax*, *Aurora* and *Black Prince*.

For the next few days, while thickly sown minefields were being swept, delaying the landings, the boats carried out patrols and on 7/8 October had their one surface action of any significance. 667, 647 and 646 came across a group of small craft they identified as MAS boats and R-boats, and claim to have sunk two of them.[9]

The actual 'assault' was a misnomer, as there was no opposition. Rather the British forces were received with great joy by the Greeks, whose Resistance forces had been harrying the German Army as it retired

[9] MO1352 and MO1027/45; ROP at PRO in ADM 199/268.

northward. The Dog Boats performed a major part in the landings, as all the troops aboard the cruisers, which anchored about a mile off Piraeus, had to be ferried into the harbour, and this was the task allotted to them.

The only descriptive account available is that in the unpublished memoirs of David Conquest, who was the Pilot of 651. Extracts give some of the background:

Each of the boats was to come under the direct control of one of HM Cruisers. We in 651 were allocated to *Black Prince* and we tied up to her at 2200 on 14 October and were briefed. She was carrying hundreds of troops, and the codename for the operation was, rather appropriately, 'Manna'. We sailed at dawn, fourth in line of five cruisers and one MTB, as we had rather cheekily tucked ourselves (in the way we had interpreted our orders) close astern of *Black Prince*.

As the minesweepers got close to Piraeus, they put up more and more mines, and suffered damage and casualties. The cruisers were ordered to reverse course and stand off for a time, but not us! *Black Prince* flashed us up and told us to disregard the order and press on to rendezvous with a badly damaged Fleet Sweeper and to lift off Captain M/S (SO of the minesweeping force) and his staff and take them to a newly designated flagship.

It was obviously (and optimistically) assumed that as a shallow draught wooden boat we would be immune – but the evidence of the sinking and damaged ML sweepers we had passed gave the direct lie to that assumption.

We weaved our way through moored mines visible just below the surface and floating mines which had been cut. I was

MGB 645 of the 60th Flotilla, with HMS *Stalker, en route* from Salonika to Skiathos. (IWM)

given the unenviable task, as the junior officer on board, to stand in the bows and give directions. It was not funny! We crept along – backing and filling – at very low revs, and after what seemed hours got alongside the Fleet Sweeper which was 15 degrees down by the bow. Repeating the process, we took Captain M/S to his new abode, and then returned to *Black Prince* after the most hazardous hour of our commission!

At 1400, course was set again for Pireaus, and when *Black Prince* had anchored we began ferrying troops, 100 at a time, into the harbour. For the rest of the daylight hours our four boats (647, 667, 651 and 646) continued until at dusk we were told to stay alongside.

Conquest goes on to describe how, after

two days acting as a 'trot boat' for the cruisers, the situation in Athens was sufficiently stable for leave to be granted. Officers and men in immaculate white uniforms were soon receiving adulation and hospitality from the celebrating citizens of Greece's capital city.

Over the next few days, the boats remained at Piraeus but were sent out to islands near and far (647, for instance, records visits to Khios, Syros and Skiathos) and to make patrols well to the north, in the Gulf of Salonika. These culminated early in November with yet another 'ferrying' assignment, when a whole commando battalion was lifted into the region of Salonika. There, Basil Bourne received orders to sail with one boat (651), very close to the coast to avoid mines, into Salonika itself to discover the military and political situation there. A tall order for one Dog Boat dispatched to the second city of Greece!

They entered the large but apparently devastated port, with wrecks everywhere, and suddenly realized the approach to the harbour wall was packed with excited civilians waving Greek flags (and a few Union Jacks). All was calm except for their exuberance, which proved later to be the major problem. 651 reported to the control ship by plain language W/T, and was told to remain in the harbour to keep a watching vigil until the main force arrived. It was nearly three weeks before any major group arrived although 651 was joined by the other three boats, and the crews meanwhile enjoyed exuberant Greek hospitality once again.

It was 19 November when they returned to Piraeus, and found that the early stages of the internecine struggle between the ELAS factions and the ELAN forces, which was to tear Greece apart for months, had surfaced. They were finally sent back to Brindisi via a coastal route to investigate conditions in small ports, and the flotilla was back in Italy by the New Year, once more preparing to return to the Dalmatian Islands.

Not all the boats had an uneventful passage. 646 (Knight-Lachlan) and 645 (Martin) left Piraeus after the others, and were weather-bound over Christmas in a tiny inlet halfway between Poros and Kithera. They continued on passage, and when they looked into Nauplion they found that ELAS troops were still in control. They moved on westward and arrived at Katakolon in the afternoon of 4 January.

There had been a bad error in the briefing by intelligence. Katakolon was expected to be held by British troops but in fact they had been evacuated by LCI on 12 December. When 645 and 646 entered the harbour, the town was silent and there was no sign of any military or civilian activity. There were two

caiques moored there, one alongside the outer mole and the other bow-on to the town quay.

645 investigated the first and 646 the other. Both were found to be full of ammunition, and a decision was made to 'cut them out'. Lines were put aboard each, and 645 pulled the outer one away without difficulty. 646 was not so fortunate: her caique was secured by a padlocked chain. A boarding party was sent over to try to start her diesel engine, without success. They were able to cut the chain link, but as they did so, ELAS forces opened fire with small arms from the buildings on the quayside. The boarding party scrambled back aboard 646, but Lt M.J. Roberts on the foredeck received a head wound from which he died several hours later. A/B Daley did not manage to get back aboard, and was taken prisoner by the ELAS forces. He rejoined the boat in mid-January at Patras, having been forced to walk the 90 miles over mountain tracks in mid-winter in the light gear he had been wearing when captured.

Even when the boats reached Patras, they found ELAS troops very much in evidence. But reinforcements arrived and on 8 January British troops secured the upper hand, and fighting all over southern Greece, including Athens, ceased. It had been an unpleasant and seemingly irrelevant episode for the boats, beginning as a Greek internecine struggle which pulled in an Allied response.

HMS *Ajax* and four destroyers arrived in Patras, and Mike Roberts was buried at sea. Even the return to Brindisi was interrupted: an LST in company was mined 5 miles out and had to be escorted back to Patras.

The 60th Flotilla's three months in Greek waters and the Aegean had been memorable in many ways, and full of the unexpected incidents which were by no means uncommon for the Mediterranean Dog Boats. (Appendix 1, Note 28)

Gunnery trials off Malta in MGB 674 to try out the new 6-pdr and 2-in rocket flares. (Courtesy, C.E.R. Hind)

In the Dalmatian Islands, operations by November 1944 were concentrated firmly in the northern area. Morale had just been boosted by a signal from C-in-C Mediterranean.

I have observed with pleasure the conduct of the light coastal forces operating from Bastia and in the Adriatic during recent months. The constant harassing of the enemy's sea routes has had a direct bearing on the successes of the armies fighting in Italy, and highest praise is due to the officers and men whose uniform vigilance, daring and skill has been responsible for the destruction of many tons of enemy shipping and escort vessels, as well as to base personnel who have maintained our craft in fighting condition.

Such signals were appreciated by the crews because they tended to have a general impression that their efforts were not sufficiently understood or even known about by the 'top brass', and it was gratifying to realize that was not so.

Early in November, Morgan-Giles's urgent requests had finally been met, and FOTALI had sent Hunt class destroyers to his area, particularly as there had been constant reports of the arrival of at least two German destroyers (or possibly torpedo boats) to

Fiume (Ryeka), whence they were able to create a threat to the Coastal Forces craft and Partisans that needed to be neutralized. Almost at once, HMS *Wheatland* and HMS *Avon Vale* found first the German corvettes VJ 202 and VJ 208, and later TA 20 (the *Audace*), a German torpedo boat, and sank them off Lussin with excellent gunnery, making a very important strategic contribution to the situation in the area.

By the end of November, Burke had the majority of the 56th Flotilla with him in the islands: 658, now with American SO Radar, and commanded by Reynolds, 633 with Lt Kenneth Golding having replaced Steve Rendell, and Derrick Brown (until the loss of 663 her First Lieutenant), the new CO of 655, now that Cam MacLachlan had returned to Canada.

Their first operation in the new phase was on 18/19 November when Burke led six boats, three of them MTBs, in an attempt to intercept or flush out and attack the enemy craft, using Cigale Cove on the west coast of Lussin Island. Morgan-Giles had information that the E-boats or MAS boats and Explosive Motor Boats (EMBs) there were planning an attack on the coves in Mulat, not much further south, which he was using as his temporary anchorages for MTBs and MLs: this was his attempt to pre-empt such a strike. Six torpedoes were fired into the cove, but nothing stirred.

On 2/3 December, Morgan-Giles planned a more ambitious attack on Lussin which was deemed to have become, at this time, of great strategic importance as the northern islands were soon to be attacked in the relentless move up the coast by the Partisans and Allied forces. The main harbour of Lussin was deep and large, and made an excellent base for enemy craft, supplemented by Cigale Cove, used by the EMBs and one-man torpedoes which were more significant in the threat they

posed than in any achievements so far (just as had been the case at the Normandy beachhead several months earlier). There was also a strategically important bridge from Lussin linking it to the north end of the island of Cherso at Ossero, a fair sized German garrison in the town of Lussinpiccolo, and some heavy calibre coastal batteries with an all round arc of fire making this an important enemy stronghold.

With the support of FOTALI, Morgan-Giles had been given an impressive naval force to command in an attack on this complex. He established his headquarters aboard his current 'mobile base' LCH 282 (Landing Craft – Headquarters), an LCI specially adapted with sophisticated radar and communications. At his disposal were four Hunt class destroyers (*Lamerton*, *Wilton*, *Brocklesby* and *Quantock*), three LCGs and an LCF (Landing Craft, Flak), four Dog Boats (two MGBs and two MTBs) led by Burke, three MLs and two HDMLS, and the cooperation of Hurricanes and a group of thirty-six rocket-firing Beaufighters. Operation Antagonise was considered a great success. The Beaufighters made the first attack and effectually silenced the Asino battery. *Lamerton*, *Wilton* and the LCGs bombarded Lussin, and *Brocklesby* and *Quantock* went close to the entrance to Cigale Cove and poured 600 rounds into the buildings and jetties. At last it was the turn of the Dog Boats: Burke in 633 (Golding) with 649 (Hughes) in support, volunteered to investigate Cigale Cove more thoroughly. He decided straight away to go inside the narrow entrance and probe right to the far end where there were clearly boats, some under camouflage. Immediately one EMB headed at speed towards the entrance (and 633) and fire was opened.

The craft altered course and ran herself hard into the rocks. Further in there was one

Three Yugoslav partisans at Zara. (Courtesy, F. Martin)

boat circling: she was sunk and two others alongside destroyed. Burke's report introduces a lighter touch (not uncommon with the Canadians):

The coxswain of the first boat evidently decided things were getting too warm for him. No one had seen him escape from his boat when it crashed into the rocks, but he suddenly leapt up from behind a rock and sprinted for cover in the nearby woods, hotly pursued by shot and shell of various calibres. This character was seen to be stark naked and it was agreed by one and all in 633 that the speed of his flight over the rough ground was truly phenomenal. Although the woods were thoroughly sprayed as he disappeared again, no definite hits can be claimed.

633 came under fire from light machine-gun and rifle fire from concealed positions on shore, and three casualties were suffered (one later died) as she left the cove. Two engines were put temporarily out of action by .303 bullets, showing how vulnerable wooden craft with petrol engines could be.

In general, Morgan-Giles was well pleased with the results of Operation Antagonise, which certainly restricted German activities for some time and unquestionably damaged morale.[10]

The use of coves and anchorages at this time was made far more hazardous by the increasing frequency of the Bora, as expected in these winter months. This sudden and

[10] ROP of Cigale Cove action, held by author; *Western Mediterranean*.

Lt Cdr J.A. Montgomerie (V59). (Courtesy, N. Taylor)

violent northerly wind could be lethal to small craft, and on some occasions blew continuously for several days. As Ancona was now working fully, even the passage to and from the operational area became an unpleasant experience. When Zara was taken by the Partisans, in the northward thrust up the coast, a far better port became available, well protected and with good berthing, and new ground was broken when HMS *Colombo*, an anti-aircraft cruiser, was able to berth there and provide additional facilities for the boats. SNONA (SNO Northern Adriatic), Captain N.V. Dickinson, was based there, and as he had been at Bastia and Leghorn, was a helpful and understanding senior officer to the Coastal Forces boats.

In December, the first reinforcements for the Dog Boat flotillas arrived in Malta from the UK in the shape of the 59th Flotilla. Whereas the first four flotillas, when they arrived in the Mediterranean in the spring of 1943, had all been new and untried boats, the 59th had already operated for over a year in home waters and were seasoned campaigners. It took a little while for them to be accepted by the other crews, who listened to stories of 'D-Day' and then politely asked 'which D-Day is that? We've had several!', but when they arrived in the islands in January they proved to be a valuable addition to the Dog Boat force.

They were led by Lt Cdr J. Alastair Montgomerie in 699, and the other boats were:

697 (Lt D.H. Booth)
698 (Lt P. Wraite)
700 (Lt R.S. Mortimer)
703 (Lt N.W.G. Taylor DSC)
705 (Lt P.M. Davies)
706 (Lt M.H.S. Hume)
710 (Lt A.W. Bone)

Before they arrived in the operational zone, there were very few significant patrols, but on 22/23 December, Bligh in 662 led 643 (Bird), 674 (Bowyer) and 638 (Lummis) in a follow up to Operation Antagonise, codenamed 'Antagonise Two'. Once again it was aimed at the harbour of Lussinpiccolo and this time there were two 'Hunts' bombarding, and Bligh took his boats right into the harbour and attacked an E-boat berthed at a quay and EMBs alongside. (By early December the E-boats of the 1st and 2nd Groups had resumed operations in this area.)[11]

Just before Christmas, the 56th Flotilla was relieved and sent to Malta. Several of the boats had been operating for months with wing tanks filled with water, broken frames and engines requiring replacement, and the opportunity was taken to give them the new armament which the Dogs were receiving: a semi-automatic 6-pdr replaced the pom-pom for'd, and the MGBs also had one aft in place of the old Hotchkiss 6-pdr. Some boats of the flotilla were back in the islands by February, but the opportunity was taken once again to fill gaps in the other flotillas, and as 'Corny' Burke was returning to Canada (after a second two year period on operations), no new SO was appointed.

The first action of the New Year was, appropriately, by Montgomerie's 59th Flotilla when 699, 706 and 698 were despatched to Unie Island, off the northern end of Lussin. Three E-boats had been sighted by aircraft firmly aground, obviously having run ashore in bad visibility the previous night.

On 15/16 January the 59th found the three boats and destroyed them, making sure they could never be salvaged and put back into service. Strangely this was an almost exact parallel with the fate of two 'short' MTBs

[11] MO1070 and MO1919; ROP at PRO in ADM 199/257; *German Coastal Forces in WW2*.

that had gone aground on Levrera Island a few miles west of Unie two months earlier, which had also had to be destroyed by Dog Boats. Both islands were low and a navigational hazard in bad visibility. German records show that the E-boats which suffered this fate were S33, S58 and S60.[12]

The 59th Flotilla bore the brunt of patrols from Zara during February, with some help from the few operational boats of the 57th. CCF's monthly report records sixty-four patrols by the Dog Boats in the month – a record for the Mediterranean – and yet the only recorded action was on 13/14 February when Walter Blount as SO in 634, with 660 and 710, met a group of heavily armed F-Lighters in the Quarnero Channel, near the east coast of the Istrian Peninsula. The port of Arsa had become very important as a supply port for the northern islands, and this was to be the scene of several bitter battles in the next few weeks.

On this night, helped by the new SO Radar at his disposal, Walter Blount plotted three large F-Lighters and was able to make a close range gun attack and sink one having achieved surprise. In a second attack one more was sunk, but 710 suffered an 88-mm hit on the engine room coach roof just abaft the bridge and fragments killed two men, wounded two others and put three engines out of action. Blount persisted in the attack and the third F-Lighter was sunk by torpedo, aimed by radar.[13]

Another significant development was the beginning of operations right inside the islands where a narrow coastal channel (the Planinski Channel) had enabled the enemy to avoid interference. To get access to the channel involved a hair-raising creep between islands, where everyone felt they would be

trapped if detected. These patrols made possible an attack on the small port of Karlobag on the mainland, and on 17/18 February, 699, 703 and 655 fired torpedoes into the harbour with no obvious results.

March began well on 6/7th when Basil Bourne led a mixed unit in a patrol off the Arsa Channel in 656 (Masson), which had been fitted with SO Radar, and 703 (Taylor) and 705 (Davies). Once again the excellent radar echoes enabled a careful plot of a convoy that was detected and 656 was able to fire two torpedoes at 1,200 yd and hit a merchant ship which was seen to sink. 703 and 706 attacked with guns, and suffered some damage from heavy fire while inflicting some on the enemy.[14]

It was Montgomerie's turn on 12/13 March when in his own 699 and with 703 (Taylor) and 710 (Bone), just back from repair, he sighted two F-Lighters and a tug rounding the southern point of the Istrian Peninsula and entering the Arsa Channel. The enemy opened fire first, but Montgomerie forced them to retire although his unit had to make smoke to avoid heavy damage. He bided his time, and an hour later saw that more ships had joined the convoy so he fired four torpedoes and star-shell. Mines were detonated, and once again the enemy were prevented from making progress. Two hours later, more vessels came from the north, the remaining two torpedoes were fired, and one hit was thought to be obtained on an F-Lighter. It was a prolonged and patient attempt at the blockade of the Arsa Channel, which was the object of the patrol.

It became obvious from the events of the next few weeks that the enemy was mining the channel intensively, and sadly they achieved considerable success. On the 16th, 710 detonated a mine that damaged her

[12] MO4087; *German Coastal Forces in WW2.*
[13] MO4693; Summary of actions.

[14] MO5411; Summary of actions.

MTB 705 sinking after being mined in the Islands. (Courtesy, W. Last)

shafts: she was towed into Mulat. But worse was to come. On 22/23 March, Basil Bourne in 674 (Bowyer) with 655 (Brown) and 643 (Lt D.G.T. Hill had just taken over from Bird) patrolled off Arsa but found no evidence of enemy movements. They set off at 0300 to return to Zara, and at 0425, 655 hit a mine which struck midships, under the bridge. She broke in two, burning petrol spread over the sea, and survivors appeared swimming away from the flames. 643 picked up twenty-three including the CO and First Lieutenant, but seven were missing, including the Pilot and the Coxswain.

Derrick Brown, the CO, who had broken his left femur, felt particularly deeply the loss of his Coxswain. Petty Officer Laurie Nicholl had been in Coastal Forces since 1941, and had first been Mentioned in Dispatches in MGB 67, one of Hichens's flotilla in that year. He had become Tom Ladner's Coxswain

in MGB 75 in the same flotilla, and won a DSM in an action off Cherbourg in August 1942. He had loyally followed Ladner to 663 as his Coxswain early in 1943, and won a bar to his DSM. When 663 had been mined and sunk in September 1944, Nicholl had been injured, but had volunteered to join Derrick Brown when he was appointed CO of 655 a month or two later. That he should lose his life in a second mining so near the end of the war, as a result of such loyalty, was a bitter blow.[15]

Mines struck again the same afternoon, when 705 was sunk on passage from Ancona to Zara in the Maknare Channel. Her stern was blown off and she floated for about twenty minutes. Two men were missing, and one seriously injured.

[15] MO4677 and MO5180; Sir Derrick Holden Brown (then CO of 655).

April for the Dogs, apart from some skirmishes in the Planinski Channel, again proved that the enemy had added even more fire-power to its escorts, and that although the number of convoys with supplies was very much reduced as the recipient areas in the northern islands and the mainland dwindled, when they did sail they were very strongly defended.

In particular, Tim Bligh, in 662's last direct action, with 634 (Blount), 638 (Lummis) and 633 (Golding) fought a bitter battle with F-Lighters on 9/10 April in the Arsa Channel.

He had the advantage of his SO Radar, and picked up the enemy (four F-Lighters) at 8,000 yd. This enabled him to plot their course and plan his attack, and he decided to get inshore of them before attacking from an advantageous position. Unfortunately, the unit was detected, and the F-Lighters illuminated and were able to avoid the six torpedoes which were fired. There followed a very fierce gun fight, with hits on two of the F-Lighters but no opportunity to use Bligh's successful tactics at Vir in October, of close station-keeping and concentrated fire at short range. The conditions were very different. The F-Lighters were able to keep pounding away with their 88-mm guns, and almost at once disabled both 633 and 638. 633 was hit on the bridge, and Ken Golding the CO was seriously wounded, with his Coxswain beside him killed. 638 was hit in the bows by an 88-mm shell and was unable to go ahead at any speed. Bligh attacked again with 634 close astern, and this time it was 662's turn to be hit by three shells and she suffered serious casualties – three killed and five wounded. By now the F-Lighters had reached the entrance to the channel and safety, so the action was broken off and attention concentrated on saving 638. She was towed stern first back to Ancona by

634 – yet another feat of seamanship by the irrepressible Walter Blount and his crew.[16]

The threat of the F-Lighters' 88-mm guns was underlined again the following night, when Mountstephens in 647, with 643, penetrated the Planinski Channel and attacked three 'F's with, they thought, two E-boats in support, and 647 received a direct hit which blew off most of her stern. This was to be 647's last operation, as she needed extensive repairs. She had been one of the first Dog Boats in the Mediterranean, and Maurice Mountstephens (together with his First Lieutenant, Sub-Lt E. Lonsdale, who had begun in January 1943 as the Midshipman Pilot) was one of the very few COs in Dog Boats who served throughout the whole of his boat's life. 647 had had a distinguished and unusually varied commission, in every area of the Mediterranean Dog Boats' activities from Gibraltar to the Levant.

The same day, 710 (Tony Bone) of the 59th, joined the sad catalogue of boats lost to the pernicious danger of the thickly sown mines. She sank off Sansego Island, with the largest list of missing in any of these disasters – fifteen – including the CO Tony Bone, who had commanded her since December 1943, right through the UK section of her commission.

There was one last success for the Mediterranean Dog Boats, on 12/13 April. The imminent activity at this time was the taking of the islands of Rab, Krk and Cherso by the Partisans, and small units of Dog Boats were being used to support them.

On 12 April, SNONA dispatched Montgomerie, in 670 (Hewitt) with 697 (Booth), 643 (Hill) and 658 (Reynolds), on a patrol clearly motivated by intelligence received. 670 and 658 had SO Radar; 670 and 697

---

[16] MO306; Summary of actions.

were MTBs, and 643 and 658 MGBs. At this stage, boats were lying up in a small cove on the mainland side of the Planinski Channel, and 658 had only just arrived there to join up with the others after her long refit. The unit was to move to the northern end of the channel and be prepared to attack any vessels coming south from Fiume, the major port less than 30 miles to the north, which might be attempting to reinforce or evacuate Rab.

By 0130 the unit was lying out, close to the coast of Krk, opposite the mainland port of Novi. At 0215, 658's radar detected two large targets, the operator thought destroyers, at 4 miles, coming south. Montgomerie lined up his MTBs, plotted course and speed very carefully, and when the two ships (they were destroyers) could be seen, he ordered the spread of four torpedoes to be fired, at 1,500 yd. After the usual long agonized pause, there was an enormous explosion and one of the destroyers disappeared from the radar plot. A star-shell burst overhead and Montgomerie decided not to hang about now all his unit's torpedoes were fired, and left the scene at 22 knots.

It is only recently that detailed information has been obtained of actual results from the German records, but in a most unusual way. The author received a letter from a Yugoslavian diving enthusiast and writer, who had followed up reports from Novi that crews of the fishing boats were talking about fine catches in the channel (renamed after the war as the Velebit Channel) in an area where 'old men reported a naval battle in 1945'. He made some preliminary dives and found the wreck of a destroyer 60 metres down. Most astonishingly, he discovered that the ship was in two pieces, with the stern section ahead of the forward half, and the bows smashed to pieces. Clearly, two torpedoes had struck – one breaking her in half and the other at the bow. The engines must have propelled the

stern half, sinking very rapidly, under the forward half.

He decided to research the background of the battle, and secured an extract from the German war diary of the Commander of the First Escort Fleet (Adriatic) stationed in Trieste. The sunken ship was identified as the TA 45. The letter A indicates that the ship did not have a German origin. When the Germans occupied Fiume and Trieste in September 1943, they found six unfinished Italian destroyers under construction, and decided to complete them. The class was named Ariete and the TA 45 was named *Spiza* – being built in Fiume (later renamed Rijeka). Although the prefix 'T' indicates a torpedo boat, boats of this class were large enough to be regarded as destroyers. She was

Kpt Wuppermann, SO of the Adriatic E-boats, aboard 658 off Ancona, May 1945. (Courtesy, A.T. Robinson)

completed on 20 June 1944 and had never operated in combat until 12/13 April 1945, which was her first and last patrol, lasting less than one hour!

The war diary of Fleet Commander Fridrich Birnbaum reveals that he left Fiume with his two destroyers – TA 40 and TA 45 – on an operation designed to interrupt the progress of the Partisans who had reached Senj and were known to be about to attack Rab. He wrote:

We were in line, with TA 40 followed by TA 45, about 100 metres apart. Suddenly the starboard lookout reported white marks on the water towards Krk, and we concluded that they must be the wakes of English MTBs. Almost at once, the 'bugging device' detected torpedoes rushing towards us. We turned to starboard as fast as we could, and fired star-shell. A few seconds later torpedoes passed each side of us. A second later we heard two explosions, one after the other. We turned round. The stem of TA 45 stood straight up in the air, and we could see the stern passing forward. A few seconds later, she had sunk and we in TA 40 turned at full speed, firing at the MTBs, and returned to Fiume.

Survivors of TA 45 swam to both Krk and to Novi, and gradually made their way north, many of them on foot. Eighty officers and men out of the complement of 150, including the Captain, had lost their lives.[17]

But even the elation over this success was short-lived, as three days later, on 16/17 April, Montgomerie in 658 (Reynolds) with 697 (Booth) and 633 (F.E. Dowrick), sailed from Rab Town (liberated two days earlier)

to patrol north-west of Krk (now under Partisan land attack). They were within 30 yd of the Krk shore when 697 – second in line – blew up in a sheet of flame. Mines were bobbing about on the surface and the task of rescuing survivors (ten were missing) and then getting out of this minefield was nerve-racking.

During the next few days the last remaining serviceable Dog Boats, now in Rab Town, assisted in the taking of Cherso, the last of the northerly islands, and effectively the Dalmatian campaign was over.

There are three 'postscripts' to the story of the Mediterranean Dog Boats.

The first occurred at 0600 on 3 May, off Ancona. Without warning, seven E-boats appeared and just hove to near the harbour entrance. There was a great flap, and boats were dispatched, with 658 in the lead and several of Jerram's Vospers of the 28th not far behind. 658 closed the leading E-boat which was flying a white flag, and a senior officer came on board. He turned out to be Kpt Wupperman, the senior E-boat officer in the Adriatic, and he explained that he had brought troops over to surrender them as prisoners of war, and wished to be allowed to make a return visit to Pola to collect more before surrendering his boats. He did not wish to leave prisoners in the hands of the Partisans. Naturally, NOIC Ancona refused the request and the seven E-boats were escorted into Ancona. They were S30, S36 and S61 of the 1st Group (formerly the 3rd Flotilla) and S151, S152, S155 and S156 of the 2nd Group, formerly the 7th Flotilla.

It was a proud moment for a Dog Boat to receive the surrender of the very E-boats that had been longest in the Mediterranean. To see them alongside in the base was tremendously satisfying.

Just before this, Bligh had sailed north

[17] MO6623; ROP held by author; diver's report on wreck on TA45; German report.

with three of his flotilla on what proved to be another remarkable episode in his illustrious career – this time a success resulting from cerebral diplomatic skills rather than leadership in action.

He embarked in 634, the boat of his closest ally Walter Blount, with 651 (Ennis) and 670 (Hewitt). Charles Jerram, with seven of his extraordinarily successful 28th Flotilla Vospers, also sailed independently, but had to turn back as the weather deteriorated. Bligh's orders from SNONA were as follows:

> Proceed to intercept an enemy convoy reported as twenty-plus F-Lighters accompanied by tugs and E-boats with other small craft which left Trieste on Tuesday morning and were reported to be making for Grado between Trieste and Tagliamento. It is believed these vessels are willing to surrender and that their original intention was to make for Ancona. Use your best efforts to bring these craft to Ancona. Spitfire reconnaissance aircraft will be over the area and a striking force of aircraft will be available if called for.

When the Dogs reached the head of the Adriatic, they saw in front of them a very large number of ships around and within the tiny harbour of Tagliamento. Some were aground, and not one was wearing a white flag. The Spitfires reported that some were hostile and advised the Dogs to 'get the hell out of it'. But Bligh stoically approached, with each of his boats wearing the largest

Surrendered E-boats at Ancona.

237

white flags that could be found (wardroom sheets were pressed into service).

There was a great sense of uncertainty everywhere. Might they fight? Would they scuttle? Was there any chance that they could be persuaded to return to Ancona? Bligh was apprehensive but calm, and his boats were ordered to show no signs whatsoever of any aggression. The odds against them were so great that there was no other possibility than to parley.

An attempt was made to do just that in a very difficult meeting aboard an R-boat. Bligh used his main card, which was to suggest that a passage to Ancona was far preferable to surrendering to the Partisans who, he told them, would reach Tagliamento before the Allies. He met with a mixture of blatant antagonism from a Nazi, indecision from an Admiral and possible cooperation from a Yugoslavian royalist with more to lose than most! The Admiral finally said that it was up to individual boats and crews to scuttle or leave as they decided, and Bligh and Blount returned to 634 to await developments. A few craft made friendly noises and seemed prepared to leave, and others began to burn or to sink in the shallow water. Sadly for Tim Bligh's main lever of influence, a small unit of New Zealanders arrived before the Partisans and complicated matters.

Bligh had asked SNONA to send up more Dog Boats, and five more arrived that evening. To get things moving, he ordered them to take in tow any F-Lighters that seemed to have been abandoned or to escort any which were willing to go. Gradually convoys were formed (very necessary as everyone was well aware of the minefield to be traversed) and, having averted any disaster and achieved whatever results seemed possible in an impossible situation, eight Dogs set off for Ancona towing and escorting

five F-Lighters, twelve other small craft and taking in 500 prisoners.

When they were handed over at Ancona, the apprehension felt throughout three harrowing days was found to be justified: all the guns aboard the German ships were found to be loaded and every safety catch set to 'fire'. It took over twenty-five hours to complete their slow voyage before the Dog Boat crews could relax, with their war at an end.

The Admiral, in forwarding Bligh's report to C-in-C, commented, 'This was probably one of the strangest operations of the war, and I consider that Lt Cdr Bligh's handling of a situation almost without precedent is deserving of the highest praise,' Bligh was subsequently awarded the OBE.[18]

The third and final postscript is another almost unbelievable story, concerning the fate of the Dog Boats after they had paid off to reserve. In January 1946, twelve of them were prepared to be towed by destroyers to Alexandria to be sold there, possibly to the Egyptian government as Excise boats or for other purposes. Their engines and guns had all been removed.

Rumour began to filter through in the following months that all had been sunk, although by this time, virtually every officer and man who had served in these boats was either in the UK or some other appointment, or had been demobilized. It was not for many years that those concerned gathered that the only official statement was that which appears in the various lists of the fate of Coastal Forces craft: 'Lost on passage between Malta and Alexandria, 30th January 1946.' It seems to have been of little consequence to the Admiralty. There were apparently no casualties, and the boats were

18 Sir Walter Blount and the late Gordon Surtees of 634; digest of Bligh's ROP in WIR 286 (September 1945).

Lt Cdr Tim Bligh, V57 (right) with Lt Walter Blount, Lt Leonard Ennis and Lt Eric Hewitt aboard a surrendered E-boat after Tagliamento. (IWM)

supposedly of little value at this stage. But to the 60 officers and 500 men who had lived and fought in these boats, many of them for almost three years, the news came as a great shock, and they demanded an explanation. The author, who was personally involved as his boat MGB 658 was one of the eleven, undertook to investigate, and wrote (in 1989):

The boats were 633, 634, 637, 638, 642, 643, 658, 659, 698 and 700 – and almost certainly 674 – and all of them had very distinguished operational records.

Research unearthed four men who could give direct evidence of the events of late 1945 and early 1946. First were two seamen from 643 who had been in the 'Care and Maintenance' party living aboard 674 – one of the twelve boats all lying in Pieta Creek near HMS *Gregale* in Malta. They had been involved in making up the towing bridles to be used.

Next was a Telegraphist previously in 705, who had been on watch in the Operations Room of *Gregale* during the night of a great storm, and who recorded signal after signal as boats were reported first as 'breaking tow' and later as 'sunk'.

Then a seaman who had served in the 28th Flotilla and had just been drafted to HMS *Chequers* came forward and reported that he remembered vividly the scene as the four destroyers – *Jervis*, *Chevron*, *Chequers* and *Chaplet* – towed the boats out of Marsamaxett. He remembers the storm brewing up and the tows parting, and most poignantly of all, remembers the boats being sunk by gunfire from the destroyers as navigational hazards.

And finally, someone discovered that the incident had been mentioned in G.G. Connell's book, *Mediterranean Maelstrom* (Kimber, 1987). Mr Connell was contacted, and supplied the addresses of the Gunnery Officer of *Jervis*, Lt Peter Boissier and her Signalman, Peter Coney, who were able to seal the story in most respects.

It seems that each of the four destroyers was to tow three Dog Boats in line astern. They would all wallow in their very light state. A bad weather forecast led to a request from the Captain of *Jervis* to the Flag Officer, Malta, to postpone the sailing in view of the imminence of storm conditions. This was curtly turned down – 'Sail in accordance with my orders!'

Within three hours, the boats began to corkscrew wildly as the weather deteriorated, and some broached to. Tows began to part. All began to founder. One by one, the hulls were sunk by gunfire, and the destroyers made short work of the task. The CO of *Chequers* collated reports and recorded the loss of each boat in turn. It was a very violent storm which caused a troopship to founder further east.

It was indeed a sad ending for twelve such proud boats. But it was perhaps a more fitting end than rotting on the beach. They became, in a way, a memorial to the men who died out there in the Mediterranean: they joined not only the wrecks of Phoenician and Roman galleys in that classic sea, but also the enemy vessels that had been sunk, together with the fifty-three boats of Mediterranean Coastal Forces which had themselves been sunk in battle, by mines, and in air attacks over five years of war. (Appendix 1, Note 29)

CHAPTER 11

C CLASS MGBS, SGBS AND CAMPER AND NICHOLSON MGBS

It is the author's hope that a full history of all MTBs and other attack craft of Coastal Forces in all operational areas will in due course be written.

Although this volume clearly concentrates on the activities of the 209 Dog Boats built for the RN and RNorN, it is logical to ensure that the very significant contributions of the other 'long' boats of Coastal Forces are covered. There were not many such boats but they were extremely active in the Channel and North Sea from 1941 to the end of hostilities. This supplementary chapter attempts to accord them the respect they deserve.

THE C CLASS FAIRMILE MGBS

The story of the progressive development of the Fairmile organization is told in Chapter 1. After the twelve A class boats, which were mainly used in minelaying operations from Dover, Felixstowe and Harwich, came the B class motor launches of which 696 were ordered worldwide. No attempt has been made to cover the operations of these two classes, which deserve a history of their own.

The C class boats – of which twenty-four were built (MGBs 312–335) – were direct descendants of the A class, using virtually the same design, but with improvements in the light of experience. As in all Coastal Force boats, their original armament was increased in stages from 1941 to 1945.

They were originally to be classified as motor launches, but almost at once were designated motor gunboats and served as such throughout the war. The hull was hard chine, 110 ft in length and 17 ft 5 in in beam, giving a long slim configuration. They were powered by three Hall-Scott 900-h.p. supercharged petrol engines, giving them a maximum speed of 26.6 knots, and a handy continuous cruising speed of 23.6 knots. They were originally fitted with a 2-pdr pom-pom for'd, two twin 0.5-in power turrets midships, and a 2-pdr Rolls gun aft, with twin Vickers machine-guns on each side of the bridge.

Unfortunately, it is quite impossible to give as much detail of the C class MGBs' operations as has been done for the Dog Boats. They did carry out some offensive sweeps to both the Dutch coast and in the Channel, but the vast majority of their time was spent as the invaluable close escorts of vital coastal convoys, mainly operating from Yarmouth. Their sterling work in that role did bring them into some notable actions

MGB 335, showing the long, narrow hull of the C class. (IWM)

with E-boats, but for the great majority of the time their efforts were largely unsung. One division was based at Dover, and during 1942 saw contact with the enemy on a number of occasions.

Perhaps their most colourful and significant operations were on clandestine missions to the enemy coast, landing and retrieving agents. Their low silhouette and slim lines made them very suitable for such duties, but the very secret nature of these activities and the fact that they were handled by authorities other than Coastal Forces means that the very considerable part the 'C' boats played in this role is largely unrecorded.

Chapter 9 of this volume has been devoted to the part MTB 718 – the only Dog Boat exclusively involved – took in the operations of the 15th MGB Flotilla, which came under the aegis of DDOD(I). In fact, the C class MGB 318 had an even longer membership of that flotilla, together with MGBs 502 and

503, Camper and Nicholsons boats that will be mentioned later. 318 took the place of the original 'cloak and dagger' 314, which achieved lasting fame as the headquarters ship for the St Nazaire raid. But during 1942 particularly, a large number of the C class boats were seconded for occasional clandestine operations, and also participated in such major raids as those at Bruneval and Dieppe. Several other daring operations that involved transporting raiding parties were rehearsed, but postponed through adverse conditions until finally aborted.

Even the participation of C class boats in the van of the assault force for Operation Neptune from D-1 on 5 June 1944 is poorly documented and cannot be given the prominence it deserves.

All the Fairmile 'C's were completed between June and October 1941, having been built in thirteen yards around the coasts of Britain. They were formed into three flotillas, the 12th, 14th and 16th MGB Flotillas, each

The armament of a C boat (MGB 321) looking aft – 0.5-in turrets and the Rolls-Royce 2-pdr. (Courtesy, V. Clarkson)

of eight boats, although movement between flotillas was common.

The 12th Flotilla was based at Great Yarmouth at the Coastal Force Base HMS *Midge*. Its first SO was Lt P.G. Loasby RN, who led the flotilla from its formation in August 1941 until February 1942. It is interesting, in studying the appointments to the boats, as in all the C class flotillas, to note how many of the SOs and COs went on to play distinguished roles in Coastal Forces, particularly in Dog Boats: many of them have featured in earlier chapters. In fact, the next two SOs of the 12th Flotilla went on to command Dog Boat flotillas, Lt H.P. Byrne RN and Lt Cdr N.H. Hughes RNVR, as did no fewer than seven of the COs. Clearly this group of COs were mainly derived from the early 'yachtsmen' RNVR officers who gathered experience from the very start of the war.

The 14th MGB Flotilla was led by officers who were every bit as experienced and whose later service in Coastal Forces was similarly distinguished. Unusually, the flotilla operated in two separate divisions – one at *Hornet* in Portsmouth and the other from *Wasp* at Dover. Later, the *Hornet* based division became the '1st Coastal Force Flotilla' and units were often used, between normal gunboat duties, on special operations, including raids on Dives, Courseilles, Merlimont, Le Touquet, St Vaast, St Laurent, Bruneval, Hardelot, Boulogne and Dieppe. Boats were added frequently and then moved back to other flotillas as operations required.

The first SO was Lt Cdr W.G. Everitt RN, and he was followed by T.N. Cartwright, A.R.H. Nye and J.H. Coste. At Dover, the first divisional leader was Lt K.A. Cradock-Hartopp RN.

A C class MGB under way. (Courtesy, G. Gregory)

The 16th Flotilla at Great Yarmouth had a similarly varied constitution. At one time or other eighteen of the twenty-four 'C' boats joined the flotilla, often leaving again shortly after. Its well-known SOs included Lt E.M. Thorpe RN, Lt Cdr G.C. Fanner and Lt Cdr D.G.E. Probert. Other COs of the flotilla who feature prominently in the Dog Boat story were Lt P.N. Edge, Lt F.R. Lightoller, Lt D.G. Bradford RNR, Lt J.H. Hodder, Lt D.G. Dowling and Lt R.A. Forbes.

It is proper to pick out those operations where official mention is made of the C class boats, in order to illustrate their important contribution to Coastal Forces operations.

The first indication that their patrols from Dover began as early as 3/4 December 1941 comes in a report that MGBs 324 and 328 were in company with boats of the 6th MTB Flotilla when they attacked a convoy in the Dover Strait. Six weeks later, the same two boats, with 330, intercepted and attacked two armed trawlers on a night when MTB 47 was sunk in a second attack. Units led by Cradock-Hartopp in 324 were again in action in February, so clearly the division was pulling its weight in supporting the short MTB flotillas at Dover.

The first mention of the Yarmouth boats comes on 19/20 February 1942, when 319 and 329 of the 16th Flotilla, in company with three destroyers, intercepted three groups of E-boats and scored hits with their 2-pdr guns. Two E-boats were sunk and others damaged: survivors were picked up from S53, one of the two definitely sunk.[1]

In the spring and summer of 1942 came a series of three very important raids on the

---

[1] CFI (Coastal Forces Information Bulletin) 13.

enemy coast, all mounted under the direction of Lord Mountbatten, Chief of Combined Operations. They each involved boats of the Portsmouth division of the 14th MGB Flotilla. They had been specially equipped with navigational aids so that they could lead in assault craft, and painted in 'Mountbatten pink' camouflage, mauve and lilac, which was to prove extraordinarily effective.

The first was on 27/28 February 1942, and was the raid on Bruneval where the objective was to attack and overwhelm the garrison guarding the cliff-top radar station there, remove the equipment, and return with it to the UK. The operation involved both parachute troops and commandos landing from LCAs (Landing Craft, Assault), and the seaborne force was to be led in and recovered by the MGBs.

Five boats were used on this occasion – three of the Portsmouth boats and two from Yarmouth. In the lead was 316 (the SO, Lt Cdr W.G. Everitt RN); 317 (Lt J.H.Coste); 312 (Lt A.R.H. Nye); 315 (Lt P. Mason) and 326 (Lt R.D. Russell-Roberts). They escorted across the Channel the LSI (Landing Ship, Infantry) HMS *Prince Albert*, which carried eight small landing craft in davits. 316 was designated headquarters ship, and carried the Force Naval Commander. When they arrived off the landing area, the LSI dropped her LCAs, which were led in by the MGBs and she then returned to Spithead.

There were two anxious periods for the MGBs as they waited to tow the LCAs back to base. First, two enemy destroyers escorted by E-boats were sighted approaching from the east. They passed close by, but failed to sight the MGBs before turning into Le Havre. The second was when the anticipated time for return of the LCAs went by, with no sight of them. Everitt took the MGBs in closer, and to his relief, the LCAs appeared. Hastily the precious radar equipment was transferred to

Lt Cdr J.H. Coste DSC and Lt Cdr R.A.H. Nye DSC, leaders of C class flotillas. (Courtesy, E. Robertson)

Coastal Forces on their way to Dieppe, August 1942: MGB 321 is in the foreground. (Courtesy, V. Hood)

312, which set off at speed for Portsmouth. Each of the remaining MGBs took two LCAs in tow, and even though they were only 15 miles off the French coast at first light and they had no air cover, they returned safely. The raid had been a tremendous success, and the capture of the radar equipment proved of great strategic importance.[2]

Operation Chariot, the St Nazaire Raid, came several weeks later, on 26/28 March 1942. This time, the only C class boat involved was MGB 314, together with MTB 74 (a Vosper) and sixteen MLs. 314, commanded by Lt D.M.C. Curtis, acted as headquarters ship and three of those she carried on the raid were awarded VCs: the Military Commander Lt Col A.C. Newman, the Senior Naval Officer, Commander R.E.D. Ryder RN, and A/B W.A. Savage, the pom-pom gunner of 314, who died at his gun. His VC – the only one awarded in Coastal Forces operations – is regarded as representing the gallantry of thousands of officers and men who served in the boats and whose cumulative record in close action with the enemy was recognized throughout the Royal Navy.

The story of the raid is very well documented, and need not be described in detail here. MTB 74 and twelve of the MLs were sunk, and MGB 314 herself so badly damaged that although she managed to sail out of St Nazaire riddled with shell holes and full of wounded, she had to be sunk by HMS *Atherstone*. 314 had entered history for her exploits, and the 'C' boats – with the MLs and Coastal Forces in general – had achieved a special place in the archives of Combined Operations.

The main objective of the raid, to block the only dock on the Atlantic coast of France large enough to take the battleship *Tirpitz*,

2 Article, J.H. Coste, 'The Bruneval Raid'.

using the old destroyer *Campbeltown* as a block ship, was entirely successful.[3]

The raid on Dieppe (Operation Jubilee), on 19 August 1942, had stronger naval and military forces than any landing earlier in the war. It had a chequered background of planning and preparation, and many opposed it on a variety of grounds. It seemed that the biggest benefits were likely to be the experience provided by a large-scale landing (which Churchill later described as a 'reconnaissance in force'), together with the much overdue employment of the Canadian troops, who had been waiting for action since arriving in Britain late in 1939.

Coastal Forces were heavily involved, and were represented *inter alia* by eight C class MGBs and four SGBs. They were used in a great variety of ways, but those most concerned with the actual landings were the experienced boats of the 14th MGB Flotilla and the newly commissioned SGBs. Once again they formed the vanguard, leading in the fleet minesweepers right to the beaches, and covering the landing ships HMS *Princess Beatrix* and HMS *Invicta*. 317, with John Coste in command, carried the Colonel of the South Saskatchewan Regiment, Colonel Merritt (later to win a VC), and the Beachmaster for Green Beach, and his unit was kept busy carrying out minor bombardments, rescuing damaged landing craft, and picking up RAF pilots and casualties. Another group of 'C's and SGBs were very active on the right flank, and their activities are described in great detail by Peter Scott, CO of SGB 9, in *The Battle of the Narrow Seas*.

It is, of course, sad to relate that militarily the operation was regarded as a defeat and a disaster for the Canadians, who lost 65 per cent of their personnel. But the lessons learned may well have contributed massively to the success of the landings in North Africa and Sicily, and in Normandy.[4]

However, these raids were not the only notable operations involving the C class MGBs. In chapter two, there is a full description of the first action in which a Dog Boat took part, when 601 was severely damaged having joined 322 and 328 in a patrol from Dover. The unit attacked a heavily escorted enemy tanker off Cap Griz Nez on 20/21 July 1942. It was led by Lt H.P. Cobb in 328, and she was sunk when attempting to break through this greatly superior force of escorts to attack the tanker with depth charges.

Only a few days later, on 30/31 July, Lt E.M. Thorpe RN, SO of the 16th MGB Flotilla from Yarmouth, led a unit to patrol off the Dutch coast. He was aboard 335 (Lt R.A. Forbes) in company with 332 (McCallum) and 327 (Wilkinson). They met and attacked five heavily armed trawlers off Ymuiden and set one on fire. In the attack, 332 was hit repeatedly and disabled, with half the crew killed or wounded. Thorpe went in and took her in tow and got her back to Yarmouth.[5]

The Dover 'C's were in action on 16/17 August, and once again they were joined by a Dog Boat – 609, the second to be completed. The story of the action appears in chapter two, but from the 'C' boats' point of view deserves a little more detail. The SO of the unit, Lt Sidebottom, in MGB 330, attacked the rear of a line of six R-boats. Visibility was excellent, and he was astonished to get close and into a good firing position before the R-boats reacted – even though they had a six to three advantage. When he opened fire, the

---

[3] ROP at PRO in ADM 199/680; *The Attack on St Nazaire*.

[4] CF Periodic Review 1, article by J.H. Coste, 'Dieppe – The Dawn of Decision'.

[5] MO107841/42; ROP at PRO in ADM 199/782; Battle Summary 58 at NHB.

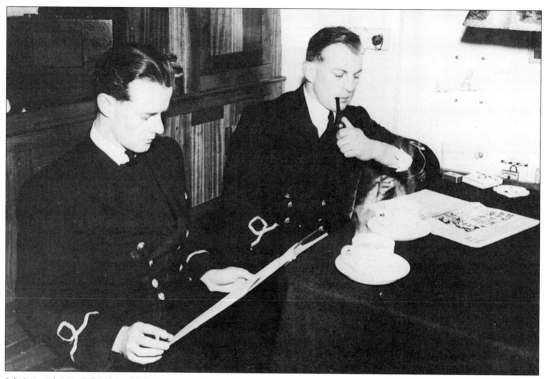

S/Lt R.M. (Mike) Marshall (right) and S/Lt P. Irvine, CO and No. 1 of MGB 321, early 1942. (Courtesy, V. Clarkson)

reply was instantaneous and intense, and in no time both targets and attackers were suffering crippling damage. With all his starboard guns out of action and many casualties, Sidebottom decided to ram. He hit the R-boat's port quarter and nearly cut her stern away. He pulled clear and watched the other two boats of his unit carrying on the fight, then both of them were forced to disengage. The battle was successfully continued by the 'short' gunboats and eventually the three boats limped back to Dover.[6]

On 10/11 September, another group of boats from the 16th Flotilla, led by their SO 'Micky' Thorpe, were involved in a bruising battle, once again off Ymuiden. Thorpe had

listened on his radio to reports of the short MGBs in action with E-boats further west. He positioned himself to await their return to harbour at first light and found himself in contact with two groups of E-boats, nine in all. 335 ('Tufty' Forbes) turned out of line to close on the enemy and she was hit, seriously damaged and stopped. Suddenly she was surrounded by a ring of E-boats all concentrating their fire. Thorpe in 334 led his MGBs in to beat them off and attempt to rescue 335. By now there were even more E-boats, but some were taking a hammering, and eventually he broke through the ring, got alongside 335 and began to take off the wounded, including the CO. When it was clear she would have to be abandoned, an attempt was made to sink her with pom-pom shells, and everyone believed she was

[6] Battle Summary (BS) 64 at NHB.

doomed. Unfortunately she did not sink, and next day was towed into Den Helder by the enemy.

For his leadership and personal gallantry in the rescue attempt against great odds, Lt Thorpe was awarded the DSO, and the coxswain of 335, Petty Officer G.H. Plenderleith, received the very rare award of the CGM (Conspicuous Gallantry Medal).[7]

The description of this continuous stream of actions throughout 1942 makes it very difficult to understand why, from September 1942 onwards, there are very few entries involving the 'C' boats in the Admiralty list of engagements by Coastal Forces. For the next six months none were recorded.

It seems clear that on the arrival of the Dog Boat flotillas with their heavier armament and slightly higher speed, the 'C' boats were switched largely to the convoy defence role in which they were already well versed, to the exclusion of the offensive patrols off the enemy coast in which they had, whenever the opportunity arose, acquitted themselves gallantly.

But on 28/29 March 1943, it was one of the customary defensive patrols that brought the opportunity for confrontation with the E-boats against which, night after night, the boats lay in wait ready to repel their attacks. Lt D.G. Bradford RNR was leading the unit in his own 333, with 321 (P.L. Stobo) in company. While lying 'cut' (i.e., stopped with engines not running to enable a listening watch for E-boat engines), he suddenly heard them, started up, intercepted their course and having sighted them, tracked a line of five moving slowly. Why so slow, he could not fathom. He was able to approach very close, pour a broadside into the last in line, and then take on the next ahead. Stobo in 321 had

gone after the others, so Bradford decided to ram, and sheared off the last twenty feet of her hull, which broke away. He circled back and could find little trace of either E-boat, so chased off to find the first three. When he found them stopped in a group, he opened fire and they were away at full speed.

A group of prisoners of war later admitted that their E-boat, S29, had been scuttled after action damage from British MGBs.

Soon after, Bradford joined the 31st MTB Flotilla of Dog Boats, and became the SO almost at once.[8]

It may seem churlish, having earlier devoted the whole of chapter nine to MTB 718 as the one Dog Boat in the 15th MGB Flotilla engaged in clandestine operations under the aegis of DDOD(I), not to acknowledge the very distinguished service of MGB 318, which for even longer occupied a similar position as the only 'C' in the flotilla.

However, the story of MGB 318 is well told by Harold Pickles, the editor of the Coastal Forces Veterans' Association Newsletter for many years, in his book *Untold Stories of Small Boats at War*, a privately published collection of articles taken from many of the newsletters. 318 operated from 1942 to 1945 on clandestine work, mainly to the coast of France and ultimately exclusively to Brittany.

To conclude the story of the 'C' boats, mention must be made of the part they played in Force J in the opening stages of Operation Neptune, when they led in the initial waves of LCAs on D-Day. However, in the absence of documented information, no real detail can be given.

Perhaps it is true to say that what cannot be recorded, through lack of archive information, is the ceaseless activity of all the flotillas of this small group of twenty-four

[7] ROP at PRO in ADM 199/680; CFI19; BS71 at NHB; *Seedie's List of CF Awards*.

[8] MO4278; ROP at PRO in ADM 199/536.

Lt Cdr Peter Scott MBE, DSC, RNVR, SO of 1st SGB Flotilla and CO of HMS *Grey Goose*. (Courtesy, E. Robertson)

boats over four years of war in a great variety of roles. The respect in which they were held in Coastal Forces far outweighs the brief record of endeavour reported here.

THE STEAM GUNBOATS

The steam gunboats were built as a totally different concept from the wooden, petrol-engined boats which typified all other Coastal Forces craft. They were steel-hulled, powered by two-shaft, geared, steam turbine engines, originally giving 8,000 SHP, were 137 ft in length and displaced 165 tons. Later, when their machinery was found to be vulnerable to machine gun fire, armour plate was fitted to the sides of the boiler and engine rooms, and armament was considerably enhanced. As a result the displacement increased to 260 tons, leading to a reduction in maximum speed to 30 knots.

In many ways, they were mini-destroyers in appearance, and were clearly an experiment to maximize fire-power. Only seven were built, and although their early vulnerability is often quoted as the reason for the decision not to build more, the major reason was that priority for the use of slipways was given to more urgently needed destroyers.

SGBs 1 and 2 were never laid down due to bomb damage at Thornycroft's Woolston yard. The remaining seven (SGBs 3 to 9) were all completed between February and July 1942. By mid-1943 they had their armour plate and finally had an armament of one 3-in, two 6-pdrs, and three twin 20-mm guns, with two 21-in torpedoes – formidable indeed. SGB7 was sunk on 18/19 June 1942 so that for the majority of its existence, the 1st SGB Flotilla had six boats.

The first SO of the flotilla was Lt R.G.L.

HMS *Grey Goose* (SGB 9). (Courtesy, V. Clarkson)

Pennell RN who handed over to Lt Cdr P.M. Scott MBE at the beginning of 1943. By July 1943 he had prevailed upon the Admiralty to allow the boats of his flotilla to be given names instead of numbers. SGB 3 became *Grey Seal*, 4 was *Grey Fox*, 5 *Grey Owl*, 6 *Grey Shark*, 8 *Grey Wolf* and 9 (Peter Scott's boat) was *Grey Goose*.

The flotilla appears in the list of recorded Coastal Forces actions on seventeen occasions between June 1942 and October 1944. These included a major part in the Dieppe Raid on 19 August 1942, which was Peter Scott's first operation in command of SGB 9, newly commissioned and worked up. In each of the previous three actions, the boats had been badly damaged, and indeed the details of all the actions up to this time, and many that came later, show that they suffered heavy casualties.

Peter Scott handed over command of *Grey Goose* to Lt P.N. Hood on 15 November 1943. After a spell as an instructor and training director at HMS *Bee*, the working-up base, he joined the team planning the Coastal Forces' complex role in Operation Neptune. The SGBs played their part in that operation and spent much time in the Assault Area.

The original edition of Peter Scott's autobiography, *The Eye of the Wind*, contains very detailed accounts of many of the SGB actions. They also feature widely in *The Battle of the Narrow Seas*. In this supplementary chapter it is not possible to enlarge further on those actions, but a survey of the seventeen engagements does indicate an enormous amount of gallantry and of attacks pressed home whatever the odds. There was, however, a surprising shortage of positive results. Considering the tremendous fire-power of the SGBs, this must

Four boats of the 50th Flotilla, with base staff aboard, celebrate VE Day. (Courtesy, L. Sprigg)

have been disappointing to the crews and to those operating the boats.[9]

THE CAMPER AND NICHOLSONS MGBS

These nine lovely boats with their elegant yacht-like lines were originally ordered for the Turkish Navy and were used in a variety of ways when requisitioned. The first Camper and Nicholson boat MGB 501 had three Packard engines. She was followed by 502 to 508 with three Davey Paxman diesel engines, and 509, which also had Packards. 510 was an experimental Vosper boat, with four Packards coupled to two shafts.

In fact, only four Campers operated as MGBs, and all these were allocated to the 15th MGB Flotilla, attached to DDOD(I) for clandestine operations rather than to Coastal Forces. 501 was sunk on 27 July 1942 by an internal explosion off Land's End. 502 and 503 carried out many of the missions to Brittany from 1943 to 1945. 509 was not completed until 1945.

The boats originally numbered 504–508 became the mercantile blockade-runners named *Hopewell*, *Nonsuch*, *Gay Viking*, *Gay Corsair* and *Master Standfast*. They were manned by merchant navy officers and men (or seconded as such), and achieved fame in bringing precious cargoes of ball-bearings and special steels back from Sweden, through the German blockade of the Skagerrak.

Master Standfast was captured by Vp 1606 off Hako, Norway, on 2 November 1943; *Gay Viking* was abandoned on 6 February 1944 after being in collision with *Hopewell* in the Skagerrak.

In 1945, near the end of the war in Europe, the blockade runners were returned to the RN for refit and were intended for use in the Pacific under DDOD(I). The surviving boats of the 500 series were re-numbered as 2002 to 2005, 2007 and 2009. The sad end of 2002 when mined a week after the end of the war off Norway has been described in chapter nine.[10]

A list of awards to the personnel of the 'C' MGBs, the SGBs and the Camper and Nicholson MGBs is given in Appendix 2.

---

[9] *Battle of the Narrow Seas*; *The Eye of the Wind*.

[10] *Warships of WW2*; *The Blockade Busters*; *The Secret Navies*; *On Hazardous Service*.

EPILOGUE

It behoves all historians of military matters to avoid the trap of overestimating results or reaching simplistic conclusions. In these pages, descriptions of actions taken from reports of Proceedings frequently refer to losses and damage inflicted upon enemy ships: wherever possible, evidence has been sought from enemy or post-war intelligence Reports to substantiate claims.

Most of the statistics produced during the war or immediately after its close had perforce to be based largely on claims made by participating ships. But such claims were, with the best will in the world, made (in the case of MTBs) on return from a series of night attacks, often with twists and turns, interruptions caused by damage during which enemy dispositions changed, targets appeared and disappeared, and individual boats lost contact and regained it. Such confused situations were purpose built for duplicated and distorted claims, however hard the debriefing meetings tried to eliminate them. A blazing ship frequently did not sink; an explosion might not be the end. The only really safe criterion was to see a target sink

MTB 5020 – the last Dog Boat in commission – in August 1956 at Portsmouth. (Courtesy, Art Webster)

beneath the waves, and boats rarely had the luxury of hanging around to watch without interruption from the enemy.

Occasionally the intelligence services could provide confirmation: much more rarely the enemy would admit that one or more of their ships was sunk. The safest statistics are those admitted specifically to have been sunk in each navy's own lists. And estimates of 'damaged' ships are virtually useless: there were countless examples in all navies of ships limping home – towed or on one engine, with pumps going full blast – after being seriously disabled.

So there will be no attempt here to claim that the 'long' MTBs/MGBs, whose operations are described in this book, sank a specific number of ships. It is certain they sank many. It is just as difficult to quantify the number of patrols they carried out or the number of engagements with the enemy they had, although there are pointers to the latter.

The list of recorded actions involving Coastal Forces boats was compiled in the Admiralty in about 1952, and should provide much of the evidence. Unfortunately it is rather incomplete and inconsistent, as each command used different methods to report, and there were in any case no specific criteria to define 'an action'. But as it is the best documented evidence available, a simple count based on classifications of types of enemy contact is possible, and may be of interest.

The list indicates that all types of Coastal Forces craft were in contact with the enemy on 967 occasions. The MTBs, MGBs and SGBs were involved in 761 of those incidents; the remainder were mostly by MLs. Three-quarters of those contacts (about 570) were in the form of what can be simply described as surface battles – exchanges of fire, usually at short range, with enemy ships. In addition, there were about 150 reports of engagements with aircraft, mining incidents, and close attacks by shore batteries. Landings and clandestine operations were rarely reported adequately.

To be more selective, the Dog Boats were involved in 273 of those battles: 136 in home waters, 104 in the Mediterranean, and 33 in Norwegian waters. The C class MGBs, despite their heavy commitment to convoy protection, were in twenty-one, and the SGBs in seventeen. These broad figures at least convey the high level of aggressive commitment to seek out and engage the enemy. It has been estimated that the ratio of patrols when there was no enemy sighting to those resulting in contact was possibly as high as 10 to 1: the concentration and expenditure of nervous energy was hardly less when awaiting enemy contact than when that contact was made.

One last assessment can be attempted. As the Dog Boats were originally conceived with the intention of combating the enemy's E-boats, it is interesting to reflect on the outcome of that intention. It has frequently been said in the description of operations that the ability of the E-boats to speed away from Dog Boats was a grave disadvantage. That, together with the tactical truism that the primary aim of the E-boats was to torpedo larger targets, and to avoid bruising battles with the MTBs and MGBs, meant that it was only on rare occasions that they met, as it were, on even ground. Whenever intelligent positioning, or good radar direction, or weather conditions such as fog banks, or just sheer chance, led to the opportunity for the Dog Boat to mount a gun attack on E-boats (even in superior numbers), their far heavier armament was frequently too much for the enemy, who could be expected to retaliate bravely, but more often sought to break off as quickly as possible. But the high-speed diesels of the E-boats, the comparative safety of the fuel and their low silhouette were all recognized as enormous advantages to the enemy.

Even before the end of the war, an

'The other face of war.' Fifty years on, Coastal Forces veterans honour their dead at Komiza, Vis, Yugoslavia. (Courtesy, P.J. O'Hare)

assessment began of factors that should be considered when plans were made for post-war development of the ideal fast patrol boat. Agreement was immediate that it was essential that the mistakes following the First World War, when all the lessons learned were lost, should not be repeated.

A concensus was reached that the need was for a 'long' boat with sufficiently high power/weight ratio engines to be able to attain high speeds and yet have long range, good stability in a seaway, and ability to accept a heavy armament.

In 1948 the Admiralty produced a programme which included research to develop those engines, with preference for diesels or gas turbines to reduce vulnerability. It also contemplated the use of an existing 17-pdr gun to be capable of sinking an E-boat with one hit. Flexibility was to be sought by making the boats easily convertible by their own crews for use as torpedo boats, gunboats, minelayers or raiding craft.

By 1950, hastened by the Cold War and the Korean War, and with the production of the Deltic diesel engine, the Dark class of short fast patrol boats were built in quantity, but never proved satisfactory. Vosper were then invited to produce a 100-ft boat with 50 knot Proteus gas turbines, called the Brave class, with a similarly convertible capability. But in 1958 the Admiralty reduced Coastal Forces to a four-boat Trials Squadron, which, following their completion, incorporated the two 'Braves'. Vosper continued their own programme, building for foreign navies, and in fact, the development of lightweight surface-to-surface weapons like Styx and Exocet made such boats potentially extremely effective units in the 1960s and 1970s.

However, satellite and AWACS surveillance of any war area waters reversed the balance from the late 1970s, so that it is currently generally held that offensive Coastal Forces craft are no longer practicable except perhaps in very small localized conflicts.

When the Second World War ended, the disposal of the force of Dog Boats began very quickly. Many of them, of course, had already come to the end of their useful lives by the end of 1944 and had been 'paid off to Reserve'. But those that had come from the yards in 1944 and 1945 were still in demand. Only a small number were retained in service: the majority went to a variety of destinations. Many were loaned to Sea Cadet units and Sea Scout groups. Another large batch was handed over to the RAF to be converted as 'Long Range Rescue Craft' (LRRC). Others were sold to be used as houseboats (the common asking price was between £300 and £500). The most degrading end was to be sent to the breakers' yards and all useful fittings sold.

The majority of the men were demobilized by 1946, and most waited with a mixture of anxiety and detached interest to see whether the Navy would retain a peacetime force of boats, and hoping that if it did so, they would reflect the operational lessons learned in 1939–45.

In longer term retrospect, the veterans of the boats have retained their affection for their ships and loyalty to their shipmates. Many meet regularly and the Coastal Forces Veterans Association helps them keep in touch with each other. They find it difficult to come to terms with the fact that major histories of the war at sea in the Second World War have given scant recognition to their endeavours in which about one thousand of their number gave their lives.

It is particularly strange that in the major work entitled *Engage the Enemy More Closely*, there is just one single mention of MTBs and MGBs, the naval units which undoubtedly *did* engage the enemy more closely than any other.

A symbolic end to conflict.

GLOSSARY

A/B	Able Seaman	MAS	Italian Motor Torpedo Boat
ACOS	Admiral Commanding Orkney & Shetland	MGB	Motor Gun Boat
		ML	Motor Launch
CBs	Confidential Books	MTB	Motor Torpedo Boat
CCF	Captain Coastal Forces	NID	Naval Intelligence Department
CFVA	Coastal Forces Veterans Association	NOIC	Naval Officer in Charge
CFW	Commander, Coastal Forces Western (Mediterranean)	OBE	Officer of the Order of the British Empire
C-in-C	Commander in Chief	PO	Petty Officer
CO	Commanding Officer	POMM	Petty Officer Motor Mechanic
CSA	Chloro-sulphonic Acid (smoke apparatus)	PPI	Plot Position Indicator (Radar screen)
CTL	Constructive Total Loss	PT	Patrol Torpedo Boat (USN MTB)
DDOD(I)	Deputy Director Operations Division (Irregular)	RANVR	Royal Australian Naval Volunteer Reserve
DSC	Distinguished Service Cross	RCNVR	Royal Canadian Naval Volunteer Reserve
DSM	Distinguished Service Medal		
DSO	Distinguished Service Order	RNorN	Royal Norwegian Navy
GM	George Medal	RNR	Royal Naval Reserve
HDML	Harbour Defence Motor Launch	RNVR	Royal Naval Volunteer Reserve
IFF	Interrogative Friend or Foe	RNZNVR	Royal New Zealand Naval Volunteer Reserve
Ju	Junkers		
LCA	Landing Craft Assault	SANF(V)	South African Naval Forces (Volunteer)
LCG	Landing Craft Gun		
LCI	Landing Craft Infantry	SGB	Steam Gun Boat
LCT	Landing Craft Tank	SNOVIS	Senior Naval Officer, Vis
L/MM	Leading Motor Mechanic	SO	Senior Officer (of a flotilla)
L/Sea	Leading Seaman	SOIS	Senior Officer Inshore Squadron
LSI	Landing Ship Infantry	TLC	Tank Landing Craft
LST	Landing Ship Tank	V56, V57, etc.	Senior Officer, 56th MTB Flotilla . . . 57th, etc.
MA/SB	Motor Anti-Submarine Boat		

NOTES

Abbreviations: PRO: Public Record Office; NHB: Naval Historical Branch; MO numbers are Admiralty references, found at NHB; ROP: Reports of Proceedings; the ADM 199 series refer to operational reports at the PRO; WIR: War Intelligence Reports; NID: Naval Intelligence Department; CFPR: Coastal Forces Periodic Review; CFI: Coastal Forces Information Bulletins; CCF: Captain Coastal Forces.

CHAPTER 1

NOTE 1

Throughout the text, any names of officers may be taken as RNVR unless they were RN (Royal Navy), RNR (Royal Naval Reserve), RCNVR (Royal Canadian Naval Volunteer Reserve), RANVR (Royal Australian Naval Volunteer Reserve), RNZNVR (Royal New Zealand Volunteer Reserve), SANF(V) (South African Naval Forces, Volunteer), FFN (Free French Navy), RNethN (Royal Netherlands Navy), RNorN (Royal Norwegian Navy), and USN (United States Navy).

CHAPTER 2

NOTE 2

Lt Cdr Robert P. Hichens DSO DSC RNVR, the first RNVR officer to be given command of a flotilla. He was SO of the 6th and 8th MGB Flotillas until he was killed in action on 12/13 April 1943, and is acknowledged as having had a profound effect on MTB and MGB operational tactics.

NOTE 3

Operation in the Skagerrak: Operation Cabaret. Sources: a) Letters from Lt D.G.E. Probert DSC RNVR, CO of MGB 610, and from A/B (Radar)

John W. Harrop, Radar Operator of MGB 610; b) Confirmed by a passage in *The Secret Navies*, A. Cecil Hampshire, William Kimber, 1978.

NOTE 4

For detail of action: MO35422; ROP at PRO in ADM 199/537.
For detail of results: NID OD5084/45.
N.B. The reports of the actions on 9/10 and 12/13 March were submitted by Lt K. Gemmell and are signed by him, spelt in this way. Other books spell his name culminating in a single 'l'.

CHAPTER 3

NOTE 5

General note on source of information: Although many of the operation reports are available at PRO, it is doubtful whether, without help from Norwegian sources, this account could have been as complete. Through the assistance of Rear-Admiral Bj Grimstvedt, the Inspector-General of the Royal Norwegian Navy in 1988, a comprehensive report was written for the author by Vice-Admiral H.B. Gundersen RNorN, who himself served in the two Norwegian MTB flotillas from the earliest days, first as a Midshipman and ultimately as CO of MTB 618 and 716. He translated reports and verified accounts of enemy ships sunk or damaged, with reference to German reports after the war. In addition, Rear-Admiral Grimstvedt provided details of every boat in the Norwegian flotillas from *Norwegian Naval Ships 1939–1945*, Frank Abelson, Oslo, 1988. ISBN 84-7046-050-8.

NOTE 6

The CMBs of 1919 and operations in the Gulf of Finland.

This operation is described in two books by Captain Augustus Agar VC RN, the first, *Footprints in the Sea*, and then in greater detail in *Baltic Episode*, Hodder and Stoughton, 1963; Conway Maritime Press, 1983.

It is a remarkable fact that many of those involved in that operation were to serve significantly in Coastal Forces in the Second World War. Agar himself was Chief of Staff to Rear-Admiral Piers Kekewich (Rear- Admiral Coastal Forces) during the vital formative years in 1940–1; Admiral Sir Walter Cowan, who commanded all British Forces in the Baltic in 1919, was still seeking action in the Dalmatian Islands at the age of eighty with Tito and his Partisans in 1943–4; and Commander A.E.P. Welman DSO DSC RN, who served in CMBs at this time, not only formed and commanded HMS *St Christopher*, the Coastal Forces training base at Fort William, but also became Commander Coastal Forces Western Mediterranean (CFW) in 1943.

NOTE 7

MTB 345's capture and murder of her crew. Report compiled from German and Norwegian records by relatives of Telegraphist Rennie Hull, the only Royal Navy member of MTB 345.

NOTE 8

The 'Chariot' and 'Welman' operations.
Sources: a) a letter from L/MM Thomas M. Robinson of MGB 675; b) extract from *The Naval Record*, Vol. 33, 1945, 'A gallant venture' (MCR).

NOTE 9

17th Flotilla Senior Officers:
18.5.42 to 4.4.43 Lt Cdr H.M. Duff-Still RNVR.
4.4.43 to 1.8.43 Lt Cdr D.G.E. Probert RNVR.
1.8.43 to 18.5.44 Lt Cdr G.L. Cotton RNVR.

CHAPTER 4

NOTE 10

Sinking of U-639 and U-439 on 4 May 1943 in the Atlantic after attack on Coastal Forces convoy.
Sources: a) *The Month of the Lost U-boats*, Geoffrey Jones, William Kimber, 1977. ISBN 07183-0205-2; b) The author's recollections, in

Gunboat 658, L.C. Reynolds, William Kimber, 1955; c) ROP at PRO in ADM199/1317.

NOTE 11

Action, 25/26 April 1943 off Bizerta by MTBs 639 and 635.
No report of this action was submitted at this time, although Mediterranean signal 272346 refers to it. It was later described by Lt E. Hewitt when Captain Coastal Forces (Mediterranean) – Captain J.F. Stevens RN – realized in December 1944 that his predecessor had never received a report. Hewitt, who in April 1943 was a Sub-Lieutenant and First Lieutenant of MTB 635, was by the end of 1944 a highly respected and experienced CO (of MTB 670) and was asked to fill the gap. This was passed to Admiralty in CCF's letter, 5.12.44.

NOTE 12

The daylight action by MTBs 639, 633 and 637 on 27 April 1943.
Because the SO, Lt P.F.S. Gould DSC RN, was killed, the reports of this action were delayed, and pieced together mainly by Lt E.F. Smyth. They were submitted by Commodore G.N. Oliver RN, at the time Senior Officer Inshore Squadron (SOIS) at Bone. The earliest published account was by two war correspondents, George Palmer and Frederic Sondern Jr, in *Saturday Night*, the Canadian weekly, on 4 September 1943. It was later repeated in condensed form in the *Reader's Digest* under the heading 'These, too, were expendable'. The author now has the advantage of two personal accounts, one by a survivor of 639's crew, Telegraphist (wireless operator) John Hargreaves, and the other by his friend Telegraphist Andy Falconer of 635 who were prevented from joining the unit because of engine trouble. Falconer played a significant role in this operation back in Sousse by keeping radio watch throughout. Every account varies slightly in detail.

NOTE 13

8 May 1943: MTB 637 and MGB 643 attempt to enter Bizerta Harbour with Commodore Oliver.
This account is derived from reports from Lt E.F. Smyth (637) and Lt G.M. Hobday (643) and

Commodore Oliver (copies held). A personal account by Lt Hobday appears in his book, *In Harm's Way*, IWM, 1985, and more detail is derived from *Western Mediterranean 1942–5* by 'Taffrail' (Captain Tapprell Dorling DSO RN), Hodder & Stoughton, 1947.

NOTE 14

The invasion of Sicily (Operation Husky).

The detail of Coastal Forces' continuous activity during Operation Husky is rather patchily described in official documents. ADM 199/541 and ADM 199/1318 at PRO are helpful on specific incidents. Taffrail's *Western Mediterranean 1942–5*, using C-in-C's records extensively as an immediate semi-official history, is a valuable and accurate source. The work of the 20th MGB Flotilla is well covered as the author was Navigating Officer of MGB 658 throughout, and is described in his book *Gunboat 658*. He also had the advantage of a handwritten draft of the report by the SO of the 20th Flotilla, Lt Cdr N.H. Hughes of the patrols in the first ten days of the operation.

NOTE 15

The September 1943 special operations at Salerno, the Galita Islands, Capri, Ischia, Procida, and the surrender of Sardinia to two MGBs.

It has been very difficult to piece together accurately the chronology and the detail of events. The author has received personal accounts from officers and men who took part in each of these successive and dramatic events, but they rarely contain dates and rely on recall at almost fifty years' distance. But once again Taffrail's *Western Mediterranean 1942–5*, Hobday's *In Harm's Way* and Dudley Pope's *Flag 4* are very helpful and the last of these includes accounts (e.g. from Lt T.J. Bligh of 662 at Cagliari) recounted much nearer to the events.

CHAPTER 5

NOTE 16

Petty Officer Frederick Coombes DSM.

PO Fred Coombes was Coxswain of MTB 621 and was awarded the DSM for the action on 19/20 September 1943. He had a twin brother, Petty Officer Frank Coombes, who was Coxswain of MTB 624. He was awarded a DSM for Operation Neptune, in the initial landings in Normandy. For twin brothers to be coxswains in the same flotilla was a remarkable coincidence, and for both to be awarded DSMs even more so. They attended a presentation ceremony at Buckingham Palace together on 26.6.45 to receive their awards. They together wrote a fascinating unpublished autobiography of their naval careers, beginning as seaman boys at HMS *St Vincent* in the 1930s, copies of which are held by the author and at the Imperial War Museum.

NOTE 17

Action by MGBs 603 and 607, and MGBs 609 and 610, off Smith's Knoll, 24/25 October 1943.

For a full list of awards see, *Seedie's List of Coastal Forces Awards*, under each of these four boats. It is sad to note that neither Lt Marshall nor Lt Lightoller survived the war. Lt Mike Marshall, a pre-war English rugby international, was lost when in temporary command of MGB 2002 in May 1945 off Norway (a few days after the surrender of German forces), the boat having hit a mine. Lt Frederic Lightoller was killed ashore in March 1945 when the German garrison in the Channel Islands carried out a commando raid on Granville.

CHAPTER 6

NOTE 18

The detail of operations by the 30th/54th MTB Flotilla in this chapter is derived mainly from the report compiled in 1988 for the author by Vice-Admiral H.B. Gundersen as described in note 5.

The flotilla operated under the command of the Admiral Commanding Orkney & Shetland (ACOS), and where available the reporting signal prefixed 'ACOS' is quoted, and also the Admiralty List number prefixed MO— as in all Reports of Proceedings. The Reports are to be found at the Public Record Office in ADM 199/270 (for 1943–4) and ADM 199/997 (for 1945).

The report is quoted very extensively, and the results of actions, with the details of ships sunk, are clearly totally reliable. It is noticeable that no 'claims' are made in respect of enemy vessels 'damaged' rather than those verified as 'sunk'.

CHAPTER 7

General note: the fact that the author served in MGB 658 in the Mediterranean throughout this period, and recorded many observed events soon after the war with the help of Reports of Proceedings held personally, is of great assistance.

Flag 4 – The Battle of Coastal Forces in the Mediterranean, Dudley Pope, William Kimber, 1954, is a valuable source. The author helped Pope in the preparation of material. It is valuable particularly because Pope had direct access at the time for comment and description of events from T.J. Bligh, R.A. Allan, and Capt A.E.P. Welman who have since died.

In Harm's Way (op. cit.) is a useful source in that it contains material, particularly on Aegean operations, for which there are no other accounts.

Our Lady of the Pirates by Kenneth Horlock, privately published in about 1989, is valuable for its descriptions of Adriatic operations and a personal account of the boarding incidents of April 1944.

The main source of information throughout is the collection of ROPs held at the PRO in Kew in ADM 199/268 and /269, together with CCF (Mediterranean)'s reports in the Coastal Forces Periodic Reviews.

NOTE 19

The MTBs available to CCF on reorganization of flotillas in late 1943 were:

7th MTB Flotilla (in the process of being re-equipped with new boats as follows):
  MTBs   375 376 377 378 (Vospers)
  MTBs   419 420 421 423 (Higgins)
10th MTB Flotilla:
  MTBs   260 261 263 266
         307 309 313 315 (Elcos)
20th MTB Flotilla:
  MTBs   287 288 289 290
         295 296 297 298 (Vospers)

24th MTB Flotilla:
  MTBs   81 85 86 89 97
         226 242 243 (Vospers)
32nd MTB Flotilla:
  MTBs   633 634 637 638 640 (D class)
33rd MTB Flotilla:
  MTBs   649 651 655 656 667 670 (D class)
A total of 32 'short' MTBs and 11 Dog MTBs.

NOTE 20

Details from one of a series of ROPs of the 15th PT Squadron (Ron 15) of the United States Navy by their SO, Lt Cdr S.M. Barnes USN and held by the author.

NOTE 21

Three actions on successive nights by the 56th MTB/MGB Flotilla from Bastia in January 1944.
i) On 21/22 January 1944 off Civitavecchia by MGBs 657, 658, 659, 663 and MTB 655.
ii) On 22/23 January 1944, south of Leghorn, by MGBs 657, 659 and 663.
iii) On 23/24 January 1944 off Vada Rocks by MGB 658 and MTB 655 with PT 217.
Sources: a) MO3983; b) ROPs at PRO in ADM 199/268; c) additional detail in *Gunboat 658*, L.C. Reynolds.

CHAPTER 8

NOTE 22

General note on sources.

The descriptions of the complex operations detailed in this chapter, and particularly of the part Dog Boats played in Operation Neptune – the landings in Normandy and their aftermath – depend on a large number of sources. They include:
(a) the report of CCF (Channel) as part of the Portsmouth Command Report on Operation Overlord; (b) the report on Coastal Forces in the Plymouth Command on Operation Neptune; (c) the account in *Battle of the Narrow Seas*, particularly because Lt Cdr Peter Scott was directly involved in the planning and operational aspects under CCF (Channel); (d) Lt Cdr D.G. Bradford's manuscript of his memoirs, *Day In, Night Out*, including descriptions of the 55th Flotilla's operations during the period May to August 1944; (e) *Chronology of*

the War at Sea 1939–1945 vol. 2, J. Rohwer and G. Hummelchen, trans. Derek Masters, Ian Allan, 1974; (f) numerous personal accounts; (g) reports of Proceedings either held by the author or at the Public Record Office, Kew; (h) the chronological summary list of all Coastal Forces actions compiled in Admiralty in about 1952.

NOTE 23

The protection of the anchorage and supply routes from E-boats out of Le Havre during the period 4–16 July, by the 55th MTB Flotilla.

Sources: (to prevent repetition, the Admiralty list number is given beside each night's activity rather than a series of separate notes.) All appear in the Summary of Coastal Forces Actions. All are amplified in Lt Cdr Bradford's *Day In, Night Out*, and references in *Chronology of the War at Sea*, pp. 433–5.

NOTE 24

Actions fought between 15 and 25 July 1944 both in the Channel and off the east coast by the 64th, 63rd, 50th, 58th and 54th and 52nd Flotillas.

Sources: again, these five actions are identified by the Admiralty list number. Each appears in the Summary of Coastal Forces Actions at the relevant date. Most are referred to in *Chronology of the War at Sea*.

NOTE 25

Comments by an E-boat CO Harry Garmsen, later a naturalized Canadian. Garmsen emigrated to Canada in 1953 and became a film cameraman with CBC. He became known to members of the Canadian CFVA and was invited to speak at their Annual Reunion in Toronto in 1989.

Sources: a) notes of the speech sent to the author; b) quoted in *Champagne Navy* by Nolan and Street, Random House, Toronto, 1991. ISBN 0-394-22149-9.

CHAPTER 9

NOTE 26

The material for this chapter has been obtained directly from the CO of MTB 718, Lt Ronald

Seddon DSC, who supplied copies of his Reports of Proceedings, and from the Telegraphist of 718, Charles Milner DSM, who has been the chronicler and correspondent for the boat's crew since the war. He is well known in Coastal Forces as the Treasurer of CFVA. His personal view of the clandestine missions and comments from the point of view of the ship's company are invaluable.

As much of this material was also made available to A. Cecil Hampshire, author of *The Secret Navies*, William Kimber, 1978, ISBN 0-7183-0195-1, and used in Section 1 of that book 'Freedom Ferry', reference to that book for material which puts the activities of MTB 718 in the overall context of the 15th MGB Flotilla has also been important. But since 1978 more reports have come to light and accounts here are more accurate.

NOTE 27

The loss of MGB 2002 on 12 May 1945 off southern Norway.
Source: notes from Charles Milner. N.B. The text of a letter written by POMM Tom Sheehan to friends in 2003 from hospital in Kristiansund while he and Norman Hine were facing major operations is a most wonderful expression of the irrepressible spirit of the British matelot. It describes the horrors and privations of four days on a raft in northern waters. Shortly after, Sheehan had both legs amputated, and Hine lost all his toes.

This letter is given in full in *Untold Stories of Small Boats at War*, Pentland Press, Durham, 1994, ISBN 1-85821-176X, a collection of articles from the newsletters of the CFVA edited by L/Sea Harold Pickles DSM of MGB 318, who edited the newsletters for many years.

CHAPTER 10

NOTE 28

The events from September to December 1944 in Greek waters including the liberation of Athens and Salonika, involving the 60th Flotilla.
Sources: a) extracts from *Western Mediterranean 1939–45* by 'Taffrail'; b) the unpublished memoirs of David Conquest who served as Navigating

Officer in 667 and 651 in this campaign; c) notes by Michael Hayes, from 1943 to 1945, an A/B in 660, on the detached service of MGB 660 at this time; d) notes by Norman Finch, Navigating Officer of 646 when Lt Michael Roberts was killed at Katakolon by ELAS troops on 4 January 1945.

NOTE 29

Description of circumstances of the loss of twelve Dog Boats while being towed from Malta to Alexandria on 30 January 1946.
Sources: a) research by the author through an appeal in the quarterly newsletter of the CFVA (Coastal Forces Veterans Association) leading to letters from: i) Jack Fearon and M.W. Coan (of 643); ii) Robert Westwood, (of 705) on duty in the Operations Room at HMS *Gregale* on 30 January 1946; iii) Ken Rogers (of MTBs 85 and 410) aboard HMS *Chequers* on the night of 30 January 1946; iv) G.G. Connell, author of *Mediterranean Maelstrom*; v) Peter Boissier, Gunnery Officer of HMS *Jervis*; vi) Peter Coney, signalman aboard HMS *Jervis*; b) article published in the CFVA newsletter.

TABLES

TABLE 1: AWARDS OF DECORATIONS
(From *Seedie's List of Coastal Forces Awards*)

IN HOME WATERS

DISTINGUISHED SERVICE CROSS

MTB	602	Lt H. Battson
		Lt J.D. Robinson
	608	Lt R.W. Ball
	611	Sub-Lt T.E. Atkinson
	613	Lt W.M. Marley
	617	Lt J.R.H. Kirkpatrick
		Sub-Lt D.R. Rotherham
	620	Lt J.A.H. Whitby
	622	Lt F.W. Carr
	624	Lt K. Gemmell
		Lt S.D. Marshall
	628	Lt R.E. Cunningham
	630	Sub-Lt W.G. Dalziel
	632	Lt C.W. Ford
	652	Lt G.W. Claydon
	666	Lt D.N. Buller
	675	Lt F.W. Bramwell
	677	Lt A.H. Clayton
	681	Lt E.S. Forman
	682	Lt W. Beynon
	684	Lt D. Storrie
	687	Lt J.V. Fisher
	690	Lt R.D. Marlow
	691	Lt J.W. Lambert
	693	Lt Cdr D.H.McCowen
		Lt S.B. Taylor
	694	Lt W.K. Foster
	695	Lt D.L. Macfarlane
	698	Lt J.D. Dempster
		Lt J.R.L. Best

	702	Lt F.T. Goodfellow
	704	Lt J.V. Balfour
	713	Lt J.A. Reeves
	714	Lt J.A. Lyall
	717	Lt B.H.C. Robinson
	718	Lt M.I.G. Hamilton
		Lt R.F. Seddon
	720	Lt J.N. Wise
	721	Lt J.O. King
	723	Lt K.E. Le Voi
		Lt A.M. McDougall
	724	Lt J.F. Humphreys
		Lt F.N. Thompson
	733	Lt J.C. Cain
	738	Lt Cdr D.Wilkie
	743	Lt M.C. Knox
	750	Lt Cdr J.A.C. Findlay
	764	Lt A.M. Watson
	772	Lt C.J. Wright
	5002	Lt D. Currie
	5007	Lt E.E.J. Whyfe
MGB	601	Lt A.A. Gotelee
	603	Lt F.R. Lightoller
	607	Lt R.M. Marshall
		Sub-Lt J.N. Arkell
	608	Lt J.H. Hodder
	609	Lt P.N.G. Edge
	610	Lt W. Harrop
	611	Lt Cdr I.D. Lyle
65th Flot		Lt J.W. Collins

BAR TO DISTINGUISHED SERVICE CROSS

MTB	611	Lt Cdr I.D. Lyle	MTB	693	Lt S.D. Marshall
	617	Lt D.G. Bradford		698	Lt Cdr H. Bradford
	632	Lt C.W. Ford		755	Lt B.H. Robinson
	683	Lt J.P. Perkins	52nd Flot		Lt Cdr T. Cartwright

SECOND BAR TO DISTINGUISHED SERVICE CROSS

MTB	617	Lt Cdr D.G. Bradford	MTB	673	Lt Cdr T. Cartwright

DISTINGUISHED SERVICE ORDER

MTB	632	Lt Cdr D.G. Bradford	MTB	693	Lt Cdr D.H. McCowen
	687	Lt Cdr K. Gemmell	MGB	605	Lt Cdr H. Duff Still

DISTINGUISHED SERVICE MEDAL

MTB	602	POMM T.W. Shufflebotham
		A/B K. Warburton
	606	LMM R. Mulrooney
	608	L/Sea F.H. Abram
		A/B R. Brunt
		PO N. Crompton
	611	CMM W.M. Peak
	614	A/B A. Mawson
		A/B J. McLaughlin
		L/Sea L. Pringle
	616	CMM E. Wain
	617	A/B A.R. Morgan
	619	L/Sig R.V.F. Collins
	620	Tel E.J.W. Slater
	621	PO Fred W. Coombes
		A/B G.F. Anderson
		L/MM F.H. Daw
		PO J. Barnes
		A/B E. Barber
		A/B R.H. Benham
	622	A/B H.J. Leader
	624	A/B W. Wilson
		PO Frank Coombes
		CMM J.S. Simmister
	628	PO F. Griffiths
	629	PO J.H. Richardson
		CMM M. Illingworth
	630	POMM E.E.V. Bailey
		Tel T. Barrett
		L/Sea C.F. Churchill
		PO H. Curry
		A/B F.C. Holmes
	632	Sto W. Wilson
		PO J.G. Huntley
		MM P.C. Roe

		CMM J.B. Sidebottom
	650	Sto E.G. Lamb
	652	A/B W. Scade
		CMM G.T. Walker
		POMM H.J. Wright
	666	A/B A. Hastie
		PO R.A. Jolliff
		CMM L.P. Stanton
	671	A/B A.R. Day
	673	Sig A.C. Westcott
		L/Tel J.W. Pearson
		CMM A. Baxter
	675	A/B G.R. Harrison
		POMM D.W. Knowelden
		O/Sea B.E. McNeill
	677	A/B D. Dynes
		PO A.J. Skinner
	679	PO C.R. Osborne
		Tel G.T. Smith
	680	A/B E.C.G. Musk
		POMM J.A.A. Shenton
		Sig D.M. Stein
		A/B H. Whittle
	683	PO A.E.L. Moulder
		A/B H. Davies
		CMM G.W. Stopps
	684	A/B J.H. Brewer
		A/B S. Smith
		CMM L.T. Terry
	685	CMM H.W. Norman
	687	Wire C. Bardsley
		Tel R. Harrison
		Sig F.W. Hollingdale
		L/Sea R. Tomlinson
		POMM H.G. Tuff
	689	A/B J.D. Etherington

	690	A/B R.P. Taplin		724	O/Sea K.G. Dix
		POMM D.G. Wilton			A/B F.R. White
		Wire V.P. Johnston			A/B C. Brockwell
	691	A/B R. Last	MTB	5002	L/Tel F.G. Merrill
		PO F.J. Tydeman			L/Tel R.A. Stent
		PO G.E. Cottman			Sto J. West
	692	CMM J.A. Minshull			PO R.J.S. Dwyer
	693	A/B G.R. Phillips			L/Sto C.J. Hart
		PO J.F. Horley		735	PO R.A. Hempshill
		A/B J.R. Barr		737	CMM J.R. Gibbs
		A/B R. McCulloch		743	A/B S.J. Anderson
	694	PO J.J. Billings			PO H.L. Harrison
		POMM H. Shaw		746	POMM A. Juckli
	695	L/Sea E. Leah		750	A/B J.A. Carter
		PO S.J. Mears		753	A/B T.L.K. Ford
	697	PO E. Reason			A/B E.H. Leigh
	698	L/MM R.H.C. Goldney		766	L/Sea F. Huntingford
		CMM L.F. Jarvis		771	L/Tel S.F. Coppin
		PO J. Rogers		772	A/B R. Gorman
		L/Sea W.H. Jones		776	CMM V.J.W. Hoban
	700	CMM P. Rankin			L/Sto J. Adams
	704	L/Sea A. Whalley	MGB	601	A/B A.R. Harris
	705	A/B J.H. Alexander			Tel E.H. Hensey
	706	PO J.N. Hutchinson		603	A/B A.R. Cherry
	710	Sto C. Lydon			PO H.Manson
	716	O/Sea G. Smith		607	A/B L. Cousins
	717	O/Sea E.L. Morris			A/B A. Hinchcliffe
		POMM J. Thomson			A/B R.H. Peter
	718	POMM W.R. Cartwright			PO H.B. Merriman
		L/Sea A.E. Dellow		608	A/B R.E. Dearing
		L/Tel C. Milner		609	PO R.E. Varnall
		L/Sea C.A. Stanley			A/B J.R. Beaumont
	721	Sto M.N. Peacey			CMM R.J.A. Bunce
	723	A/B J. Dixon		612	CMM A.H. Morrison
		Wire W.E. Sowden			A/B J. Parlour
		O/Sea T. Walkingshaw			CMM J.H. Thompson
		A/B W. Hopkins			

BAR TO DISTINGUISHED SERVICE MEDAL
MTB   687   PO R.W. Evans

BRITISH EMPIRE MEDAL
MTB   735   CMM G.H. Jones

CROIX DE GUERRE
MTB   652   PO W.J. Talbot   MTB   617   Lt P.W.J. Simcox

ROYAL HUMANE SOCIETY BRONZE MEDAL
MTB   729   L/Sto D.R. Colbron   MTB   729   A/B R.J. Wright

In Mediterranean Waters

DISTINGUISHED SERVICE CROSS

MTB	637	Lt E.F. Smyth		659	Lt K.E.A. Bayley
		Sub-Lt R.G.J. Cutting			Lt P.D. Barlow
		Lt R.C. Davidson		660	Lt A.T. Robinson
	638	Lt D.R. Lummis		661	Lt R.M. Cole
	651	Lt K.M. Horlock			Sub-Lt R.S. Smith
	655	Lt E.T. Greene Kelly		662	Lt Cdr T.J. Bligh
	670	Lt E. Hewitt			Lt W.R. Darracott
	697	Lt D.H. Booth		663	Lt T.E. Ladner
	699	Lt J. Redgrove	60th Flot		Lt Cdr B.L. Bourne
	710	Lt A.W. Bone			
59th Flot		Lt Cdr J.A. Montgomerie			
MGB	643	Lt G.M. Hobday			
	647	Lt M. Mountstephens			
		Sub Lt E. Lonsdale			
	657	Lt J.D. Maitland			
	658	Lt C. Burke			
		Sub-Lt C.A.M. Brydon			
		Lt L.C. Reynolds			

BAR TO DISTINGUISHED SERVICE CROSS

MTB	634	Lt W.E.A. Blount
	637	Lt R.C. Davidson
	670	Lt E. Hewitt
MGB	657	Lt Cdr. J.D. Maitland
	658	Lt C. Burke
	662	Lt Cdr T.J. Bligh
		Lt W.R. Darracott
	663	Lt T.E. Ladner

SECOND BAR TO DISTINGUISHED SERVICE CROSS

MTB	634	Lt W.E.A. Blount	MGB	658	Lt C. Burke
61st Flot		Lt Cdr T.G. Fuller			

DISTINGUISHED SERVICE ORDER

MGB	662	Lt Cdr T.J. Bligh

OFFICER OF THE ORDER OF THE BRITISH EMPIRE

57th Flot   Lt Cdr T.J. Bligh

CROIX DE GUERRE

MGB	657	Lt Cdr J.D. Maitland	MGB	659	Lt P.D. Barlow

GREEK WAR CROSS

MGB	645	Lt Cdr B.L. Bourne	MGB	647	Lt M. Mountstephens
	646	Lt B.L. Knight-Lachlan			

ROYAL HUMANE SOCIETY BRONZE CROSS

MTB	697	Sub Lt G.W. Herd

DISTINGUISHED SERVICE MEDAL

MTB	634	POMM R. Colthorpe			PO R.A. Dix
		A/B F. Smith		637	PO V.E. Clark
		L/Sea A.K. Bleach			CMM W.L.H. Gitsham
		A/B R.C. Craig			A/B V. Hood
				638	A/B J. Vaughan

	639	PO P.F. Crossley
	649	Tel J. McMillan
MTB	655	CMM D.R. Barber
		A/B S.J. Cowley
		PO C.H. Matthews
		A/B F. Allen
		A/B W. Jinks
	656	A/B D. Peters
	667	POMM J.H. Lacey
	670	A/B W. Turner
	697	CMM B.T. Richardson
		A/B C.N. Murch
MGB	643	L/Sea S. Kinnear
		POMM J.W. Stephens
		A/B L.E. Brewer
	647	O/Sea N. Matheson
		CMM J.R. Deeming
	657	A/B R.W. Charter
		A/B J.S. Armit
		PO H.R.P. Burton
		POMM T. Gardner
		A/B W.C. Wray
	658	A/B G.E. Howe
		POMM W.J.E. Last
		A/B N.C. Preston

		L/MM A.O. Burrows
		A/B K.W. Duffill
	659	POMM G.H. Daley
		PO P.J. O'Hare
		A/B W.A. Love
		L/Tel R. Ackers
MGB	660	PO W.F. Dodd
		PO D. Stevenson
	661	CMM J.D. Chaplain
		L/MM A.R. Hayter
		L/Tel L.J. Pegler
		L/Sea E.J. Nicholls
	662	PO W. Briddon
		A/B W.E. Allbright
		L/MM N.J.H. Hughes
		A/B A.H. Loryman
		POMM P. Reeves
		A/B R.S. Whiteley
		L/Tel S.A. Breen
		A/B P. Menzies
		A/B S.G.F. Ridler
	663	L/Sea B.L.M. Nash
		A/B D.H. Pain
60th Flot		L/Tel W.T. Page

BAR TO DISTINGUISHED MEDAL

MTB	637	POMM J.C. Jones	MGB	662	A/B R.S. Whiteley
	655	A/B S.J. Cowley		663	PO L.S. Nicholl
MGB	646	CMM F.N. Dowson			

BRITISH EMPIRE MEDAL

MTB	710	PO J.R. Stiff

TO NORWEGIAN PERSONNEL

DISTINGUISHED SERVICE CROSS

MTB	619	Lt B. Christiansen	54th Flot	Lt C.O. Herlofsen
	711	Lt A.F. Sveen		Lt K. Bogeberg
	715	Lt F.N. Stenersen		

BAR TO DISTINGUISHED SERVICE CROSS

MTB	711	Lt A.F. Sveen

DISTINGUISHED SERVICE MEDAL

MTB	619	PO S. Gjelsten	MTB	711	L/Sea J. Johansen
		A/B H.F. Olsen			PO/Eng F. Solberg
				715	PO K.J. Wahgren

IN C CLASS MGBS, CAMPER AND NICHOLSON MGBS AND STEAM GUNBOATS

DISTINGUISHED SERVICE CROSS

MGB	312	Lt A.R.H. Nye
	314	Lt D.M.C. Curtis
		Sub-Lt R.T.C. Worsley
	316	Lt Cdr T.N. Cartwright
		Lt The Lord Selsdon
	317	Lt J.H. Coste
	318	Lt C.E.C. Martin
	321	Lt M.L. Hirst
	322	Sub-Lt L.H. Blaxell
	323	Lt G.C. Fanner
		Lt Cdr D.G.E. Probert
	326	Lt N.A. Breeze
	328	Lt H.P. Cobb
	329	Lt Cdr C.H.W. Andrew
	330	Lt D.C. Sidebottom
	333	Lt D.G. Bradford
	15th	Lt D.L. Birkin
	Flot	Sub Lt D.N. Miller
		Lt J.T. McQuoid-Mason
		Lt M.P. Salmond
		Lt K.M. Uhr-Henry
		Lt Cdr P. Williams

Lt L.F. Bott
Lt A. Smith

SGB 3/ *Grey Seal*
    Lt J.S. Southcott

SGB 4/ *Grey Fox*
    Lt J.D. Ritchie
    Sub-Lt P.E. Mason
    Lt J. Erskine-Hill
    Lt T.J. Scott
    Lt R.G. Gaunt

SGB 5/ *Grey Owl*
    Sub Lt R.T. Davey
    Lt R.B.F. Hawkey

SGB 6/ *Grey Shark*
    Lt P.M. Scott

SGB 8/ *Grey Wolf*
    Lt I.R. Griffiths
    Lt R.G. Pennell

C & N Blockade-Runners
    Ch/Off R. Thornycroft
    Ch/Off S.B.J. Reynolds
    Ch/Off E.B. Ruffman
    Ch/Off The Earl Fitzwilliam

BAR TO DISTINGUISHED SERVICE CROSS

MGB   503   Lt R.M. Marshall   1st SGB Flot Lt Cdr P.M. Scott

DISTINGUISHED SERVICE ORDER

MGB   334   Lt E.M. Thorpe   C & N Blockade-Runners
                                           Cdr (Sp) Sir G. Binney

BAR TO DISTINGUISHED SERVICE ORDER

15th MGB Flotilla: Cdr E.A.G. Davis

VICTORIA CROSS

MGB   314   A/B W.A. Savage

CROIX DE GUERRE

MGB   324   Lt A.R. Birrell   MGB 316 CMM B. Barry

LEGIONNAIRE OF THE ORDER OF MERIT (USA)

SGB 3/ *Grey Seal*
        Lt J.S. Southcott
SGB 4/ *Grey Fox*
        Lt Cdr F.D. Russell-Roberts
SGB 5/ *Grey Owl*

                    Lt R.M. Hall
SGB 6/ *Grey Shark*
                    Lt R. King
SGB 8/ *Grey Wolf*
                    Lt C.E.C. Martin

MILITARY WILLEMS-ORDE (NETHERLANDS)
MGB 320 Sub-Lt F.T. Goodfellow

DISTINGUISHED SERVICE MEDAL
MGB 312 PO W.J. Caine
CMM J.W. Hulbert
314 POMM F.S. Hemming
L/Sea F. McKee
A/B F.A. Smith
315 A/B J. Lee
316 L/Sea H. McBain
PO A.B. Dawkins
317 O/Sea D.G. Mackenzie
PO C.E. Turner
L/Sea G.A.I. Camburn
318 CMM T. Barker
PO T. Boyle
319 PO C.S. Tate
320 A/B E. Luttig
321 PO E.P. Cast
322 PO J. McConaghie
A/B J.G. Price
324 L/Sea R.T. Winter
325 PO P.A. Traynor
326 CMM R.R. Dawson
L/Sea L.R. Jones
A/B D. McFarlance
327 CMM R. Bone
328 L/Sea A.L. Buttle
Sto L. Coles
332 PO A. Smith
333 LMM R.D. Gilbert
A/B G.W. Jennings
O/Sea S. Paxton
L/Sea J.J. Phillips
334 A/B G. Houghton
502 A/B O. Bleasdale
PO G.C. Chambers
A/B J. Daglish
CMM C.F. Hearn
503 A/B N.T. Hine
A/B J.G.S. Pringle

A/B A.L.G. Turner
A/B C. Wren
15th Sto A.A. Andrews
Flot Tel H. Banks
A/B R. Bartley
Sto R. Bracey
Tel C.K. Gadd
A/B J.J. Gordon
A/B J. Hayden
L/Sea A. Hibbert
A/B P. Lumsley
A/B J.S. Markham
Sto K. Peel
A/B H. Pickles
PO F.S. Smith
PO W. Webb and A/B G.I. Hill
SGB 3/ *Grey Owl*
ERA E.N. Serridge
A/B J.E. Hughes
CERA P.H. Humphrey
SGB 4/ *Grey Fox*
Sto PO V. Landon
A/B J.B. Rees
A/B A.Edwards
SGB 5/ *Grey Owl*
ERA R.J. Eastlake
A/B F.F. Ferguson
SGB 6/ *Grey Shark*
A/B N. Clegg
Sig J.D. Stanway
SGB 7 O/Sea R. Barnes
A/B W. Gough
L/Sto R.W. Muir
SGB 8/ *Grey Wolf*
ERA F.M. Merwood
SGB 9/ *Grey Goose*
A/B R.D. Wenden

BAR TO DISTINGUISHED SERVICE MEDAL
15th Flot PO H.E. Mould
SGB4/ *Grey Fox*
ERA E.N. Serridge

SGB 5/ *Grey Owl*
ERA R.J. Eastlake
SGB 8/ *Grey Wolf*
PO T. Boyle

CONSPICUOUS GALLANTRY MEDAL
MGB 335 PO G.H. Plenderleith

TABLE 2: WAR LOSSES

(N.B: 'CTL': 'Constructive total loss' – beyond economic repair)

DOG BOATS

MTB	(Flot)	Date	
605	51st	17.2.45	Sunk in collision with wreck off Ostend.
606	50th	4.11.43	Sunk in action off Dutch coast.
622	31st	10.3.43	Sunk in action off Terschelling.
625	54th	8.2.44	CTL after storm in Scottish waters (RNorN).
626	54th	22.11.43	Lost by fire and explosion at Lerwick (RNorN).
631	30th	14.3.43	Stranded on Norwegian coast. Captured by enemy (RNorN).
635	32nd	–.7.43	CTL: split keel as result of weather on passage to Gibraltar.
636	32nd	15.10.43	Sunk by gunfire from 658 in identification confusion.
639	32nd	28.4.43	Sunk in Sicilian Narrows after air attack.
640	56th	26.6.44	Mined off Vada, Italy.
654	33rd	–.6.43	CTL after internal explosion, Bone.
655	56th	22.3.45	Mined in Arsa Channel east of Istria.
665	33rd	15.8.43	Sunk by shore battery in Messina Straits.
666	58th	6.7.44	Lost by explosion in Ymuiden after damage in action.
669	58th	26.10.43	Sunk off Norway by German surface craft.
671	55th	24.4.44	Sunk off Cape Barfleur by German destroyer.
672	52nd	29.5.44	CTL: mined off Berry Head.
681	58th	10.6.44	Sunk off Dutch coast by German surface craft.
686	58th	22.11.43	Lost in Lerwick by fire.
690	53rd	28.1.45	Lost by collision with wreck off Lowestoft.
697	59th	17.4.45	Mined in Krk Channel, Adriatic.
705	59th	23.3.45	Mined in Adriatic.
707	63rd	18.4.44	Lost in collision with French frigate off Ireland.
708	63rd	5.5.44	Sunk in error by Beaufighters.
709	54th	19.5.45	CTL after explosion alongside 715 at Fosnavag, Norway (RNorN).
710	59th	10.4.45	Mined in the Adriatic.
712	54th	25.1.45	CTL after grounding off Scapa Flow (RNorN).
715	54th	19.5.45	CTL after explosion at Fosnavag, Norway (RNorN).
732	64th	28.5.44	Sunk in error by French frigate in Channel.
734	50th	26.6.44	Bombed in error by Allied aircraft off Normandy.
776	63rd	14.2.45	Lost by fire and explosion in Ostend harbour.
782	63rd	19.12.44	Mined off the Schelde.
789	64th	14.2.45	Lost by fire and explosion in Ostend harbour.
791	52nd	14.2.45	Lost by fire and explosion in Ostend harbour.
798	52nd	14.2.45	Lost by fire and explosion in Ostend harbour.
5001	68th	7.4.45	Sunk in North Sea by E-boat.
601	17th	27.7.42	CTL: blew up in Dover after action 24.7.42 in Dover Strait.
641	19th	14.7.43	Sunk by shore battery in Messina Straits.
644	19th	26.6.43	Mined west of Sicily.
648	19th	14.6.43	Sunk by aircraft off Pantelleria.

657   56th   12.9.44   Mined off Rimini.

663   56th   10.10.44   Mined off Rimini.

A total of 42 war losses from the 228 boats built.
19 in home waters; 15 in Mediterranean; 8 in Norwegian waters.

C CLASS MGBS

MGB	(Flot)	Date	
313	12,16	6.8.44	Mined off Normandy.
314	Indep	28.3.42	Sunk after damage at St Nazaire.
326	1st CF	28.6.44	Mined off Normandy.
328	16,14	21.7.42	Sunk in action, Dover Strait.
335	14,16	10.9.42	Lost in action, North Sea.

CAMPER AND NICHOLSON MGBS

501	15th	27.7.42	Sank after explosion near Land's End.
502	15th	12.5.45	Mined in Skagerrak.
Gay Viking		6.2.44	Abandoned in Skagerrak after collision.
Gay Corsair		22.5.45	Grounded off Aberdeen.
Master Standfast		2.11.43	Captured by Vp 1606 off Norway.

STEAM GUNBOATS

SGB 7   19.6.42   Sunk in action off Etaples.

TABLE 3: THE DOG BOAT FLOTILLAS

17th MGBs	June 1942 to Oct. 1943. Became 50th MTBs. Great Yarmouth.
MGBs	601, 603, 604, 605, 606, 607, 609, 610, 612.
SOs:	Lt Cdr H.M. Duff-Still RNVR to April 1943. Lt Cdr D.G.E. Probert RNVR to August 1943. Lt Cdr G.L. Cotton RNVR (then SO 50th MTBs).

18th MGBs	Feb. 1942 to Oct. 1943. Became 51st MTBs. Portsmouth, Newhaven.
MGBs	602, 608, 611, 613, 614, 615, 616, 680, 689.
SOs:	Lt H.P. Byrne RN to April 1943. Lt Cdr I.D. Lyle RNVR (then SO 51st MTBs).

19th MGBs	Jan. 1943 to Dec. 1943. Became 60th and 61st Flots. Mediterranean – Bone, Malta, Augusta.
MGBs	641, 642, 643, 644, 645, 646, 647, 648.
SOs:	Lt E.M. Thorpe DSO RN. Lt Cdr A.D. McIlwraith RNVR. Lt Cdr B.L. Bourne (then SO 60th MTBs/MGBs).

20th MGBs		Feb. 1943 to Dec. 1943. Became 56th and 57th Flots.
		Mediterranean – Malta, Sicily, Maddalena, Bastia.
	MGBs	657, 658, 659, 660, 661, 662, 663, 674.
	SO:	Lt Cdr N.H. Hughes RNVR to Dec. 1943.
21st MGBs		June 1943 to Oct. 1943. Became 52nd MTBs.
		Dartmouth.
	MGBs	664, 673, 676, 677, 678, 679.
	SO:	Lt Cdr T.N. Cartwright RNVR (then SO 52nd MTBs).
22nd MGBs		May 1943 to Oct. 1943. Became 53rd MTBs.
		Lowestoft.
	MGBs	693, 694, 689, 690, 692.
	SO:	Lt Cdr D.H.E. McCowen RNVR (then SO 53rd MTBs).
30th MTBs		Sept. 1942 to Oct. 1943. Became 54th MTBs.
		Lerwick. Manned by Norwegian crews.
	MTBs	618, 619, 620, 623, 625, 626, 627, 631, 653, 688.
	SO:	Lt Cdr R.A. Tamber RNorN.
31st MTBs		Sept. 1942 to Oct. 1943. Became 55th MTBs.
		Great Yarmouth.
	MTBs	617, 621, 622, 624, 628, 629, 630, 632, 650, 652; later 668, 671, 682.
	SOs:	Lt I.R.P. Goodden RN to May 1943.
		Lt L.J.H. Gamble RN to Sept. 1943.
		Lt D.G. Bradford RNR (then SO 55th MTBs).
32nd MTBs		Dec. 1942 to Dec. 1943. Became part of 56th, 57th, 61st Flots.
		Mediterranean.
	MTBs	633, 634, 635, 636, 637, 638, 639, 640.
	SOs:	Lt P.F.S. Gould DSC RN to April 1943 (killed).
		Lt Cdr E. Rose RNVR (temporary).
33rd MTBs		Jan. 1943 to Dec.1943. Became part of 56th, 57th, 60th, 61st.
		Mediterranean
	MTBs	649, 651, 654, 655, 656, 665, 667, 670.
	SOs:	Lt Cdr R.R. Ashby DSC RHKNVR to July 1943.
		Lt Cdr J.D. Archer RNVR to August 1943.
		Lt Cdr E.T. Greene-Kelly RNR to Oct. 1943 (killed).
34th MTBs		June 1943 to Oct. 1943. Became 58th MTBs.
		Lerwick after Lowestoft.
	MTBs	666, 669, 672, 681, 683, 684, 685, 686, 687.
	SO:	Lt Cdr K. Gemmell RNVR (then SO 58th MTBs).
35th MTBs		Gathering when re-numbered 59th MTBs.
	MTBs	697, 698, 699, 700, 703, 705, 706, 710.

Appointed SO: Lt Cdr H.O.T. Bradford RNVR (see 59th Flotilla), to 59th MTBs.

Re-numbered flotillas from October 1943. All designated MTB flotillas except four Mediterranean flotillas, where MGBs retained as such, and called MTB/MGB flotillas.

50th MTBs		Oct. 1943 to May 1945 (previously 17th MGBs). Yarmouth, also Dover, Newhaven, Ostend.
	MTBs	603, 604, 605, 606, 607, 609, 610, 612; later 673, 676, 677 and 678 from 52nd & 734, 751, 756.
	SOs:	Lt Cdr G.L. Cotton RNVR to April 1944. Lt Cdr H.W. Paton RNVR to Nov. 1944. Lt Cdr J.H. Hodder RNVR.
51st MTBs		Oct. 1943 to May 1945 (previously 18th MGBs). Portsmouth, Newhaven, Dover, Ramsgate.
	MTBs	602, 608, 611, 613, 614, 615, 616, 680 and 689.
	SOs:	Lt Cdr I.D. Lyle RNVR to Dec. 1944. Lt Cdr W.B.G. Leith RNVR.
52nd MTBs		Oct. 1943 to Nov. 1944 (previously 21st MGBs). Dartmouth.
	MTBs	664, 673, 676, 677, 678 679; later 619, 620, 720, 713, 717, 719, 672, 716, (755, 721, 704 allocated).
	SOs:	Lt Cdr T.N. Cartwright RNVR to August 1944. Lt Cdr F.D. Russell-Roberts RNVR.
52nd MTBs		(A second formation) Nov. 1944 to Sept. 1945. Gathering at Yarmouth and Ostend.
	MGBs allocated:	511, 512, 513, 514, 515, 516, 517, 518.
	MTBs	758, 762, 764, 791, 798, 5020.
	SO:	Lt Cdr A.R.H. Nye RNVR.
53rd MTBs		Oct. 1943 to June 1945 (previously 22nd MGBs). Lowestoft, Portland, Portsmouth, Ostend.
	MTBs	689, 690, 691, 692, 693, 694, 695; later 740, 755, 772, 775, 675, 664; from 52nd 696, 768, 774, 775, 778.
	SOs:	Lt Cdr D.H.E. McCowen RNVR to March 1944. Lt Cdr S.D. Marshall RNVR.
54th MTBs		Oct. 1943 to late 1945 (previously 30th MTBs). Lerwick, Lowestoft and Yarmouth; Norwegian.
	MTBs	618, 619, 623, 625, 626, 627, 653, 688, 709, 712, 715, 722, 711, 713, 717, 716, 723, 704, 719, 720, 721.
	COs:	Lt Cdr R.E. Tamber RNorN to April 1943. Lt Cdr C. Monsen RNorN to Sept 1944. Lt Cdr C. Herlofsen RNorN.
55th MTBs		Oct. 1943 to June 1945 (previously 31st MTBs). Yarmouth, Portsmouth from May 1944.

MTBs	617, 621, 624, 628, 629, 630, 632, 650, 652, 668, 671, 682; later 741, 759, 773, 771.
SOs:	Lt Cdr D.G. Bradford RNR to August 1944.
	Lt Cdr J.A.H. Whitby RNVR.

56th MTB/MGBs	Jan. 1944 to March 1944 (previously 20th, 32nd, 33rd). Mediterranean – Bastia, Brindisi, Komiza, Ancona.
MGBs	657, 658, 663, (642); MTBs 655, 633, 640, 649.
SOs:	Lt Cdr J.D. Maitland RCNVR to Sept. 1944.
	Lt Cdr C. Burke RCNVR.

57th MTB/MGBs	Jan. 1944 to August 1945 (previously 20th, 32nd, 33rd). Mediterranean – Bastia, Brindisi, Komiza, Ancona.
MGBs	634, 638, 659, 670 637; MGBs 660, 662, 674.
SO:	Lt Cdr T.J. Bligh RNVR.

58th MTBs	Oct. 1943 to June 1945 (previously 34th MTBs). Lerwick, Lowestoft.
MTBs	666, 669, 675, 681, 683, 684, 685, 686, 687, 723; later 629, 701, 702, 704, 713, 719, 721, 714, 720, 673, 676, 677, 678.
SOs:	Lt Cdr K. Gemmell to August 1944.
	Lt Cdr D.G.H. Wright to May 1945.

59th MTBs	Oct. 1943 to July 1945 (previously 35th MTBs). Home Waters (Yarmouth, Dover, Newhaven); Mediterranean.
MTBs	697, 698, 699, 700, 703, 706, 705, 710.
SOs:	Lt Cdr H.O.T. Bradford RNVR.
	Lt Cdr D. Mason RNVR.
	Lt Cdr J.A. Montgomerie RNVR.

60th MTB/MGBs	Jan. 1944 to July 1945 (from 19th and 33rd). Mediterranean – Aegean, Adriatic.
MGBs	643, 645, 646, 647, 661; MTBs 656, 667, 651.
SO:	Lt Cdr B.L. Bourne RNVR.

61st MTB/MGBs	Jan. 1944 to Oct. 1944 (then redistributed). Mediterranean – Brindisi, Komiza, Ancona.
MTBs	637, 649, 651; MGBs 642, 661, 674.
SO:	Lt Cdr T.G. Fuller RCNVR.

62nd MTBs	Dec. 1944 to Feb. 1945 (never operated together). Redistributed as below.
MTBs	709, 711, 712, 715 to 54th; 716, 717, 719 to 52nd.

63rd MTBs	Dec. 1943 to June 1945. Dover, Portsmouth, Yarmouth.
MTBs	701, 702, 704, 707, 708, 720, 721; later 696, 730, 753, 729, 741, 751, 756, 761, 763, 766, 769, 771, 776, 782, 777, 779.

SOs: Lt Cdr G.C. Fanner RNVR.
                Lt Cdr H.W. Paton RNVR.
                Lt Cdr P.C. Wilkinson RNVR.

64th MTBs   Dec. 1943 to June 1945 (minelaying for Operation Neptune).
                Portsmouth, Portland, Felixstowe, Yarmouth.
    MTBs   724, 725, 728, 738, 739, 742, 749, 759, 766, 773, 787,
                784, 788, 795, 5015.
    SO: Lt Cdr D. Wilkie RNVR.

65th MTBs   May 1944 to June 1945 (all Canadian crews).
                Dartmouth, Yarmouth, Ostend.
    MTBs   726, 727, 735, 736, 743, 744, 745, 746, 748, 797.
    SO: Lt Cdr J.R.H. Kirkpatrick RCNVR.

66th MTBs   August 1944 to July 1945 (anti-submarine).
                Portland, Plymouth, Ramsgate.
    MTBs   731, 733, 737, 747, 750, 752, 757, 760.
    SO: Lt Cdr J.A.C. Findlay RNVR.

67th MTBs   Dec. 1944 to June 1945
                Yarmouth.
    MTBs   765, 767, 783, 785, 786, 796, 5002, 5005, 5010.
    SOs: Lt Cdr J.H. Hodder RNVR.
                Lt Cdr D.G. Dowling RNVR.

68th MTBs   Jan. 1945 to June 1945.
                Yarmouth, Ostend.
    MTBs   754, 770, 781, 794, 5001, 5013.
    SO: Lt Cdr D.G. Dowling RNVR.

72nd MTBs   May 1945 to Sept. 1945.
                (Gathering at Portland on VE Day).
    MTBs   774, 779, 783, 785, 786, 790, 793, 794.
    SO: Lt Cdr D.G. Dowling RNVR.

73rd MTBs   May 1945 to Sept. 1945.
                Post-VE Day Portsmouth, Portland.
    MTBs   5002, 5003, 5005, 5007, 5008, 5009, 5013, 5015, 5020.
    SO: Lt Cdr D.G.H. Wright RNVR.

Detail obtained from Red Lists, Pink Lists, and personal information from veterans.

BIBLIOGRAPHY

PUBLISHED SOURCES

Abelsen, Frank. *Norwegian Naval Ships 1939–1945*, Sam and Stenersen, 1986

——. *Footprints in the Sea*, Evans Brothers, 1961

Agar, Captain Augustus, VC DSO RN. *Baltic Episode*, Conway Maritime Press, 1983

Barker, Ralph. *The Blockade Busters*, Chatto and Windus, 1976

Barnett, Correlli. *Engage the Enemy More Closely*, Hodder and Stoughton, 1991

Beaver, Paul. *E-boats and Coastal Craft* (Second World War Photo Albums), Patrick Stephens, 1980

Bruce-Lockhart, Sir Robert, KCMG. *The Marines Were There*, Putnam, 1950

Chatterton Dickson, Captain W. RN (Retd) ('Seedie'). *Seedie's List of Coastal Forces Awards for World War 2*, Ripley Registers, 1992

Churchill, Winston S. *The Second World War*, Volumes 1–6, Cassell, 1948–54

Connell, G.G. *Mediterranean Maelstrom*, Kimber, 1978

Cooper, Bryan. *The Buccaneers*, Macdonald, 1970

——. *The E-boat Threat*, Macdonald and Jane's, 1976

Dickens, Captain Peter, DSO MBE DSC RN. *Night Action: MTB Flotilla at War*, Peter Davies, 1974

Dorling, Captain Taprell, DSO FRHistS RN. ('Taffrail'). *Western Mediterranean 1942–1945*, Hodder and Stoughton, 1947

Fairbanks, Douglas, Jnr. *A Hell of a War*, Robson Books Ltd, 1995

Hampshire, A. Cecil. *On Hazardous Service*, Kimber, 1974

——. *The Secret Navies*, Kimber, 1978

——. *Undercover Sailors*, Kimber, 1981

Hichens, Lt Cdr Robert Peverill, DSO DSC RNVR. *We Fought Them in Gunboats*, Michael Joseph, 1944

Hobday, Geoffrey, DSC. *In Harm's Way*, Imperial War Museum, 1985

Holman, Gordon. *The Little Ships*, Hodder and Stoughton, 1943

Jones, Geoffrey. *The Month of the Lost U-boats*, William Kimber, 1977

Lambert, John. *The Fairmile 'D' Motor Torpedo Boat* ('Anatomy of the Ship' Series), Conway Maritime Press, 1985

Lambert, John, and Ross, Al. *Allied Coastal Forces of World War 2*, Volume 1, 'Fairmile Designs and US Submarine Chasers', Conway Maritime Press, 1990

Law, Cdr C. Anthony, DSC CD RCN (Retd). *White Plumes Astern*, Nimbus Publishing Ltd, Halifax, Nova Scotia, 1989

Lawrence, Hal. *Victory at Sea: Tales of His Majesty's Coastal Forces*, McClelland and Stewart Inc., Toronto, 1989

Lenton, H.T. and Colledge, J.J. *Warships of World War 2*, Ian Allan, 1964

McCoville, Michael. *A Small War in the Balkans*, Macmillan, 1986

Millar, George. *The Bruneval Raid*, Bodley Head, 1974

Mordal, Jacques. *Dieppe: The Dawn of Decision*, Souvenir Press, 1963

Nolan, Brian, and Street, Brian Jeffrey. *Champagne Navy – Canada's Small Boat Raiders of the Second World War*, Random House, Toronto, 1991

North, A.J.D. *Royal Naval Coastal Forces 1939–1945*, Almark Publishing Co., London, 1972

Pickles, Harold, L/Sea DSM. *Untold Stories of Small Boats at War*, The Pentland Press, Bishop Auckland, 1994

Pope, Dudley. *Flag 4: The Battle of Coastal Forces in the Mediterranean*, William Kimber, 1954

Rance, Adrian. *Fast Boats and Flying Boats* (a biography of Hubert Scott-Paine), Ensign Publications, 1989

Reynolds, Leonard C., OBE DSC. *Gunboat 658*, William Kimber, 1955

Rohwer, J. and Hummelchen, G. *Chronology of the War at Sea 1939–1945*, Volume 1, 1939–42; Volume 2, 1943–45, The Military Book Society by arrangement with Ian Allan Ltd, 1972

Roskill, Captain S.W., DSC RN. *History of the Second World War: The War at Sea 1939–1945*; Volume 1: *The Defensive*, HMSO, 1954; Volume 2: *The Period of Balance*, HMSO, 1957; Volume 3: *The Offensive*, Parts 1 & 2, HMSO, 1960

Ryder, Cdr R.E.R., VC RN. *The Attack on St Nazaire*, John Murray, 1947

Scott, Lt Cdr Peter, MBE DSC RNVR. *The Battle of the Narrow Seas; a History of the Light Coastal Forces in the Channel and North Sea, 1939–1945*, Country Life Ltd, 1945

——. *The Eye of the Wind*, Hodder and Stoughton, 1961

White, W.L. *They Were Expendable*, Hamish Hamilton, 1942

Whitley, M.J. *German Coastal Forces of World War 2*, Arms and Armour Press, 1992

UNPUBLISHED SOURCES

PRIVATELY PRINTED AND DISTRIBUTED MEMOIRS

Blaxell, Lionel H., OBE DSC. *Through the Hawse Pipe 1939–1946*, 1990

Horlock, Kenneth M., DSC. *Our Lady of the Pirates*, 1991

Lewis, Arthur H., RD FRICS. *A Caul and Some Wartime Experiences*, 1992

Lynch, Mack. *Salty Dips, Volume 1* (Section 11: T.G. Fuller, 'MTB Skipper and Flotilla Commander'), compiled by the Ottawa Branch of the Naval Officers' Associations of Canada, 1983

Tomlinson, Randall L., DSM. *To the Shores of Scandinavia*, 1994

MEMOIRS IN MANUSCRIPT OR ARTICLE FORM

Board, Robin W.V. (as CO MTB 610). *Jottings*, 1944

Bradford, Donald Gould, DSO DSC**. *Day In, Night Out*, date unknown

Conquest, L. David. Manuscript of memoirs, section on Mediterranean Operations in MTBs 651 and 667, date unknown

Coombes, Frank and Fred. Both DSM. *Reminiscences of World War Two, Part 2*, date unknown

Falconer, Andrew. Manuscript of memoirs, *Reminiscing*, date unknown

Gundersen, Vice-Admiral Hans B., RNorN (Retd). *The 30th and 54th (Norwegian) MTB Flotillas in World War Two*, manuscript prepared for the author, 1958

NAVAL RECORDS

At the Naval Historical Branch.
ADM 187: 'Pink Lists': Weekly lists of movements of minor war vessels overseas.
ADM 199/2327: Rear Admiral Coastal Forces Information Reports.
ADM 208: 'Red Lists': Weekly lists of movements of minor war vessels in home waters.
Battle Summary Reports.

Card Index of all MTBs and MGBs.
Coastal Forces Monograph.
Coastal Forces Periodic Reviews.
Draft of lecture by W.J. Holt RCNC on 'History and Development of Coastal Forces Craft'.
List of Recorded Coastal Forces Actions.
Navy Lists.
Naval Historical Branch Search Documents.
War Diaries.
War Intelligence Reports.

AT THE PUBLIC RECORD OFFICE, KEW

ADM 199/257	Operations in Adriatic and Aegean	1943–5
261	Coastal Forces Actions	1943–4
262	"	1944
263	"	1944
264	"	1943–4
265	"	1944–5
266	"	1944
267	"	1944–5
268	Coastal Forces in the Mediterranean	1943–4
269	Coastal Forces Actions, Adriatic	1944
270	Norwegian Coastal Forces	1943–45
536	Coastal Forces Operations	1942–3
537	"	1943
677	" in the Mediterranean	1941–5
680	" actions	1942–3
782	" actions	1942
784	" against E-boats	1942
858	Operation Husky	
891	Reports of Surrender of German Naval Forces in Northern Adriatic	1945
943	Operation Husky	
944	"	
945	"	
947	"	
997	Operations by Norwegian C.F. Lerwick	1945
1036	Coastal Craft actions in English Channel	

1550–1688 (index) 1689) Operation Overlord
2195–2326 War Diary Summaries 9/39–12/45
London Gazettes.

OTHER SOURCES

Article 1, 'Narrow Waters in War', by Captain P.G.C. Dickens DSO MBE DSC RN (Retd.), in the *Journal of Royal United Services Institute*.

Newsletters of the Coastal Forces Veterans' Association.

Questionnaires from Veterans – all sources.

Report of CCF Portsmouth on Operation Overlord.

Report of CCF Plymouth on Operation Overlord.

'War and peace.' (Courtesy, A.T. Robinson)

INDEX

FAIRMILE D MTBS/MGBS

601: 4, 7, 16, 17, 247

602: 96

603: 25, 86–8, 262

605: 6, 22, 27, 74, 82, 188

606: 25, 27, 78–81, 89

607: 25, 74, 84–6, 208, 262

608: 96, 98, 175

609: 18–19, 57, 74, 86–7, 93, 247, 262

610: 22, 25, 27, 74, 74–82, 86–7, 91, 93, 260, 262

611: 77, 82, 96

612: 22, 25, 27, 74, 76, 78–80, 169

613: 96, 175

614: 74, 96, 175

615: 74, 96

616: 77

617: 23–4, 25, 80, 88, 93, 95–6, 98–100, 173

618: 37, 78, 104, 109, 260

619: 35, 39

620: 37, 39, 41

621: 26, 78–81, 88–90, 93, 95, 173, 262

622: 23–4, 25

623: 37, 109, 111, 113

624: 23–4, 26, 78, 95–6, 173, 262

625: 37, 105, 107, 118

626: 38, 42, 106, 118

627: 38, 104–5, 107, 109, 111, 113

628: 24–5, 74–5, 173

629: 25, 74, 93, 95, 173

630: 26–7, 88–90

631: 35, 37, 39, 118

632: 27, 74, 88, 98, 100, 172

633: 52–5, 62, 68, 132, 145–6, 218–9, 234, 236, 240, 261

634: 50–1, 55, 64, 134, 143, 157, 217, 220–1, 228, 232, 234, 237–8, 240

635: 48, 51–2, 55, 261

636: 39, 68–9

637: 52–7, 130, 134, 151, 217, 219–22, 240, 261

638: 50, 57, 59, 68, 134, 220–2, 231, 234, 240

639: 51–5, 59, 261

640: 48, 51–2, 61, 64, 65, 132, 141, 144–6, 148

641: 57, 63–4, 130

642: 58, 218–9, 240

643: 50, 55–6, 60, 63, 63–4, 125, 134, 151, 216, 231, 233–5, 240, 261

644: 48, 51, 60

645: 125, 128–9, 134, 154, 223, 226

646: 55, 63–4, 125, 134, 153, 155, 223–6

647: 125, 128–9, 134, 151–3, 155, 223–5, 234

648: 57–8

649: 59, 130, 134, 150–1, 156, 219, 228

650: 88, 172

651: 60, 61, 64, 134, 150–3, 156–7, 223–6, 237, 265

652: 78, 80, 95, 173

653: 42, 106–7, 109, 111–12

654: 48, 60, 127, 134

655: 6, 57, 62, 125, 132, 136, 138–40, 146, 148, 218, 228, 232, 233

656: 51, 57–8, 62, 134, 155, 232

657: 48, 50, 60, 66, 131, 139, 146, 211–14, 217–19

658: 7, 61–2, 64, 68–70, 123, 131, 138–42, 144–5, 148, 209, 211–17, 228, 234–6, 240

659: 58, 59, 61, 125, 136, 138–43, 156, 216, 222–3, 240

660: 7, 61, 68, 123, 134, 143, 146, 157, 223–6, 232, 265

661: 59, 134, 153–4, 223

662: 59, 61, 68, 69, 123, 134, 143–6, 150–1, 156–7, 211–12, 217, 220–2, 231, 234, 262

663: 61, 66, 125, 132, 139–40, 148, 211–16, 219

665: 59, 65–6

666: 105, 107, 170–2

667: 48, 66, 134, 151, 154, 156–7, 211, 223–5, 265

668: 82, 95–6

669: 105

670: 61, 64–5, 123, 124, 134, 156–7, 211–12, 234, 237, 261

671: 88, 98–100

672: 101

673: 102, 166

674: 60, 134, 135, 151, 154–5, 217, 222, 231, 233, 240

675: 7, 42, 261
677: 102
679: 175
680: 98, 175
681: 105, 109, 168–70
682: 173
683: 105, 169
684: 105, 169–70, 176–7
685: 105
686: 42, 105–6
687: 105, 169, 170, 175–7
688: 105, 109, 111
689: 93
690: 93–5
691: 163
693: 93–5, 163, 186
694: 93, 186
695: 93–5
697: 231, 234, 236
698: 231, 240
699: 231–2
700: 90, 231, 240
701: 98
702: 98
703: 231–2
704: 165
705: 90, 162, 231–3, 240, 265
706: 231
707: 98
708: 100
709: 109, 111, 113–14
710: 67, 231, 232, 234
711: 109, 113, 116–17
712: 109, 110–13, 118, 169
714: 165
715: 109, 111, 114–15, 169
716: 109, 113–15, 260
717: 102, 109, 111–13, 115–16
718: 191–208, 242, 249, 264
720: 100–1, 176
721: 98
722: 109, 110–13
723: 117, 170–1, 176–7
724: 182

728: 182
729: 170–1
730: 6
732: 101
734: 169
736: 190
738: 174
739: 101
745: 166, 183, 190
746: 190
748: 185
755: 186
763: 176–7
767: 189
769: 176–7, 185
772: 186
775: 187
776: 187–8
779: 188
781: 190
782: 186
789: 188
791: 188
794: 89
795: 188
796: 189
797: 190
798: 188
5001: 189–90
5003: 189
5005: 190
5020: 256

C Class Fairmile MGBS

312: 245
314: 3, 193, 242, 246
315: 245
316: 245
317: 12, 245, 249
318: 193, 242, 249
319: 244
321: 249
322: 16–17, 247

323: 15
324: 244
325: 245
326: 245
327: 247
328: 16, 244, 247
329: 244
330: 19, 244, 247
331: 19
332: 247
333: 249
334: 15, 248
355: 248–9

Steam Gun Boats

SGB 3 (Grey Seal): 74
SGB 7: 251
SGB 9 (Grey Goose): 250, 252

Camper & Nicholsons MGBS

501: 193, 253
502: 193, 196–7, 200, 208, 242, 253
2002: 262, 264
503 (2003): 193, 208, 242, 253
509: (2009): 208, 253

Other MTBS ('short' boats)

54: 29, 31
56: 29–31, 104
97: 150
226: 150
297: 130
345: 39–41
485: 188

USN PT boats

202: 146
203: 142

217: 140
218: 146

Landing Craft

LCG 14: 142, 146
LCG 19: 142, 146
LCG 20: 142, 146
LCH 282: 222, 228

Allied Ships

Greek: *Adrias* 128, 129
Norwegian: *Draug* 29, 31
Canadian: HMCS *Haida* 101
United States: USS *Knight* 67
French: *La Combattante* 101
Polish: *Dragon* 173
Italian: *Miraglia* 149

RN Ships

HMS *Ajax:* 226
 Antwerp: 61
 Atherton: 246
 Avon Vale: 228
 Bickerton: 57
 Black Prince: 224
 Brocklesby: 228
 Campbeltown: 247
 Cato: 173
 Chaplet: 240
 Chequers: 240
 Chevron: 240
 Columbo: 231
 Coverley: 48
 Cubitt: 190
 Curzon: 186
 Dido: 137
 Duff: 163
 Eglinton: 93
 Garth: 93
 Invicta: 247
 Jervis: 246

Lamerton: 228
Magic: 173
Newfoundland: 61
Prince Albert: 245
Princess Beatrix: 247
Pytchley: 86
Quantock: 228
Retalick: 185
Stayner: 182
Tetcott: 61
Torrington: 187
Ulster Monarch: 61
Vienna: 129, 149
Vivien: 93
Walpole: 186
Warrior: 47
Wheatland: 228
William Stephen: 86
Wilton: 228

Dog Boat Flotillas

MGB FLOTILLAS
15th: 182, 191–208, 242, 249, 253
17th: 18, 20, 25, 26, 42, 72, 78
18th: 21, 43, 72–4, 77
19th: 44, 46, 48, 50, 55, 57, 59, 63, 125
20th: 44, 46, 50, 57, 59, 60, 61, 63, 67, 131, 262

MTB FLOTILLAS
30th: 21, 22, 28, 29, 104, 262
31st: 21, 22, 24–5, 26, 42, 72–5, 78, 249
32nd: 23, 44, 46, 48, 50, 55, 57, 64, 130
33rd: 44, 46, 48, 50–1, 57, 59, 62, 64, 67–8, 130
50th: 42, 82–3, 88, 93, 96, 168, 175, 181
51st: 43, 82, 96, 98, 159, 174–5, 182

52nd: 83, 96, 101, 166, 175–6, 182, 188
53rd: 83, 93, 96, 159, 163, 175, 181, 185–6, 188
54th: 96, 98, 104–19, 168–9, 204, 262
55th: 42, 82–3, 88, 93, 94, 96, 98–9, 159, 162–3, 172–4, 182, 263
56th: 132, 136, 137–41, 143–4, 148, 209–11, 216, 218–19, 263
57th: 132, 134, 143–4, 148–50, 155, 157, 210, 217, 219–22, 251–2
58th: 42, 83, 96, 105–10, 168–70, 175–6, 181, 188
59th: 83, 90, 96, 160, 162–3, 174, 182, 230–32
60th: 134, 151, 154–5, 210, 217, 223, 264
61st: 134, 151, 156, 209
62nd: 109
63rd: 83, 98, 100, 160, 163, 174–6, 181, 185–8
64th: 83, 90, 96, 101, 165, 174–6, 181–2, 188
65th: 96, 166, 181–3, 185, 188, 190
66th: 164, 177–8
67th: 189
68th: 190

C CLASS MGB FLOTILLAS
12th: 242–3
14th: 242–3, 245
16th: 242, 244, 247–8
1st CF: 243

1st SGB Flotilla: 250–1

Allied Personnel

Cdr R.A. Allan RNVR: 50, 61, 69, 121, 123, 139, 142–3, 145–6, 148

Capt Andrews USN: 67–8

Lt A. Andresen RNorN: 32, 37, 41

S/Lt J. Arkell RNVR: 85, 88

Capt H.T. Armstrong RN: 181

Lt M. Arnold-Forster RNVR: 93, 177

S/Lt B. Arrandale RNVR: 56

Lt H.E. Ascoli RNVR: 165

Lt Cdr R.R.W. Ashby RNVR: 46, 57

Lt R. Ball RNVR: 74, 175

Lt P. Barlow RNVR: 142, 156, 222–3

Lt Cdr S.M. Barnes USN: 123–4, 138–9

Tel. T. Barrett: 26–7

Lt W.O.J. Bate RNVR: 148

Lt K.E.A. Bayley RNVR: 57, 125

Lt P.A. Berthon RNVR: 21, 74

Lt W. Beynon RNVR: 25, 161, 173

Lt D.G.E. Bird RNZNVR: 216, 231, 233

Lt L. Blaxell RNVR: 17

Lt Cdr T.J. Bligh RNVR: 61, 68, 134, 143–5, 146–9, 150–1, 155–7, 211–12, 217, 219–22, 231, 234, 236–9

Lt A.W. Bone RNVR: 231–2, 234

Lt W.E.A. Blount RNVR: 134, 157, 220–2, 232, 234, 237–9

Lt R.W.V. Board RNVR: 91

Lt K. Bogeborg RNorN: 32, 38, 39, 110, 112–13

Lt P. Boissier RN: 240

Lt D.H. Booth RNVR: 231, 234, 237

Lt J. Borresen RNorN: 113

Lt Cdr B.L. Bourne RNVR: 125, 129, 134, 151, 154, 217, 219, 223–4, 232–3

Lt M.G. Bowyer RNVR: 150, 154–5, 222, 231

Lt T.W. Boyd RNVR: 21, 74

Lt Cdr D.G. Bradford RNR: 43, 78–82, 83, 88, 90–1, 95–6, 98, 100, 159, 161–3, 172–4, 182, 244, 249

A/B L. Brayshaw: 139

Cdr Brind RN: 78, 80, 90, 183

Lt D.H. Brown RNVR: 228, 233

Lt D.N. Buller RNVR: 107, 170–1

Lt Cdr C. Burke RCNVR: 48, 68–70, 131–2, 140–2, 144, 212–16, 217–18, 229

Lt H.P. Byrne RN 21, 43, 243

Lt F. Carr RNVR: 23, 25

POMM R. Cartwright: 207

Lt Cdr T.N. Cartwright RNVR: 83, 97, 101–2, 161, 166, 176, 182, 243

Lt A.C.N. Chapman RNVR: 21

Lt B. Christiansen RNorN: 32

Lt Col J.M.F.T. Churchill: 155

Lt G.W. Claydon: 78, 173

Lt (E) H. Coatalen RNVR: 136

Lt H.P. Cobb RNVR: 16–17, 247

S/Lr L.D. Conquest RNVR: 224–5

PO Fred Coombes: 81–2

Lt R.M. Cole RNVR: 134, 153–4

Sig P. Coney: 240

Lt Cdr J. Coste RNVR: 243, 245

Lt Cdr G.L. Cotton RNVR: 42, 82

Lt J.A. Colvill RNVR: 94

Lt Cdr K.A. Cradock-Hartopp RN: 243–4

Adm. Sir A.B.C. Cunningham: 9, 52, 56

Adm. J.D. Cunningham: 221

Lt R.E. Cunningham RNVR: 21, 24, 74–5, 173

Lt D. Curtis RNVR: 193, 246

A/B Daley: 226

S/Lr W.G. Dalziel RNVR: 27

Lt P. Danielsen RNorN: 29, 32, 104, 111, 115

Lt R.C. Davidson RNVR: 130, 134, 151, 220

Lt P.M. Davies RNVR: 231, 232

Cdr E. Davis RNR: 194

A/B A. Day: 100

S/Lt J. Dean RNVR: 157

L/Sea A. Dellow: 199–200, 207

Lt P.G.C. Dickens RN: vi, 93

Capt N.V. Dickinson RN: 125, 139–40, 218, 231

Lt Cdr J.D. Dixon RNVR: 177

Lt Cdr D.G. Dowling RNVR: 78, 81, 88–9, 244

Lt F. Dowrick RNVR: 152, 236

Lt C.W.S. Dreyer RN: 62, 159

Lt Drummond RNVR: 65

Lt Cdr H. Duff-Still: 18, 20, 25–7

Lt W.N. Dye RNVR: 176

Lt A.B. Eason RNVR: 50

Lt P.G.N. Edge RNVR: 86–8, 244

Gen. Eisenhower: 44

Lt L.H. Ennis RNVR: 134, 156, 224, 237, 239

Lt Cdr C.P. Evensen RNVR: 126

Lt Cdr W.G. Everitt RN: 243, 245

Lt J.D. Fairbanks USNR: 68

Tel. A. Falconer: 51, 55

Lt Cdr G.C. Fanner RNVR: 98, 100, 161, 174–5, 181, 244

Lt W.L. Fesq RANVR: 101

Lt Cdr J.A.C. Findlay RNVR: 177

Lt J.V. Fisher RNVR: 167

Lt C.J. Fleming RNVR: 21, 23

Lt J. Fletcher RNVR: 105

Lt R.A. Forbes RNVR: 63, 125, 244, 247–8

Lt C. Ford RNVR: 172

Lt E.S. Forman RNVR: 168–70

Lt Cdr T.G. Fuller RCNVR: 48, 62, 134, 151–4, 156, 209

Lt Fulton RNVR: 172

Major Fynn RM: 38

Lt L.J.H. Gamble RN: 74

Lt Cdr K. Gemmell RNVR: 21, 23–5, 83, 96, 105–8, 167–71, 175, 181

Lt K. Golding RNVR: 228, 234

Lt I.R.P. Goodden RN: 21

Lt D. Goodfellow RNZNVR: 224

Lt A.A. Gotelee RNVR: 16–17, 20, 21

Lt P.F.S. Gould RN: 14, 21, 23, 46, 48, 50–5, 57, 132, 219

Lt Cdr E.T. Greene-Kelly RNR: 57, 62–4, 68–9

V-Adm. Sir P. Gretton: 212

R-Adm. Bj Grimstuedt (RNorN): 260

Lt H.B. Gundersen RNorN: 113, 115

Lt G.A. Guthrie RNVR: 21, 27

Lt A. Haavik RNorN: 32, 37

Lt M.I.G. Hamilton RNVR: 194, 196, 207

A/B F. Hargreaves: 53

Tel. J. Hargreaves: 52

Tel. R. Harrison: 66

Lt W. Harrop: 78, 81, 86–7

L/MM A.R. Hayter: 155

Lt H. Henricksen RNorN: 32, 38, 104, 107

Lt Cdr R. Herlofsen RNorN: 32, 109–11, 113, 115–16

Lt E. Hewitt RNVR: 156, 211–12, 234, 237, 239

S/Lr F.L. Hewitt RNVR: 89

Lt A.G.D. Heybyrne RNVR: 55

Lt Cdr R.P. Hichens RNVR: vi, 14, 21, 26, 72, 93, 132, 233

Lt D.G.T. Hill RNVR: 233, 234

A/B N.T.J. Hine: 208

Lt G.M. Hobday RNZNVR: 50, 55, 60, 63, 125, 128, 134, 151

Lt Cdr J.H. Hodder RNVR: 21, 181, 190–1, 244

Lt S. Hoddevik RNorN: 111, 113

Holt, William J.: 3, 4

Lt P.N. Hood RNVR: 252

Lt K. Horlock RNVR: 60, 61, 134, 150–3, 156

Lt P. Hughes SANF(V): 63, 130, 134, 151, 154, 156, 228

Lt C.J. Jerram RNVR: 48, 66, 134, 151, 154, 156, 211, 223, 224, 236, 237

Lt G.N. Johnstone RNVR: 77

Lt A.P.G. Joy RCNVR: 62, 68

Lt P.J. Kay RNVR: 134

Lt W. Keefer RCNVR: 132

Lt J.O. King RNVR: 20

S/Lr I. Kinross RNVR: 89

Lt Cdr J.H.R. Kirkpatrick RCNVR: 89, 97, 161, 166, 181, 183, 185, 190

Lt B.L. Knight-Lacklan RNVR: 125, 134, 153, 155, 226

Lt E. Kristiansen RNorN: 117

Lt T.E. Ladner RCNVR: 48, 66, 125, 132, 148, 211–16, 219, 233

Lt Cdr B. Lancaster RNVR: 130

POMM W.J.E. Last: 214

Lt Cdr C.A. Law RCNVR: 21, 25, 172

A/B H. Leader: 25

A/B G. Lesslie: 27, 188

Lt A.H. Lewis RNVR: 90, 162

Lt F.R. Lightoller RNVR: 20, 86–8, 244

Lt P.G. Loasby RN: 243

S/Lt E. Lonsdale RNVR: 234

PO F. Loy: 101

Lt D.H. Lummis RNVR: 220–2, 231, 234

Lt Cdr I.D. Lyle RNVR: 21, 43, 77, 95, 159, 161, 174, 182

Lt McCallum RNVR: 247

Lt C. MacLachlan RCNVR: 132, 144, 148, 218, 228

Capt. P.V. McLaughlin RN: 159

Lt Cdr D.G.E. McCowen RNVR: 83, 93–5, 96, 159, 161, 163, 181

Lt A. McDougall RNVR: 106, 170–1

Lt Cdr (Cdr) A. McIlwraith RNVR: 19–20, 21, 57, 63, 125, 128–9, 132, 134

Lt N. McLeod RNVR: 60

Lt O.B. Mabee RCNVR: 91, 166, 183

Lt Cdr G. Macdonald RNZNVR: 93

Lt D.L.W. MacFarlane RNVR: 93–5

Lt Cdr C. Macintyre RN: 171

CMM R.M. MacKintosh: 77

Noel Macklin: 1, 3

Lt Cdr J.D. Maitland RCNVR: 48, 60, 66, 131–2, 138–40, 141–2, 145, 146, 148, 211–16, 217–18

Lt Col J.C. Manners RM: 155

Lt R.D.F. Marlow RNVR: 94

Lt R.M. Marshall RNVR: 21, 74, 75, 84–8, 208, 248

Lt S.D. Marshall RNVR: 161, 173, 181, 185

Lt S. Marthinsen RNorN: 107–8, 111

Lt P.G. Martin RNR: 154, 223, 226

Lt Cdr D.H. Mason RN: 160, 162, 174

Lt P.E. Mason RNVR: 21, 74, 245

Lt W.E. Masson RNVR: 134, 155, 232

Lt E. Matland RNorN: 32, 37, 39, 107–8

PO S.J. Mears: 95

Col. Merritt: 247

Lt W. Messenger RNVR: 93

L/Tel. C. Milner: 196, 198, 204, 207

Lt Cdr C. Monsen RNorN: 98, 109, 114

Lt Cdr J.A. Montgomerie RNVR: 230–1, 232, 234–5, 236

Lt A.H. Moore RNVR: 68

Lt Cdr M. Morgan-Giles RN: 129, 149, 216, 222, 227–9

S/Lt C. Morley RNVR: 100

S/Lt J.W. Morrish RNVR: 95

Lt R.S. Mortimer RNVR: 231

Adm. Lord Mountbatten: 245

Lt M. Mountstephens RNVR: 125, 129, 134, 151, 153, 155, 223, 234

Lt Col. A.C. Newman: 246

Lt D. Newman RNVR: 175

PO L. Nicholl: 233

Lt Cdr R.H. Nye RNVR: 182, 243, 245

S/Lt O'Brien RNVR: 206

PO P. O'Hare: 57–8

Commodore G. Oliver RN: 55–6

Lt A.H. Olsen RNorN: 111, 113, 115

Lt Cdr H.W. Paton RNVR: 21, 168, 181

L/Tel L. Pegler: 155

Lt P.G.L. Pennell RN: 252

Lt R. Perks RNVR: 51–2, 55

Lt H.M. Pickard RCNVR: 125, 132, 148

L/Sea H. Pickles: 249

PO G.H. Plenderleith: 249

Lt A. Prebensen RNorN: 32, 37, 39, 105

Lt A. Price RNVR: 16

Lt Cdr D.G.E. Probert RNVR: 21, 22, 74, 244

Lt I.A. Quarrie RNVR: 61

Lt A.H. Randall RNVR: 101

Lt A.S. Rendell RCNVR: 132, 145, 218, 228

Lt L.C. Reynolds RNVR: 211, 218, 228, 234, 236

Lt G.D.K. Richards RN: 14, 20, 74, 93

Lt M.G. Roberts RNVR: 226

Lt A.T. Robinson RNVR: 134, 157, 223

Lt J.D. Robinson RNVR: 21

LMM E. Robson: 82

AR H. Rockwood: 199–200, 205

Lt E. Rose RNVR: 50, 57

Lt G.L. Russell RNVR: 51–3

Lt Cdr F.D. Russell-Roberts RNVR: 182, 245

Cdr R.E.D. Ryder RN: 246

Lt M.P. Salmond RNR: 198

Capt Bell-Salter RN: 32

A/B Sandalls: 197

A/B W. Savage: 246

Lt P.M. Scott RNVR: vi, 159, 165, 177, 191, 247, 250, 252

Lt R. Seddon RNVR: 194, 197–208

Lt D. Shaw RN: 177

POMM T. Sheehan: 208

Lt D.C. Sidebottom RNVR: 19, 247–8

Capt. F. Slocum RN: 22, 192–4, 197–8, 204, 206

Lt R.R. Smith RNVR: 61, 173

S/Lt R.S. Smith RNVR: 155

Lt E.F. Smyth RNVR: 55–6, 218

L/Sea C.A. Stanley: 207

Lt F.N. Stenersen RNorN: 114

Capt J.F. Stevens RN: 64, 71, 120–31, 134, 144, 148

Lt S. Stewart RNVR: 176

Lt P.L. Stobo RNVR: 249

Lt D. Storrie RNVR: 170, 176

Lt W.S. Strang RNVR: 75, 82, 95, 163

Lt A. Sveen RNorN: 111–13, 116–17

Lt B. Syvertsen RNorN: 111, 113

Lt R. Tamber RNorN: 31–2, 36, 39, 42, 98, 104, 109

Lt D.G. Tate RNVR: 57, 62

Lt N.W.G. Taylor RNVR: 231, 232

Lt P.A.R. Thompson RCNVR: 65

Lt F.N. Thomson RNVR: 182

Lt E.M. Thorpe RN: 46, 48, 57, 244, 247–9

A/B R. Tomlinson: 170

Lt L. Toogood RNVR: 100

Adm. J. Tovey: 78, 80

S/Lt J. Townend RNVR: 194, 202

Lt I. Trelawney RNVR: 93

Lt E.D. Truman RNVR: 21

Adm. Sir Philip Vian: 163

Villiers, Alan: 11

Midn Walmsley RNVR: 174

Lt F.A. Warner RNVR: 68–9

Lt N.R. Weekes RNVR: 19

Cdr A.E.P. Welman RN: 129–30

Lt Cdr J.H. Whitby RNVR: 78, 95, 173–4, 182

Lt D.T. Wickham RN: 95

Lt Cdr D. Wilkie RNVR: 90, 96, 101, 160, 161, 165, 174, 181

Lt P.C. Wilkinson RNVR: 78, 169, 175, 181, 247

Lt Cdr P.A. Williams RNVR: 21, 22, 193, 197

A/B W. Wilson: 25

Lt J.N. Wise RNVR: 101, 176

S/Lt E. Wood-Hatch RNVR: 90

Lt P. Wraite RNVR: 231

Lt Cdr D.G.E. Wright RNVR: 167, 175–7, 181, 191

Lt A. Yates RNVR: 90

Lt M.J.R. Yeatman RNVR: 176

Midn Youalt RNVR: 53

OPERATIONS

Agreement: 44

Antagonise: 231

Aquarius: 202

Barbro: 207

Brassard: 148

Cabaret: 22

Cartoon: 37

Chariot: 246

Cygnus: 197, 202

Gun: 143

Haven: 200

Husky: 60

Infatuate: 185

Knockout: 201

Korda: 200

Lola: 204

Lurcher One: 137

Maple: 160

Neptune: 96–7, 100, 157–60, 165–6, 249, 252

Newt: 146

Overlord: 158

Reflexion: 199

Retribution: 56

Scaramouche: 196

Selma: 206

Torch: 44, 50